ALSO BY MARK WYMAN

*Hard Rock Epic: Western Miners and
the Industrial Revolution, 1860–1910*

*Immigrants in the Valley: Irish, Germans, and Americans
in the Upper Mississippi Country, 1830–1860*

DPs: Europe's Displaced Persons, 1945–1951

*Round-Trip to America:
The Immigrants Return to Europe, 1880–1930*

The Wisconsin Frontier

HOBOES

HOBOES

BINDLESTIFFS, FRUIT TRAMPS, AND

THE HARVESTING OF THE WEST

MARK WYMAN

HILL AND WANG

A DIVISION OF FARRAR, STRAUS AND GIROUX

NEW YORK

Hill and Wang
A division of Farrar, Straus and Giroux
18 West 18th Street, New York 10011

Library of Congress Cataloging-in-Publication Data
Wyman, Mark.
    Hoboes : bindlestiffs, fruit tramps, and the harvesting of the West / Mark
Wyman.— 1st. ed.
        p.   cm.
    Includes bibliographical references and index.
    ISBN 978-0-8090-3021-7 (hbk. : alk. paper)
    1. Tramps—West (U.S.)—History.   2. Migrant labor—West (U.S.)—
History.   3. West (U.S.)—History—1860–1890.   4. West (U.S.)—History—
1890–1945.   I. Title.

HV4504.W96   2010
305.5'68—dc22
                                                                2009020834

Designed by Jonathan D. Lippincott

www.fsgbooks.com

1   3   5   7   9   10   8   6   4   2

*This book is dedicated
to all those who have
helped me know,
and love, the American West*

CONTENTS

THE NEW WEST

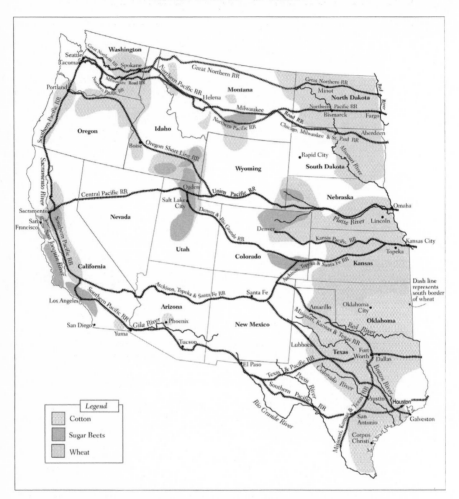

Major railroads and important areas of cotton,
sugar beets, and wheat.

GREAT PLAINS AND THE SOUTHWEST

Wheat, sugar beets, and cotton dominated different areas.

PACIFIC NORTHWEST

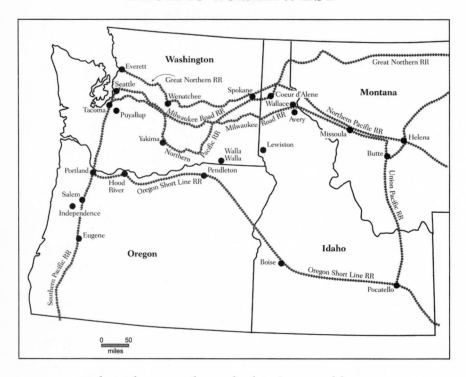

*Wheat, hops, apples and other fruit, and logging
became major products after the arrival of the railroads.*

TEXAS

*Railroads helped cotton spread west from
the Gulf Coast and Piney Woods.*

CALIFORNIA

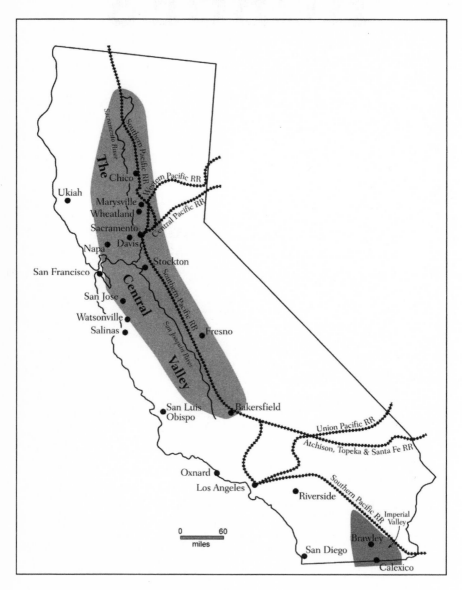

Wheat gradually gave way to fruit, hops, and cotton.

HOBOES

INTRODUCTION

It was not just the long line of men—some two hundred of them—being marched by Aberdeen police from one railroad crossing to another and told to grab a freight out of town. And it was something more than seeing the Aberdeen Commercial Club "packed full of men, honest-looking men, begging for work with no questions as to wages," while farmers in that area of South Dakota "for miles around in all directions were supplied with all the harvest hands they could use."

No, in that summer of 1914 what mainly bothered the agent from the U.S. Commission on Industrial Relations was that only a few weeks earlier the federal government had called for thousands of harvest hands to come to the Great Plains—12,000 to 15,000 for Oklahoma, it was said, then 30,000 more for Missouri and 40,000 for Kansas. Notices calling for more and more workers were sent to postmasters to affix in "a conspicuous place," and the *Aberdeen Daily News* announced that 82,000 more men were needed throughout the wheat belt: "Harvest Fields Offer Opportunity for Unemployed of the Cities."

Special Agent William A. Duffus had to ponder all this as he surveyed the Aberdeen scene, with its saturation of harvest hands, even as calls went out for more: What kind of system would urge thousands of men to leave their homes and head to the harvest fields—when they were not needed? What basic design led men to "flock blindly into the grain states, crowding into the larger and more easily accessible railroad centers," where labor needs were already filled, while "smaller and more remote communities on the branch lines" might be "desperately in need of harvest hands"?

If his employers at the Commission on Industrial Relations had doubts of the truth of his report, Duffus had a suggestion:

The commission should walk up and down the streets of little cities like Oakley and Colby, Kansas; Huron and Redfield, South Dakota; and Casselton, North Dakota, and watch the men who sit along the curbs in long rows, crowd the side walks, lean against buildings, and hang around the railroad stations waiting, waiting—always waiting—for some farmer to come into town to hire a hand; and note the hungry, tired, despondent and some-times sullen looks on the faces of these men.

The probing questions asked by Agent Duffus that day in Aberdeen went to the heart of the transformation of the American West that be-gan in the latter nineteenth century and ran fully two decades into the twentieth. It was brought first by the railroad as it coursed through plains and mountains and coastal districts, opening vast stretches to farming. Then came irrigation canals that, together with the railways, made possible new kinds of intensive agriculture with often strict de-mands on horticulture and science. Arizona cotton growers needed wa-ter from irrigation ditches and a nearby railroad to haul their product to distant markets—as did growers of Washington berries, Colorado sugar beets, and California oranges. The insects that thrived amid closely planted fruit trees had to be combated with the latest sprays. And once the fruit was carefully picked and packed, it had to reach consumers— but the markets for western produce were located far away, in the Mid-west, in the East, even in Europe. With the iron horse, growers could now reach those markets. The pioneer West of Indians and mountain men had emerged into a Second Frontier, beyond the fur trade and cattle drives, where riches came not only from underground mines but also from topsoil. It was truly a new West, and it would soon become the nation's granary, its bountiful orchard, the Cotton West, the Garden West.

What this new frontier lacked was laborers. The large scale of this new agriculture and the lack of nearby cities meant that not only was a hired hand inadequate for a farm's summer and fall needs, but also that the vast numbers of seasonal harvesters required were not available close by. Instead, transients would have to do the work. They would have to show up in time and in large enough numbers to bring in the crop; then when the work was finished, they would have to clear out of the area; but, next season, they would be expected to return. The railroad's role in moving them would be crucial.

Special Agent Duffus saw the worst side of this situation when he stumbled upon the police roundup at Aberdeen. Most of the new crops had only days to be harvested, and growers had no way to guarantee whether labor would be scarce or, as at Aberdeen in 1914, in over-supply. For western newspapers often told the opposite story: in 1906, just when Puyallup, Washington, was expecting one of its biggest raspberry crops, the *Republican* gave out the alarming news that "some farmers have abandoned whole fields and some parts of fields because they cannot get pickers." The following summer in Fresno, California, the *Herald and Democrat* lamented, "Loads of fruit going to waste in need of men." And in Spokane, Washington, in 1910 there were "fully $2000 worth of strawberries rotted on the ground . . . due to a lack of labor," the *Inland Herald* reported. The same stories, the same headlines, ran over and over in western newspapers—harvests were unpredicted and unpredictable. These facts lay in the background that summer of 1914, when Agent Duffus looked out over Aberdeen: too many workers in some areas, too few in others, some needed, some not wanted.

For the railroad that made the new intensive agriculture possible could not pick the cotton, apples, and hops; pull and top the sugar beets; fill the trays with raisin grapes and apricots; or stack the wheat bundles in shocks to be pitched into the maw of the threshing machine. The railroad network may have been hailed as a crucial link between the West and distant markets, but the iron horse that galloped over those steel rails was unable to gather the produce flowing from this new cornucopia.

Which meant that finding workers to shock the wheat, pick the hops, and dig the beets was crucial to western development. While harvesters were required on every farm in every country, there were important differences in the American West. In the Midwest and East farm help often came from family members, neighbors, or occasionally men hired in nearby towns. But this was not the case in much of the West where large fields or groves were common; as a Texas farmer explained when asked about federal attempts to restrict the migration of

Mexicans who picked his cotton: "We need them and they need us. We are sparsely settled here, and have not enough people." A contemporary western investigator summed up the new situation bluntly: there was an "immense reserve labor force because there must be."

Dominated by American whites and European immigrants at the start, soon this army of migrant workers became multicolored: there were Navajos and Klickitats, African-Americans and Chinese, Japanese, Mexicans, Hindus, Filipinos, and Puerto Ricans, among others. And they came in different sizes, genders, and ages, including children who picked berries and also topped beets with sharp machetes. Women flocked to the packinghouses, and frequently entire families could be seen bending among the rows.

But most harvesters were men, and they became closely identified with the western scene, hopping off freights, traipsing along roadways searching for work, ganging up around employment agencies. Later scholars would define them as "agricultural nomads" or "indispensable outcasts." They often carried a rolled-up blanket known variously as a bundle or "bindle"—hence their nickname, "bindlestiffs." And they were called "hoboes," "fruit tramps," "harvest gypsies," "floaters," "transients," "drift-ins," "apple glommers," "almond knockers," and "sugar tramps."

Other names reflected the faraway origins of many. The Japanese soon had their own word for bindlestiffs: *buranketto* boys ("workers who carried blankets with them and went from place to place to work," as one *Issei* explained). Mexican *pizcadores* picked cotton and *betabeleros* dug sugar beets. Names were tossed about in sultry days along vineyard rows, invented in long evenings when they sat in the shade and talked of their new lives, sang old songs, and remembered families left behind when they took up the hobo life.

This ethnic jumble helped produce the food that fed much of the nation and no small part of the world. Their part of the region's story is often glossed over by those seeking the vicarious excitement of a cowboys-and-Indians West. And even when the harvest story is presented, it is often shown as a romantic tale of picturesque people who suddenly appeared and then just as suddenly disappeared, leaving behind only quaint tales and songs.

William Duffus saw a different story as he walked around Aberdeen at the height of the 1914 wheat harvest. He saw that a system with men "beating their way" on freight trains was both dangerous and demoralizing, and he asked how hoboes could "feel a keen interest in the welfare of a community" when they were lured by the promise of good wages and then arrested for vagrancy—or as in Aberdeen, run out of town?

For this was the reality of western harvest labor: it was eagerly recruited—warmly welcomed—then cast off, often chased away, forgotten until next year's harvest. These stark contrasts of the Second Frontier will be explored in these pages. It is a story that must be told if the twenty-first century is to understand western harvest labor development and its continuing challenges. For a large part of the western economy simply could not have developed without them. Victors generally write history, and harvest workers' near-total exclusion from written history might lead one to the conclusion that they were not the victors in this story. But that absence cannot erase their roles in creating the new West.

The chapters that follow will focus on their lives as they harvested the major crops across the West, from the arrival of the railroads starting in the 1870s until automobiles came into widespread use among migrant workers in the mid-1920s. This story will proceed by regions: workers bringing in crops in different western states and territories, requiring some repetition in describing the impact of broader events. The anti-immigrant mood that followed World War I, for example, hit Arizona cotton in different ways than Washington hops. This means that throughout, several major themes will be followed, as the book traces hoboes "beating their way" on railroads, new groups brought in by desperate growers, harvesters' struggles over wages and working conditions, the crisis of World War I and the postwar period, and the arrival of the "gasoline gypsies." It is a story at the center, at the very heart, of the Second Frontier, when the Garden West was created. And within that garden at harvest time was the western hobo, the bindlestiff, the fruit tramp.

1

GREAT EXPECTATIONS

The terms "hobo miner," "hobo lumberjack," "the blanket
stiff," are familiar and necessary in accurate description of
Western labor conditions.   —Carleton Parker

It all depended, at the outset, on the railroad.

"What made Pennsylvania?" a Kansas editor asked one day in mid-
1867. His answer: "Railroads." He asked again: "What made Illinois?
Railroads. What has extended our country from the Atlantic coast to its
present distance west of the Mississippi? Railroads."

A construction crew was then laying down rails approaching town,
and he threw out another query: "What fills Junction City with strange
faces, who crowd our boarding houses and hotels, making five or six
times the life and stir there was one year ago?" The answer was obvious:
"The Union Pacific . . ."[1]

Great expectations preceded the railroad everywhere. To the east,
cities and towns and even crossroads from the Atlantic Coast to the
Mississippi fought long, hard, and with great ingenuity to lure the iron
horse. Now similar efforts were called for as the Union Pacific (UP),
Kansas Pacific (KP), Northern Pacific (NP), Great Northern (GN),
Atchison, Topeka & Santa Fe (called simply the "Santa Fe"), and other
lines pushed on to the Plains and into the mountains in the decades
following the Civil War, while the Central Pacific (CP) and later the
Southern Pacific (SP) were laying tracks eastward from the Pacific
Coast. In ensuing years others were built through the West—the D&RG,
the MKT, the Milwaukee Road, and many smaller lines.[2]

They were awaited with much anticipation. "The effect of a railroad through Plumas [County] would be like touching the gas jet on the dark and somber stage, when all becomes light and animation," predicted the *Oroville* (California) *Register*. "It would be like the whistle in a great mining camp after a period of idleness . . . It would be like the effect of daylight upon the masses of a great city when everyman springs at once to active work of some character." Communities still lacking rails lamented the riches they were being denied. Humboldt County in northern California raised wonderful peaches—"as large as a teacup, and of most luscious flavor"—but without rail connections they had to be packed out on horses or mules "and, from the tenderness of their flesh, are unable to withstand this rough transit."

Desire for a rail link was almost palpable in these towns, whether they were barely populated start-ups platted by eager capitalists or ongoing settlements in ranching and mining districts. And so capitalists were feted; congressmen were cheered. Town after town, county after county, voted bonds overwhelmingly for a promised rail line. Council Grove, Kansas, cast its ballots 78–0 for bonds to fund a southern branch of the Union Pacific, the result only slightly more lopsided than Smoky Hill Townships's 147–7 vote to aid a Kansas Pacific branch from Salina to Lindsborg, running—of course—through Smoky Hill. As the historian of the Southern Pacific observed of such projects, "Some were even built." Failure could mean disaster: Leavenworth, Kansas, was said to be "one-half the size it was fifteen years ago" because a rail connection had slipped through its fingers. And so the town fathers in Dayton, in eastern Washington, promised to ship fruit, grains, flour, even soap and beer worth $100,000 on any railroad that would come their way.

But constructing rail lines to reach these distant outposts—crossing plains, mountains, and deserts, mostly unsettled—required vast amounts of money, difficult to raise in any setting but especially so after the Civil War. Congress recognized quite early that running rail lines to the Pacific would take more funds than capitalists could come up with on their own. The U.S. government was indeed "land poor"—it had land but lacked money. The solution was to give unsettled acres to the railroads as an enticement to financiers: initially lines crossing the West were to receive ten sections (a section is one square mile, 640 acres) of land for each mile of track laid; this was eventually increased to twenty sections, later to forty. The first transcontinental—the Central Pacific–Union Pacific—received 6,400 acres per mile across flatland, more through the mountains. As further encouragement, the UP and CP also were given loans of $16,000 to $48,000, depending on difficulties of the terrain. Later the Northern Pacific won Congress's approval to issue bonds of up to $50,000 for *each mile* of track laid.

Land grants made the difference. They provided tangible collateral for lenders, beyond the promise of eventual riches, for land could be sold right away to the thousands of settlers already chafing to head west. These settlers would one day be shipping produce on the railroads, riding as passengers on the railroads, and purchasing goods hauled from the East and Midwest on the railroads. The possibilities seemed endless. They brought gleams to the eyes of eastern capitalists.

Company directors immediately seized upon the key role of land in fitting together the financial requirements. The Southern Pacific's land agent told the Pacific Railway Commission in 1887, "Here is an instance where the owner of the land is interested in the progress of settlement. The land pays the company, perhaps, much better after it is settled than it does by the price of it." Land sales soon were bringing large sums to railroad cash boxes—totaling almost $12 million for the Central Pacific by 1903, $12.3 million for the Southern Pacific—but those amounts were almost dwarfed by the earnings made hauling freight and passengers. As historian Richard Orsi notes, "Into the twentieth century, company leaders viewed land sales primarily as a stimulus to that vital traffic."

Not only Congress was being solicited for funds, and not only Congress was eager to help. Idaho boosters eagerly backed the Union Pacific in hopes of promoting settlement by Gentiles, to fend off the Mormons colonizing the territory's southern regions. In Texas, El Paso became the major port of travel and trade between the United States and Mexico—but only after it welcomed two railroads from the north and one from Mexico.[3]

When lines were actually constructed, lucky communities often found their great expectations borne out. It seemed true for Fargo, Dakota Territory, after the Northern Pacific arrived in 1872, for "from that day on Fargo seemed to grow by leaps," reaching 800 population by 1878 and 2,753 by 1880, rising to 7,394 in the special 1885 census. A similar story was told in Schuyler, Nebraska, where the Union Pacific's main line came through early in its march from Omaha: in its first year the town gathered in some 400 residents, with two hotels, several stores, and town lots selling for up to $500. New Chicago, Kansas, revealed its dreams in the choice of town name, and the appellation seemed justified after it welcomed its first trains in 1870: three weeks following incorporation, fifty houses and a two-story hotel were completed or under construction; within a few months the population reached 500 and the community had gained a newspaper, a lumberyard, and another hotel.[4]

In the Pacific Northwest along James J. Hill's Great Northern, the town of Wenatchee, Washington, boomed from 451 inhabitants in 1900 to more than 4,000 within a decade after the railroad chose it as a regional hub. Nearby Yakima became an early hops center with the Northern Pacific's arrival, as did Puyallup once it too lured the NP. And when steam engines finally puffed into southern Oregon, Medford saw thirty-six new buildings constructed within three months. As an editor in Ashland announced, his community "is now connected by rail with the great cities of the continent."[5]

That was the major point: the new rail lines with their parallel telegraph wires brought links to the outside world, connecting to people miles and miles away, and—most important for future growth—connecting to markets.

Agricultural possibilities suddenly opened, and in the Central Valley of California the transformation was especially dramatic. As late as the early 1880s Fresno had been, according to a settler's recollection, "without a solitary shrub or tree"—but twenty years later there were 3,000 raisin grape vineyards of 10 to 40 acres each within twenty miles of the city—all because of the railroad. Soon more lines besides the CP-UP route carried California fruit to markets far beyond the West. The Southern Pacific arrived in Yuma on the Arizona border in 1877, then pushed west across Texas to El Paso and beyond to New Orleans by 1881. The Santa Fe provided links between Chicago and the Pacific Coast, through the Southwest, by 1885. To the north, the Northern Pacific reached Portland in 1883, and the Great Northern arrived in Seattle in 1893, in the process stimulating large-scale wheat raising and "bonanza farms" across the northern tier of states, as well as fruit raising in Wenatchee, Okanogan, Yakima, and other districts in Washington State.[6]

No wonder the celebrations were so elaborate, the excitement so intoxicating. Just as parades had erupted across the nation with the marriage of the UP-CP rails at Promontory Summit, Utah, in 1869, similar outpourings appeared across the West wherever lines were completed or even merely authorized. "A grand blowout" marked the initial work with shovels and picks on Texas's Denison & Southwestern Railway in 1877, and when two sections of the Northern Pacific were joined in Garrison, Montana, in 1883, ex-president U.S. Grant was on hand for the festivities. Beams from the headlight of a newly arrived locomotive illuminated the dance floor at Sprague, Washington, as townspeople whirled and cheered the opening of the NP's new roundhouse.

An up-and-coming town without a railroad? Preposterous to think of. And that explains the unusual moves by some communities: The Kansas City, Pittsburg & Gulf Railroad missed the Choctaw town of Scullyville, Oklahoma Territory, so inhabitants picked up and moved two miles to build a new town right beside the tracks. Residents of Yakima, Washington, were no different, although they had been bypassed by the Northern Pacific through their own fault: the city had refused to provide land for a depot. Miffed, the railroad located its depot farther on. Yakima residents then relocated there.[7]

Could any enthusiasm seem extreme in such settings? Were not European buyers already showing up in Portland to personally order apples? A Hamburg, Germany, commission merchant "was so impressed with the fine quality of these apples, that he came over in person to make arrangements for his future supply," the *Northwest Pacific Farmer* reported with pride. The evidence was everywhere: a California horticulturist noted that the rise of Siskiyou County as a major apple producer had occurred only "since the completion of the railroad through the county. Before this time no notice was taken of fruit . . ." The journal pointed out what was happening everywhere: "The completion of the railroad, and the opening of a market thereby, have had the effect of turning attention to fruit growing as a business . . ."[8]

The *Northwest Pacific Farmer* was right. The railroad was creating a new West, a fruit-growing, wheat- and cotton- and beet- and hop-growing West, a West transfixed by the profits ahead. For this was the launching of a new era, brought into existence by the railroad. The iron horse promised solutions to the West's weaknesses, drawbacks dating back to the beginnings of American control: its towns and farms sat at great distances from markets; rapid communication was impractical to impossible; arid climates presented agricultural difficulties; and its population was sparse and widely dispersed.

In the East, settlement had preceded the railroads, and so both customers and markets had been ready when loading platforms went up at the railheads. But major markets for the West remained hundreds and even thousands of miles away, and transportation was extremely costly. Expensive shipping around the Horn, or carting by stagecoach or freight wagons, argued against transporting anything but the most important goods. When Ben Holliday's freighting company took only three months and four days for a round-trip from Junction City, Kansas, to Denver, an editor observed, "No such time was ever made on the Platte route . . ." Speed was not yet a part of Western life.

It arrived with the railroad, reducing to inadequacy or even futility many of the traditional systems of transport. The *Atchison* (Kansas) *Free Press* rang the final bell for Ben Holliday's freight wagons in December 1866:

> At about noon to-day the last of the trappings of the Holliday Overland Stage Line, consisting of about a dozen four mule teams and covered wagons, moved quietly from Second street, up Commercial street, and on westward to where the star of the empire in stage business is in the ascendant. Its movements were melancholy—the funeral aspect only enlivened by the white canvas covers of the great lumbering wagons. Very well; the iron sinews of commerce are stretching out across the prairies from the "Gate of the West," and will soon send the great stage route far into the wilderness again to keep its braying mules beyond the stirring scream of the steam whistle.[9]

It was more than tragic, it was also symbolic when a Southern Pacific locomotive smashed into an Arizona wagon train one day in November 1880, killing the mules and destroying two wagons. The incident was just one more discouragement for the mule team owners—they were charging 5½ to 14 cents per pound transporting goods for the twenty-day haul from Yuma to Tucson. The new SP took only a day to complete the trip, charging 1½ cents per pound.

Farmers who had rushed to the Plains in the early corn and wheat frontier days had a special, immediate need for the railroad. "When our first sod corn was raised father went eighty miles to mill in an ox wagon, and for two years we had this to do," a Kansas woman recalled of her family's 1857 settlement in Morris County. Other early Kansas reports told of settlers traveling fifty to seventy-five miles, then waiting up to ten days for their wheat to be milled. In the rolling country around Pendleton, Oregon, one farmer described hauling grain to be threshed up to forty miles away at Umatilla at a cost of 17 cents per bushel. But that, the *Northwest Pacific Farmer* explained, was "before the advent of the railroad . . ."[10]

The railroad changed it all. It ended the total reliance upon ox team or riverboat for a farmer wishing to market his wheat outside the immediate area. Those near water had advantages, of course, and at one point some six hundred sailing ships were carrying wheat from San Francisco to Liverpool for British consumers—wheat raised adjacent to rivers running into San Francisco Bay. But with the railroad at hand, many of those wheatlands were being carved up for orchards and new crops, and access to water transportation was no longer important. On learning in 1890 that California vegetables were being raised for the New York market, the state agricultural society declared with evident pride that the state's "radius of profitable production sweeps over a limit of land transportation three thousand miles long." Just a few years earlier it had been twenty-five or thirty miles.[11]

Besides drastically extending the market's reach, the railroad was a catalyst for further technological change. Helping lift the Dakotas to prominence was hard, red spring wheat, the new variety demanded by Minneapolis millers who could now tap the northern Plains. By 1915 Minneapolis was milling 20 million barrels of flour annually. On the Palouse, the rolling prairies in eastern Washington and Oregon, new seeds and harvesting machinery produced a crop so enormous in 1890 that the supply of cars was inadequate to haul it away, and piles of wheat lined the tracks well into winter. Mechanical advances with one crop encouraged inventions for others. The raisin seeder, an important advance for Fresno's raisin grape yards, was developed by growers who had observed how the new reapers and threshing machines were simplifying wheat harvests nearby.[12]

Areas that had been agriculturally barren now became known for new crops, for different crops. Cotton raising spread across Texas. "Cotton picking has already begun in the lower [southern] list of counties in the State," noted a Fort Worth reporter interviewing an official in August 1894, "and is being ginned and he expects that by August 15 there will be a decided increase in the traffic of the Santa Fe in consequence of cotton seeking the markets." Soon sugar beets, well established in Europe and grown elsewhere in the United States, were being produced in several western districts, especially in California, Utah, Idaho, Colorado, and Nebraska; hops expanded into the Pacific Northwest and California. Cantaloupes, whose weight made them especially dependent upon cheap transportation, became important in Colorado and southern California, and a wide variety of fruit became identified with the coastal states.[13]

Railroad companies pushed agricultural settlement, irrigation, and scientific experiments. William H. Mills, who held the position of chief SP land agent from 1883 to 1907, urged farmers toward specialization in their districts, based on the region's sharp differences in soils, moisture levels, and climate. These campaigns produced results quickly, and Ventura County's experience was not unusual. N. B. Smith of Buena Ventura told the California State Agricultural Society in 1891 that the county had 84,000 apricot, 5,000 fig, 50,000 prune, 5,000 lemon, 36,000 orange, and 100,000 walnut trees. He hardly needed to add: "Since the advent of the Southern Pacific Railroad we have made rapid and progressive growth . . ."

New crop after new crop appeared because now the railroad could carry it to a waiting public. Wheat had once been the only major agricultural product that left California, but this changed as the fledgling orange industry became established. Soon other fruit joined the rush, as in Oregon, where a minister in Ashland estimated in 1888 that 200,000 fruit trees had been planted in Jackson County in a single season, and "every body, young and old, rich and poor, saint and sinner, is engaged in picking, drying, packing or shipping fruit." When an historian later surveyed the changes there, he concluded, "A new industry had been born in the year of the railroad."

The transformation brought more than fruit trees; the *Northwest Pacific Farmer* noted that 1904 was "the first year that a special berry train was ever run out of Hood River, the O.R. & N. furnishing a special strawberry train, running straight through from here to Omaha on passenger time." In Puyallup, Washington, in 1908, wagons and carts packed with crates of raspberries "were often lined up in a long string on the streets waiting their turn to deliver the product" at the loading platform. It was a common scene, for in the days of harvest many western freight depots became congested, as wagons filled with cotton bales, hops bales, or fruit containers jostled to unload.[14]

Refrigerator cars—"reefers"—made much of this possible. At first "ventilator cars" attempted to carry delicate berries and peaches at least as far as the Midwest without heavy spoilage. Producers and marketers demanded something better, however, and so ice was tried in a variety of experiments, especially during fall's cooler temperatures. Finally midwestern meat packers achieved a breakthrough that produced effective refrigerated cars, and western fruit packers rushed in. By 1900 the Southern California Fruit Exchange was contracting with three firms: the Santa Fe's refrigerator car line, the California Fruit Express, and Armour Car Lines. In 1906 the SP and UP joined to form Pacific Fruit Express, which immediately ordered 6,600 of the new cars. Shipping on them was expensive, for six to eight re-icings were often required for apple shipments between Washington State and Chicago. But a need had been met, and the growers cheered, although they continued to complain about high freight charges. Nationwide, some 110,000 refrigerator cars were in use by 1915.[15]

Insect scourges were frequent, though rarely as serious as the 1874 grasshopper invasion that wiped out crops on the Plains and led the Kansas Pacific Railway to provide free seed to farmers. But they could be devastating and drew quick scientific assistance. "We have the pests of the entire world," lamented one California grower in 1884, "and from present appearances they have come to stay." As historian Steven Stoll has catalogued, California fruit district threats included fifteen different parasites attacking pear and quince trees; fourteen that hit grapevines; and many others targeting specific fruits, including the woolly apple aphid, the codling moth, red scale, and Hessian fly. "Stinking smut" attacked the wheatfields, while "chinch bugs" turned cornstalks black—two early menaces fought by the new state agricultural experiment stations. Here again railroad companies rushed to give assistance, especially the Southern Pacific, which worked with California's university scientists. A later writer characterized the SP as "one of the leading patrons of scientific farming in the West, as well as of advanced agricultural research and education."[16]

The large-scale capitalism behind railroad expansion was quickly turned to other activities benefiting agriculture, especially irrigation. Railroad companies were among the foremost institutions encouraging water development projects, partly from an immediate, operational need. Early steam engines needed to stop every twenty-five miles for water (or carry their own); photos of giant windmills drawing water along the westward-building Union Pacific dramatically demonstrate that requirement. But once rail lines were in full operation, the focus was on making water available for farmers so that they could move beyond planting dryland wheat. The Northern Pacific helped launch the Northwest's largest project, the Sunnyside Canal in Washington, that opened up much of the Yakima area for fruit raising. The same need existed in the desert or near-desert areas to the south—in much of the Great Basin, California's Central Valley, and especially the extremely dry regions of southern California. The federal government soon stepped in to build dams and reservoirs. These projects—extensive and expensive—opened vast areas to agriculture, areas previously classed as little more than waste deserts.[17]

That was the case in Arizona, where pioneer boosters soon realized there would be no agricultural advance without irrigation. The territorial governor saw irrigation and agriculture as "indissolubly linked together, as all success in agriculture depends entirely upon irrigating enterprises carried to a successful conclusion." Maricopa County, site of the territorial (later state) capital of Phoenix, saw early irrigation canals tapping the Salt, Gila, and Verde rivers. An 1890 U.S. Census report claimed that early results showed that some parts of Maricopa "when properly wet, can produce enormous crops," rivaling portions of California. Further, the report added, when hauled to eastern markets the Arizona fruit—thanks to the Southern Pacific—would be "saved a day's journey through the hot desert" which California fruit had to endure en route east. Maricopa became the major Arizona county vigorously pushing irrigation, but there were others, and from 1890 to 1900 the territory saw 545 miles of irrigation canals and ditches constructed, many with railroad support. The key role played by railroads in irrigation as well as other development was being repeated across the region, and each state and territory could echo a Colorado Bureau of Labor Statistics report for 1909: "Upon the transportation companies depend, in a large measure, the prosperity of our state."[18]

These new irrigation projects, the attacks on insects, the land purchases, and the land clearing—all meant that western farmers' start-up costs could be enormous. When almond trees were first planted around Davisville (now Davis), California, it turned out that the trees took up to five years to bear. When sugar beets were started in Lehi, Utah, in 1891, the promoters discovered they had to spend $30,000 just training local farmers—totally unfamiliar with the crop—during their first two years. Proprietors of an early Washington State hop operation learned that their 611 acres in the Puyallup area would need tens of thousands of climbing poles for the vines, some 8,000 pounds of twine, 1,500 gallons of whale oil, and 2,500 pounds of caustic soda for spraying.

Further, because the West's new crops were now sold on both national and world markets, they were beset with sudden, sharp price swings, during growing season and between seasons. Oregon hops went for 25 cents per pound in 1921, then 9 cents in 1922. ("I would not advise people to go into hop culture unless they own the land and have a bank account upon which to draw during low prices," one California expert warned, noting that three or four years of low prices "are enough to break most growers.") The high costs often forced farmers to stake everything on intensive plantings that would provide the returns they needed to survive. In this regard fruit raising and other endeavors were no different from western mining and logging, which also had heavy start-up requirements and suffered frequent shutdowns over collapsing prices. Disasters from price swings showed that the West remained a colony of the East, for decisions made in faraway centers held strangleholds on many of the new agricultural endeavors.[19]

There was one other major concern: growers were operating in a labor desert. The issue loomed large over the new western farmers as they sought to reduce expenses—many of which were beyond their ability to control. But labor costs at least held the potential for control. At all steps their need for hired help was great—pickers, loaders, graders, packers, men, women, and even children who could help bring in the crop and process it and pack it, then send it to consumers thousands of miles away. While every crop in every section of the nation had extra labor needs at harvest time, western growers were launching their enterprises in lightly populated districts. That this could lead to disaster was often not recognized at start-up.

"Loads of fruit going to waste in need of men," announced the *Fresno Herald and Democrat* in 1907, hardly an unusual report around the region. "Tons of peaches are dropping on the ground for want of pickers . . . ," the newspaper explained, quoting a fruit packer: "The reason for the congestion is that the fruit is ripening all at once . . ." The California Fruit Canners manager told the Industrial Relations Commission in 1914 that this type of agriculture was different from manufacturing, "in that the product does waste if you do not handle it immediately . . . Any thing that is not canned the day it comes in, it is deteriorating immediately."[20]

That was the problem. Having large numbers of harvesters was crucial, and the dependence upon a single fruit in one district meant that vigorous competition among growers for harvesters was unavoidable, even desperate. Cattle could be kept in a feedlot or range for longer periods; potatoes could be dug later or even stored. But many crops that were overripe were lost. Even cotton would lose color, declining in quality, after going unpicked past its prime; wheat ran the risk of shattering or being caught in a rainstorm. A U.S. Department of Agriculture specialist explained what often happened regarding labor needs in such a situation: without rotating plantings from one year to the next—impossible in most cases—"some of the most important crops . . . compete strongly with one another in the matter of labor required at certain seasons of the year." He added that while usually little labor was needed at other seasons, during the harvest rush "it is necessary to depend on transient labor, which is almost always of an undesirable character."[21]

The U.S. Bureau of Labor Statistics's 1884 report probed deeper into what was becoming a perplexing situation:

> We have heard and have indeed known of fruit remaining unpicked on the trees and grapes remaining ungathered in the vine-

yard. Grain has remained in the fields exposed to the rain because men could not be secured to thrash [sic] it, and hay has rotted in the stacks because there were no farm hands to handle it. Farmers have been compelled to take what help they could get, whether they were white or Chinamen, nor has it been a strange sight to see in California women and children labor in the fields. Boys and girls, in fact, have been in great demand in the vineyards, on the hop farms, and in the berry gardens . . .

Hitherto the one great objection to an increase of the unskilled white labor population in California has been that necessary as it was to have more help during Summer and harvest, the manner of husbandry in this State was such as to assure those who labor for others, work only for three, or at the highest, five or six months during the year. It was admitted to be an unnatural condition of affairs, and one which should be remedied . . .[22]

Requiring large numbers of workers who showed up only for harvest was a novel experience for many newcomers, especially those who had come from small farms in the Midwest and East. It was so different that many sensed danger in the new system. The threat for a society dependent upon hoboes was put bluntly by Mrs. Anna Morrison Reed, of the Sonoma-Marin district: she told delegates to the 1891 meeting of the California State Agricultural Society that back east, farmworkers ate with the family; "they are self-respecting citizens of this republic." But the situation developing in California, she argued, meant different treatment for farm laborers. There seemed to be no space in the new system for workers walking out from town, no more hiring of locals. "They were required to furnish blankets and sleep in straw," Mrs. Reed complained. "Make the employment of men brutal and you must depend upon a brutalized class . . ." But some held out hope for change, and those 1891 delegates heard the organization's president glowingly predict that the dominance of large ranches would someday lessen, and "the pursuit of horticulture may be the happy means of dotting the land with small holdings, which will be the seat of happy homes . . ." Rearrange the rural landscape, he emphasized, and "small farms will solve the labor question."[23]

But the issue would not die, and each year the goal of re-creating the midwestern farm scene became less reachable. As early as 1890 the

Southern Pacific's William Mills admitted before the California State Agricultural Society that when the railroad opened up the fruit industry, it also gave birth to a major problem: "the irregular character of employment." As an example, he cited Senator Leland Stanford's 3,000-acre vineyard, where 500 men were added for two months at the start of picking, then up to 700 men during a three-week period within those two months. Across California, the grape harvest required ten times as many men as were employed year-round—but "it would be impossible to have the labor of nine men available for a few months in the vintage season for one man who might find steady employment." The single-crop emphasis of most intensive farming left few options.[24]

As sugar beet cultivation expanded in the West—first in California, then in Utah, Nebraska, Kansas, Colorado, Idaho, and eventually Montana—this situation appeared over and over to challenge growers. Surveying sugar beet cultivation in 1909, one expert concluded, "The sugar-beet sections of the country are greatly in need of more labor, and in a great measure of more intelligent and reliable labor." Filling this need required importing immigrants and people from the cities, he noted, adding a crucial final point: "Probably the uncertainty of continuous employment in the country is one of the most potent factors in this connection."[25]

The result: achieving success with sugar beets, as with most other crops now sprouting and blooming across the West's intensive-agriculture districts, depended in the final analysis upon transient labor—specifically, its availability in large numbers, at low cost, easily discharged, and sent away when work was done.

Labor requirements of this Second Frontier were creating new realities, but the transient nature of harvester requirements may have seemed less innovative to some because of the traditional mobility of frontier folk. Moving, and moving on, was already in the genetic makeup of many who traveled west during this, the final chapter of America's westward movement. Well before the railroads hauled settlers in special emigrant trains, a Kansas editor in 1867 looked out on people traveling through Junction City. "Some ten families of Texans passed through town on their way to Oregon," he reported in the *Union*. "They were a migratory

set, having lived in Illinois, Missouri, Arkansas and Texas." It was already an old tale, already a way of life on the cattleman's frontier and the mining frontier. And so testimony by a miner in a Nevada court case was not out of the ordinary: Charles MacKinnon had come West from Pennsylvania and had mined in British Columbia, at two sites in Colorado, at Tonopah, Rhyolite, and other small mines around Nevada, in addition to working in Mexico, Texas, the Indian Territory, and Arkansas. All in the course of just over two decades. "I was rambling a good deal during them years," he explained.[26]

A rambling population meshed well with the new western agriculture. A harvest job would not last; it would always be seasonal, short term, erecting barriers to anyone who was trying to save up to buy a nearby farm (part of the midwestern tradition of going up the "agricultural ladder"). And once these "floaters" finished work, they "hibernated," or trekked to a city fleabag hotel for the winter. Historian David Vaught notes how conditions of fruit harvesting in California enforced these cycles for transients: "little, if any, job security; temperatures near 100 degrees; dry and dusty terrain; and, with vineyard work, constant stooping or squatting. Regardless of the skill, experience, or knack required, orchard and vineyard work attracted only those with limited options."

Such was harvest life in wide areas of the West, where laborers following crops over many years came to know no other type of life and to consider nothing else as possible. Railroads had helped create an agriculture that ensured their options were indeed limited.[27]

While poets talked blithely of the freedom of the open road, others closer to the scene saw "the whip of economic necessity" driving migrant workers on, always moving to another job in another orchard or field or yard. It became a habit, and while railroad engineers could praise hoboes for their wide knowledge of the different problems of constructing new lines, the engineers also admitted that hoboes were "a very unreliable class of men, their length of service averaging from three days to six weeks . . ."

This carried over to agriculture: a California fruit grower called seasonal laborers "an uneasy class of people, and many of them don't even work out the time I would like to have them work; they will work a week or so, and when they have got a little money they will move on—ask for their money and move on to other places." They had a "gypsy spirit," a hopyard owner told the Industrial Relations Commission, driven by the fact that "there is not enough work to go around, and the people get in the habit of moving, and they keep moving . . . If there was more steady employment we would have less of that wandering sort." But whatever the motivation, their existence was "essential under the present organization of industry on a seasonal, irregular basis," explained Carleton H. Parker, the era's leading expert on casual labor. In agricultural work they may have been called "fruit tramps" or "harvest gypsies," Parker agreed, but they were everywhere in the West, in many occupations: "The terms 'hobo miner,' 'hobo lumberjack,' 'the blanket stiff' are familiar and necessary in accurate description of Western labor conditions."[28]

Eventually, in the mid-1920s, many in this seasonal labor force would start using the automobile, ushering in another era in western history. But before the automobile they traveled on the railroad. Watching "a hundred or several hundred men on a single freight train in open daylight and in plain violation of law" was "grotesquely humorous" to an Industrial Relations Commission investigator in 1914, but it had been going on for years by then, all across the West at harvest time.[29] Those riding the rails probably saw no humor, grotesque or otherwise, in what they were doing; they were just traveling to the next job. Perhaps they did not realize they were being carried on the very form of transport that had opened the West to intensive agriculture—a form of agriculture that demanded thousands and thousands of them to bring in the harvest. As one observer wrote, there was a migratory class of harvesters "because there must be."[30]

2

"WHEAT FARMS AND HOBOES GO TOGETHER"

They were desperate as wheat ripened across Kansas that hot summer of 1881. "Any culprit that refuses to work" on the wheat harvest would be put in jail "and fed on twelve ounces of bread per day, and water until discharged," the Manhattan City Council ordered—with ball and chain attached if the city marshal "sees proper to do so." Police in nearby Atchison announced that "idlers" would be arrested for vagrancy as long as local farmers were pleading for harvest help.

The threats coming out of Kansas in 1881 demonstrated that the wheat frontier had migrated again on its westward trek, this time across the Missouri onto the Great Plains. Now it was moving into a region that seemed perfect, with large, rolling, fertile fields made available by the Homestead Act and also offered by the railroads—seldom interrupted by woodlands, with enough moisture for grain to thrive, exactly suited to the new machinery being developed. An investigator for the U.S. Industrial Relations Commission declared that Kansas was "almost a one crop country—Winter wheat." The same was soon an accurate description for most of the Great Plains. Now it would also be called the "grain belt."[1]

Many events, many factors, made this possible. New immigrants from Russia—the much-sought "German-Russian Mennonites"—brought wheat seeds named Red Turkey that could survive even the blistering southern Plains summers by being planted in the fall, then hibernating through winter, to germinate the following spring and ripen by midsummer. To the north, farmers in the Dakotas and Montana learned to plant spring wheat, which was ready for harvest by late August or September.

Corn, the other crucial frontier crop, also was planted immediately by the settlers pushing onto the Plains, and it did well, especially in Nebraska. But wheat remained the major cash crop, and now the railroad could move it out to waiting buyers—which made all the difference.[2]

As settlers began showing up in these newly opened lands west of the Mississippi, they moved quickly to plow, even as they built their "soddies"—sodhouse dwellings—for they found wheat easy to plant and requiring little care. Success came quickly and bred imitators. As a farmer in Ellsworth County, Kansas, enthusiastically explained to the local newspaper in the fall of 1870, "Mr. Hudson's success has caused much interest to be taken in wheat, and many have sown this fall quite largely, considering the quantity of lands under cultivation and the fact that no flouring mill has yet been built in this part of the country."[3]

As farmers were arriving on the rolling Plains, midwestern inventors were perfecting machinery to solve some major challenges: drills, for planting seed into dry ground; John Deere's famous self-scouring plow; and harvesting miracles such as the reaper, the grain binder, the header, and the threshing machine. Now ripe grain could be cut by a machine that tied it into bundles, leaving crews to come along afterward to stand the bundles in shocks for further ripening while cap bundles gave some protection from rain. That remained the primary system for decades, although headers were sometimes used: the header would clip the grain below the head, dumping it into wagons that hauled it away for threshing.[4] Threshing machines, powered first by horses, then by steam engines, and ultimately by gasoline engines, opened the way for large-scale farming on the Great Plains. They were costly but worked well for harvesting vast acreages. The farmer became ever more a businessman seeking to expand production. Not a subsistence farmer (which, in fact, he had never been), he was more than ever a small capitalist.

Many who had started out farming the Homestead Act's quarter-section did some calculating and figured they could handle more than 160 acres. All they needed was access to one of the new harvesting machines and a crew of helpers. As early as 1870, the census found 55 farms in Kansas and 11 in Nebraska with more than 500 acres; 13 of those in Kansas had over 1,000 acres. The trend continued, and at century's end the census takers counted 21,111 farms with 1,000 acres or more in the Dakotas, Nebraska, Kansas, Oklahoma, and Texas.

It has been said that "statistics don't bleed," but they also don't awe and cannot reveal the excitement stirred by the sight of these extensive farms. A visitor in 1902 found spots in Kansas "where one can stand upon a knoll and count from eleven to fifteen quarter-sections in one field." An immigrant who returned to Norway recalled a neighbor on the Great Plains of America who "had a farm, him alone, which he ran by himself, which was as large as the whole of Selje parish." Another report told of a returned Norwegian who said that when plowing, "he had to take a sight on some landmark in the distance to keep the furrow straight. He plowed with one or two teams of horses. And he only plowed one round, back and forth each day. His fields were that big."[5]

Such extensive tracts soon produced enough wheat to overwhelm local markets, even to occasionally glut the Chicago grain market. Mill construction finally caught up, but for the first two decades after Kansas achieved statehood in 1861, the landscape featured only small mills, none with a daily capacity over 150 barrels, and "exportation of flour was unheard of, and almost unthought of." But the arrival of the railroad and the expansion of wheat acreages led to a surge in flour mill construction in the 1880s. Soon flour from the region's wheat—increasingly milled on rollers in the new "gradual reduction process"—was being exported widely, leading the Santa Fe railroad to build in Kansas City a mill whose daily capacity of 5,000 barrels placed it among the world's largest.

Census figures reveal that in 1870 Kansas and Nebraska each were producing more than two million bushels of wheat, but by 1900 these totals had grown to 38,778,450 bushels for Kansas and 24,924,520 for Nebraska. They were not the national leaders, however, far from it, for by century's end North Dakota held that title with 59,888,810 bushels, while neighboring South Dakota produced 41,889,380 bushels.[6]

A ready supply of harvest hands made such output possible. Wheat's expansion could take place only with the required ingredients present: fairly level or gently rolling land, adequate moisture, seed adapted to the Plains climates, railroads conveniently running nearby—and enough workers at harvest time. Earlier in the American experience, single-crop plantations had relied upon importing African slaves, a labor system that produced the powerful, wealthy cotton kingdom of the antebellum South. But such a solution was not available in the western lands that railroads were opening from the 1870s on. As historian Allen Gale Applen put it, "The development of the wheat growing industry on the Great Plains following the Civil War occurred in what was essentially a labor vacuum . . . The western Prairies and High Plains had no indigenous labor force suitable to the needs of the large-scale wheat producer."[7]

Earlier wheat frontiers depended on farmers working with their families and neighbors at threshing time, with an occasional hired man brought out from town. But as larger farms appeared on the Plains, more than neighbors were required to fill out threshing crews. Kansas editor William Allen White found that Dakota wheat harvests in 1879 were drawing transients from states to the south and from such large cities as St. Paul, Chicago, Omaha, St. Louis, and Milwaukee. The number hired is impossible to determine accurately for any year, for statistics become a jumble of "shockers" who set the wheat bundles into shocks to ripen or "cure"; "spikers" who tossed the bundles into the wagons; "bundle pitchers" who tossed the bundles into the maw of the threshing machine; and many others handling wagons and horses.

The "Great Dakota Boom" that ran from 1879 to 1886 drew massive numbers of workers to the "bonanza farms" that thrived under the Northern Pacific land department's encouragement as it sold large chunks from its extensive land grant. While the standard field on a bonanza farm was one section—640 acres—individual farms reached mammoth sizes: the Dalrymple farm had a total of more than 30,000 acres at one point but was eclipsed in size by the Grandin farms, which took in more than 75,000 acres; the Grandin holdings were broken up and sold after 1894.

Hiring workers only when needed was seen as an advantage over the midwestern custom of keeping hands around even when their labor was not required. On the Plains, however, wages rose and fell with the abundance or scarcity of workers, leading to sharp variations year by year: "In the slack periods in the summer, men could be secured for from $0.60 to $0.75 per day," historian Hiram Drache found. Lower wages were paid to shockers, spike pitchers, and bundle wagon drivers; the higher pay went to the men running the threshing machines, a much-sought position—one report said such a man "often slept under the separator at night for fear of losing his job."

With heavy investments in men, horses, and machines, wheat production in the Red River Valley shot up from 4,500 bushels per 100 inhabitants in 1879, to 121,500 bushels per 100 in 1884. Such abundance encouraged the Great Plains equivalent of Paul Bunyan tales, especially "furrow" stories. One son recalled his father plowing "a furrow that was over 40 miles long, and so straight you could snap a chalk line in it from one end to the other without touching either side." A similar tall tale claimed that a man on a bonanza farm was sent out with a plow in the spring and plowed steadily until fall; "Then he turned around and harvested back."[8]

Bonanza farms needed hundreds of workers—one farm of 4,000 acres hired 20 men just to set up shocks. An 1897 report told of requiring 15 extra workers for every 1,000 acres of wheat, with Grandin bringing in 250 extra men for harvest. The Dalrymple operations in 1884 hired 1,000 men for its harvest fields, operating 200 self-binding reapers pulled by 800 horses. The wheat from 30,000 acres was threshed by 30 steam-operated threshing machines; output was 600,000 bushels.

Much attention has been focused on bonanza farms, then and now. A touring journalist commented on the condition of the dormitory where crews stayed, where clean beds, a smoking and loafing room, and a supply of hot water made it quite different from the usual housing for farmhands. At the Keystone farm, however, the bunkhouse with forty men was termed "verminous"—at odds with the condition of the barns, which were often cleaned twice a day. At harvest time at Keystone the extra crew often slept outdoors, on straw.[9]

Outsiders unaccustomed to such massive labor crews—their near equivalents existed only in the South—could be critical: on such fields men were employed "in squads," the 1901 Industrial Commission was told, a system that "eliminates all the individuality and independence of these men." The bonanza farms' need for workers meant that any shortage could bring disaster—and the inadequate labor supplies of the World War I era have been cited as a major factor in their decline. By then, however, rising land values, a round of dry years and falling prices, and the use of new machinery by the large farms' competitors throughout the Grain Belt had been encouraging sell-offs and breakups. Little by little the bonanza farms were divided and sold.[10]

While many Plains farmers tended to settle on 320 acres as the best size, still manageable by a family and requiring few transient workers, over time many others went for larger holdings. The variations in harvest needs could be enormous, making planning difficult. The annual wheat harvest began in the Texas and Oklahoma fields in early summer, edged steadily northward as the grain was ripening at some twenty-five miles a day, and ended in the autumn fields of Saskatchewan. All along the way the weather had numerous opportunities to help or hinder or even destroy a crop. Rainy weather could produce long straw if the storms were abundant in the growing season, requiring more harvest help; but a protracted period of hot, dry days could doom the grain. "Wheat is dieing," a Nebraska farmer wrote in his diary for June 12, 1893. "There will be no harvest this year from present indications."[11]

Later historians' estimates put the annual harvest labor total for the Grain Belt in the neighborhood of 100,000 men—for a "normal crop season." A 1921 study determined that 40 percent of the harvesters were family or immediate neighbors, who might be trading labor, and 44 percent were hired from the outside. Great Plains newspapers and other contemporary accounts reveal that sharp shifts in demand went beyond season to season, coming even week to week and day to day. A Kansas official told of a decision made one morning that harvest would come in two weeks—but "the next morning we knew it would start within 24 hours." In Salina, Kansas, laborers were abundant in June 1879 when harvesting was "in full blast"; two summers later, however, nearby areas were reporting "a scarcity of help . . ." In Dickinson County, Kansas, the farmers in 1881 "say they have lots of work to do and no one to do it"—and when they went to town hunting for laborers, nine out of ten times "their search is fruitless." Don D. Lescohier, a researcher for the U.S. Department of Agriculture, tried in the early 1920s to calculate these shifts in demand but finally concluded that "there seems to be a striking variation in the amounts of labor used in different areas using the same machinery."[12]

The early 1890s were particularly disastrous in the Grain Belt, and after farmers lost production in 1891 from inadequate numbers of harvesters, South Dakota newspapers in 1892 described farmers as "panic stricken" over labor shortages. In Ellis County, Kansas, that year, the call went out for 500 laborers to harvest some 1,000 acres of wheat; some farmers offered to board any early arrivals while they waited for work to begin. A farmer in Stockville, Nebraska, wrote during 1892's threshing, "Run short of men at dark and I had to do about two men's work until 10 p.m. Without supper too."[13]

Labor shortages called forth dramatic, sometimes desperate measures. One Kansas farmer ignored the sunup-to-sundown tradition and was "cutting and caring for his wheat day and night . . . It was a strange sight to see the harvest operations by lamp and torch light." Shortages were so bad in 1897 in southwestern Kansas that wages shot up to $4 and $5 a day—unheard of then—and in Crowley and Sumner counties women and girls were brought into the harvest crews. The *Nebraska State Journal* reported that "harvest hands have never been so hard to find" in Kansas as that year. The National Farmers' Alliance business agent testified in 1899 that "at this time now, in Minnesota and in the Dakotas, we have the greatest difficulty in getting sufficient farm laborers to go out into the wheat fields to save the crop," partly because men preferred the steadier employment of railroad construction.[14]

When wheat was rotting in the fields, anger mounted at men who would not answer recruitment calls. Particularly galling to farmers was what greeted them when they came into town: idlers lazily slouching around Main Street while a few miles away a wheat crop needed saving. Editorials blasted such loafers, and a rural reporter in Cambria, Kansas, asked, "Could not Salina spare a few of those gentlemen of leisure who daily haunt the corners of the streets, under awnings, and think store boxes good seats?" The *Salina Herald* was especially vexed, noting that two local men had been offered $1.25 a day but "'the work was too hard.'" The editor lashed out: "Any able-bodied man or boy applying for something to eat should be summarily bounced."[15]

Railroad construction crews were sometimes a source of emergency help, and Kansas coal miners occasionally showed up. For more than farmers could serve: in Cherokee, Oklahoma, the county agent urged shopkeepers "to get out and help in the harvest . . . Every store in the county could run with less help during the harvest period . . ." He also urged that boys be tried in the fields, although he added, "They should not of course expect a man's wages unless they can do a man's work." Such extensive recruiting could mean that crews sometimes contained different ethnic varieties, with African-Americans, Mexicans, and Indians starting to appear.[16]

At times during particularly bad years, farmers gathered around the jails, offering to pay fines so they could acquire prisoners to come out and work. In mid-July 1912 a Nebraska reporter talked with farmers trying to recruit at the Grand Island jail—"The heaviest part of the harvest is now on and there is a big scarcity of help." The jailer at Alliance, Nebraska, released two men in August 1923 "to go to work for L.N. Worley 8 miles west and 2 mi. south"; and a month later the fine for another arrested vagrant "was suspended to allow him to go to work for L.E. Bliss with an understanding that Mr. Bliss would hold 2.00 from his wages to finish paying cost . . ." Sometimes frustrated farmers went not to the jailhouse but instead sneaked around neighboring fields to recruit, and a participant in a rural meeting drew applause when he said, "I had rather a man would come to my corn crib in the night and steal my corn than to have them bid my pickers away from me . . ."[17]

Such desperation appeared because each year's harvest was all important in the economies of the Plains states, affecting the lives of individual farm families, neighboring communities and their businesses, and the state government itself. "Well, every man, every business and every calling depends upon the wheat crop in our state!" the Kansas Commissioner of Labor told an investigator. For the farmer, losing a crop could be tantamount to having to leave, to give up farming; there was no safety net. And the costs were great also for those who depended upon the farmer as customer, supplier, and taxpayer.[18]

The worker who was so sought after had problems that seldom bothered the farmers. Beyond difficult sleeping conditions on the farm (often in the barn), inadequate food, and low pay, he had to think about the next job. For when threshing was completed on one farm, he had to move on to another place, which usually meant walking, sometimes long distances or, if lucky, catching a ride on a train. The complexities often frustrated the transient's job search and crushed hopes of saving up a nest egg from a summer's labor. As an Illinois congressman recounted after talking with men in his district who had worked on the Plains wheat harvest, "The wages they drew for a day's work was fairly satisfactory, but the work was so scattered that it took all they made for living expenses and they generally 'bummed' their way back home, and if they had enough to get home they were lucky."[19]

At this juncture in the history of the American West, three factors came together to produce the opening act in the drama of the western hobo: the extreme importance of wheat, with the likelihood of disaster if it were not harvested on time; the absence of a large local pool of workers on the Plains; and the newly laid rail lines connecting directly with more populated states just to the east. These elements provided ingredients for the popular saying "Wheat farms and hoboes go together." They went together because unless enormous numbers of workers could be brought in from the outside, much of the grain would remain in the fields. As a grain belt investigator reported to the U.S. Industrial Relations Commission in 1914: "The existence of such a class is essential under the present organization of industry on a seasonal, irregular basis."[20]

Nels Anderson experienced this life, observed the changes in the West, and wrote about them. After working western harvest jobs and railroad construction, he traveled to Chicago, enrolled at the University of Chicago, and became the first scholar to place the hobo in historical context. In extensive writings he pointed out the importance of these men who "worked and wandered, carrying their beds on their backs . . ." The crucial fact was that "they worked in places where no labor supply existed." Arriving too late to be part of the pioneer generation, the hobo in Anderson's view was instead playing an "in-between role related to the two frontiers. He came on the scene after the trailblazer, and he went off the scene as the second frontier was closing."[21]

Into the wheatlands the hobo "beat his way"—that was the preferred term for his type of travel, although outsiders sometimes called it "freighting." That is, the men caught rides on trains, usually without paying. The Kansas Supreme Court in 1891 confronted the case of a hobo who had entered a boxcar "to beat his way over the road . . ." When

Northern Pacific workers found a body beside the tracks at Logan, Montana, in 1907, they reported that the man had been trying "to beat his way lost his hold fell injuring back of head." And an investigator who interviewed wheat workers during the summer of 1914 found that most "beat their way" on freight trains for at least part of the trip. This had become "an established system and the farmers of the grain states depend upon it to furnish them with sufficient men to do the work of the harvest fields."[22]

Riders beating their way west learned what parts of the railyards to frequent for the best chance of grabbing a spot on the next freight. Most popular were the outskirts, where trains still moved slowly, before gaining speed. Some hung by the sandhouse, where the locomotive was loaded with sand to be sprayed under the wheels when extra traction was needed. If his speed and timing were right, a hobo might rush out and steal a ride in "blind baggage," the baggage car's platform, where he was somewhat safer from discovery because baggage piled up inside the car blocked the doorway. This was often a mail car—locked and inaccessible to the train crew or passengers, so no one would be coming through the door. Many would "ride the bumpers," standing on couplers between two cars, while locking their arms onto the brake rod. This method required both strength and unending vigilance.

Jack London described riding on top of a boxcar, warning anyone who thought it easy: "Just let him walk along the roof of a jolting, lurching car, with nothing to hold on to but the black and empty air, and when he comes to the downcurving end of the roof, all wet and slippery with dew, let him accelerate his speed so as to step across to the next roof, downcurving and wet and slippery." Riding inside a boxcar was preferred, although shifting freight could also make that a dangerous trip. Least safe was "riding the rods," hanging onto a crossing rod that was part of the underframe truss installed to keep wooden cars from sagging or becoming twisted. Sometimes the illegal rider inserted a supporting board, but he was still never more than inches from being maimed or killed.[23]

It was all illegal. Police reports from throughout the West during the era document the prevalence of these trespassers, as do coroners' reports, railroad company correspondence, and newspaper accounts. "Was climbing up between cars to steal a ride, and while bracing himself train slacked, catching his arm breaking same," the Union Pacific reported on a case at Julesburg, in eastern Colorado, in 1897. John Rollie Mitchell spent two days in the jail at Grand Island, Nebraska, in October 1915 for "stealing ride on R.R." Among the numerous notes in the North Pacific's special agent books are such items as "Arrested for riding trains—Spokane to Belgrade [Montana] . . . $25 each"; and "Stealing ride on train no. 2 [from Seattle]—Compelled to pay fare."[24]

It was tempting for railroad employees either to throw the freeloaders off the trains or to let them continue riding as long as they made a financial contribution to the employees' welfare. The standard fee was a dollar, which John R. Johnson paid in 1891 to a Santa Fe Railway brakeman when he got into a boxcar in Purcell, Indian Territory, heading for Guthrie. (He later was injured and sued the company.) Peter Speek's 1914 interviews found that before the harvest the railroad companies were generally happy to let the men ride free to the harvest fields, but individual railroad employees often charged 25 cents to carry a nonfare passenger "a short distance" and $1 for travel across a hundred-mile division. Hoboes called the freight ride from Salt Lake City to Pocatello the "Silver Dollar Route," because that was the brakeman's charge. Harry O'Banion went to court after a brakeman threw him off a Missouri Pacific train leaving Leavenworth; he had refused to keep paying every brakeman he encountered as he climbed back over the cars. He sued the company after the head brakeman, whom he refused to pay, "grabbed hold of my shoulder and pushed me in such a manner as to make me fall beneath the train."[25]

Police and railway records from the West are filled with similar stories. "Nine hoboes beating their way on freight east bound Aug. 17 [1917] claim to have been stuck up by train crew," an NP special agent reported from Casselton, North Dakota. The Denver & Rio Grande discharged numerous employees (usually conductors or brakemen) for "carrying tramps," from whom they had usually collected money. Josiah Flynt told of being accosted by a Southern Pacific brakeman who demanded money; when Flynt showed that he had none, the brakeman angrily ordered him to jump off, yelling, "Well, hit the gravel! I can't carry you on this train." Sometimes riders would pay in other ways, as old-time Montana railroader Warren McGee recalled. McGee's father, an NP fireman, had to shovel thirteen tons of coal during his run across

Montana: "He would get a hobo to help him, shoveling that coal from the back of the tender toward him, to get closer to the fire box door." Also, if the crew needed to get a car re-railed, they would get the accompanying hoboes to help pile up material to raise the car, often paying them $1 apiece.

The need to move laborers early in the summer led several rail lines running from the Midwest to the Plains to offer special rates for men going west for harvest work. Three railroads from cities of the Upper Mississippi charged $5 each for groups of at least five; the Santa Fe and the Rock Island offered a "one and one-sixth" rate from the Missouri River to Kansas wheat towns—full fare westbound, one-sixth for the return, but only to men in groups of ten or more.[26]

More than simply being illegal, cadging rides was extremely dangerous. Railroad and local records alike are filled with reports of the injuries and deaths, although few show up in court documents because hoboes seldom filed lawsuits. "Load shifted in M. & St. L. 6346 lumber killing J.E. Davis of Spokane who was stealing ride in car," noted a 1907 Northern Pacific report from Montana. The Union Pacific's agent described the injuries to a fifty-eight-year-old trespasser: "Running his way to harvest fields, fell from train & wheel passes over both feet mashing three toes." The body of a seventeen-year-old was found east of Topeka: "Walking over top of train fell between cars legs cut off mashed hands. Died same day."

Many injuries were due to the deliberate acts of others. A Union Pacific employee was the antagonist of a Denver man riding through Oakley, Kansas: "Was in box car, watchman struck him on arm with club, breaking arm." Often the UP paid $1 to the victim in such cases. The El Paso & Southwestern likely had to pay something to John Conchin, after the Arizona Territorial Supreme Court ruled that one of its watchmen acted with reckless disregard when he shot him in the knee as he crossed the El Paso & Southwestern yards at three a.m. one night.[27]

It is no easy task classifying these men who for varied reasons trespassed on the railroads while en route west to work the harvests. A basic definition was provided early in the twentieth century by Dr. Ben

Reitman, who like Nels Anderson became identified with Chicago's "Hobohemia" after experiencing life on the road: "There are three types of the genus vagrant: . . . The hobo works and wanders, the tramp dreams and wanders, and the bum drinks and wanders." A fellow worker with Reitman at the Chicago Hobo College similarly called the hobo "a migratory worker. A tramp is a migratory nonworker. A bum is a stationary nonworker."

Peter Speek was aware of these divisions during his 1914 interviews for the Commission on Industrial Relations, when he defined hoboes as "a rank of casual laborers earning most of their living by labor, willing and desirous to work, but in the time of unemployment, when hard pressed, supplementing their living by such means as begging, application for charity, and stealing . . ."

The attempt to distinguish between *hoboes* and *tramps* was often complicated because it was easy to move back and forth between the two groups, and many did. A hobo might tire of looking for work; a tramp might decide that he had to work to survive. A writer in *The Survey* titled his article "How to Tell a Hobo from a Mission Stiff" and explained, "In the East the average public confuses the hobo with the tramp, but in the West, where he obtained his nickname, he is often a welcome guest at the farm in harvest time." The writer told of encountering a "Hobo Employment Bureau" in Philadelphia, whose leader welcomed hoboes as itinerant laborers but rejected bums as derelicts, while defining "mission stiffs" as those who would not work but were "willing to exchange 'conversion' for bread, coffee, and a free bed."[28] Romantic notions of hoboes as simply wanting a free and easy life could not survive the inspections of investigators who followed them into the harvest fields. Such studies all concluded that they were goaded by "the whip of economic necessity."[29]

The terms *hobo*, *tramp*, and *vagrant* and the images they evoked all drew on the age-old popular fear of wanderers from outside the community. English laws had begun dealing with vagrancy by the late Middle Ages, and by the early sixteenth century unemployment itself was termed a dangerous crime, "the very mother of all vice," according to a writer in 1509. A. Lee Beier, historian of England's "masterless men," writes that this attitude was consistent with both contemporary law and public opinion. A *vagrant*, or the earlier *vagabond*, came to be defined as a person with no fixed residence or employment. In 1577 a writer said that the *vagabond* "will abide nowhere but runneth up and down from place to place . . . to and fro over all the realm"—a definition that later could have been applied to American tramps and hoboes. In fact, a writer in *The North American Review* in 1909 argued that the wording in the vagrancy laws of early England paralleled those of early 1900s America because "up to the middle of the sixteenth century rural England was very much in the same circumstances as rural America today," with a dispersed population, weak police protection, and growing numbers of the unemployed on the roadways.

The word *tramp* was widely used in England after *vagabond* and then in the early United States, usually as a synonym for *vagrant*. *Hobo* came into use later—possibly to distinguish between those traveling about to work and those who did not work. Different origins of the word *hobo* have been advanced, from an eighteenth-century English term *hoe boy* (referring to a bonded servant who hoed all day), to an employer's shout of "Ho! Boy!" By the time *tramp* and *hobo* crossed the Atlantic, both were fastened with negative connotations, which became attached to any man forced to move about hunting for work.[30]

The tramp in America emerged from the early wanderer, such as the Civil War–era vagabond along rural roadways, then loomed suddenly as a new, dangerous threat in the industrial world developing in the 1870s and 1880s. Looking back almost half a century later, the president of the Minneapolis, St. Paul & Sault Ste. Marie Railroad noted that "the tramp was unknown until the Civil War. We have had them ever since . . ." Various historians have charted the links between the agitated, boom-and-bust economy of those postwar years and the numbers of men on the road. *The New York Times* first used the term *tramp* in 1874; that same year the city marshal in Lynn, Massachusetts, referred to men lodged overnight in the jail as tramps. Press accounts during that decade's Molly Maguire violence in the Pennsylvania coalfields compared tramps to the violent Mollies who had been apprehended and hanged.

Poet Walt Whitman saw something he "had never seen before" one day in early 1879—"three quite good-looking American men, of respectable personal presence, two of them young, carrying chiffonier-bags on their shoulders, and the usual long iron hooks in their hands, plodding along, their eyes cast down, spying for scraps, rags, bones, &c." He predicted disaster if the numbers of such poor and nomadic persons kept increasing, for then the American experiment would be "at heart an unhealthy failure." Indeed, just six years later readers of the *American Law Review* were told that the vagrant was "the chrysalis of every species of criminal." He lacked home ties, was idle, and had no means of support—so "what but criminality is to be expected from such a person?"[31]

Whitman was really lamenting the fading of an idealized agricultural America, for he wrote in the era of economic convulsions and violent strikes. State legislatures began to respond. New Jersey and Pennsylvania came first, passing anti-tramp legislation in 1876, both resting heavily upon earlier vagrancy statutes. Pennsylvania's act defined tramps and vagrants as outsiders coming into a state with "no labor, trade, occupation or business, and have no visible mean of subsistence, and can give no reasonable account of themselves." Their penalty was to be put to work for a period from one to six months. The movement caught fire and spread across the East—to Rhode Island in 1877, to Delaware and New York in 1879, then to other states nearby. A critic noted that the Delaware law ordered policemen "to arrest tramps wherever found," and he summed up the impact of the new law: "To have no home and to seek employment is a crime in many parts of the United States." Applying the old vagrancy statutes to the new class of unemployed grew in popularity until a study in 1898 found only four states without any tramp legislation, many of them making felonies of what had earlier been classified as misdemeanors for beggars.[32]

The public ridicule, fear, and scorn that gave birth to these laws along the eastern seaboard joined the westward movement. But the crucial role hoboes played in wheat harvests perhaps complicated the issue in Kansas: the *Salina Herald* hailed the Connecticut tramp law in 1879, noting that it "was not as stringent as some of those passed by other States" but "seems to have served its purpose," namely that "wandering vagrants" had to move on. But the editor, writing from his perch in the center of the Grain Belt, added—somewhat inaccurately—that under the law "no injustice has been done . . . to honest workingmen traveling in search of employment." A year later the *Herald* reported on the new Massachusetts tramp act, which "classes as tramps all persons who rove from place to place begging or living without labor or visible means of support," excluding women, children, the blind, and those asking charity. Tramps were to be put in a "house of correction or state work house for not less than six months nor more than two years." Massachusetts, it noted, even had a state "tramp officer."[33]

These acts meshed with American public opinion, if reminiscences and printed items may be believed. A woman recalling her childhood on a Wisconsin farm near railroad tracks said, "There was always the lurking fear that a tramp might take refuge in the barn—a tramp with a pipe or cigarette." Texas, after the railroads arrived, saw an increase in reports of arrests of tramps, sometimes linked to robberies. A reporter for the *Nebraska State Journal* joined Lincoln policemen late one night in mid-1894, when they raided the Rock Island yards and arrested seven vagrants sleeping in empty boxcars. "It was the same old story of human misery, of misfortune, of degradation and despair," the reporter wrote:

> It seemed hard that they should be taken from their miserable bed on the floor of the box car and lodged in the city jail, but such are the precautions which the authorities find it necessary to take to preserve an immunity from the tramp nuisance. Crimes, too, have been committed, attempted robberies have been reported, and while many innocent persons suffer, a great many of the guilty are caught.[34]

The *Denver Times* called tramps a low level of humanity, and each Denver policemen knew "as well as he knows his beat" that the tramps would beg, insult, burglarize, and even assault "before they would work for their bread . . ." In Kansas, the *Salina Herald* peppered tramps with various slings. Above all, they were criminals: "Many tramps have shown themselves in this section, much to the dislike of women and children. Too much care cannot be taken in securing premises over night." When tramps were caught, the city jailer restricted their diet to "a bucket full of water twice a day" in hopes of deterring them from ever coming back.

Almost universally, hoboes were tarred with the same brush as were tramps; an article in *Century* in 1884 referred to *hobo* as "the nickname of the American tramp." Nels Anderson recalled from his years beating his way around the West that "suspicion and hostility are the universal attitudes of the town or small city to the hobo and the tramp." When the *Nebraska State Journal* complained in June 1915 of the seriousness of the "tramp problem," it added that "hoboes do not show vicious tendencies unless they are cornered and are forced to make a fight." The so-called "King of the Hoboes," Jeff Davies, pointed to the problem: "It is the tramp who steals the farmer's chickens—the hobo gets the blame. It is the hobo who prevents the railroad wreck—yet newspapers, unthinkingly will give credit to the tramps."[35]

These were the men who converged on the Great Plains for the wheat harvest, then often went beyond to pick apples or hops in the Northwest or cotton in Texas, to dig sugar beets, or to head on to the orchards of California. Despite their important role, however, they would meet much opposition, whose source lay at least in part within the biases carried west by settlers. These attitudes were then passed on. A western hobo who had no problem locating the source of his troubles complained to a labor newspaper in 1910 that "the little school boys are not to blame when they throw clods at us; they have been taught that a hobo is everything that is vile and degraded . . ."[36]

Upon a foundation built of such contradictions, the New West began to emerge from its frontier era.

3

THE WESTERN HOBO

The subtle danger of casual work, which silently accomplishes
serious results, is that it develops a habit of irregular work in
those who depend upon it for a livelihood.
            —Don D. Lescohier, *The Labor Market* (1923)

The California hobo was disgusted. It was now ten years since he had
quit teaching in a rural school to become a hobo, and in his travels from
job to job he had viewed the world from different angles. He disliked
what he saw.

Hoboes, Ned Bond stressed in a 1910 letter to a Seattle labor paper,
had an "historic mission" to build railroads and canals, to harvest crops,
"to level the land of the great Southwestern deserts for irrigation," and
to fell trees in the Northwest. "I have helped to build railroads," he
wrote, "and have had so little conscience as to steal rides thereon, hither
and thither, during my ill starred career." But he aimed his arrows mainly
at farmers, who might be hailed as "the backbone of this nation" but in
reality could only claim to make up part of the national frame:

> They may be the dorsal vertebrae, but the hoboes, the wayfaring
> laborers, who have not where to lay their heads, except on bun-
> dles of old shirts in cold tents or in the open air, who imagine
> that they are taking a vacation in the lap of luxury when they eat
> ham or beef and get plenty of condensed milk for their coffee,
> and sleep in a warm shanty, these may at least claim to be the

lumbar vertebrae . . . If the farmers raise the crops and get in
debt, the hoboes harvest the crops and get hell.

Bond was not alone in his anger. After decades of harvesting the
new crops poking up through western soil, as well as constructing the
region's railroads and building its dams and irrigation canals, hoboes
were still dismissed around the West as "necessary nuisances" and
jailed as vagrants when harvest was finished. They saw themselves as
different from hoboes and tramps in the East, facing different challenges, surviving in an often hostile political and economic environment. Another western hobo, T. J. O'Brien, explained:

> In this western country the conditions differ a great deal from
> those of the East. A majority of the workers in this part of the coun-
> try do not know what a home is. The only home most of us have
> is the roll of blankets which we carry on our backs. In ninety-five
> cases out of one hundred he is single and his work often compels
> him to travel often as far as three hundred miles in search of
> employment, while in the East a majority of the workers are mar-
> ried and therefore not transients. We must look at the worker
> from a different point of view here west of the Rockies.[1]

These hobo writers told the truth. Their environment was different,
and it created a hobo lifestyle at odds, in some key ways, with those
who followed a rootless existence in the East. Distances were great
between western communities, and freight trains were even more important for transients with such large expanses of territory to cover;
riding a train was usually the only alternative to walking and "counting
ties." Elsewhere in the nation men stole rides in or beneath boxcars,
but a 1914 investigator concluded that they used "freighting" more frequently in western states. And a sudden end to this rail-based system of
hauling harvest hands would be more than a calamity for the West's
seasonal industries, the U.S. Industrial Relations Commission predicted:
growers then "would face an unexpected scarcity of labor and the possibility of consequent heavy losses."[2]

In western states and territories the population centers were generally small and scattered. Lengthy travel in unheated rail cars meant that

weather was important: western weather ranged in extremes from desert to mountain, or fog-shrouded coastal inlet to alkali plain—the cold-
est January days averaging 40°F above zero in San Antonio, Texas, but
40°F below zero in Minot, North Dakota. If some districts had nothing
but prairie and sky, others, towered over by mountain majesties, lay in
valleys so narrow that railroads could barely fit, like the mining town of
Burke in Idaho's Coeur d'Alenes region. One former hobo insisted that
the distances and harsh climate made "truck-riding" necessary in the
West—that is, riding beneath the cars rather than hanging onto a boxcar in the open breeze or finding room inside.[3]

In addition, the push of construction westward after the Civil War
laid out a rail system in east-west corridors, which held important im-
plications for legions of hobo job seekers. These routes became fixed
in the popular imagination: as the Texas Supreme Court stated in an
1892 case, railroad lines, once established, became "notorious and in-
disputable" and were seen "as fixed and permanent in their course as
the rivers themselves." Hoboes would talk of "riding the old D&RG" or
"catching the SP," just as an earlier generation might have talked of
floating down the Ohio. But the east-west layout meant that riders
often had problems going in other directions, and frequently during
harvest this led to hobo frustration and congestion in railway centers. In
turn, the resulting concentrations frequently upset the locals.

"Tramps strike the town," the *Nebraska State Journal* reported from
Fremont in 1894, after "a whole flock of tramps struck the city" in late
July—probably the result of an oversupply of men seeking work, or
even weather shifts that had upset the harvest schedule. Fremont police and townspeople were frantic at first, but soon "the whole caboodle
of tramps was escorted out of town . . ."[4]

William Duffus traveled throughout the wheat areas for the Industrial Relations Commission and sometimes found railroad towns "flooded
with men." These conditions were often a result of the rail system's
layout. As Duffus wrote, "Men flock blindly into the grain states, crowding into the larger and more easily accessible railroad centers in the
grain-growing districts." The consequences were predictable. While
around those hubs the demand for laborers was often filled, the smaller
and more remote communities were left without enough harvest help,
complaining when newspapers in the bigger cities reported a statewide

oversupply. Redfield, South Dakota, witnessed one aspect of this imbalance: investigator Peter Speek watched as a train rolled in with over 300 "freighters" clinging to the boxcars. They were met by the sheriff and some 100 deputies armed with clubs, "to prevent the men alighting. The men were not wanted either in the town or by the nearby farmers . . ." Such instances were frequent during Great Plains summers, providing vivid demonstrations of the absence of any system for distributing harvest labor.[5]

In many ways a one-crop West had developed—but one crop for different sections. It was wheat on much of the Great Plains, but some western areas of that terrain became one crop with sugar beets. In many western districts the diversified farming of the Midwest was little known, replaced by areas where intensive farming of a single crop in orchard, field, or patch dominated. This meant that most of the farmers in an area needed workers at the same moment, and when harvesting was finished, the vast numbers of harvesters who had traveled there had no other nearby employment. Alternate, easily accessible jobs were needed—but in much of the West a migrant worker might discover that his time between paydays could stretch into many days and weeks.[6]

The West taking shape during this Second Frontier presented a different ethnic pattern than the rest of the country. In much of the United States, a population made up of immigrants and the children of immigrants was scarcely unusual, but hoboes coming to harvest Great Plains wheat were the advance party of great variety—a heterogeneous conglomeration of thousands of harvesters, specializing in different crops. They were drawn from Indian tribes of the western states and territories, Alaska, and British Columbia, as well as from China, Japan, Mexico, India, and eventually Puerto Rico and the Philippines—and all parts of the United States and Europe.

This ethnic variety had an impact on migratory labor life; California especially would be marked by shifting stereotypes that at times dictated which racial groups would harvest which crops. Ethnic awareness runs through western jail records, where police often cared enough about national identities to list them in arrests for vagrancy, the usual charge against transients. A major exception was the Great Plains wheat harvest, where the native-born and immigrants from northern Europe predominated. A study of Omaha's 1887–1913 vagrancy record, likely heavily skewed toward men beating their way west, showed slightly more than three-fourths of those arrested were U.S. natives; of the remainder, the Irish were at 11.2 percent, and 4.5 percent German, 2.6 percent Scandinavian, and 1.5 percent from England or Scotland. In the Northwest, Spokane was a key hobo stopping-off point; police records of the 492 who were arrested after harvest was completed in December 1913 showed that 111—almost one-fourth—were held for vagrancy (second to drunkenness, with 197). Arrest totals for all charges gave this December ethnic/nationality breakdown, which probably mirrored the ethnic breakdown for vagrants: native-born whites, 260; Swedes, 36; Irish, 30; Canadians, 15; Norwegians, 14; Chinese, 13; English, 13; Germans, 11; Scots, 10; Japanese, 10; Negroes, 7; Italians, 5; Austrians, 4; Indians, 4.

In Grand Island, Nebraska, however, the jailer during 1914 listed an ethnic identification for each inmate—24 Irish, 5 Germans, 1 Greek, 1 Pole, 1 Swede, 1 Dane, 1 English, 1 Irish-German, 1 Russian Jew, 1 Hebrew, 1 Scot, 1 Romanian, 1 Japanese, but only 2 "Americans." Obviously, the origins of transients were no more predictable than their employments.[7]

The general dominance of the native-born among migrant workers may have been the case only for grain harvest labor on the Plains, because information on hoboes in other western areas reflects a wider diversity. Peter Speek's visits to Montana labor camps in 1914, concentrating on railroad construction crews (often a detour for hoboes), found that immigrants made up roughly half, with northern and southern Europe equally represented. But in the Pacific Northwest, the Southwest, and California, far different scenes played out. This different ethnic mix has usually been overlooked in the West because writers used a more limited focus; as historian Howard Lamar has noted, "Those who do discuss Western labor tend to write about it regionally or in terms of craft or race; they treat, for example, the Chinese laborer, the Mexican worker, the Basque sheepherder, the cowboy, the hardrock miner, and the Anglo and Chicano migratory worker." The West's polyphony of ethnic change—shifting between occupations and regions, leaving wage labor entirely, leasing farmland, then returning to the road—has often been neglected.[8]

Western hoboes' rich diversity may have been difficult at times for passersby to notice, given the workers' similarities in clothing and in the layers of dust they picked up while beating their way. Men doing similar work had similarly calloused hands. One morning in December 1906, when a railroad telegrapher was walking along the Southern Pacific tracks near Sacramento, he came upon a man lying facedown, dead. The *Sacramento Bee* determined him to be "evidently of Danish descent," about thirty-five, with red hair; he carried a "thin, worn comfort as his only covering" and wore "a common bicycle cap, a thin overshirt, a pair of overalls and heavy-soled shoes." In his hip pocket were a Turkish towel and a copy of the previous day's *Yolo Independent*. To the *Bee* reporter he was "a typical hobo." Often the fact that the deceased had been carrying rolled-up blankets in a "bundle" or bindle helped define him as a hobo, but sometimes other clues helped with identification. The Custer County coroner, when confronted with a body found in August 1915 along the Milwaukee Road tracks near Montana's Tongue River, noticed laced boots, khaki clothes, black hat, and also "the pillow such as Russian trampers are known to carry," which "would indicate he was a Russian." The body was buried in "pauper field."[9]

Records of western jails as well as newspaper reports reveal that hoboes' lives were heavily salted with violence. The "wild frontier" continued to be a reality for more than cowboys and Indians, partly because of the lack of police protection over wide areas, but also because frontiers in America always attracted many living outside the law. Josiah Flynt in his far-flung hoboing witnessed some of this, concluding that "the Western tramp is rough, often kind-hearted, wild and reckless . . ." Westerners looked down on eastern hoboes and tramps as tenderfeet, he added, and "they laugh at law, sneer at morality, and give free rein to appetite. Because of this many of them never reach middle age." And lawmen were frequently part of this frontier style: a Montana Indian named Prairie Chicken left his name in the Custer County Jail register after he was discharged on a grand larceny charge in 1884: "Killed By Butting to [*sic*] hard against Six Shooters in the Hands of Conley and Johnson."

Railway as well as police records reflect this violent life. "Was stealing ride on 1st, #3, and was stabbed by some other tramp," the Union Pacific's Kansas ledger recorded for October 1900, and such entries were frequent. Investigators for the Industrial Relations Commission found that the wheatlands attracted not only men looking for work but also criminals intent on "harvesting the harvest hands." Peter Speek ran into a group of five such "harvesters" in Kansas City, two Italians, two native-born, and one Russian. "They had recently arrived from the West and had held up several harvest hands," one of them getting arrested along the way.[10]

Dangers of life on the road were often extensions of a migrant worker's work life. Investigators discovered quickly the sharp contrast between the public's interest in hoboes at the start of a Plains harvest season and attitudes after the work was finished. When the wheat was all threshed, not only did railroads begin charging hoboes fees to ride in, upon, or even underneath boxcars, but everyone—railroad employees, farmers, shopkeepers, and town dwellers alike—seemed to look at the harvest hands "as intruders, public nuisances, worthy of kicking and hated only." While the *Carrington* (North Dakota) *Record* could warn, at the outset of the 1915 wheat harvest, that "an immense number of men" were needed to handle a bumper crop, it still labeled the laborers arriving on boxcars as a "necessary nuisance."[11]

Some applause might have been expected, for it was difficult work. When three Nebraska youths quit harvest jobs after only one week and signed up with the navy, they admitted that they expected navy life to seem like a vacation: "When it comes to harvesting they [the farmers] don't know what the clocks are," they told a reporter. "They work by the sun."

The navy-bound Nebraskans' harvesting experience was not unusual. Men worked extremely long hours in the ripening fields of grain, with eleven to thirteen hours per day the average, although up to fifteen hours was often the case. (William Allen White commented on the men's work schedules on the bonanza farms in 1879: "Death from natural causes up on the big farms seldom occurs.") Water from Great Plains wells was frequently alkaline. Usually the food offered was substantial, "but the meals are always the same, mostly eggs, salted meats and canned stuff." Sleeping accommodations were generally crude and sparse, in a barn or out on the grass; sometimes no blankets were provided. Thomas Isern reports a thresherman's findings at Kingfisher, Oklahoma, in 1912: "The straw pile is everybody's bed here. Sometimes we don't get near a house all week." Harvest workers expected to sleep outside, the farmers insisted, adding that the workers "don't mind it." But William Duffus found that "many of the men do mind it"—sleeping in granaries filled with rats and mice, amid odors from the stable. "They object, even when the physical discomforts are not serious, to the attitude which the farmer assumes when he sends them to the barn or the straw stack to sleep," or even to a bunkhouse that was often unsanitary and crowded. Common drinking cups were the rule; bathing facilities were absent.

Conditions changed little for hoboes as they moved across the West—to logging camps, hopyards, citrus groves, hardrock mining, apple orchards, berry patches, and railroad construction. When California investigated labor camp conditions in the World War I era, it found conditions little short of disastrous—so bad as to beg the question as to why men would stoop to such employment. One typical report came from a "ranch camp" (the name given to California farms, whether with orchards, vineyards, wheatfields, or cattle) that was "filthy," according to one worker's complaint—the ten employees "have no plates or pots with which to do the cooking, but have to use old tin cans that are found around the camp . . . the tents and the bedding in which men have to sleep are all wet . . . No toilets. No bathing facilities."

The heat of a Plains summer could be oppressive. "A Swede was sunstruck last week while working in the hayfield," it was reported in Riley County, Kansas, in September 1881. "He was just from Sweden and perhaps was not aware that he was so warm." In Oklahoma the term was that the men "burn out" from working in high temperatures. "Hot blasts" from the South could wilt plants as well—daily temperatures over 100°F baked Nebraska and Kansas through much of August 1894, and in Beatrice, Nebraska, "even the leaves on the trees curled up and plainly showed the effect of the intense heat."[12]

U.S. Department of Agriculture wage records might have given some Plains farmers a feeling of justification for providing few amenities for their employees. Western harvest wages were found to be clearly above those of the rest of the nation, and harvest labor hired only for the day constituted a much larger portion of western farmers' annual employment of hired labor than was the case elsewhere. In 1910 daily wages in the North Atlantic states averaged $1.63; $1.07 in the South Atlantic; $1.14 in the South Central; and $1.75 in the eastern North

Central states. But in the West it was substantially higher—$2.01 for North Central west of the Mississippi (including Kansas, Nebraska, and the Dakotas), and $2.02 in Far Western States. Thus pay in both sections of the West was more than a third higher than the national average of $1.45 for daily harvest labor with board. And by 1918, during the war, the spread was even greater—the national average was $2.65 per day, but the Plains states and other North Central states west of the Mississippi were 40 percent higher at $3.72, while the Far Western states were 28 percent higher at $3.39.[13]

But a hobo's daily wage meant little if work time was restricted and he wasted days or weeks searching for the next job. The Industrial Relations Commission's investigators in 1914 said men heading into the harvest fields generally found employment "limited to a few weeks at best" and then had to move from job to job with the search often taking considerable time. William Duffus wrote that he and Peter Speek "repeatedly met men who had not succeeded in finding a day's work in the harvest fields although they had spent days and even weeks in the grain growing districts looking for the three to four months' work at good wages so glowingly described by the publicity agents . . ."

Farmers sometimes complained about the lackadaisical activities of workers. A later investigator, however, placed their laments in context: employers who point to the harvesters' unreliability, Don D. Lescohier wrote, "would do well to remember that the chances of employment which they offer are as unreliable as the men who accept them . . ." In addition, the total income they receive for a summer's labors "is as insufficient for their needs as the work they perform is insufficient to satisfy the employer."[14]

When harvesting was completed in a district and hoboes headed for the railroad yards to snag a ride, they were no longer hailed as a godsend for the farmer. "Back in those days, they arrested someone that just hung around and didn't work," George Dawson recalled of his western hoboing days after World War I. "Some towns was pretty strong with those laws and made life pretty unfriendly for a man without a job."

Police registers and court dockets from Great Plains communities show that in general, postharvest treatment was the same for all transients: hoboes who had been working nearby, tramps and bums just passing

through—all were handled identically. If they were seeking employment it usually meant nothing to the police: hoboes were indistinguishable from the work-avoidance class. And in the towns the various charity
groups traditionally limited their efforts to caring for residents. Non-
residents' problems—such as finding a place to sleep in cold weather—
were left to law enforcement. Anyone without work was considered a
vagrant.[15]

Overwhelmed with vagrancy arrests, the police chief in Lincoln,
Nebraska, put the prisoners to work. "The rock pile proved a success,"
cutting their numbers in town sharply. Farther along the UP line in
Grand Island, the judge regularly sent vagrants to do several days "of
hard labor on streets," or in one case "three days of hard labor ball &
chain." One case revealed the wide net used by police in their arrests,
and also the judge's breadth of sentencing power: the judge found the
vagrant "wandering about the streets and other public places . . . therefore considered by me that the defendant be placed at hard labor for
seven days." The jailer in Alliance, Nebraska, reported for a single week
in August 1923 that "we have received a total of 21 days work from
prisoners working out their fines and costs." A common vagrant's sentence was to serve a short jail term—one day, two days, five or ten days.
One man got ten days for simply being "without visible means of support or employment and giving a good account of himself."

But more frequently the judge simply moved hoboes out of town as
quickly as possible. In Miles City, Montana, a vagrant was "told to skip the
town." One day in July 1923, with the jail's vagrant population exploding,
the Alliance jailer "released all vags from the city jail, returned all property,
ordered them to move on." The Grand Island police judge suspended sen-
tences for five men "provided defendants leave the city immediately."

A survey of police courts in several western areas showed that such
outcomes were common. In Sacramento, jail registers used the initials
"W.H." for "was held," and from midsummer through fall "floaters" regularly had "W.H. 5 minutes," "W.H. 3 hours," or similar time allotments
written after their sentence, regardless of how long the sentence was
for. There were almost no vagrancy arrests in Sacramento in October,
one of the busy months for the area's vineyards and hopyards, but in
winter there were always men listed in the jail register as "lodgers"—
transients who were allowed to sleep in the jail on cold nights. In this
respect, at least, police showed some compassion.[16]

While train crews generally did little to bother hoboes beating their way *into* the Grain Belt for harvest work, they treated them differently later on. Railroad "bulls," the private agents hired by the lines to police their yards and trains, became known for their viciousness toward trespassers, as did "shacks," the brakemen. "The bull in Omaha carries a big stick," a bruised boxcar rider told George Dawson as they hopped a freight out of St. Louis. "I took it in the face before he threw me off the train." In another city a bull shot at Dawson and a group of hoboes.

The meanness of the bulls and shacks often seemed to know no ends. Jack London, the chronicler of hobo life, told of shacks trying to oust men riding underneath a boxcar, on the underframe, by positioning themselves on the car ahead and lowering a long cord weighted with a coupling pin:

> The coupling-pin strikes the ties between the rails, rebounds against the bottom of the car, and again strikes the ties. The shack plays it back and forth, now to this side, now to the other, lets it out a bit and hauls it in a bit, giving his weapon opportunity for every variety of impact and rebound. Every blow of that flying coupling-pin is freighted with death, and at sixty miles an hour it beats a veritable tattoo of death. The next day the remains of that tramp are gathered up along the right of way . . .

It was called a "bo-teaser," and a young midwestern railroad telegraph operator recalled a hobo's response when asked its effects: "'Plenty.' His unshaven jaw set hard. 'To a 'bo ridin' the rods—' He broke off, and for a long moment his eyes focused on a point in space. Then, with bitter reminiscence: 'The goddam thing bounces up an' damn near kills him.'" The telegrapher added, "'Obviously he knew this from experience.'"[17]

Higher courts usually took a dim view of railroad employees' violence toward hoboes and tramps. An Arizona judge ruled that if someone trespassed on company property, the rail company owed him "no duty" except to refrain from "willfully or wantonly injuring him," but still ruled that when a brakeman with a gun threatened an illegal rider with "instant death," this was a wanton act even if the hobo was not pushed but simply jumped off the moving train. A Montana court cited considerable precedent to rule that if a brakeman used unnecessary violence in removing a trespasser, the railway company was liable for any injuries. However, the Kansas Supreme Court asserted that if a rider—unthreatened by any employee—leaped from a moving car rather than waiting until it slowed down, the conductor who was aware of the rider's presence was not liable for the resulting death. Cases of hobo injuries on railroads seldom appeared on court dockets, however, for hoboes were generally not in any position to seek legal redress— lacking local residence and acquaintances, with few funds, and without the power needed to take on some of the nation's most powerful corporations.[18]

Railroad officials countered that not all men beating their way were merely catching a ride, that some of their crews' acts were justified in self-defense. Those stealing rides occasionally robbed, beat, and sometimes killed railway employees, and "pilfering" of equipment and freight was frequent. Incidents of tramp violence occurred often enough that employees had reason to be leery of those they encountered trespassing on the train. That was the experience of a Montana trainman when he stopped the ore train to remove two tramps he had previously ordered off. One of them "drew a 38 Calibre Colts revolver and with the words 'You son of a bitch, I'll fix you!' deliberately . . . fired two shots into the back of Conductor Chauncey W. West . . ."

While railroad company leaders were fully aware of such crimes by hoboes and tramps when Peter Speek questioned them in 1914, their written answers to his queries revealed a high level of ignorance regarding reasons for the hoboes' trips. "The prevailing opinions in the answers," Speek wrote, "were that the annual migration of floating labor is not necessary and the method of travel is not necessary. Those who travel are usually tramps and will not work if offered the opportunity . . . The opinion is that the hoboes could be eliminated; that, if they were arrested whenever possible and put to work they would soon disappear."[19]

Although investigators sometimes saw demoralization resulting from such treatment—whether by railroads, farmers, police, or townspeople— others were fascinated (and continue to be fascinated) by hobo culture. Some who studied labor migrants focused on the subculture of homeless men, overwhelmingly single and young, mainly white and unskilled or semiskilled. Because of the shared aspects of life on the road, they came to form a distinct group in American life. Students of subcultures often point to different words and customs as keys to developing a separate identity. Among hoboes, such words might include the terms for different jobs and people—"apple knocker" for apple picker; "pearl diver" for dishwasher; "mission stiff" for a bum who got his food from the "Starvation" Army and other religious charities; "clover kicker" for farmer; "shack" for brakeman. A "scissorbill" was one who did not believe in fighting back against poor treatment; a "splinter belly" was a carpenter; the "shovel stiff" worked with a shovel; the "rust eater" worked on the railroad—and of course, the "bindlestiff" was a hobo.

Transients also became known for signs they would mark on fences, warning others of what lay ahead—"Go to back door," "Will make you work here," "Bad dog," "Danger steer clear." And when onetime hobo Carl Sandburg collected songs for his *American Songbag* in 1927, he published seven "Hobo Songs" but left out others that a modern collector would likely include, such as "Big Rock Candy Mountain" and "The Preacher and the Slave" (which Sandburg placed in the "Prison and Jail Songs" section).[20]

Along the railways, never far from stopping points, were the "jungles," where the men beating their way gathered. Once when Peter Speek saw "jumpers" being pushed off trains by railroad employees, he noted that their "jungles" were nearby, "where they rested and cured the wounds and bruises received from the blows of the carmen or by some accident in getting on or off the cars." African-American George Dawson found the jungles clear of racial segregation. "Some of the men were white and some were colored . . . Funny thing was, though, poor as they were, they were always generous. If one of them had any food, no one went hungry." Riding the rails, Dawson said, "we was all one, but outside the yards, it was a world of white and colored."

Several jungles were enormous—some in California were a mile long—but most were small affairs, where in addition to resting up there was drinking, singing, storytelling, and mulligan stew. Investigator William Duffus in 1914 said a visitor to a "jungle" was likely to meet "professional gamblers, petty criminals of various kinds, degenerates, bums, and tramps," which would likely bring "weakening to the character." But his co-worker Peter Speek saw something else. Speek took a survey of the 225 men in a hobo jungle near Redfield, South Dakota, and found 12 college men, 4 college students, 2 lawyers, 19 "old-time immigrants—Irish and German," 1 boy under sixteen years of age, 2 men over fifty years, 43 homeless men "(their only home was the jungle)," and 26 army veterans. Further, Speek's interviews turned up that 8 had been cheated out of wages by farmers during the harvest season, 39 had been arrested in town for vagrancy, 51 had been beaten on freight trains by carmen, 80 were without money, 70 had one dollar or less, and 50 "had at some time learned a trade."[21]

Although the men were thrown together, on trains, at work, in "jungles," one aspect of hobo life that shouts out across the decades is the anonymity: the men who spent hours and days together did not seem to know much about each other. They did not inquire. Repeatedly, coroners' inquests over bodies found along the tracks could come up with no identity; even fellow hoboes had no idea who they were. They appear in records only as "unknown man"; coroner's jury members "are unable to find anything from which the identity of the man or who the man was that was killed . . ." When a coroner's jury sought the identity of a body found near Spokane Falls in the winter of 1890, one nearby resident testified that he had earlier taken the old man some food but did not know his name: "I never learned it and never asked it. It is a peculiarity we have in this western country, to get acquainted with a man, talk to him, & transact business with him, without asking for his name." Employers also sometimes preferred not to know: the *Omaha Daily Bee* carried the story of a farmer reporting that one of his harvest hands died from a sunstroke: "As the man had been in his employ but a few days he could not give his name."

Pockets of these deceased hoboes and tramps usually held no more than a few cents or a few dollars, plus a razor, perhaps a knife, and what was described as "junk." Seldom was there a letter or other paper with an address; usually there were no friends or relatives to contact. "Nothing could be found to identify him . . ." "No personal property. Nothing to identify him." Sometimes the railroad agent would have to guess: "Appearance of Hobo evidently trying to steal ride on freight . . ." Seldom was the body of a female found along the tracks; few women rode the rails, although some hid their gender by wearing men's clothing and cutting their hair short.

Names and histories had been jettisoned long ago; the hobo wished to remain anonymous.[22]

An inquest over a body found in a Spokane lodging house in 1891 put these issues on display, even though the deceased had had local friends and acquaintances. But they apparently knew little about him— not even his full name. First came a cook who had once employed him:

Q. Do you recognize this body[?]
A. Yes I know his name is Finn; his first name I don't remember to have heard, I don't think I heard it.
Q. Are you sure you never heard it?
A. I don't think he ever told me his first name. All the name I ever heard was Finn.
Q. How long have you known him.
A. Seven (7) weeks, or near that.

The manager of the lodging house where he stayed was also of no help:

Q. What was his first name?
A. I don't know what was his first name.
Q. Is it not your habit to keep a Register of the names of your lodgers?
A. Sometimes I keep a register of the names and sometimes I don't, register the names.
Q. Is it not a custom among lodging House Keepers to register all guests occupying rooms?
A. Well, if they want it I register their names, if not I don't.
Q. Is that your way of doing business?
A. Yes that is the way I do business; if a man wants to register I take his name but if he don't, it is all right, any how, I don't make it any of my business.

A friend of two and a half years' standing, in whose cabin he had recently stayed, also drew a blank on the name:

Q. You have no knowledge of his full name?
A. No, I never heard it, nor saw the initials in writing . . . No I don't know where he was born.
Q. Do you know if he has any relatives?
A. No, I don't know if he has any relatives; I never heard him say so.

Q. Where did you meet him?

A. When he came back from the work on the construction of the new road, from the neighborhood of Moscow, Idaho.

Q. Where did you last see him?

A. It was about ten (10) days ago.

Q. Where was he stopping?

A. He stopped and slept with me till a few days ago. A while back he went away to work, but came back one day after being absent. He came and stopped with me 1 day, and then I understand that he got in company with a woman, and we saw less of him.

Only the woman friend had answers:

Q. What was his full name?

A. His name was Zachery Finn . . . He was very much of a gentleman, as far as I know.

Q. Were his habits dissipated?

A. No, he had no bad habits whatever, was quiet and gentlemanly.

She knew his age—forty-two; his birthplace—Norway; and his nearest relative—a sister in Iowa.

Q. Had he any property that you know of?

A. No property that I ever heard of. I don't think he had anything.

Asked her occupation, she replied, "I am a sporting woman."[23]

Zachery Finn's profile fits many of the men who supplied the West's migratory, transient labor. If more information could be learned, it would probably reveal that he had beaten his way west on the railroads at some time, had worked on harvests, and had lived in a "jungle" at some point. He had no settled home, even in Spokane, which had a thriving YMCA; it tried to appeal to migrant workers who would agree to live more Christian lives. Finn seems not to have visited there. The welcome for migrant workers in western towns often came only from the saloon and "sporting women." In several major western cities Christian-based charities sought to provide alternate welcomes for transients; in Portland it was Scadding House, with a club room and lodging "where the men have all the freedom of the saloon without any of its temptations and vices." Such institutions occasionally reached the transient population, but not in large enough numbers to depopulate the "jungles." Most lived their lives akin to that of Zachery Finn, always drifting, with friends but still scarcely known to them.[24]

Finn's varied job travels seem to have been driven by "the whip of necessity," but sometimes those who took to the road had other goals, as can be seen in the recollections of a hobo who left a detailed personal account: the poet Carl Sandburg. For some western migrant workers, a summer riding the rails to work in harvests was an adventure as well as a chance for a job, especially for the few women hoboes whose experiences have been chronicled.[25]

Carl Sandburg had such dreams for his hobo summer. He was nineteen when he decided to leave his home in the Swedish center of Galesburg, Illinois, "to head west and work in the Kansas wheat harvest," as he explained in his autobiography, *Always the Young Strangers*. It was 1897, and his travels that summer in most ways followed typical hobo activities of the era. Sandburg climbed into a boxcar leaving Galesburg, got off across the Mississippi River in Missouri, and beat his way west— picking apples and pears, threshing, washing dishes, waiting tables, sawing and chopping wood, pulling weeds, blacking stoves, and working on a steamboat and a railroad section gang. He met friendly folk who gave him food, and unfriendly folk who called him a "bum."

And he encountered all sorts of men also beating their way. "I had talked with hoboes enough to know there is the professional tramp who never works and the gaycat who hunts work and hopes to go on and get a job that suits him," Sandburg explained. He met several professionals, including a man raised in a Brooklyn orphan asylum who did not work: "'A real tramp can't even think about work,' he said, 'and it gives him a pain in the ass to talk about it.'" There were homosexuals, thieves, and panhandlers, one of whom told him "what kind of faces to ask for a dime or a quarter." Another tramp showed him a gun he used to rob harvest hands. Riding in the boxcars and on the bumpers, Sandburg experienced the viciousness of the "shacks" as well as their occasional kindness ("'If you're going to ride, keep out of sight,'" one told him.) But another "shack" hit him in the jaw when Sandburg refused to pay him 25 cents, and snarled, "'Stay where you are or you'll get more.'"

He finally reached the Kansas wheat fields, where he worked on a threshing crew in Pawnee County for three days at one farm, two days at another, pitchforking bundles of wheat onto the tables of the roaring threshing machine. In contrast with what the Industrial Commission investigators found in 1914, Sandburg seemed to have no complaints: "It was hard work but the crew was jolly, the meals and cooking good, the barns clean where four of us slept on hay, the pay a dollar and twenty-five cents a day and board." Then he had a five-day search for more work, finally catching onto a crew for three weeks that harvested on different farms around Lakin, Kansas.

After his wheat labors were finished, Sandburg's experiences continued to follow the hobo pattern. When he arrived in McCook, Nebraska, a policeman hanging about the yards confronted him: "'We don't want the likes of you in this town. You get back on that train.'" Sandburg obeyed, catching the same freight out and jumping off thirty miles farther on in Oxford, Nebraska.

Although he encountered unsavory characters in some of the "jungles," he generally had good memories of these stopovers, dominated early in the summer with "a keen and clean lot of travelers . . . most of them heading toward the wheat harvest." In one spot visited at the end of summer, en route back to Galesburg, he even admitted, "I was sorry to leave that friendly jungle" where during a restful three days he washed his clothes, ate corn stolen from nearby fields, and talked for long hours with four other travelers. Sandburg arrived back home on October 15, 1897, having gone as far west as Colorado, working in Nebraska and Missouri and harvesting wheat in Kansas. He knew something of hobo life.

Carl Sandburg's experiences in 1897 summed up many of the themes that ran through the experiences of western harvest labor. He was drawn by reports of Kansas wheat-harvesting jobs, rode the rails to reach them, met a variety of men along the way, lived in "jungles," tangled with railroad employees and town police, and in general was part of the developing hobo culture of the American West.

If he had wanted to continue on farther west, he would have found many things the same in the Pacific Northwest, but with several sharp differences, because of different types of agriculture and different groups of workers.

4

"LABOR SHORTAGE MENACE" IN THE NORTHWEST

Pickers are plentiful, the *Puyallup Republican* announced as the Washington State hops harvest began in 1907—"whites, Indians and Japs."[1]

Whites—including some hoboes as well as local people—had been showing up for work in the area's hopyards for years. More recently small numbers of Japanese had appeared also.

Indians were veterans of the Northwest's hops-picking labor force, paddling their long canoes from Alaska and British Columbia along the inner passages down to Puget Sound, entire tribes making their way to Puyallup and other hops centers. They merged this paid labor into ancient traditions and autumn rituals.

The ocean passageways they used were one of several characteristics that set apart Washington and Oregon, a section of the West marked by sharp differences in both topography and climate. West of the Cascade range, reliably heavy rainfall made possible an agricultural abundance along the Willamette, Umqua, and Rogue rivers in Oregon and on the coastal floodplain along Washington's Puget Sound. But east of that mountain range the rainfall was uncertain: known variously as the Columbia Plateau, the Columbia Basin, or the Inland Empire, this vast area runs from the steep, forested slopes of the Cascades on the west, to the Okanogan River on the north, bending southward to Camas Prairie in central Idaho and looping west again to Oregon's Umatilla and Deschutes country. While the Cascades steal most of the rainfall from clouds moving inland, nature benevolently provided the semi-arid Plateau with alternate moisture possibilities drawn from the Columbia and Snake rivers, which carry abundant water from the Rockies and adjacent ranges. One historical geographer refers to the area as a sort of "great interior sea" of rich but dry soil resting on a volcanic ash base, creating "an unusual land."[2]

Another important factor in the Northwest's development came simply from the transit history of wheat: as the grain frontier moved west from the Great Plains, the Inland Empire was an obvious next stop for wheat raising, and southeastern Washington and northeastern Oregon—the "Palouse"—became a breadbasket. But the region was already well on the way to becoming an agricultural cornucopia, starting in the early nineteenth century, when the Hudson's Bay Company governed the region and blackberry plants were first brought from the Sandwich Islands (Hawaii). Later the wagons of incoming Americans carried seeds and grafts for berries, apples, pears, and other fruit. Oregon's lush river districts west of the Cascades proved productive early on, and in 1853 apples were being shipped down the coast to gold-rush San Francisco. These traveled by sea, and before long the American consul in Manchester, England, reported in 1897 that Oregon apples were being sold there. In 1900 the *Northwest Pacific Farmer* announced that "nearly the entire output of Southern and Eastern Oregon's grown Newtowns and Jonathans" had been shipped to England and Germany. By 1906 an estimate put the total number of trees bearing apples, apricots, cherries, plums, and peaches in the state at 6.5 million, and in 1911 Oregon's orchards sold over $4 million worth of fruit—mainly apples but also peaches, pears, cherries, prunes, loganberries, grapes, strawberries, and even 300,000 pounds of English walnuts.[3]

Fruit production developed more slowly across the Columbia Plateau, but once proper conditions were created, agriculture thrived. In 1895 Washington's apple production was "absolutely a negligible factor" in national totals, but by 1917 it was proclaimed "the heaviest commercial apple-producing State in the Union." The U.S. Department of Agriculture that year termed the productivity and planting intensity in the Yakima and Wenatchee valleys to be "unsurpassed by other apple regions in this country"—and Washington alone shipped 16,000 railroad cars of apples, a fifth of the 1917 U.S. total.[4]

More than apples poured forth from this cornucopia. In the summer of 1917 the *Yakima Morning Herald* proudly reported that a carload of Yakima cherries had just sold in New York for $3,115—the Lambert

cherries for $3.20 a crate, the Bings for $2.50, and the Black Republicans for $2.25: "This is the greatest little fruit story of its kind that
was ever told in Yakima." And there were Yakima strawberries, blueberries, apricots, peaches, pears, and cranberries, and soon sugar beets
and potatoes.

And—hops. Both Oregon and Washington became major producers
of hops, a necessity in providing beer with its taste. The two states and
California jockeyed for national leadership in hops production; the lush
Willamette Valley hopyards enabled Oregon to hold the lead from 1905
to 1915. But beyond bragging about their sales, businessmen soon found
that the influx of workers boosted the local economy as well. When a
Puyallup newspaper proclaimed, "The whole world is invited to come
and help us pick hops," the store owners were prepared: shops in Puyallup
and other hops areas such as Independence, Oregon, and Yakima, Washington, kept busy selling "hop pickers' supplies" that included gloves,
work clothing, finger tape, sun hats, hop baskets, hop thermometers, hop
scoops, hop forks; groceries; and such camping gear as stoves, dishes,
eating utensils, and lantern oil, plus shoes "built for rough wear."[5]

Reports of this agricultural wealth erupting from the Northwest's soil
began to reach readers outside the region. Settlers arrived in large
numbers by the 1880s, and their numbers kept increasing, their communities expanding. Still, as late as 1913 the Industrial Relations Commission's investigators could observe that "the population is sparse,"
and despite continuing population growth, orchard men and farmers
frequently found that workers were scarce. The recruitment of harvesters was persistent, desperate, and an ongoing feature of Pacific Northwest agriculture.

The crews they enlisted showed a changing mix of ethnic origins
as well as differing work histories, genders, and ages. Because of the
Northwest's location at the far end of the westward movement, recruitment styles there were varied and often relied heavily on the lure of a
vanishing frontier, as federal investigator Peter Speek found in 1913.
Speek did not visit orchards and berry patches, however, but stuck to
railroad and logging camps, two of the main stopping points for transient workers—who generally would land at some point in an orchard

or hopyard job. What he saw consisted of "quite a number of former clerks, bookkeepers, stenographers, actors, and so forth, from the large cities of the East and Middle West—New York, Boston and Chicago. They explained that they had come West for various reasons—to find an opportunity of business on a small scale, to settle on land, to improve their health."[6]

Labor recruitment for several of the Northwest's crops was complex, because even more than with wheat, knowing the exact ripening times for hops and most fruits was crucial in hiring for picking, sorting, packing, and shipping. Fruit-picking costs occupied a "strategic position" in the world of the employer, one labor expert would later explain, for unless harvest labor "is available in adequate amounts when the product is ripe, the crop soon becomes unsaleable, and all the work and investment expended have been in vain." Furthermore, fruit prices changed frequently—often day to day—exasperating the orchardist or hopyard owner in dealings with workers who were sometimes too slow, too careless, or simply too few.

This unregulated swarming of men ebbed and flowed, and different areas were often left short of threshermen, hops pickers, and apple glommers. "Labor shortage menace to inland empire," the *Coeur d'Alene* (Idaho) *Evening Press* warned in May 1910, calling for 40,000 men to harvest the wheat crop of eastern Washington and Oregon, north and central Idaho, and western Montana. The situation was so bad that year around Ritzville, Washington, that the city council freed prisoners from the city jail to work in the fields. Similar warnings and pleas were heard frequently, especially in the newspapers of Spokane, the rail and commercial center of the Inland Empire. The city's major newspaper, the *Spokesman-Review*, ran numerous articles on fruit growers threatened with serious losses by the scarcity of labor, and throughout the era reports of strikes, inclement weather, and nearby forest fires often included extra paragraphs gauging their impact on the harvest. Workers' abundance—and willingness to work—were always uncertain. In July 1920 the newspaper headlined with alarm that two-thirds of the region's plum and prune crop would be lost "unless they can get pickers and packers . . ."

Such were the factors that went into creating a Northwest harvest labor force of great diversity, complexity, and mobility during the decades before the automobile came into widespread use. White hoboes rode the rails, but families from the region showed up as well, especially in berry-picking time; large numbers of Indians were fixtures for years in the hopyards, and later small numbers of Chinese and Japanese arrived, sometimes followed by "Hindoos" (from India), later by Filipinos. And eventually Mexicans reached the region.[7]

Climate, soil, and topography were all important in creating an agriculture that needed such a labor force, but as on the Great Plains, the Northwest also demonstrated the crucial role of the railroad. Although wheat and some other agricultural products had been leaving Portland on sailing ships and steamships from early days, the boom years for fruit and hops awaited rail lines. The Northern Pacific, propped up by congressional land grants, reached Spokane in 1881, setting off a settlers' rush into the Palouse with dreams of raising wheat. The line reached Tacoma in 1883 and provided the Northwest, finally, with its long-awaited transcontinental connection. And when the NP decided to bypass Yakima City and stop instead four miles away in North Yakima, some of the Yakima City residents transported their few structures four miles to establish a railhead. The NP rolled through on Christmas Day 1884. With the opening of the NP's Cascade Tunnel in 1888, Yakima began a boom that saw its population swell to 41,000 by 1910.

The Oregon Short Line Railroad provided connections to the Union Pacific through Idaho's Snake River Valley, but the major link eastward after the NP was James J. Hill's Great Northern. Lacking the land grants that made the UP and NP possible, Hill began building westward from St. Paul by encouraging settlement and therefore economic activity, first in the Red River Valley between Minnesota and the Dakotas, then at every stop on the way west. His immigration promotions drew thousands of settlers, feeder lines linked new farms to the GN's rails, model farms were set up, and credit banks and scientific agriculture were offered—all part of Hill's drive to the Northwest.

After its formal launch in 1889, GN engineers and surveyors were soon plotting a direct route, so the line could pay its own way as it edged along North Dakota's bonanza farm districts, into the mining sections of northern Montana, then through Idaho's Coeur d'Alenes into Washington, seeking always—as Hill cautioned his chief engineer—"the best possible line, shortest distance, lowest grades, and least curvature that we can build." Along the way towns were established and new life breathed into spots existing mainly in speculators' dreams, such as Havre and Kalispell, Montana, and the future apple center of Wenatchee, Washington. Finally, on January 6, 1893, the last spike was driven where the GN's rails crossed the Cascades near present-day Scenic, Washington, and James J. Hill provided the Pacific Northwest with another connection to the East. Completion of the Milwaukee Road in 1909 would give the region yet another link to the outside.[8]

With so many railroads competing for farmers' shipping, agriculture's future was looking brighter and brighter. River transport had often required transshipments—the Willamette was usually not navigable above Salem, and those trying to run the Columbia expected to portage. Overland freighting costs were high. Encouraged by the new opportunities the railroads promised, incoming settlers sought out plots in the abundant vacant lands. During the 1890s the number of farms in Washington State nearly doubled, reaching 33,202 by the end of the century and 56,192 by 1910; Oregon had 35,837 farms in 1900, 45,902 in 1910. Prices zoomed for lands in the wheat belt, while state populations shot up as well—by 1910 Oregon had almost 673,000, Washington over 1.1 million.[9]

Distant markets began to open for the region's fruit, largely because of the refrigerated railway car but also because of new marketing campaigns. Old-timers interviewed by the *Wenatchee Advance* in 1894 spoke proudly of sales to faraway consumers and only grudgingly admitted earlier troubles, leading the editor to point out, "The reader must remember that this land has been wholly void of markets until within the last year, that before the whistle of the Great Northern was heard in this country that it was sixty miles from railroads and on the wrong side of a mountain range besides." Some Northwest communities were still barred from becoming success stories, however. Someday the isolated Okanogan country to the north could become a great fruit area, a Wenatchee editor agreed in 1901, but there was a prerequisite: "When reached by a railroad orchards will be planted in every nook and corner."[10]

•

Wheat—not apples or hops—was the Northwest's early cash crop, grown especially for distant export, and as acreages expanded, there were corresponding calls for more harvest hands. The Pacific Northwest wheat belt developed east of the Columbia's "Big Bend," taking in the Palouse hills and the Walla Walla area, stretching southwestward to Pendleton in Oregon's Umatilla country. Slighted by rain clouds for much of the year, the district still received enough moisture for grain. Early farming was concentrated in the valleys, where riverboats could carry away much of the output. Large stretches of the country east of the mountains were also open range, and cattle raising competed with wheat. Experimentation with grains began in the 1880s, fallowing a field every other year, sometimes adopting Great Plains dry farming methods.

Eventually farmers found they could sow upon the hillsides, and wheat production on the Palouse grew from almost 1.5 million bushels in 1880 to some 52 million for 1909—by which time not only had railroad assistance arrived but a new "Walla Walla" wheat variety was developed, better adapted to the region, and per-acre production climbed to 40 bushels. At that point horse-drawn binders were still the dominant harvest system in use in the eastern Palouse, but Case tractors were starting to appear elsewhere along with combines and headers. Weather was uncertain and as always could be friend or foe; a Great Northern official noted that "hot winds coming at an inopportune time destroyed fully one-third of the wheat crop" in 1906—but then did not occur again in 1907, he added with apparent relief.[11]

Labor was the other uncertainty. Wheat prosperity depended heavily upon the thousands of men who gathered annually to work the harvest. Hayes Perkins was one such harvester: born in Coos County on the Oregon coast in 1878, he followed the hobo cycle for several years, and summer of 1898 found him jumping off a train in Walla Walla, Washington. Some three thousand other potential harvest hands had arrived in that Palouse center as well, lured by newspaper advertisements. Over the next few months Perkins worked on several crews in the area, finding as always that conditions for both working and living varied sharply. In July he was writing in his diary that the hours were long, "but we have ample food to hold us up, and everyone is healthy on such a job as this." A month later near Colfax, Washington, the crew was sleeping in a straw stack, and Perkins soon quit, then was hired at a new harvest job with a fifty-cent raise—only to discover that "this outfit works endless hours; begin at three in the morning and quit at nine at night. We have poor food, too." Employed on yet another farm at the end of September, Perkins was again rising at three a.m., having four food breaks before it was dark: "Then we work by flares until nine or even ten. No overtime, just plenty of work."[12]

Conditions were little changed twenty-three summers later, when Frederick Bracher of Portland took a train out to the eastern Oregon wheat fields; he noted the grain elevators that by 1921 were posted every fifteen miles along the tracks. In Pendleton the seventeen-year-old was soon employed driving a team of horses pulling a headerbox. The crew slept on the ground and was awakened at five o'clock each morning. Bracher then took care of his team of horses before heading for breakfast at six; then again at midday lunch the men "tried, again, to cram in enough fuel to last through five more hours of hard physical labor"—in afternoon temperatures that often hit 100 degrees.

Two of his fellow harvest workers that summer were cowboys from the area who followed the wheat harvest north, but another was "a true bindle stiff." Old Tom had no permanent residence; all his belongings "went along with him, rolled up in his bindle, and he moved from one job to another as ripening crops or his inclination suggested." Tom's record was varied and included employment on a Puget Sound ferry, in lumber mills, on logging and construction crews, a gold dredge, a salmon cannery, a sheep ranch, and a sternwheeler on the Willamette and Columbia. Old Tom referred to their group as "working stiffs."[13]

The experiences of Hayes Perkins, Frederick Bracher, and Old Tom were in many ways representative of the different harvest labor conditions across the Palouse. Harvests featured a variety of machines going over terrain that ran from flat, dry ancient floodplains to the slopes of the Blue Mountains and the rolling Palouse hills. These machines encouraged larger wheat acreages, but farmers who planted extensively now had to call for larger crews, never guaranteed at harvest time. The ebb and flow to the labor supply defied predictions. In the Ritzville area in 1910 it was a "serious situation," with farmers offering up to three dollars daily for stackers and pitchers. The previous year had been different—then, "the curbstones were lined with men waiting to go out." But in 1910 even local construction crews were decimated by the absence of men gone to harvest wheat. With labor supplies there was no predicting.

Because different employers needed crews at the same time, in any Palouse town competition for local workers was fierce—as when an "immense crop of swamp hay" on Wilson Creek near Wenatchee could not be put up because too many farmhands quit "to go to the harvest fields." That same year—1907—the Washington State grain inspector reported there was a "staggering problem" of finding "sufficient harvest hands to save the crop." Left unharvested in the fields, wheat could be ruined by rains. When faced with such a crisis one year, Walla Walla closed its saloons on Sundays, responding to a petition signed by all farmers within ten miles of the city: "For years the harvest hands have worked all week and on Sundays have gotten drunk and have been intoxicated for several days," the *Spokesman-Review* reported. The consequence was "heavy loss especially when hands were short," as it was that summer, leading to the farmers' pleas.[14]

Wheat could succeed in a dry region, but further agricultural progress east of the Cascades "was mainly a matter of developing irrigation projects." Wheat thrived with minimal moisture; most fruit and hops could not. Early farmers devised various methods to distribute small amounts of water over sagebrush country, which seemed to bring results. The *Yakima Herald* would later claim that the takeoff point for large-scale projects was 1881, and after that "irrigation canals have been built at an amazing rate." It cited the Selah Valley canal north of Yakima, the Gleed ditch, the Hubbard ditch, and the Selah-Moxee ditch. But soon men had even bigger dreams.

A bottle of champagne smashed on a canal headgate off the Yakima River in 1892 launched the Sunnyside Canal, destined to become the region's largest irrigation project. The champagne's splatters and the accompanying band music inaugurated the first twenty-five miles of the effort; its Northern Pacific promoters dreamed it would eventually consist of some 550 miles of lateral canals that would water 40,000 acres. Caught the following year in the 1893 national financial depression, Sunnyside eventually rebounded under new financing. Soon eastern capitalists were lured, and everywhere across the sagebrush country of eastern Oregon and Washington the talk was of irrigation. Yakima County, in fact, saw its irrigated farms increase tenfold over a twenty-year period. By the 1920s, wrote historian John Fahey, "every one of Washington's nineteen counties east of the Cascades contained irrigation systems . . ."—including Yakima County, with 93 percent of its farms irrigated; Benton, 85.2 percent; Chelan (which included Wenatchee), 81.3 percent; and 79.4 percent of those in Kittitas County.[15]

The NP touted Yakima as one of its prizes for pushing west; soon the GN had Wenatchee to point to with pride, and irrigation was at the top of its list of priorities there. J. J. Hill's planners launched the Gunn Ditch in 1891, eventually bringing water to 12,000 acres in the Wenatchee vicinity, while other nearby projects covered thousands of additional acres. Spokane-area boosters quickly got on the irrigation bandwagon, although Fahey notes that many pushed "speculative schemes devised to sell land otherwise unsaleable—and at immoderate profit." Their extensive promotions drew hundreds, soon thousands of settlers, but "few knew how to farm." Fahey found in examining earlier Yakima projects that "nearly three-fourths of the original buyers of irrigated tracts sold their land within three years . . ."

Similar troubles developed in the Spokane area: problems with dependable water combined with lack of farming know-how to produce failure, frustration, and anger. A spokesman for nearby Arcadia Valley Fruit Growers lamented in 1914, "Not one in fifty people coming in . . . for the express purpose of making a business of apple culture, ha[s] ever before . . . owned and cultivated a bearing apple tree."[16]

In Oregon other problems developed. In the summer of 1909 heavy upstream draining by irrigation companies caused the Umatilla to run dry in three locations. Unlike Washington's situation, in some years half of Oregon's irrigated acres were served by runoff from spring floods, temporarily stored behind dikes and dams.

Frequent disappointments and failures—though eventually giving way to some successes—led to federal intervention. It appeared in the form of the National Reclamation Act of 1902, the Newlands Act. In 1905 the U.S. Reclamation Service bought the struggling Sunnyside project, expanded it, then launched others with long-term financing. The government would also build needed dams, such as the Minidoka on the Snake River in 1909. By 1910 more than a quarter of Washington's irrigated acres were watered by federal projects. Fahey contends that troubles of the various Spokane Valley projects seem "to confirm the general opinion of western historians that irrigation survived chiefly because of government intervention."

Irrigation stimulated new dreams among entrepreneurs. One of Wenatchee's eloquent boosters predicted that when the High Line ditch was completed and the "peerless valley" fully irrigated, "then the big red apple will grow where now nods the sage brush and the lovely peach will blush where now plays the chipmunk." Economists agreed that these projects gave an enormous impetus to the Inland Empire's intensive agriculture—while pointing to the western irrigation report in the 1900 census, which cautioned that "irrigation properly conducted means intensive farming with great care in the application of water, followed by thorough cultivation of the moistened soil."[17]

Wheat farms kept expanding with the new machinery—on the Palouse in 1910 the average wheat farm covered 384 acres—but small orchards were the rule for fruit raisers. It was big business on a small scale, for by 1910 almost 5,400 Washington farms, and almost 3,150 Oregon farms, had only 10 to 19 acres. A 1914 U.S. Department of Agriculture survey examined eighty-seven typical Wenatchee orchards, which had an average size of 11.4 acres, with 6.5 acres in bearing trees. Production averaged 591 boxes of apples per acre. But to achieve such output, irrigation was needed, and its costs were high, capitalization was high, and mortgages were high.

As farmers studied their expenses, they were drawn again and again to the costs of labor. It was a complicated question, in the Northwest as everywhere: how to cut expenses while still attracting workers?[18]

As with wheat, the centers of commercial hops production had migrated westward—from New England to New York, on to Michigan and Wisconsin, then jumping to the Pacific Northwest when a newly arrived settler from Wisconsin transported some roots after the Civil War. From the colonial era onward, beer breweries had depended on hops, but this specialty crop required considerable knowledge of technology and plant science and was affected by sudden dips and turns of the market. And hops men faced another problem: the growing Prohibition movement.

The fragrance of hops plants comes from lupulin, drops of yellow resin found at the base of leaves forming the cone. And it is lupulin that provides the flavor for which beer drinkers thirst. To retain that flavor, cones had to be dried soon after picking, either spread out in the air and sunlight or carried to kilns. As hops historian Michael A. Tomlan stresses, "Drying hops was decidedly the most critical operation."

Because the small cones had to be pulled from the vines as soon as they were ripe—usually during September in Oregon and Washington—the availability of pickers at that moment became extremely important; a large portion of the hops story involves their recruitment. Statistics underscore this need: a Washington State College study found that although hops were grown "on only about one-ninth as large an acreage as that devoted to fruits and one-seventeenth that devoted to general crops, they nevertheless require 1.5 times as much hired labor as do apples, 4.2 times as much as do the soft fruits, and 3.9 times as much as do general crops."[19]

As early as 1883 Ezra Meeker, the pioneer Washington hops grower, saw that the future of hops in the Northwest rested entirely on the number of workers. With the region's railroad connections and soil, he predicted, "we could raise hops enough to supply the world"—but "just how many can be picked is a problem that will be speedily tested by the increased acreage being planted."

That was always the crux. At times the issue even crowded out the newspapers' headlines trumpeting hops prices in European and New York markets. Noting that certain nearby areas found enough workers but others did not, one editor cautioned that rumors about the supply of workers should not be repeated "because the labor problem is sufficiently perplexing as it is." Amid such conditions, employers had to coax, as one did in his advertisement in the *Yakima Herald* in 1917:

WANTED:—Fifty hop pickers, starting Sept. 12; low trellis, any picker can pick from 1 to 1 1/2 boxes more per day than on high trellis; old hop boxes hold only seven lime barrels; come and examine hops, finest stand in county; $1.25 per box.

Towns saw business pick up as soon as the hops pickers began arriving. It was a time of crowded streets, busy shops, and frantic activity. Evangelists were brought in for weekends, and a Puyallup church even offered special Sunday-afternoon services for harvesters. Hops operations were of such size and complexity, and underwent such changes, that evaluating field conditions required much more than looking merely at production figures. When Oregon produced more than 20 million pounds of hops in 1905—more than doubling Washington's production, and almost 60 percent above California's—the state's labor commissioner estimated that the 34,000 hops pickers had been paid $1,011,500, or an average of $29.75 apiece. But two years later the commissioner admitted that "some yards were not picked," and payments to pickers fell to $871,305, while in 1916 he blamed the shortage of workers on "the wages paid, and particularly . . . the poor accommodations provided by the employers for their help."[20]

To harvest this complicated crop, northwestern growers first turned to Indians, a dependence that gave way only gradually as white settlers moved into the region in numbers. In 1909 the U.S. Immigration Commission would note that most workers in the yards along the Willamette were Americans and European immigrants. But at least from the late 1870s and possibly earlier, Indians were the labor force that established hops in the Northwest.

Their canoes became familiar late-summer sights along the Tacoma and Seattle bayfronts. Native Americans were the stable base of crews in the annual autumnal hops harvest. In 1882, when Meeker looked back on the season just completed, he estimated that 2,500 Indians had worked in the hopyards, where they picked "the bulk of the hops . . ." In the *Washington Farmer's* 1890 report on the Snoqualmie Hop Ranch—"conceded to be the largest hop ranch in the world"—it found 800 Indians and 100 white men employed.

Soon after hops propagation arrived after the Civil War, the word on employment in the new hopyards spread rapidly among the region's tribes. It quickly reached the Northwest's interior tribes such as the Muckleshoots, and before long drew Siwashes and Makahs from the coast, Chimsyans and Haidas from British Columbia, and Thlinkets from the southern tip of Alaska, as well as those clustered about the Cascades foothills. Some canoed down to Puget Sound after salmon canning had ended; others arrived on steamers, following a route already familiar to those experienced in sawmill jobs.

The tribes' journeys themselves seemed linked to ancient traditions. Meeker recorded that

> they come from far and near, some in wagons, some on horseback, a few on foot, but the greater number in canoes . . . These were from all parts of Puget Sound, from British Columbia, and even from the confines of Alaska. The furthermost tribes come in their large canoes (made from the immense cedars of that region), so large that they dare and do venture to sea in them, in their seal-fishing season, manned with twenty men or more. The voyage to the hop-yards is all by the inland channel and among the islands of Puget Sound. Often-times a month is occupied in making the trip, leisurely working their way, camping here and there to hunt or fish, as their inclination prompts.[21]

Over several decades the journey to the hopyards became an important part of the tribes' yearly activities: when the Nuu-cha-nulth chief Sayach'apis' tried to invite members of the Songhee, Saanich, and Cowichan tribes to come to a potlatch in the mid-1880s on Vancouver Island, he was told, "You are too late . . . we are going to the hop fields," and "we might be late for the hops."

The infant city of Seattle grew to depend upon the Indians stopping off en route to the hops fields and on their way home. Many of their relatives were working there already—as historian Coll Thrush concludes, "Let there be no mistake: without the labor of Indians, Seattle would have been stillborn." In August 1878 scores were camping at the foot of Washington Street, a layover on the way to nearby hop fields, and in later years they came through to harvest berries, vegetables, herbs, and even flowers. These stopovers benefited Seattle shopkeepers, for sometimes before returning north the Indians would fill their canoes with goods for the potlatch, the coastal tribes' ritual in which wealth was displayed, status reaffirmed, and gifts distributed to strengthen ties between relatives and tribal members.

The numbers traveling to the hops districts for work meant a massive influx into small rural communities, enough that even their brief presence increased trade and spawned a new form of tourism: whites were attracted from a wide area, hoping to view exotic sights. As picking season got under way in Puyallup in early September 1906, many rode the train over from Tacoma—"'to see the Indians,' they said."[22]

With their predominance in the hops crews, Indians were in a strong position to make demands, and records show several labor disputes erupted over the years—for higher pay midway through the 1877 season, and for a return to the use of smaller boxes in 1903, for example. But lack of unity among the different tribes, as well as appreciation for the amenities provided, may have worked against the protests. In addition, with a family able to fill two or even three boxes with hops in a single day, receiving one dollar per box, the purchasing power of their earnings may have seemed substantial to a people used to a barter economy.

While entire families were usually involved, Indian women did most of the hops picking in the Northwest; men frequently took nearby farm jobs or went hunting and fishing. As Paige Raibmon has found, the migration of British Columbia Indians southward to the hops fields was so great that at times in the mid-1880s their numbers may have reached one quarter of the province's native population. With families coming to stay for weeks, living conditions could be crucial, and records indicate some moved on rather than accept poorly constructed huts with poor food possibilities. Raibmon quotes one Indian's written complaint about a hopyard on Cedar River: "Place looks like empty no potatoese turnips cabbages [c]arrot onions all nothing to our use"; the hops they were to pick were "no good to eated." He and his family moved on to another site.[23]

The white tourists flocking to gaze at Indians each September were probably not aware that what they were observing had roots in the distant past. Accounts from across North America tell of Indians holding summer berry-gathering festivals, and records indicate that Northwest tribes were no different. The Yakama[*] had traditionally held ceremonies preceding their annual huckleberry harvest: they prayed and fasted, then headed up into the mountains to the berry fields, staying as late as mid-October. After being dried to become raisinlike, huckleberries

[*] This early spelling of the tribe's name was later changed by whites to *Yakima*, and the city follows that spelling. Today the tribe has reverted to *Yakama*.

would easily keep through the winter, giving the berry a central role in Indian nutrition. Missionary Henry Perkins complained in 1843 that the Indians "preferred to spend their summer Sundays in the meadows of 'Indian Heaven' instead of listening to sermons that promised a Christian paradise." But they were in their own paradise, picking huckleberries. Although warfare between tribes marked Indian life throughout the presettlement era, peaceful multitribal gatherings took place at such central areas as the Twin Buttes district near Mount Adams, and it is recorded that tribes from the western and eastern slopes mingled in Cascades huckleberry fields. They were coming together on mutual ground, sharing a resource rather than competing for it.

The hopyards provided a way to continue these traditions. As white settlement converged on the region, many tribes found their accustomed lands being taken away. Clearings that had been developed over generations by the Snoqualmies proved ideal for whites' farming, and the tribe was pushed off. "We were just tramping around; we didn't know where to go," one aged Snoqualmie leader later recalled. But the hops boom in the 1880s and 1890s opened a doorway to survival, and the tribe set up villages on Lake Sammamish (close to Seattle), near the hopyards where they could obtain work. As historian Kent Richards explains, in many respects these Snoqualmie hops harvests replaced earlier mountain gatherings that were vanishing as tribes were moved to reservations, and their traditional social structures severely disrupted. With up to twelve hundred Indians coming together for the season, Richards points out, hops picking marked "the largest number of natives gathered in the upper valley during the historic period."

Among some tribes the late-summer mountain gatherings continued, however, and it is likely that these were remnants of the huckleberry collecting of yore. But down in the valleys the hops harvest brought together Indians from far and near for a yearly celebration. Along the White and Green rivers as well as in the Snoqualmie Valley, hops harvests "became a time of gathering" for the tribes, as well as providing cash income. Tribal interaction was fortified by the Chinook Jargon, a trade language that was developed among coastal tribes before whites arrived, then enriched with words from English and other languages. Further, some tribes brought elements of their customary potlatch celebrations and other traditions with them to the hopyards.[24]

The Klickitats were one tribe hired by the Snoqualmie Hop Growing Association, and when a *Seattle Times* reporter visited their camp in
August 1891, he was especially impressed with the nonharvest activities: they played music, danced jigs, and gambled in a game "as unpro-
nounceable as its methods are mysterious . . . ."[25] A reporter with the
Pierce County News surveyed the Puyallup hops fields—"Indians from
all over Washington Territory and Oregon flock there"—and saw it as a
"peculiarity" that the Indians wanted to be paid each night after work.
Upon investigation, he found that with as many as 2,000 Indians gathered around on Sundays at the "Devil's Play Ground," "the Indians in-
dulge in horse racing and every species of gambling." The Indians'
devotion to gambling attracted much notice, but it often led to violence
when combined with their twin devotion to alcohol.

The regional exodus to the hops fields sometimes ran counter to
U.S. and Canadian government efforts to "civilize" the Indians. Lengthy
journeys to jobs around Puget Sound kept Indian children out of agency
schools—but it also brought families into contact with the new culture
being imposed by the Americans. Coll Thrush argues that these canoe
trips "actually helped Native people integrate themselves into settler
society."[26]

This large-scale involvement by Native Americans with Northwest
hops harvesting has been largely ignored by historians, who until recently continued portraying western tribesmen as somehow untainted
by Euro-American ways. Newer studies, however, have brought out the
extensive Indian involvement in wage labor, perhaps part of their "secret history," as interpreted by Philip J. Deloria. Playing a key role in an
important economic activity, the hops pickers were "Indians in unexpected places," part of the "Indian anomalies" that challenge stereotypes
depicting them in passive positions untouched by the forces of modern-
ization. The world around them was changing and they adapted to it; the
money economy held openings for them as well as for white settlers.
Native American hops pickers created for themselves a different world
than has been assigned to them in novels, movies, and television.

And there were other aspects of this "secret history." Examining Indian participation in the nineteenth-century labor force across the West,
Martha C. Knack and Alice Littlefield point out that this wage labor
"was largely self-motivated. Native people did not wait for government

agents to direct them to wage opportunities; rather, they perceived those openings and sought them out." Often the agents opposed their hiring, as in 1887 when the Indian agent with the Siletz in Oregon criticized their trips to the Willamette hops fields because "they come into contact with some of the worst class of white people," weakening their morals. But, the agent admitted, "it has been the custom for years to allow them this privilege," and entire families found employment picking hops. The tribe was not passive; the agent had not pushed them into hops work.

Indians needed such employment for survival, Littlefield and Knack argue, relying on "the one resource they still controlled: the strength of their hands and the sweat of their backs." As Paige Raibmon noted, behind their long canoe trips from Alaska and British Columbia to labor in Washington hopyards were "reasons unrelated to the White economy," including visiting, trading, gambling. "These gatherings were embedded in local Aboriginal politics and culture," and in some aspects—such as racing their canoes as they headed home—the hops picking actually helped them expand traditional activities.[27]

Hops picking appears to have been held in low repute by many white males, for it required few skills, did not rely on strength, and was done by the very young and the very old, two age groups largely excluded from other harvesting. Washington's governor at one point issued a special call for whites to consider hops picking as a worthy enterprise, evidently because of fears of growing labor shortages. Further reducing the importance of such work in white males' eyes, some tribes were believed to be carrying slaves along with them on their journeys to Puget Sound, putting them to work in the hopyards.

Also dampening the enthusiasm of many white males was the fact that some Japanese and Chinese picked hops, although their labor mainly went into other farm and urban pursuits; they appear in Northwest hops-picking histories mainly in the oratory of anti-Asian politicians. Indians sometimes joined in campaigns against the Chinese, claiming that they did so to protect their own jobs. The Immigration Commission reported in 1909 that some Japanese worked in the major Oregon hops area around Independence.[28]

Over the years, hops work was developing an image at odds with other types of western harvest labor: many regarded it as a happy, almost carefree activity, for young whites as well as for the Indians, with their gambling and horse racing. In some areas white women and children were recruited; at one point schools in the city of Yakima delayed their fall opening date to encourage students to take jobs in the hopyards. To recruit large numbers of youths, the work could not carry an aura of gritty, dismal plodding. Accordingly, the *Pacific Northwest Farmer* referred to hops picking as "a holiday for the young people," noting that the ranch with the best dance floor was most sought by incoming youths. A U.S. Department of Agriculture report added that while hops picking provided a chance to make some money, it was also regarded as a "frolic."[29]

An effort to expand awareness of what hops picking involved, as well as perhaps to stimulate some reform, occurred in 1907. In that key year of the Progressive reform era, a YWCA specialist worried about the treatment of female workers took it upon herself to hire on at Independence, in the Willamette River Valley, an area where white hops workers were numerous. She was Annie Marion MacLean, of Adelphi College in Brooklyn, who traveled to Portland in 1907 to use the investigative approach favored by many contemporary reformers: she went to work herself. Scanning newspaper advertisements, she noted one that she termed "unusual": "Perfect accommodations, good food at city prices, free whiskey, dance five nights in the week, evangelists on Sunday and a hell of a time." Another advertisement claimed it had the "largest and best-equipped hop yard in Oregon; all on trellis wire; perfect accommodations; grocery store, bakery, butcher shop, barber shop, dancing pavilion 50x150 feet, telephone, physician, beautiful camping ground; three-acre bathing pool, restaurant, provisions sold at Portland prices."

The next morning, Saturday, found her riding with some eight hundred others in a "hop special" train destined for the Independence hopyards, in a crowd that included families as well as "several hundred young men and women off for a lark with a chance to make some money," many from Portland's "floating working population." Young men courted the girls en route, piling off the train at each stop on the four-hour trip to steal apples and prunes from nearby orchards, returning to share the bounty with their newfound favorites.

Arriving at Independence, and following a six-mile ride on a "spring-less hay rack," Annie MacLean picked up denim and filled it with fresh straw to make a tick to sleep on, in a tent occupied by herself and nine other young women. Sunday was spent getting acquainted, and she was repeatedly impressed by "the democracy of the hop field" as her fellow workers opened up about their lives and goals. Registration that after-noon, however, proved to be a shouting, shoving, tawdry event, as some one thousand pickers were assigned yards: MacLean was number 185 in Yard B, Company 4, pinning on her pink badge with pride. That eve-ning a poorly presented stereopticon lecture on the "Parables of Jesus" closed out a long day, although sleep proved difficult "for men were drinking and carousing until early morning . . ."

Pickers began to rise at four a.m., but MacLean did not get to her yard until nine a.m. because of first-day requirements. She was im-pressed "to see the various companies form and march off to victory, for everyone expected to make a lot of money—from three to seven dollars a day, I was told when I engaged work in Portland." In the field "wire men" came to cut down the trellises, and the pickers began pulling cones off the vines. A fellow worker told her, "Strip the vines, leaves and all,'" while another added, "Throw in some sand, it weighs good." But the yard boss warned: "Pick clean or you get no money." MacLean found that while it may have been healthful to work outdoors, "it is hard with the reaching and stooping and tramping over the rough, ploughed ground." She picked 53 pounds in two and one-half hours, earning 56 cents, but by lunchtime her throat was choked with pollen. Few made $2 a day; some did not cover their expenses of 65 cents a day for meals and bed. "There was much dissatisfaction, too," she added, "over the fact that the weighers frequently gave the young and pretty and flirtatious girls ten or twelve pounds extra weight."

MacLean carefully observed her fellow workers:

In one row a man and his wife picked together while small chil-dren crawled around in the dirt at their feet; over a little was a woman with six offspring picking in her basket; just beyond was a giddy girl with a forward boy she had met on the train— both picking away and passing cheap compliments; away to the right was a red-cheeked German girl crying already because her clumsy fingers made work slow; near her were two bright high-school girls eager to earn money for clothes; not far away was a widow of nearly fifty with her aged mother, making small headway with the hops; I taught them what I had learned and then things went better.

MacLean took notes about her twenty-seven fellow female hops pickers, eight of them Germans, two Swedes, and the rest Americans, all from the Portland area. Six were housewives seeking to earn money for their children, or to provide a family outing, or (a twenty-year-old German) because she "ran away from home." Six were high school students; most of the rest were employed in shops or factories. Their reasons for traveling to Independence to pick hops were varied—several listed earning money as the chief goal, others "to have a good time" or a "profitable vacation," and one aimed "to meet nice men."

Annie MacLean was impressed with the efforts of the Oregon YWCA to improve the situation, offering evening concerts and running the restaurant. She faulted the yard owner for weak organization and called for "more wholesome recreation" that would have to originate with an outside institution. But for all the problems she found, MacLean conceded that next hops season she would feel the urge to travel to Oregon "and don the calico frock and apron, with the picker's stout gloves and neck-kerchief, to sleep again on the bed of straw and rise in the dawn to help harvest the blossoms, and even to endure again the cruel weariness it implies, to enjoy the true democracy of the motley crowd, and to watch the future realization of betterment efforts." She closed her account: "Long live the Oregon hop pickers!"[30]

The world of hops picking that Annie MacLean glimpsed was an important part of seasonal labor in the Pacific Northwest. It involved women and children and the elderly as well as men, and in other yards it featured enormous participation by Indians. An aphid infestation in 1910 severely crippled the Northwest's first hops-growing era, but hops recovered and plantings expanded, and in the process labor patterns were established that would be repeated in other agricultural endeavors.

Hops picking and the variety within its crews provide another example of the overlapping of different Wests, fitting into the findings of historian Carlos Schwantes. He found this overlap in some places where "the gunslinger mentality of the classic West was employed in the complex new business of labor relations," but he located other overlaps where unusual juxtapositions occurred. It can be argued that hops fields provided such an overlap: tribes retained their traditional customs while still fitting into the developing world of wage labor, even forging a new pan-Indianism in the process; and white families with young children left the city and engaged in agricultural work. Schwantes was examining a predominantly male West, where men slogged on in logging, sawmills, mining, and railroading. But the concept should logically be expanded to include women, children, and the elderly, for experiences in Northwest hopyards demonstrate that they were part of the wage workers' frontier also. This West would provide many other such examples of overlapping frontiers, as Indians and housewives, hobos and high school students, Asians and office clerks and cowboys worked the harvests.[31]

5

THE NORTHWEST
BECOMES AN ORCHARD

The speaker from the Woman's Suffrage Association had just finished her talk at Puyallup's GAR Hall, stressing "the reasonableness, righteousness, justness and need of the ballot in the hands of women." She used logic as well as personal examples to back up her arguments that summer evening in 1908, as the suffrage movement gained momentum across Washington and the Northwest. But perhaps the most effective argument before that crowd came not from the visiting lecturer but later, during audience discussion, when First Baptist's Reverend A. Laurence Black drew on scenes everyone was familiar with. While admitting that he previously had believed woman's place was in the home, Reverend Black told how he had come to support the vote for women, pointing out that "conditions are such that we see her forced to labor in the berry fields and canneries, as evidenced in Puyallup," as well as taking office and business jobs.[1]

Reverend Black knew whereof he spoke. Women were visible everywhere in the berry fields around Puyallup, and at Hood River, Ashland, Wenatchee, Yakima, and numerous other spots around the Pacific Northwest. As in the hopyards, women and children and youths worked alongside the legions of men showing up for harvest each summer and fall. The extent to which fruit picking had become a family project was evident in a 1915 *Yakima Herald* report:

> The demands of the fruit crop have reached the point where entire families are going to the orchards for employment. When the time arrives that people move out in groups containing par-

ents, good sized son, lesser sized daughter, baby, dog, canary and phonograph, then it is safe to assume that the bulk of the summer has passed in Yakima and that pretty soon the Indians will be along for the hop picking. The movement has begun. They were all at the Northern Pacific station yesterday and the canary was singing.

As on the Great Plains, the search for harvest help was casting a wide net, reaching far beyond recruiting men jumping off passing trains.[2]

Behind this search for labor was the fact that the reputation of Washington and Oregon as fruit capitals was spreading rapidly, mainly through extensive organization and nationwide publicity. This rested heavily upon the arrival of the railroads, as well as on the development of irrigation canals through the sagebrush districts east of the Cascades. But it also was the offspring of hectic promotions, for the fruit business was moving beyond a farmer putting in several apple trees to produce for the local market. Now, with marketing and advertising, with the help of horticultural experts and railroad officials, it was becoming big—and profitable—business. While the first page of the *Wenatchee Advance* in 1902 bore the legend "Home of the Big Red Apple," by 1911 it was changed to "Where the dollars grow on trees." And it seemed true: in some years, Washington's apple sales exceeded its lumber earnings.[3]

The same thing was happening at Hood River, Oregon, where eastern investors began arriving in 1907 and by 1916 numbered sixty-eight from New York alone—including one Vanderbilt—each invested in orchard land. The town had three banks, with four trains passing through daily. Hood River orchardists are credited with pioneering the marketing concept of identifying produce with its locale of origin, through the Apple Growers Union, a cooperative: soon 90 percent of the district's apples were sold with the "Hood River" label. Other areas picked up the idea quickly.

Cooperatives proved to be the organizing mechanism for such approaches, and in 1910, when the Northwest Fruit Exchange was launched in Portland, it signed up some thirty affiliated organizations, such as the Puyallup Fruit Growers Association and the Yakima Fruit Growers Association. In another three years Pacific Northwest Fruit Distributors was organized. Cooperation had reached the fruit men, and just in time: starting in 1914 and running for three years, some two million apple trees came into production each year in Washington State, enlarging the 1914 output by 300 percent.

These new pressures led the apple men to realize their need for both quality control and new markets. The Northwest Fruit Exchange convinced growers to stop producing dozens and dozens of varieties of fruit and to instead limit themselves to only eight or ten—and then to perfect them, in taste and feel but also for ease in packing and distributing. Yakima apple raisers were pushing their "Big Y" brand, Wenatchee was selling under the "Skookum" label, nearby Arcadia had its "Big A," while Spokane Valley growers marketed under the "Redskin" and "Sunset" names. The cooperatives, meanwhile, set up national marketing schemes in conjunction with the GN and NP and the railways' fleets of refrigerated "reefer" cars, with heated cars in winter.

Growers joined a variety of other organizations as well, county groups and such regional aggregations as the Northwest Horticultural Association, to which they increasingly turned for help in controlling apple blight. Wenatchee staged its first Farmers' Institute in March 1895, where some sixty growers gathered—encouraged by lower GN fares given to participants—to hear experts talk on such topics as insects, fungous diseases of plants, and spraying machinery. In 1901 Chelan County's Horticultural Association convinced county commissioners to pay for a fruit inspector, who promptly condemned 450 newly imported trees containing the woolly aphid. They were burned immediately. Intensive agriculture required the help of scientists—and drastic action at times.[4]

Labor shortages seem not to have been important in these early consultations. The family farm ideal had traveled westward with the pioneers, and in the early years farmers' dreams were seldom upset by such nightmares. Most saw no need for harvest help beyond the circle of family and neighbors. And the old ways seemed to be working. Newspapers in the fruit districts were filled with examples of successes with small-scale operations, of minimal plots providing an adequate living for the owner-operators. Up the Wenatchee River in Leavenworth, the owner of a five-acre tract of mixed fruit was now able to plan a postharvest trip to Sweden with his wife. According to the *Echo* editor,

He estimates his income from strawberries and cherries at nearly $1,000. In addition there are trees bearing apples, plums and pears. All these are salable at good prices. Why, then, should the grower hesitate to make a tour of Europe from the returns of one season? He and his wife attend to the little farm. They require no large amount of capital to operate the place. No hired men are needed and the implements and machinery need not cost much. Practically the entire proceeds from the orchard represent savings that may be duplicated every year.

"No hired men are needed . . ."—these magic words melded with the American dream of a cozy cabin on a self-supporting farm; Thomas Jefferson would have cheered. The president of the Wenatchee Valley Fruit Growers Association certainly was cheering as he promoted five-to-ten-acre orchards as centers of "ideal home life," where an owner would cultivate his own land, "harvest his own crop," then work (through the association) to distribute what he had produced.

But as plantings continued and new orchards sprang up, demands for harvest hands began to rise, severely testing the farmer's ability to handle the crop with only local help. Before many crop years had passed, thousands of railroad cars and ships were waiting to be engorged with apples, pears, berries, and hops bales. Local pickers simply could not keep up.

Newspaper accounts trace the gradual shift as acreages enlarged and new owners appeared, no longer just pioneer farmers but frequently capitalists from afar. (The U.S. Department of Agriculture put the average investment for each Wenatchee orchard at almost $21,000 by 1917.) There was much to lure outsiders, for now northwestern salesmen were visiting eastern and European cities; refrigeration for both rail and steamship underwent such improvements that Yakima peaches could join Wenatchee apples in London market stalls. Statistics charted the growth: the U.S. Department of Agriculture reported that Washington shipped 1,000 carloads of apples in 1900, but in 1917 the Yakima and Wenatchee districts together shipped more than 16,000 carloads, and the state total hit 27,000 carloads two years later. Hood River alone was sending out 1,800 cars of apples yearly then.[5]

All this meant that fruit pickers were needed more than ever. In 1902 the Patrons of Husbandry noted approvingly that September's good weather brought more women and children into the hops harvest, but two years later it was lamenting the nation's "great need of farm help," and its report from Hood River showed why: a 30-acre strawberry field owned by "some capitalists at The Dalles" had required eighty pickers and twenty-four packers—but even then a quarter of the berries were left to rot in the patches.

A headline in July 1906 in the *Puyallup Republican* summarized the changing situation:

BERRY YIELD LARGEST EVER
Increased Acreage, Heavy Crop
and Scarcity of Pickers
Causes Growers Some Trouble

Some area farmers, the article explained, "have abandoned whole fields and some parts of fields because they cannot get pickers." Never before had there been such a problem, the *Republican* added, "but so many new fields have come into bearing this year and the increased acreage has made the demand greater than could be filled." It was a recurring problem, and in 1910 the *Spokane Inland Herald* reported that "fully $2,000 worth of strawberries rotted on the ground" in a nearby berry district, "due to a lack of labor . . ."[6]

Demand kept growing as the 1910s began, and soon the European war was drawing off manpower. Canada suffered from a labor shortage as well, dispatching fifty-two special agents to try to convince at least 10,000 harvest hands from the United States to step northward into Alberta, Saskatchewan, and Manitoba, with most recruiting concentrated in western states along the international boundary. One college student wrote a term paper in 1915 on her summer's employment picking and canning berries in Puyallup: that summer 4.5 million pounds of blackberries and 3 million pounds of raspberries had been canned, and 300 carloads of red raspberries were sent out by rail. Behind such enormous output "15,000 people were employed in the fields and 250 in the cannery," she wrote. It was a big business, also a big labor business.[7]

The call for workers brought new groups into the orchards and berry patches. Women were welcomed eagerly, especially as the nation approached war. The *Yakima Herald* cheered when ninety-four women were hired under the federal wartime employment agency, noting that "cherry picking proved a popular feminine employment," with thirty-four women and girls heading into the cherry orchards. Some fruit men worked harder at recruiting Indians, deluging reservation agents with pleas. One man who began hiring Indians in 1915 continued the practice for the next quarter-century. Requests for Indian workers poured into reservation offices, often building on past connections. A typical letter arrived at the Warm Springs Agency in Oregon from Hood River in 1926 (spelling as in the original):

> Dear Sirs.
>   Will you pleas send me 10 rasberies pickers amedatly I had a few from the agency last year. I would like to have an answer by return mail.[8]

Larger crews working in bigger orchards, patches, and canneries usually meant less supervision. This was no small change, for picking berries and pears required a more sensitive touch than jerking hops cones off a vine. When the owner of "a large fruit ranch" said he believed most damage occurred before apples reached the packing shed, the *Wenatchee Republic* agreed: the fault lay in "allowing anybody and everybody who is able to climb a ladder in the picking crew"—for while those doing the packing underwent training, employers still depended largely "upon any sort of labor for the picking."

Oregon experts suggested having three gangs of apple pickers, based on age, gender, and weight (the latter group "doing the most reaching"). Pickers should be instructed to "handle the apples as though they were eggs . . . The apple should be picked by a twist of the wrist, giving either a slight upward or downward motion at the same time." But enforcing a rule to handle apples like eggs could be difficult when crews numbered hundreds of pickers. The Oregon Agricultural Experiment Station blamed "carelessness in picking" for most of the problems with prune plums, the author admitting he had "seen men knocking the fruit from the trees with clubs, handling it with shovels, and pouring it roughly from boxes in a wagon bed."[9]

As fields enlarged and the need for workers kept increasing, farms and orchards began to steal harvesters from those nearby, as on the Great Plains. Peach and hops growers in Yakima competed vigorously against each other to grab incoming workers, some claiming that since their own advertising had drawn the worker to the district, this employer deserved first chance at him. A competitor retorted, "When they step from the trains here they are the legitimate property of the first person who can get to them . . ." Railroad cars were held in the Yakima station so that incoming workers would not be turned loose to wander around, while waiting transport to the job site. At other times special railroad cars parked in the station served as hiring offices, with telephone lines running to different growers in the area; additional railway service was added to carry pickers out to work and back.

Advertising in distant cities was not always effective, for often in their desperation to recruit, the grower-advertisers were too vague or even inaccurate—in one case drawing workers from Seattle three weeks too early. A Yakima farmer was so desperate to hold workers for his upcoming potato and sugar beet harvests that he provided early arrivals with fruit, potatoes, and wood: "it all doesn't amount to much in the aggregate and insures me a harvest crew for the fruit."

As worried growers sent recruitment notices to distant cities, some local businessmen chafed that wages paid to outsiders would be leaving the city, in an outflow of wealth. The Wenatchee Commercial Club was especially vexed and urged that recruiting be concentrated on the immediate region, to "keep many thousands of dollars at home . . ." But when the district fruit inspector announced that 4,000 men and women would be needed to handle the 1912 apple crop for an expected forty-five days of labor, the Commercial Club's local hiring plan was clearly inadequate and impractical.[10]

Another result of the labor shortages was a heightened interest in hiring children. A Puyallup man helping at a neighbor's berry farm found his co-workers were considerably younger:

> There were quite a number of kids picking. It's a good chance for the youngsters to make a little pin money during school vacation. It was very amusing to hear them in their innocent prattle talk shop. The number of boxes they picked, etc., what they were going to do with their earnings. They had visions of wealth; something like the Rockefellers had, I presume, in their kid days. One youngster was going to buy himself a wheel;* another an

* A bicycle.

automobile. Before the day was over they had secured part of their dream—"the tired feeling." The kids were quite foxy in their methods of picking. They would skim over a row, take all the fat berries and leave the lean ones for the next picker. I noticed they carried their canneries with them; whenever they would come in contact with a great big luscious one, down it went into the two-legged cannery. But after the first day or two berries did not appeal to them.

Children had been accompanying their parents into family fields for years, but just as the larger berry patches and orchards were hiring them, their employment ran into a trio of challenges: the construction of school buildings for the first time in more and more communities across the region, a tightening of state laws on school attendance, and a growing feeling in the Progressive Era that strenuous labor could be injurious to children. When Wenatchee's classes started in September 1900 there were only 120 children present, and a reporter noted that "many pupils will enter later who are now busy on the fruit farms of the valley." The fact that much of the work took place in summertime made children's employment easier to accept, and later, during the wartime labor crunch, Oregon officials pointed to this fact: "Fortunately for the berry, hop and fruit grower, schools are out at harvest time, when thousands of children aid in saving the crop."

Since "saving the crop" was crucial to Northwest communities, compromises with the school calendar were sometimes necessary. The Wenatchee School Board had to yield to this reality in early September 1907, after hearing a local grower argue that the city had to keep growing because "the fruit which is coming into bearing is increasing faster than the population." Following his plea, the board agreed to permit "the issuance of excuses to as many of the children in the schools, by a written request from the parents during the first week."[11]

The Oregon Child Labor Commission discussed possible changes in the state's child labor law in 1910 but limited its focus to children under age fourteen employed in factories, stores, shops, and messenger services—with no mention of harvest work.

Adapting growers' needs for young people in the fruit harvest continued to occupy school boards across the region—even in the federally run Yakima Indian Agency school, which in 1911 put off opening until

October 1 to allow harvest work. When Yakima High School did its annual survey of students' summer earnings as the harvest season neared its close in 1915, the school total came to $18,467—even without including many of the biggest earners whose earnings could not be included "until hop picking season is over . . ." The average earnings for the 301 students was $61.35 apiece, topped by a sophomore boy's $300 (which included delivering newspapers, as well as working in cherry and peach orchards). The leading girl earner brought in $150, all from fruit harvesting, the source of two-thirds of all student summer earnings. In October 1916 Wenatchee schools simply dismissed grades seven through twelve for several weeks for picking.[12]

As the United States was drawn into the widening European war, labor shortages became even more frequent. Some of the blame lay in the increased acreages being planted, but a crisis developed as well when the military draft began and high-wage war industries were launched. In fall 1917 ranchers in the Yakima area were recruiting desperately to bring in their apple, potato, and sugar beet harvests—but their call for student help ran up against the fact that "in some sections the school children [meaning high school boys] have been called into service." In mid-October Wenatchee's schools had still not opened, "the children helping in the orchards," and local businessmen were sending their employees there too. In Yakima the county superintendent of schools balked at allowing grade school children to miss more classes, announcing that districts should "close the schools altogether for a certain period and then make up the time later," rather than dealing with each absent pupil's missed work. High school students could keep picking in the orchards, she noted, since the compulsory attendance law did not affect most of them. This simplified Oregon's participation in the federal wartime "Boys' Working Reserve," under the U.S. Department of Agriculture; Oregon's overall success in bringing in the crops in 1917 and 1918 was attributed to the program, and the rush of townfolk to help bring in harvests was also praised.[13]

Some years ahead of the war buildup, orchard recruiters had been casting glances at Chinese and Japanese. Previously only two races had been involved in Northwest harvests: whites and Indians. Indians had long been accepted in the fruit patches as well as in the hopyards, although mixed crews generally were segregated by race. Asians were another matter—they had suffered discrimination for some time in their dealings with whites along the Pacific Coast, especially in mining camps, where they often were relegated to working placers that had been abandoned by whites. As they filtered into the region from California, the prejudice against them spread northward also, sparking several incidents in the early years of orchard and hopyard development.

One year the opening of school in Independence, Oregon, was delayed so that children could pick hops and growers would have no need to hire Chinese. One night in the Snoqualmie area in 1885 a group of Indians and whites dynamited houses where Chinese were living and chased out thirty-seven Chinese hops pickers, killing three. The incident was the first in a series of anti-Chinese riots across the region that climaxed the following year, when federal troops were called and the mayor of Seattle declared martial law. The city's besieged Chinese were escorted to a ship and deported; convictions of the riot leaders were eventually overturned. Chinese on railroad construction crews were also chased away, many heading to Portland, where anti-Chinese feeling was less intense and did not lead to the violence of Tacoma and Seattle.[14]

Despite such incidents the numbers of Asians continued to grow. Chinese became dominant in salmon cannery work in Oregon and along Puget Sound, although not in fishing, and by the early 1890s Japanese were joining them in the canneries. There were 9,510 Chinese counted in the 1880 Oregon census, while the few in Washington Territory that year clustered in ports and across the Inland Empire in river towns—the census taker counted 1,158 in Wasco County, almost evenly split between Walla Walla and Whitman. The 1882 federal ban on further Chinese immigration assured their numbers would be falling, and the Oregon total dropped to 6,468 by 1910 and 2,151 in 1920. Washington had 3,260 Chinese in 1890—Yakima counted only 84—but this fell to 2,301 in 1910 and 1,727 in 1920. The issue became complicated because large numbers continued coming over the border illegally from Canada and remained uncounted. (The Spokane jail in 1897 held men for "smuggling Chinese" as well as for "unlawfully bringing in Japanese women." One Wing Wong was arrested for being "unlawfully in U.S.")

Century's end brought a sudden increase in Japanese workers, most having landed first in California. By 1905 Japanese had replaced Chinese in the cannery crews, and their numbers continued to grow after arrivals of "picture brides"—women allowed entry because Japanese men in the United States claimed them as their wives, even though they had selected them only from photographs supplied by go-betweens. This system meant that Japanese numbers continued growing even after the 1907 Gentlemen's Agreement negotiated by President Theodore Roosevelt, which cut off immigration of laborers from Japan. The census taker had found only a single Japanese man in Washington in 1880 and only two in Oregon. The Oregon total grew to 2,522 by 1900 and 3,277 in 1910, with 468 then in Hood River County; by 1920 the census counted 3,169 in Oregon. Washington's Japanese numbered 5,769 by 1900, increasing rapidly to 12,177 in 1910 and 12,971 in 1920. Only 64 were listed in Yakima County in 1900, however, and this total grew but slightly to 257 in 1910 then to 771 by 1920, when almost two-thirds of Washington's Japanese lived in King County (Seattle).[15]

Their numbers were low, but Asians could be found in many occupations across the region—especially in salmon canneries, in sawmills, and on railroad construction crews. When twenty newly arrived Japanese men in Portland were not able to obtain promised railroad jobs in 1891, they were soon picking hops. Their pathway was not unusual: railroad labor rather than harvesting jobs became the primary Northwest employment for arriving Japanese, who comprised 40 percent of Oregon's railroad construction workers by 1907. Some section crews in the Northwest were entirely Japanese, replacing Chinese who had earlier been identified with the West's railroad construction.

To keep up with rising demand in the Pacific Northwest, two major labor contracting firms—the Tacoma Construction and Maintenance Company and the Oriental Trading Company of Seattle—arranged for ships to load Japanese laborers in Hawaii and carry them directly to the Northwest rather than to San Francisco. This connection had been developing after the United States annexed Hawaii during the Spanish-American War of 1898, and workers were soon being recruited from Hawaiian plantations, where they had been employed since first arriving from Japan. In 1905 the Tacoma contractor shipped 400 Japanese workers from Hawaii, while the Seattle firm obtained 600. The latter advertised daily summer wages in their U.S. jobs of up to $1.30 and offered to furnish work clothes and such foods as rice, bean paste, and soy sauce.

Hawaiian plantation managers and Japanese officials tried to stem this exodus, the consul in Honolulu claiming that wages and working conditions in Hawaii were better. But as historian Yuji Ichioka has pointed out, "contrary to his assertion, recruiting agents were not exaggerating nor lying. West Coast laborers in fact earned twice as much as their Hawaiian counterparts." This was no secret at home, and soon Japanese laborers were landing in Hawaii for only brief stays before continuing on to the United States. Rising anti-Japanese sentiment on the West Coast doomed the Hawaiian layover, however, and this doorway to America closed in 1907 with the Gentlemen's Agreement.[16]

For those who had already landed, farmwork beckoned, even though it generally paid less than railroad construction. Perhaps its appeal lay in the fact that most of the immigrants had been raised on farms in Japan, or perhaps they felt farm jobs offered a better chance to save money than blasting and digging to install rails, ties, and trestles. And it may have been an early indication that some were already shifting their goals away from being a *dekaseginin*, a temporary sojourner who came only to make money and return to Japan. Certainly some of the early Japanese successes in leasing orchards pointed toward prosperous possibilities. By 1909 some 400 labored on vegetable and strawberry farms in the Portland area, another 150 to 200 up the Willamette around Salem, and some 300 in Hood River's apple orchards and strawberry farms. In Polk County they went into hops; in Russellville, strawberries.[17]

In keeping with these precedents, the first Japanese working in Hood River had come not to pick apples but as laborers on the Mt. Hood Railroad, where they could scarcely miss seeing Indians working nearby, felling trees and clearing land. As elsewhere, the coming of a spur line to Hood River encouraged expansion of the apple business, and soon Japanese were needed desperately for harvest jobs rather than for building the railroad.[18]

Interviews by Linda Tamura with *issei* (the immigrant generation) who had worked in Hood River orchards in those early years reveal something of their dreams as well as their persistence through difficult times. As in peasant villages across Europe, many Japanese had been lured across the ocean by tales of people scooping up money in America. One picture bride recalled that she had been curious to see the "strange clothes" that returnees had described—"I had wonderful visions of America! I pictured that even the flies would be different."

For one man, the invitation to work in Hood River orchards came from the Japanese co-owner of a variety store, who had been pressed

into service as a labor contractor when local orchard owners—whites—
sought help finding men to pick apples:

> When start picking apples, *hakujin* [Caucasians] come to Yasui
> Store and say, "I like two to three boys to work." Mr. Yasui ask
> everybody, "Man said he like to have two to three boys. You like
> to go?" Yes, I go, I go! Everybody go. Better than do nothing and
> stay home. The main thing is I make more money.

The Yasui Store was run by three brothers, one of whom—Masuo
Yasui—had arrived in Seattle in 1903 to join his father and brothers
working on railroads. Soon moving to Hood River, this rising young
entrepreneur—who had become a Christian while boarding at a Meth-
odist mission in Portland—began seeking business opportunities and
orchard investment. When the Oregon Apple Company needed someone to both recruit Japanese workers and mediate disputes between the
firm and its employees, they turned to Yasui. He intervened repeatedly,
urging Japanese to win respect from their white neighbors by hard work
and honest dealings. And while he was working as a labor contractor,
sending Japanese out to clear land as well as to pick fruit, Yasui was also
urging his countrymen to become farmers, helping many to start leasing.

While most had worked on farms at home, fruit raising in the West
had some basic differences. The Japanese hired in orchards around
Hood River soon found there were forty different kinds of apples, and
each type had to be kept separate. The pickers recruited by Yasui earned
$3 for a ten-hour day, and many stayed in a boardinghouse he owned.
Just in time for these struggling bachelors at Hood River and elsewhere,
the picture brides began to arrive.

By 1920 a third of Oregon's Japanese were females, many working
alongside their husbands. One recalled that "our consuming interest
was to work hard, earn a lot of money, and return to Japan as soon as
possible." But picking tomatoes in Hood River was more difficult than
harvesting rice in Japan, she found, and their repeated moves—work on
five different farms in a seven-year period—was a challenge. The Japanese took steps to make their settings more like home: in Hood River,
Japanese baths were constructed, Japanese foods became available,
and they began to lease farms and then to harvest crops that they them-

selves had raised. And soon they were hiring workers—mostly Japanese, but also Indians and whites—to handle their apples, pears, and vegetables. The first recorded Hood River property deed to a Japanese came in 1908; by 1920 Japanese farmers owned 1,200 acres.

They became part of the Yakima area workforce also. By 1915 some 500 Japanese lived in the Yakima Valley and were beginning to lease land from Indians on the Yakama Reservation. This proved a more rapid route toward acquiring their own farms and orchards because the reservation was exempt from the 1889 Washington law banning alien land ownership—a law that had been originally aimed at British subjects who stayed on after the Crown gave up its claims to the area. When the Federal Council of Churches investigated "the Japanese problem" in 1915, it found that although earlier Japanese had underbid whites for farm work, most now worked for other Japanese farmers. It was the same in Oregon, with Japanese shifting from railroad work to farms: "Though at present some Japanese are employed in the hop fields and a considerable number as pickers and packers of apples in the Hood River orchards, most of them are employed on farms operated by their countrymen."

But anti-Asian feeling had not softened with the decline of Chinese in the census totals. When the Oregon Bureau of Labor Statistics in 1910–12 mailed out two thousand letters to workingmen outside the Portland area, asking their opinions on a variety of subjects, many complained about foreign workers. One replied that improvement would come "by cutting off the influx of Greek, Corean [sic] and Japanese laborers. It is almost impossible for a native born American to procure employment as a common laborer on any corporate undertaking in this section." The Northwest's growing hiring dilemma was on display in that same period when Wenatchee's district fruit inspector cried out for more apple pickers, noting that some of the larger growers were considering hiring Asians "as a last resort." He warned: "It is to be hoped that our growers will never be forced into importing Japanese and Chinese labor." After surveying the situation in Oregon, the state's bureau of labor statistics concluded that "the claim that there is work that can be done by the Orientals that our own people will not do is not borne out by the facts."[19]

America's entry into the European struggle complicated the situation. Hiring of Japanese continued; wartime needs in some areas brought larger numbers into the orchards; anti-Japanese feelings were stirred. Japanese interest in leasing farmlands rather than returning to Japan collided with the sudden eruption of wartime superpatriotism. The national drive for "100 percent Americanism" was virulent across the Northwest and caught aliens in its pincers. As early as August 1915— when U.S. participation in the conflict was still uncertain—Yakima police arrested Otto Seitz (probably a German) for publicly speaking out against U.S. involvement. With U.S. entry in April 1917, freedom of speech was further curtailed and took another hit in the Coeur d'Alenes, when Ernest Schenk was arrested on August 26, 1917, for "defaming flag and country," and a member of the radical Industrial Workers of the World spent three weeks in jail for "talking against the government." While these currents made life more difficult for the region's Japanese, U.S. State Department warnings to the superpatriots gave them some protection: Japan had been supporting Britain in the developing war, and it would hurt American diplomatic moves if Japanese immigrants were attacked here. In places like Hood River, "evidence of Japanese loyalty remained undeniable," one historian has written; Japanese made substantial Liberty Bond purchases and some Japanese boys even went into the American military draft.

But after the nation's entry into the war, even dramatic Japanese shows of loyalty to the United States proved inadequate to hold back the rising tide of racism. Near Yakima, white farmers in the McKinley, Harrah, and Wapato sections met in early 1917 to protest "further encroachment of Orientals." Japanese farmers rushed to counter this, and the leader of those leasing sugar beet lands on the Yakama Reservation attempted to cool tensions by announcing he would work to block further migration of Japanese into the area. In this overheated setting it was a German—an immigrant minister/farmer—who led the Citizen-Farmers' Protective League in clamoring for anti-Japanese legislation. This surge did not cease with the Armistice, for continued agitation led the Washington state legislature in 1921 and 1923 to ban land ownership by aliens who had not indicated intention to become U.S. citizens (foreign-born Asians were already barred from citizenship by federal law), and to prohibit such persons from leasing, renting, or sharecropping.

Similar spirits were in the air in Oregon, where Hood River whites organized the Anti-Asian Association in 1919, claiming threats from

increased landholdings by Japanese, their high birthrate, their low living standards. The campaign did not wind down quickly, even though
the Japanese population in Hood River had fallen to 362 by 1920, a drop
of 100 in a decade. Many Japanese laborers moved away—somewhat
contradicting the warnings and forebodings of the Hood River Anti-
Alien Association that the Japanese were taking over. (A 1919 report
found that Japanese owned only some 2 percent of the land available
for cultivation in the valley.) Many Japanese were harvesting fruit, but
more often on land they were leasing. In 1920 the Oregon governor
commissioned the Davey Report; entitled *The Japanese Situation in Oregon*, it told of fears of a Japanese takeover of Hood River farmland but
also noted that Anti-Alien League members "are not personally abusive
of the Japanese or bitter against them individually." It found that businessmen who feared Japanese land control nevertheless agreed that
"the Japanese are doing good work in clearing logged-off land and bringing it in a high state of cultivation with berries and fruit trees; that they
are good customers of the stores, warehouses, and banks of Hood River
and that they are quiet, well-behaved residents." The legislature finally
passed a law in 1923 against land-owning by persons ineligible for citizenship, although a later study found that such laws "had little effect on
land ownership by Japanese in Oregon."[20]

Another way to lure harvest help in a tight labor market was simply to
raise wages. Such a step had occasionally been forced over the years, as
in 1906 in Washington, when Sumner hops men were pressured to raise
pickers' pay to $1.25 a box, following raises by growers in Orting and
North Yakima. The following year apple pickers in Wenatchee saw their
pay scale increased from $2.25 to $3 a day, and some girls in the packinghouse—paid by output—made up to $2.75 daily. Harvest wages for
1912 in Oregon were 4 percent above 1909, to an average of $2.09 per
day (with board).

    Wartime sent wages even higher. In Oregon, state surveys showed
harvest pay pushed up to $4 a day. One peach packer in the Parker
district near Yakima earned $48.75 over a thirteen-day period in August
1915 "but said he worked long hours." A member of the Washington
Industrial Commission was pleasantly surprised in her summertime visit

to Yakima in 1915 to find some girls made up to $5 a day, packing some 125 boxes of fruit. When growers around Yakima that year learned that Oregon hopyards were paying 40 cents under the half-box system, they decided to go higher—up to $1 for the full box "but will be unusually particular to see that the hops are clean." They also promised to give more personal attention to conditions for arriving hops pickers, even providing room for their baggage.[21]

Such actions by employers helped workers see that they could use labor shortages to better their situation. Bad working conditions and inadequate pay might be changed if employers were having difficulties hiring enough pickers and packers. Earlier, employee anger usually erupted in brief flare-ups centered on a single farm, as when Hayes Perkins saw a disgusted feeder in a Colfax-area wheat field throw a hoe into the threshing machine. But now groups of workers began to respond. Pear packers in Yakima, part of a yearly contingent migrating up from California, went on strike, demanding 5 cents a box rather than the 3.5 to 4.5 cents prevailing that summer of 1915. Employers countered that since fruit had already passed through a sizer, the packers should be able to pack more and therefore earn more. Many packers quit, some heading for Wenatchee; the new federal employment agency, however, "was able to furnish a number" and the season ultimately concluded successfully for the employers.

With American entry into the war in April 1917, pressures on employers worsened. Rumors of huge earnings—some prompted by advertisements in Seattle newspapers—brought a flood of "inexperienced women, girls and high school students" rushing too early into harvest areas and expecting to earn $4 per day, while local growers were generally offering apple pickers $3 per day. One employer took a different approach: he paid the highest wages he had ever paid, which seemed reasonable that year of the war, and "in return he has procured excellent and dependable workers and has found the labor situation far from being the problem this year that he thought it would be."[22]

The coming of the draft, the rise in local military enlistments, and the lure of factories gearing up for war production meant that Yakima lost "a considerable number of the local young men who were expert fruit handlers." The resulting shortage affected fruit packing as well as picking. In October 1917 sixteen packers working in Yakima's Horticultural

Union warehouse struck to increase their pay of 5 cents a box up to 6 cents. The *Herald* noted, "There has been some little trouble on one or two ranches and a shifting of packers in their search for places where machine sizing is in vogue," but it counseled the employer in this case to train women for the work. The following day the newspaper reported that "girls have been put to work and business is almost normal again."

One of the *Herald*'s statements rubbed a striker the wrong way. In a line dripping with false pity, the newspaper had initially claimed that packers "are making only from $5 to $6 per day, sometimes $7 . . ." One of the strikers wrote in to protest that no one at the Horticultural Union earned as much as $5:

> I am one of the packers that asked 6 cents at the [Horticultural] union . . . There wasn't any of them that could pack more fruit than I could, and the best I would do was about $4.50 per day. Some only averaged $3 per day. If I have the fruit I can pack from 120 to 140 boxes per day, but there was only one sorter to each packer, and the fruit being so wormy one sorter could not keep up with the packer, so I would only get from 80 to 90 boxes per day. Then, too, the union wanted the fruit packed as small as 245 to the box. Women at some of the warehouses are making from $5 to $7.50 per day.

Other strikes appeared among fruit pickers and packers as the wartime scramble for workers continued, and the pattern of replacing striking men with women was sometimes repeated.[23]

From threshing crews, to laborers in hopyards and strawberry patches, to pickers twisting and grasping amid the branches of apple, peach, pear, and apricot trees—the orchard that the Northwest had become required legions of workers. The fruit packers protesting at Yakima were part of that vast army, which also included Indians, Chinese and Japanese, children and their parents, youths skipping school, migrants up from California and loggers down from the mountains, and even cowboys fresh off the Palouse. As this last frontier gradually became settled, the call for "Harvesters!" echoed across the Pacific Northwest.

6

HOBOES BATTLING FOREST FIRES

His name was Will Barnes, and the only thing to distinguish him from the thousands of bindlestiffs and other migrant workers riding the rails and picking up sporadic jobs across the Pacific Northwest was that he left a brief written memoir. Other than that, Will Barnes was not really unusual. His 1914 description could have been used over and over as the region became part of the New West:

> When I left home I started drifting. I thumbed a ride out of the logging camp in Washington that was then home, climbed into a boxcar first town on the railroad I came to, walked five or six miles after I climbed off the boxcar, washed dishes for a meal, and slept that night in someone's empty barn somewhere in the middle of Idaho. I didn't exactly know it then, but I had entered the great world of hobo America.[1]

Men like Barnes came and went, appearing just as harvest was getting under way, sometimes vanishing in the night. And this held true in all the jobs that attracted transients, part of the variety of experiences, skills, and traditions that went into "hobo America." It could be both frustrating and cheering to employers—as when members of the Spokane Loggers Club (timber and sawmill executives in the main) were concerned in 1917 over the lack of woodsmen. But a dinner speaker assured them that once harvest work was finished across the area, and crews wrapped up forest fires in the mountains, men would soon be showing up again in the logging camps and sawmills. That was the yearly pattern.

The hobo's varied job experiences made him much sought after, especially during periods of labor shortages, and this was especially true across the Pacific Northwest. There was nothing surprising in a *Spokane Inland Herald* report on July 31, 1910, that while 1,000 loggers had been laid off in Northern Idaho, "a majority of these have taken advantage of the harvest season and are now employed in the Palouse and Big Bend countries." Similarly, the Yakima county agent told wheat ranchers in the summer of 1917 that hopyards would soon be releasing crews, "and a goodly proportion of these will turn to the harvest of the other crops."[2]

That was the pattern: hops pickers did more than pick hops; miners moved on to logging jobs; railroad construction crews deserted to shock wheat; from berry patches families traveled to apple orchards. It was a kind of cycle, different from that of threshing crews on the Great Plains who worked their way north from Oklahoma to Nebraska to the Dakotas, always working with grain, and yet still akin to that migration of work.

But the cycle often created a nightmare for crew foremen, for the numbers of men shifting from job to job could leave some areas hurting for workers. Despite the growth of cities like Portland, Tacoma, Seattle, and Spokane, overall the West was still lightly populated, and so the Northwest faced periodic labor shortages. Not just in picking hops or peaches: as late as 1907 the Milwaukee Road found itself unable to fill crews as it began to dig, blast, and lay down rails through the mountains in the West's final major railroad project. "Laborers have been imported from the East" for the railroad's construction, the *Wenatchee Advance* explained, "the West not being able to supply the requisite number . . ."

With the approach of war in 1917, work in Puget Sound shipyards was stepped up and labor migration sharply increased within the region's mix of fruit, hops, and grain harvesting; logging and sawmills; salmon canneries; mining; and railroad construction. The word went out that there were many, many jobs, and the *Zillah Free Press* noted happily that these reports would attract transient harvest labor, "and they are flocking to the fields" of the Inland Empire.[3]

High turnover went with this pattern. One reason was the West's traditional "three crews" system of one crew arriving, one crew working, and one crew leaving. These "journeymen" workers were always journeying. From the days of the gold rush onward, as mining spread through the region, and as logging started in the Rockies and Cascades, mobility seemed bred into western workmen. Since both the mining and logging industries were plagued by shutdowns from time to time, however, the turnover often could not be blamed on employees. And as with the Washington logger who complained he had been "starved into berries," on many occasions the laid-off workers found their choices limited.[4]

Surviving logging and mining employment records from the Coeur d'Alenes of northern Idaho—the mountain province of the Inland Empire—drive home this reality. The western tramp logger especially was known as a member of a drifting, rootless army. The northern Rockies "short-log country" was cut almost entirely by "tramp lumberjacks," recalled "Michigan Bill" Stowell, interviewed by Samuel Schrager. Stowell looked back on his years in northern Idaho's Clearwater forests and remembered loggers "galloping" from Montana and Idaho to the coast and back, often not staying in one camp over ten days. It did not contribute to a settled family life, and the 1910 Census showed that 90 percent of the workers in West Coast lumbering were single males.[5]

Turnover rates were ferocious in the West's logging camps. One veteran logger said he had worked in thirty-eight different logging camps before he was twenty years old—starting as a "whistle punk," then as a "choker setter" putting chains around the big logs, bucking up timber for a wood-burning steam donkey, working on logging railroad crews, and on to other jobs in the big woods. The average lumber camp worker in California in 1914 stayed in a specific location only from fifteen to thirty days, Carleton Parker found. A 1917–18 survey of thirty-nine Pacific Northwest logging camps put turnover at 660 percent a year; six years later another study reported a turnover rate for the West Coast lumber industry as a whole at 500 percent annually.

Employers could not fasten blame for these high rates entirely on the whims of "journeymen." Sharp swings in the price of timber—as much as 50 percent during a single year—meant that men were often thrown out of work even if they preferred to stick around. Logging camps employing some 3,000 men in Washington's Grays Harbor shut down for thirty-seven days starting in July 1910 because of a surplus of logs. Fire danger could also force a shutdown.[6]

Or perhaps it was conditions on the job that provoked the "disruptively high rates of labor turnover," as one historian termed them. Steam power—with the aptly named "steam donkey"—and logging railroads opened up interior mountain districts after the 1890s, with chains, cables, extensive flumes, and eventually "high-lead" systems that swung logs through the air from spar poles. "Highball logging" was king, especially in long-log operations in the coastal states. Cables could snap, tongs could work loose, flatcars could spill; and as always, falling trees could carom off others. Michigan Bill Stowell admitted that he began to avoid the coast's logging camps because of highballing, preferring to work in the short-log country of the interior, where river drives were still used and the dangers seemed less life-threatening. A company spokesman in 1910 saw the issue differently, complaining of the industry's three-crew tradition: this "constant shifting of men is responsible for innumerable accidents, caused by unfamiliarity with the work . . ."[7]

Dismal, unhealthy camp life pushed the turnover rate. In 1918 a presidential commission probing the region's labor unrest pointed its finger especially at "the unlivable condition" of many logging camps in an industry "still determined by pioneer conditions of life." Father Andrew Prouty, a woods worker in the 1930s who later wrote a University of Washington master's thesis on logging accidents, relayed the reminiscences of an old-time logger from the 1890s when men slept in three-deck bunks stuffed with straw, their gunny sacks similarly filled with straw and their mackinaws laid on top. "No baths," the old-time logger told Father Prouty, unless the employee "availed himself of a river or lake . . ." And "in all except the longest days in summer, men carried lanterns to get back and forth to work." Another old-timer recalled "crowded bunkhouses, . . . dirty straw, vermin, wet clothes steaming and stinking about the central stove, men pigging together without ventilation, privacy, or means of cleanliness . . ." The 1914 California investigations classified toilets in 42 percent of the lumber camps as "filthy." Small wonder that the Spokane Rescue Mission required incoming residents to place all their clothing in an oven set at 300 degrees.

In his famous 1920 article on "The Casual of the Woods," Rexford Tugwell called the lumber camp community "a sad travesty at best," its unlighted and unventilated bunkhouses filled with "sweaty, steamy odors" that would "assassinate the uninitiated." Any veteran of such conditions could be seen plodding along a Northwest road with his bindle, Tugwell explained, his eyes "dull and reddened; his joints are stiff with the rheumatism almost universal in the wettest climate in the world; his teeth

are rotting; he is racked with strange diseases and tortured by unreal-
ized dreams that haunt his soul."[8]

The world of the logging camp thus held many similarities to that of
the harvesters. Loggers could be called hoboes of the forest. And as was
the case with transients across the West, death reports told of logging
accident victims whose "friends are unknown . . ." Their homes and
homelands, like their next of kin and often their very names, remained
mysteries to authorities.[9]

Mining camps showed parallels with the worlds of harvesters and
loggers—constant changes in the makeup of crews, and high turnover
encouraged by sudden shutdowns, as well as primitive and unhealthy
workplaces. If living conditions of miners were sometimes a bit better,
the dangers to life and limb underground were worse, starting the moment the miner stepped into a tunnel or shaft.

Records of the Hercules Mining Company in the Wallace, Idaho,
district of the Coeur d'Alenes show that a new entry in employee accounts often started by noting the man's repeated hirings and quittings:
"Worked off and on for years up to 5/25/1919," or in the case of one
man from Missouri, "This man has worked here several times and every
time he has a different name, either Mile Lee, Lee Miles, or [Miles Lee
McConnell]. Has worked off and on from 5/17/18 to 6/13/19 and generally only works a few days each time." The entry for August Beam, of
Pennsylvania, noted that he was age sixty and crippled in his right thumb:
Hired Feb. 22, 1918; left May 18, 1918. Hired June 8, 1918; left Sept. 7,
1918. Hired Dec. 28, 1919; left Jan. 10, 1920. Hired July 17, 1923; left
Aug. 17, 1923. Typical also was the account for John McCughan, a
Scottish mucker, who was thirty-eight when first employed in 1920 and
hired six times thereafter until leaving for good in July 1923. McCughan
was on the move, but Hercules records show there was nothing unusual
in his employment record. He was a typical hard-rock miner. Also typical was McCughan's status as an immigrant: one section of the Hercules personnel book records miners from Austria, Indiana, Washington,
Mexico, Pennsylvania, Italy, Jugo-Slavia, Michigan, Bohemia, Montana,
and Nebraska. Only two were married.[10]

Trying to decipher the identity of Miles Lee or Lee Miles or Miles

Lee McConnell, noted above, the Hercules personnel agent faced a situation common to those hiring migratory labor. Such workers went by nicknames primarily, which could perplex officials as well as company office workers. After an old man's body was found in his tent alongside the Spokane River, the Spokane coroner rounded up people who had seen him in the weeks before the discovery. Although many people knew him, no one could tell his name. One person who had sometimes talked with him called him only "an old miner, used to roughing it in life, and inclined to keep his affairs to himself."[11]

This was the background of many Pacific Northwest workers, whether called tramp miners, tramp loggers, hoboes, harvest gypsies, or bindlestiffs. Their lives were spent moving to different jobs, with different types of living and working conditions. They were bombarded by different noises, the varied sounds that went with migratory labor—creaking timbers and falling slate underground and the crunch of chokers being slipped around logs; and the rip of a falling hopyards trellis or the jiggle of a shaky ladder poking up an apple tree.

The labor shortages that frequently plagued employers in wheat, fruit, logging, and mining worried the new U.S. Forest Service. As its western domain expanded vastly under President Theodore Roosevelt and his successors, the national forests' need for workers could increase sharply in fire season: danger levels rose according to the previous winter's snowpack as well as spring and summer rains. When the call went out for men to fight fires, attention was directed first at nearby logging and mining camps and railroad construction crews, but as blazes spread—especially in the massive fires of 1910 and 1919—desperate recruiters also turned to migratory workers throughout the Northwest. In this way the giant firefighting efforts brought together men whose backgrounds and skills reflected labor across the region—blasting out rock but also threshing wheat, picking apples, or dropping giant Douglas fir trees.

This was the case in 1910 when summer winds came blistering off the Washington Palouse during a severe drought. On August 20 they whipped thousands of little fires in northern Idaho and western Montana into a holocaust known as the "big blowup." Eventually the areas burned in national forests that summer of 1910 equaled the size of New Jersey.

The region's scattered inhabitants had witnessed fires before but never like this. One homesteader escaping with his wife from Big Creek in the Coeur d'Alenes told a reporter that the conflagration threw giant trees into the air "like a feather," while it "traveled as fast as any train that he ever saw and that as far as noise went, he believed that if all the battleships in the world were gathered together in the path of it and fired their guns at one time, the report would not have been heard above the terrible roar of the fires." To fight such fires, the homesteader concluded, was "an absolute impossibility."[12]

Challenging impossibility was the job of the new U.S. Forest Service, and from the Montana Flathead District came a report repeated across the region: "Every man possible is being sought here today for duty on the fire line." Railroad, logging, and mining companies and even the military dispatched crews, and the mayor of Wallace threatened imprisonment for any man refusing to help protect the town.

Hoboes were already present within the logging, mining, and railroad crews thrown into action, but increasingly the Forest Service began specifically hunting men along the skid-row "jungles" of railroad towns. As Lolo Forest supervisor Elers Koch later reported, "Men were shipped from Missoula, Spokane, and Butte, until the supply of floating labor was exhausted." Most of the firefighters were transients, he said, "unknown even to each other . . ." The Spokane Rescue Mission provided 125 men.[13]

A newly arrived crew that had mistakenly been sent in with only two bedrolls spent their first night sitting around a big campfire "talking mostly about the relative merits of the different jails they had been in." The time card for a crew working out of Avery, Idaho—center of the 1910 blowup—recorded a dozen Japanese employees recruited from a Milwaukee Road construction gang, each of whom worked twelve hours a day, every day, without exception. Others on the fireline, non-Japanese, however, showed a great variety in their hours worked—usually from ten to fourteen hours a day, with several of their names marked simply "quit" or "fired." Some left before they had any hours recorded, others quit after one day, and one left after putting in four consecutive sixteen-hour days on the fire line. Rain and snow suddenly blessed the region on August 23, the beginning of the end for the big blowup of 1910.[14]

One early count put the death toll in 1910 at seventy-eight, although historian Wade Bilbrey has determined that the total reached ninety-one, including several residents of the area. Predictably, given the floating status of many and the transients' penchant for avoiding identity, large numbers of the victims left no record of family or home; some names on crew lists were found to be fictitious. Elers Koch noted that few "had a cent in their pockets when they came on a fire, nor did most of them have any permanent address to which a check could be sent." Some of those who had put in long days on the fire lines had trouble getting paid.

Only twenty-nine of the bodies discovered after the fire had enough identification for their remains and wages to be delivered promptly to next of kin. Tracing went on for years, across America and Europe. The searchers' dedication, historian Stephen Pyne suggests, came from their conclusion that in the end these "polygot mobs, mocked and maligned, bore the brunt of the fires."[15]

Nine years later the massive forest fires that erupted across the region paralleled the 1910 blowup in most ways, including the tapping of floating labor to fight them. But 1919 saw a new political environment: the Industrial Workers of the World was at full strength, especially in the woods, and after the indignities forced upon them by superpatriots during the war, they were in no mood to be challenged. One ranger recalled his confrontation with a crew that demanded "fourteen hours' pay for twelve hours' work," which he finally agreed to, to avoid their wholesale abandonment of the fire line.

The role of the IWW—known as the "Wobblies"—in the 1919 forest fires in the Northern Rockies deserves attention. Only two years earlier in the midst of the war, the IWW led a bitter two-month strike by some 50,000 Pacific Northwest timber workers, followed by an effective work slowdown that ultimately won the eight-hour day and other improvements. While the IWW drew the wrath of timber operators, a district forester pointed out to the President's Commission investigating the wartime labor upheavals that the real target of the strikes had been "conditions which a great many people admit were bad and must be remedied." In these struggles the IWW picked up many enemies; the organization was—as a later Forest Service report noted—"gaining a bad name." This was evident when the sheriff of Wallace, Idaho, arrested several dozen men in 1917 and 1918 under the simple charge of "I.W.W."[16]

Through it all the IWW became champion of the western hobo, and the crews recruited to fight forest fires were drawn heavily from men who belonged to, or were sympathetic toward, the IWW. One ranger discussing the 1919 fire crews wrote that "membership in the I.W.W. is almost universal." He complained that Wobblies on the fire lines were "unreasonable, they have no patriotic motives and look at the proposition from a strictly commercial standpoint." Another ranger encountered a fire crew led by an able IWW foreman who required every firefighter to carry the organization's red card. "He apparently handles men well," the ranger admitted, although this IWW foreman tended to overpay his crew—writing down twenty-four hours' work a day in the time book for some men, several days in succession. Thereafter the Forest Service kept a sharper watch out for "agitators."[17]

But the IWW also had defenders. An assistant district forester told the Mediation Commission that while some men were discharged for inefficiency, "we had not a single case of sympathetic strike on the part of avowed I.W.W. in such cases . . ." Another Montana forester told the commission, "When we needed men [for fire fighting] we often sent our agent directly to the I.W.W. headquarters . . ." A Forest Service engineer reported that his entire crew consisted of IWW members, most of them "really good workers." His best foreman was a Wobbly.

In fighting the 1910 and 1919 fires, the Forest Service roundup brought in many men who should have been passed over by the hiring boss. There were experienced harvesters in the mix but also unworthy derelicts. As reported by the Forest Service after the 1919 blazes, while many transients performed creditably on the fire line, recruiting drives through skid rows in Spokane and other cities often brought men of questionable use. A Forest Service officer lamented that "too little attention" had been given to hiring, "and as a result a number of cripples were sent" to the fire line, as well as many others "who were poorly shod and not used to walking or working . . ." Another claimed that among Nezperce National Forest crews was a dope fiend, a man "with a bad venereal disease," and another with "a bad rupture." After such experiences, a Forest Service officer working on the Flathead Reservation fires stated bluntly: "hoboes, or tramps, should not be engaged for this class of work . . ."

In contrast, lumberjacks and miners working on the fire line won praise from another Forest Service observer, who said such "hardened to work" veterans were preferred by foremen to "the city riff-raff." What he was unaware of, apparently, was that many of the loggers and miners would fit within the definition of hoboes, and many had spent some time in Northwest communities living among the "city riff-raff."[18]

USFS recruiters were active in Spokane because Spokane, more than any other urban center away from the coast, attracted all varieties of wandering men, job seekers, hoboes, tramps, bums, summertime adventurers, men on the run, and unemployed. It was a magnet. They came through the city because it was a major railroad point and the hub from which spokes ran out to wheat harvesting in the Palouse, apple picking in Wenatchee, hops picking and berry picking there and in Yakima, logging in the Coeur d'Alenes, mining in the Bitterroots, and railroad construction and road building throughout the vast region from Montana to the Pacific. It was—as its promoters proclaimed—the key to the Inland Empire. A *Spokane Press* story on September 17, 1910, reflected these roles: "With the wheat harvest completed and fall coming on, the annual crop of vagrants has been keeping the Union Rescue Mission officials on the jump. Jobs are exceedingly scarce and about 75 percent of the applicants are young men under 25 years of age, which is an almost unprecedented condition."

Spokane's attractions for migratory labor can be seen in many different types of local records during that era. The city's large YMCA ran a welfare department, which in November 1908 reported that more than 2,500 men had contacted it seeking employment, "most of them strangers in Spokane." Only some 850 had found work at that point, the department said. A month later it analyzed men who had turned to the YMCA for help and were given membership: 500 were single and only 90 were married; 117 stated "they had been in Spokane less than a year although probably many more than that could have said the same thing . . ." The age breakdown showed that more than half (340) were in the 21-to-30 age bracket; 119 were ages 17 to 20; and 130 were over 31 years old. Regarding nationality/ethnicity, there were 384 Americans, 41 English, 41 Germans, 39 Scandinavians, 22 Canadians, 18 Scots, 17 Irish, and many unclassified.[19]

Spokane's police records illustrate the occupational diversity. While some men arrested for vagrancy were simply called "transient," more often they were listed as "laborer," "miner," "woodsman," "salesman," "brakeman," "shipwright," "baker." Earlier the December 1898 record of vagrants assigned to the city prison listed fourteen as laborers, three as miners, three as painters, two as plumbers, two as "tramp," two as "thief," and others as salesman, machinist, cigarmaker, waiter, clerk, musician, and "confidence man." Often bits of other information are included, as in the county jail register for 1919: those arrested included a thirty-eight-year-old laborer from Canton, Ohio; a twenty-three-year-old peddler from New Brighton, Connecticut; a Norwegian gardener; and an eighteen-year-old "jack of all trades." Almost all vagrants were discharged in one or two days regardless of their sentence. "Released by chief to leave city in fifteen minutes" was recorded for thirty-one-year-old Irish laborer James Ryan on February 1, 1900, and other "vags" concluded their Spokane visits in similar fashion—one- or two-hour limits for their continued residence in the city.

Jail registers also provide further testimony to the perils of riding the rails and other dangers of hobo life: "both feet cut off at instep"; "right leg off above knee"; "left arm gone at shoulder"; "second finger on left hand gone"; "crippled in right leg"; "scar on nose, 3d finger on left hand gone." Picking hops or mucking ore, climbing shaky orchard ladders or dangling from a spar pole at a logging site—the brief entries on the vagrancy arrests as well as the coroner's reports demonstrated the inherent dangers faced by men of this "casual" labor class.[20]

The financial condition of the men arriving in Spokane was often desperate. In many winters police allowed homeless men to sleep in city hall corridors—more than five hundred during December 1897. A decade later some broke into the police station bullpen one night for a place to sleep. The Spokane mayor in 1910 threatened legal action against railroads for the lengthy delays in paying off their construction crews. "Hardly a day passes," the mayor's secretary noted, "but that from one to ten laborers call upon the Mayor and protest that they cannot draw the money due for labor on the railroads." A newspaper reported that one man who was due $22 was told to wait until the railway check arrived, forcing him to sleep in a back lot. Some were forced to wait up to ten days, the secretary said—"In the meantime they cannot ship out on other jobs and all they have earned is consumed for necessities before they receive it." A Keokuk, Iowa, man left in this situation told police in January 1911 that in the previous eighty-four hours he had eaten only an apple.[21]

Firefighters frequently faced similar problems as they came down from the mountains. Two men who had been recruited in Butte to fight fires pleaded with Spokane officials at the end of August 1910: unpaid for their Forest Service labors, they were penniless with "no fees to give an employment agency for a job." A Coeur d'Alenes crew of some one hundred men made it out of the fire lines down to Avery, but they were refused wages or time checks and were forced by soldiers to board a train. Down the line at nearby Rosalia they were welcomed by a grateful citizenry and given food; then they seized a train and rode it to Spokane. But there, the *Press* reported, "every man who came into Spokane this morning" was again refused firefighting pay.[22]

Feeling besieged at times by job seekers, Spokane sought to ferret out those who were after handouts rather than employment. In late 1907, as winter swelled the jobless rolls, the chief of police said that "suspicious" persons arrested would be quizzed: "The workingmen who are out of work will be allowed to remain, but the professional hobo and tramp will have to leave without going through the formality of spending a night in the city jail with breakfast thrown in." The YMCA and the Union Rescue Mission helped the unemployed look for work while feeding and lodging them. (Among new arrivals, a bath and "clean clothing" were required.) In the winter of 1908–9 one lodging house owner offered a night's accommodation to every idle man who would cut one-eighth cord of wood.

The city, also, sometimes attempted to make the destitute work for their keep—including pulling weeds—and in late 1911, when the city council voted authorization for six charity commissioners to handle relief works, it prohibited "unworthy begging" on the city streets. A controversy erupted in early 1915 when the Christian Home for Men—which had served 6,215 meals in December, asking an hour's work for overnight's lodging—refused a city council donation because it felt acceptance of public funds would have forced it to "take in habitual hobos." Its aim was to help men rehabilitate themselves, "not to encourage bums." The YMCA sounded a similar note from time to time, warning that indiscriminate feeding of the homeless would hurt "the worthy unemployed stranger who deserves help" while providing no real benefit "to the hobos, bums and parasites who will flock in from all sides."[23]

But still plenty of sympathy was shown sufferers of all types. Funds were collected in wintertime for the "homeless and destitute," and enough was collected in January 1909 to provide ten-cent meals for some 700 men, women, and children. Later that month the Trinity Episcopal Church girls' club gave a benefit dance to raise funds for a thousand meals for homeless men. Similar activities took place each winter in Spokane.

In contrast to some places of refuge, the Tabernacle accepted everyone; in the winter of 1908–9 it was housing up to 600 men nightly. Run by Billy Sunday, America's most famous evangelist, weekly services packed in several thousand. The YMCA urged its members, "Hear him"; the former professional baseball star "preaches much as he played baseball—with all his might and much after the same style." When a controversy arose over the discovery of vermin crawling among the men who slept and ate in the Tabernacle, Sunday and other local ministers argued that the building was fumigated daily, while attempting to convince the city to house the men in empty courtrooms. It was to no avail. Sunday then decided, "It is better for 100 people to get lousy than that one man should freeze or go to hell."[24]

Spokane's wintertime problems derived from its location at the center of the Inland Empire. The region's natural wealth could be converted into forms of wealth comprehended by the financial system only if it was harvested, logged, or mined. The city was at the juncture of the comings and goings of the people—fruit tramps, loggers, miners—who performed these tasks.

And if the entire West was being transformed by the railroad, in Spokane and the Pacific Northwest the changes were especially dramatic because of competing demands for floating labor: quite different employers often recruited among the same people. Their sudden enlistment to battle forest fires brought large numbers of them together—railroad construction crews alongside loggers, miners with wheat harvesters, apple glommers on the fire line with hops pickers. All intermixed, allied in the same endeavor, their varied employment backgrounds on display, their rootless nature often revealed. Many of these characteristics were not widely known, but firefighting revealed important facts about the bindlestiff and his place in the new economy of the Northwest.

7

KING COTTON MOVES WEST

In many areas of Texas and Oklahoma, in town after town, summer's end meant the appearance of the first bale of cotton. Wagons with their white loads jostled along country roads, headed for the gin; the cotton harvest was under way. A young witness to this grand parade in Coryell County recalled it as a glorious day for a Texas country boy, starting out from home atop the loaded wagon where "you were up high and had 1,400 to 1,500 pounds of cotton for a cushion." Then, arriving at the gin, the boy watched as the suction pipe pulled the cotton into the gin with its big steam press, soon disgorging a 500-pound tightly packed bale down into the wagon. "The cotton gin was awesome and wonderful," he remembered.

It was also sheer bedlam. On such a day in Fort Worth in October 1877, the mule-drawn vehicles "were parked so close together as to resemble a street baracade [*sic*] in times of civil war." To the north in the Chickasaw Nation in Indian Territory, a young man in Ardmore "climbed onto a wagon at the depot and walked three blocks on wagons loaded with cotton, without once getting down on the ground."[1] A joyous bedlam, for the appearance of the first bale merited celebration, as it inaugurated "the wonderful months of cash-in-hand, payment of debts, fairs, circuses, and Christmas buying." "First bale" celebrations—still being held—marked the start of a season rooted both in the local economy and in southern culture.[2]

But southerners were not the first to grow cotton in the land that eventually became Texas. Wild cotton was seen by Cabeza de Vaca, shipwrecked in 1528, and other Spanish explorers reported Indians growing and using forms of the cotton plant, a practice that incoming missionaries encouraged. When Moses Austin approached Spanish authorities in 1820, he proposed a colonization scheme in Texas under which colonists would raise both sugar cane and cotton; and when the newly formed Mexican government allowed settlement by Americans to begin in 1822, Texas had its first postnative, post-Spanish cotton crop. And the South's labor force—slaves from Africa and their descendants—began picking Texas cotton at the start.[3]

It was a natural decision because it was southerners who made East Texas a cotton land. For years East Texas remained firmly tied to the Old South and its Cotton Kingdom, and the march of cotton across Texas has been called "the last big expansion of Southern cotton." Already by 1879 some 2.1 million acres of cotton were grown in Texas, and a decade later its dominance was even more firmly established when Texas displaced Georgia as the nation's leader in cotton production. By the time of the 1920 census, when 12.3 million acres of cotton were harvested, producing 4,345,000 bales, Texas was far beyond challenge.

The southern influence would remain. In 1880, counting both whites and blacks, there were 870,645 Texas-born residents of Texas—but fully 443,985 others born in the states of the Old South.[4]

But if these natives of southern states provided links to the bygone Confederacy, Texas and its neighbor Oklahoma—by 1907, fifth in the nation in cotton production—faced west as well, the West of cattle roundups, of cowboys driving herds to railheads, of gunfights in saloons, of deserts and prairie dogs. Texas, in reality, was pulled in two directions, and cotton was involved in both. The land lay flat in the western counties, encouraging the use of new machinery and eventually moving beyond total dependence on the mule for pulling a plow. Small farms as well as large spreads became common, tenants generally occupying the former, while the latter often employed workers by the hundreds. It was a sort of hybrid economy.

But if cotton symbolized East Texas, for years cattle symbolized West Texas. Texas was Janus-faced, at once glancing back nostalgically at the Cotton South and its Confederate past, but looking confidently toward the West with men on horseback and settlers in covered wagons rolling toward the Pacific.[5]

Links to the Old South from the Indian Territory and Oklahoma were of a different sort. From the 1820s on, Indian tribes from the southeastern states were forcibly moved west—first the so-called "Five Civilized Tribes" (Cherokee, Choctaw, Creek, Chickasaw, and Seminole) and later others. These tribes already were involved in cotton culture, and after removal they resumed growing cotton on their small farms, usually 10 to 20 acres. The Choctaws planted their first cotton crop in what would eventually become Oklahoma in 1825, and eleven years later 500 bales were shipped down the Red River to market. Bigger tracts had large numbers of slaves, and at the start of the Civil War one Cherokee landlord was using some 300 slaves on his 500 acres of cotton. Following that conflict the Cherokee, Choctaw, and Chickasaw growers in the now-slaveless Indian Territory turned to tenant farmers to bring in the crop, counting 12,000 cotton tenants by 1882.

With tracts as large as 8,000 acres appearing in the Indian Territory, the labor question was becoming ever more important, and finally whites who were not members of a tribe were allowed to enter. It was illegal for them to lease land, but a solution was found that would appear elsewhere in the West: when labor was needed, laws could be bent. White lessees were paid what was called a "salary" but was in reality a share of production, or sharecropping under another name. By 1899 more than half of all farms in Indian Territory were growing cotton, and in 1906, the year before Oklahoma statehood, the Five Civilized Tribes, led by the Choctaws and Chickasaws, produced 410,520 bales of cotton.

In the earlier South the harvest labor question had had a simple solution: slaves. But now slavery was gone, and labor worries were recurring. Tradition could still provide a solution, such as calling upon neighbors for help at harvest time, but this tradition was strained as cotton was grown successively in larger and larger fields, into the Texas High Plains and in western Oklahoma, soon even farther westward, when irrigation created new cotton opportunities in New Mexico, Arizona, and California.[6]

The railroad, yet again, was the key to expansion. Even before the dislocations of the Civil War, cotton had stimulated the creation of East

Texas's first railroad, the Buffalo Bayou, Brazos, & Colorado, which by 1853 had twenty miles operating from Harrisburg to Stafford's Point, then on to Alleyton by the opening of the war. Other towns were also looking hungrily for some alternative to moving out cotton on shallow rivers and often-impassable roads, and by 1861 there were 492 miles of track in disjointed railway projects, some dependent upon the growing East Texas lumber industry. As was occurring elsewhere across the West, voters eagerly backed these new ventures: Galveston was typical, balloting overwhelmingly—741 to 11—to support a $100,000 bond issue to launch the Galveston, Houston & Henderson (the GH&H). After its completion Galveston's cotton exports predictably increased sharply, but then came war, and further railroad construction was delayed until the 1870s.

Thereafter in Texas railroad mileage and the number of railroad companies grew, often dependent on the rise or fall in the price of cotton. In 1872 the Houston & Texas Central tapped Dallas, and by the end of the decade the Texas & Pacific had reached Fort Worth; the Missouri, Kansas & Texas (MKT, or "Katy") had entered Texas from the north at Denison, and the Corpus Christi–Laredo connection was near its completion, which occurred in 1881; in that year also the Cotton Belt Railway steamed into Waco. Then came success in the race to run west–east lines across the state, with the Texas & Pacific in 1881 and the Southern Pacific's connections two years later. This meant links with the West Coast, or alternatively, one could board the Katy in Fort Worth or Waco and travel to St. Louis, and from there reach Chicago and go on to the East Coast.

Now Texans and their cotton bales had transcontinental connections at last. Even the Panhandle would eventually link up with faraway Galveston over the Atchison, Topeka & Santa Fe. Texas led the United States in rails laid down during 1877, and the following year its construction even exceeded that of the rest of the nation combined. By 1890 Texas's rail mileage ranked first in the nation and production of easily exportable cotton was booming.[7]

Shipping more cotton bales to mills in Lowell, Massachusetts, and Manchester, England, meant more cotton to be planted, more cotton to be picked. As a result, the labor needs of East Texas and the Indian Territory—and soon of areas to the west—increased rapidly, and labor shortages became frequent, serious ones, in a pattern that would remain until a workable cotton-picking machine was developed in the World War II era.

Whether on a giant operation like the Taft Ranch (which shifted from cattle to cotton in the late 1880s) or on the smallest independent farm, cotton raising required many steps before harvesting. First, stalks had to be cleared from the previous year's crop. Stalks could be quite sturdy at times, some of them inches thick. They had to be pulled, knocked down, and removed, often by hand, frequently using dragging devices pulled by mules.

Early spring plowing was done to prepare wide beds or ridges, so that seed would be more open to sun and therefore would grow more rapidly. To create a bed, a mule pulled a bull-tongue plow that first "busted out" the area between ridges; then a turning plow went on repeated swings through the field to turn soil to build up a ridge; six inches was a common height. Rows could be from three to five feet wide, depending on expectations of plant size. (The ideal was to have cotton branches from adjacent rows touching, shading the ground.) Then another turn by the plow left a furrow for seeds along the middle of the bed. Sometimes "walking planters" were used to get seed into the ground, but by the 1880s mule-drawn mechanical planters were popular in some areas. Later tractors would do the pulling.

In southern Texas cotton planting began around mid-March, but in North Texas and Oklahoma it could run well into May. The aim was to miss the last frost and any late cold spell but to ensure that the plants were up well before any summer droughts, which along with cotton worms and boll weevils constituted the major disaster awaiting growers.

Usually the plants appeared within a week, and then hoeing began, followed with "chopping" as plants and weeds grew taller. Chopping was a strenuous operation that required care and exactness. It required hoeing not only to "chop out" the weeds but also to thin the cotton plants so each row had clumps of two to four plants in a hill, each hill twelve to eighteen inches from its neighbor, each row three or four feet from the next one. They were "chopping the cotton to a stand," and as the season progressed it had to be done over and again, sometimes five or six times. A scholar of Texas cotton has written that "no work in the cotton field was harder."[8]

Cotton plants bloomed in some sixty days, evident by early May in South Texas, then bounding to late June farther north. White at first opening, the blossom closed in midafternoon and then would reappear darker the next morning before eventually falling off, pushed out by the developing boll.

The process of blossom and boll formation went through stages. Blossoms would continue to emerge in different parts of the same plant through the summer, which meant that repeated pickings were required as the bolls progressively grew to maturity. Sometimes plants were pruned to keep their height down after a rainy spell brought sharp growing spurts. Three to four feet was the usual height a cotton plant reached as bolls began opening to reveal the white fluff within, although both smaller and larger plants were common in different areas, depending on fertility and moisture. Cotton picking was under way by July in the southern counties of Texas, stretching into October and occasionally later in the north; pickings in December were reported in both northern Texas and Oklahoma.[9]

Despite the multitude of steps in transforming cotton from a seed to a 500-pound bale, picking came to symbolize the world of cotton. When a 1924 federal study of child labor blandly stated, "So simple is the task of cotton picking . . . ," it betrayed the author's lack of hands-on experience with the subject. Comments by veteran cotton pickers note the difficulties, not the ease. When J. W. Coltharp was picking cotton on his parents' farm in Coryell County before the First World War, he experienced not only the drudgery but also the pains of picking early in the morning when the dew "softened your fingers so the sharp point on the cotton burrs pricked your fingers until they might bleed, but you kept on picking . . ." Then when the sun came up "the burr points would get sharper, but you kept on picking." Coltharp's pain went beyond his fingers:

> In Central Texas, even in good cotton years, the cotton plant was typically 14 to 20 inches high, which meant you stooped over as you picked until your back ached unmercifully, then you would

straighten up briefly and very briefly, because you didn't have much time to spare if you were going to pick 250 to 450 pounds per day . . . And you are pulling an 8-foot long cotton sack whose weight as you stuff it with cotton will finally increase to 50, 75, or 80 pounds.

With the strap over a shoulder the picker walked down the rows, dragging a sack that stretched up to twelve feet long, picking the cotton and taking care not to get any pieces of the boll casings that would lower the grade. Constant bending left sore backs; in fields of shorter plants some pickers had to crawl down the long rows on their knees.

And finally the sack would hold no more, despite being punched down to lessen the time lost in repeated trips to the wagon. The picker would drag the sack to be weighed, then would pour the contents into the wagon and return to his row. Coltharp called this break from picking "a 'rest' only in the sense it is a change from the damnable stooping and picking or crawling and picking, but a welcome respite it is."[10]

Totals for a day's picking varied widely. Some accounts agree with Coltharp's 250 pounds as an adult average, but much higher totals are on record: the *Garland News* announced in September 1891 that Jesse Nelson had picked 536 pounds of cotton and Robert Cherry 512—"about the best cotton picking we have heard of . . ." Some 1,500 pounds were needed to gin a 500-pound bale, and a Nueces County report indicated that six or seven workers were needed to pick one bale of cotton in a day. In 1890 the statewide average in Texas was 0.374 bales to the acre.

After the early 1890s cottonseed became valuable; at one time discarded or used as fertilizer, it began to provide additional income as it was used to make cooking oil and cottonseed oil cakes for animal feed. Navasota's cottonseed oil factory shipped 1,700 barrels of the oil and nearly two million of the cakes to Liverpool in 1877, bringing in $623,000. By 1914 the seed and its by-products brought more profits to Texas than lumber from East Texas forests.[11]

The cry for pickers was perennial across the Cotton Belt. With the progression of picking seasons from south to north, a logical route seemed clear for seasonal migrations of pickers, but instead the fears in one section were often passed on like a spreading sickness to others, magnifying the dangers ahead. An Abilene newspaper reported ominously in 1905, "The cry has begun to go up in South Texas for cotton pickers and that reminds us that this is a problem confronting West Texas farmers that will have to be solved and that right soon. This is a knotty problem most every year and will be a more weighty one this Fall than ever. What about it?"

White hoboes appear only occasionally in the records of Texas and Oklahoma cotton harvests, as in a *Houston Post* reference to "tramp cotton pickers" working nearby. Records of the Taft Ranch show hiring of men "just drifting in," but increasingly most were recruited from border areas. Testimony by a Dallas farmer-lawyer pointed to a possible reason for the lack of white hoboes working in Texas cotton. Joe Worsham told a Congressional committee in 1920 that "a white man does not want to enter into competition with the negro, or anybody else, in the picking of cotton."[12] Added to this was the continued dim view of transient men. Over in Galveston the mayor called for return of the whipping post to handle tramps, vagrants, and similar types. Similarly, in northern Oklahoma the Carmen Commercial Club decided in 1917 "that the citizens of the town would unite on making things difficult for the professional hobo." While planning to help job seekers find work, the group "adopted the policy of discouraging citizens from feeding the hoboes who throng this section of the country during the harvest period."[13]

Absent the armies of job-seeking hoboes that followed wheat harvests farther north, cotton growers often had to scramble to find pickers. As with western orchards and fields, the threat of unharvested crops loomed perennially over the agricultural landscapes of Texas and Oklahoma. With cotton that threat became ever more ominous as plantings spread westward into former cattle ranges and cotton acreages grew sharply—a larger disaster waiting to happen every year. The *Houston Telegram* was neither original nor unique—it was certainly not breaking any new ground—when it warned in August 1880: "Very prominent farmers have said that if the yield of the crops for 1880 turns out as it now promises, there will be large amounts of nearly every product lost just for the want of labor."[14]

A common solution, at least until the 1890s, drew on the two states' southern roots: blacks. Descendants of slaves continued working in the cotton fields after the Civil War's end, and many remained for decades: by century's end in East Texas it was still true that "a substantial portion" of the cotton was picked and chopped "by African-American labor from nearby towns or distant regions." Any threat—any hint—of changing this pattern provoked high anxiety among cotton growers. A frightening report raced across Texas in late 1879, when blacks began joining the "exoduster" movement to Kansas, a state revered by African-Americans ever since abolitionists in the 1850s had sought to make it an antislavery bulwark. But the campaign failed to draw large numbers, and many returned after two rail lines reduced fares for persons traveling back to Texas. A newspaper explained, "This is done to enable planters to procure cotton pickers."[15]

Those anxieties in 1879–80 were a foretaste of the dangers that growers faced eleven years later in a threatened strike by the Colored Farmers' Alliance and Cotton Pickers' League. In 1891 blacks were still the dominant force in East Texas picking, as farmers would often need extra help beyond what their own families could supply. But family farms, such as the small holdings of 35 to 40 acres that dotted that section, now constituted only the easternmost segment of an enlarged Texas cotton world that included extensive operations in the West with greater labor needs.

In fall 1891 the price of cotton dipped to 8 cents a pound, part of the decade's nationwide decline of farm prices that eventually saw cotton bottom out in 1898 at 6 cents. It was Texas's and Oklahoma's share of the farm depression that swept across vast areas of the Great Plains, Midwest, and South, producing one of the major political upheavals in American political and economic history, eventually spawning the Populist movement.[16]

In Texas, Oklahoma, and nearby southern states the scene was set for a struggle between growers and pickers as the employers sought to hold down wages, the only cost they could control. The exact spark that set off the southern cotton pickers' strike in 1891 is uncertain.[17] Pickers' earnings ranged up to 65 cents per hundred pounds, but apparently 50 cents or even less was more common. There is evidence from late summer 1891 that cotton plantation owners around Memphis, Tennessee, and in adjacent areas across the Mississippi River in Arkansas sought to protect themselves amid the hard times by holding pickers' wages at no higher than 50 cents per hundred pounds, then requested— and won—police support to drive unemployed African-Americans into the cotton fields.

Many blacks tried to fight back, and across the South large numbers— including farm owners as well as tenant sharecroppers and laborers— sought protection through the Colored Farmers' Alliance. This alliance, one of many organized farm protests of the 1880s and early 1890s, was linked on major reform issues to the much larger white organization, the Southern Farmers' Alliance, which eventually merged with its northern partner to form the Farmers' Alliance.

The leader of the Colored Farmers' Alliance was a white Texan, R. M. Humphrey, who had been asked to head the new organization in 1886 by a group of black farmers living near his Houston County home. Humphrey, a former Baptist minister, claimed widespread support for the spin-off "Cotton Pickers' League" when he spoke with a *Houston Post* reporter the day after the 1891 strike call was first reported:[18]

"What is the League's membership?"

"There were over 700,000 names enrolled Saturday night, but I suppose by this time there are fully 800,000. It is growing very rapidly especially in Texas . . ."

"Are only colored cotton pickers permitted to join?"

"There are a great many whites as well as blacks in it, but the reports which are sent to me do not say which of the members are white or colored, and I cannot tell the relative strength of either race. I received a report from Mississippi yesterday with a list of 25,000 names, but I could not tell whether any of the members are white or not. There is nothing in the league to prohibit anyone, who is a cotton picker, from becoming a member." . . .

"What are the demands of the cotton pickers?"

"We demand $1 a hundred and board."

"When will you make your demands known?"

"On the 12th of this month."

"How will it be done?"

"Every member of the league will quit work on that date and remain out of the fields until their demands are granted by the planters."

Newspapers went on the attack immediately, against Humphrey, the league, and the idea that a strike could happen or that it would even help the pickers. Generally the main thrust of the criticism centered on two arguments: growers could not survive paying such wages when cotton prices were so low, and strikers would starve while waiting for their walkout to end. The *Bellville Times* editorialized that if the strikers met their goal, to produce the 1,500 pounds needed for a bale, the costs would run $15 for pickers, $3.50 for ginning and bagging, and $3.75 to board the pickers working the three acres that would produce a bale. As a result, the farmer's income of $35 for the bale would leave him only with $12.50—to pay for seed, planting, cultivating, rent, and implement costs. The *Times* suggested: "Why don't the cotton pickers ask the farmer for deed to his cotton farm . . . ?"[19]

Newspaper accounts made clear that many blacks were themselves farmers and would also face difficult times paying pickers above current rates. A reporter in Brenham, in Washington County, Texas, interviewed several cotton pickers and said, "They are all unanimous in the opinion that the scheme could not have been carried out here for the reason that all the members of the colored alliance in this county are farmers and it would be against their interest to encourage a raise in the price of picking, as they would have to pay it." Colored Farmers' Alliance leaders elsewhere in the South questioned the wisdom of the strike call, and Texas newspapers gave their comments prominence. Even the organization's former general organizer in Texas termed the strike call "the most serious trouble which has threatened the colored people since their emancipation."

The *Post* reported little evidence of black support for the strike, choosing instead to publicize items predicting and then proving its failure. However, some news items contained references to isolated cases of backing for the call to quit picking. At Moulton, in Lavaca County, "thirty-three have struck," a *Post* correspondent reported. At Palestine, in Anderson County, "two worthless white colored men" promoted the strike "without success," and one farmer there told of "an attempt" at striking. "He discharged them and matters immediately settled." One of the five Colored Farmers' Alliance lodges in Wharton County supported the strike, but the *Post* added, "The dissension comes from tramp cotton pickers. Leading colored men in the county are against the strike to a man."[20]

Bellicose proclamations of the strike's collapse could not completely obscure the growers' fears, however. If determination can be seen on both sides, anxiety can also, as evident in the strike's final, violent episodes in Lee County, Arkansas, across the river from Memphis.

A group of cotton strikers there were fired after demanding 75 cents per hundred pounds, but they refused to abandon the campaign and began enlisting others. As historian William Holmes found, when pickers on one plantation refused to give support, a brawl erupted and two of them were killed. A posse—with some black members—immediately took up the chase. With tensions rising, two strikers killed a plantation manager against whom they held a grudge, and at another plantation the gin was burned.

An enlarged posse finally located the strikers at Cat Island in the Mississippi River, where they were waiting to board a steamboat. Storming their hideout—in a gin—the posse killed two and captured nine; the nine were later seized by masked vigilantes and hanged. Others were hunted down and slain during ensuing days, including the strike leader who was caught on a steamboat. The strike was over.

The 1891 cotton pickers' strike revealed many points about the state of harvest labor in the cotton fields. The inability of cotton farmers who were African-American to pay more to their field crews cost the pickers potential allies. The sharp, sometimes violent reactions to the possibility of not having cotton pickers demonstrated the depth of the growers' desperation. But desperation can be seen as well in the mere decision by black cotton pickers to launch a strike, challenging the white power structure that in most communities rested on cotton. And by 1890 they were surrounded by a white society whose racism was becoming more virulent with each passing year.

For the cotton pickers had launched their strike at a time when attitudes were changing, among blacks as well as whites. With whites this meant ignoring or overturning post–Civil War legal defenses for the ex-slaves, moves now possible because of the federal government's aban-

donment of Reconstruction-era protections. Starting in the 1890s, southern whites went on a series of rampages and used both legal and violent
means to overturn earlier gains achieved by the freedmen. Their campaign was symbolized by the first southern laws requiring racial segregation in railroad cars, followed by many similar racial bans, but also by
the sharp rise of lynching. The new lynching era was on display in Paris,
Texas, two years after the cotton pickers' strike, when a crowd of some
15,000 whites watched the burning and torturing of a black man ac-
cused of murdering a white girl; many of them grabbed pieces of his
bones and clothing as souvenirs. Almost 500 blacks were lynched in
Texas from 1880 to 1930, by one estimate. Further, voting by African-
Americans came to an abrupt end in Texas with the 1902 poll tax and
the 1903 white primary, and in Oklahoma when balloting by blacks was
stopped in 1912.

But the events of 1891 showed also that blacks could fight back—
including black cotton pickers.

Something else was in the air as well, the first hints of a trend that
would eventually affect harvest labor everywhere. Several news reports
in 1891 pointed to changes under way in the makeup of the Texas cotton labor force, just as African-Americans were challenging their treatment. Minor at first, the changes can be seen as beginnings of a shift
that would lead to a major transformation. From Cuero, halfway between San Antonio and the Gulf, an initial prediction was that the
strike would meet little success there. Why? Because "a great deal of
the cotton is being picked this season by Mexicans, and if the Negroes
refused to pick it, it is not far to the Rio Grande."

The gradual, slow-moving stream of Mexicans entered a land where
families still dominated cotton picking. This was notably the case in the
Blackland Prairie or "Black Waxy"—the fertile, broad streak of farmland wending from northeastern Texas near Paris, southwesterly through
Dallas and Waco, brushing Austin and San Antonio. Families could
generally survive if all members worked, particularly the women. Indeed, the famous 1924 U.S. Labor Department study of Hill and Rusk
counties in Texas (*The Welfare of Children in Cotton-Growing Areas of
Texas*) found that more than half of the white mothers, and 85 percent

of the African-American mothers, "had worked in the fields at some time during the preceding year," and most had children under age six. The most strenuous time came during cotton picking, in which almost 90 percent participated, with ten-hour days or longer common. Texas professor Ruth Allen concluded after her extensive interviewing in the 1920s that "the labor of women in the production of cotton is woven into the warp and woof of the civilization of the Southern cotton economy."[21]

The physical demands of cotton chopping and picking held serious health dangers for women, presenting a serious paradox in the folklore and reality of cotton farming. Farm families regarded plowing and cultivating—with horse-drawn equipment—as "men's work," but these tasks reserved for the more muscular men were really "the easiest work in the field." On the other hand, cotton picking—to which women were limited—often brought problems that went beyond fatigue, especially when women or girls were lifting heavy sacks of cotton. Allen interviewed three girls "who had lifted too heavy sacks, and none of the three had been 'any good' since. Two had had operations, and the other was under the constant care of a physician." She found "general agreement" among both African-Americans and whites that the performance of field labor by women under certain conditions was expensive in the long run and had serious physical consequences. "Women who did field work during the period of pregnancy paid for it very heavily in later years."

The 1924 Department of Labor study provides glimpses into the struggles, the hardships, of farm life in the days before labor-saving machinery and appliances reached rural America: 14 percent of the white farm wives had at least nine persons to care for. (No data was provided for African-Americans, who presumably were not significantly different on this issue.) The workdays of wives on farms that the family owned differed only slightly from women's workdays on tenant farms. For all of them—family-owned and tenant—the desperation of the farm wife could be read through the lens of one typical day: "She usually got up about 4 o'clock, went to the field as soon as the morning work was done, and, except for about 1½ hours at noon, worked there till sundown; after that she had to get supper and finish the housework."[22]

"I am a farmer's daughter, 13 years old," Lee E. Baker of Van Alstyne, Texas, wrote to *Texas Farm and Ranch* in 1895. "Summer will soon be gone; then cotton picking will be here. I can pick 106 pounds in a day." Another letter writer to the publication was eleven-year-old Willie Wright of Sterrett, who announced, "I can pick 250 pounds of cotton in one day. I can chop cotton. I plow cotton and corn, and I can do most any kind of work . . ."

The young girl at Van Alstyne and the young boy at Sterrett were part of a vast army of children working in Texas cotton fields, their labors visible to anyone passing by but discernible today in yellowed pages of a bygone era. White children, African-American children, Indian children, Mexican children—children's cotton labors were as widespread as they were crucial. The 1924 federal study of two Texas counties found that "nearly all the children over ten years of age included in the study had done field work," at least eight hours a day but often twelve to fourteen hours. The reason was clear: as one father who worked 100 acres put it, "The country is ruined because you can't have your children work on the farm but such a short time in the year. Hired help is so high you can't afford it, and there you are." The study documented how far children were held back in school because of these absences— such as the eleven-year-old who had completed only second grade, or the twelve-year-old just out of first grade.

Rebecca Sharpless presented data on extremely young children being pressed into cotton picking, sometimes using flour sacks as their picking sacks. A 1917 newspaper report from Wolfe City, in Hunt County in northeastern Texas, acclaimed the accomplishment of a two-year-old boy: he picked three pounds one afternoon. Short years later Ruth Allen found that "children among the colored farm group are, if they are to any group, an economic asset." Many had picked cotton "almost from infancy," she wrote, and she encountered three mothers who "had each a child of six years trudging beside her and picking his 'hundred every day,' as the mother proudly informed us."[23]

As the Cotton South expanded following the Civil War, it brought with it a labor supply usually sufficient for the needs at hand. Sufficient, that is, as long as agriculture remained concentrated in areas where the family farm was dominant. But as it spread westward into regions where irrigation encouraged larger spreads, demands for more harvest labor forced a new, wider search for workers.

The eventual solution was Mexicans. Never found in large numbers north of the Rio Grande Valley even before the Texas war for independence, for decades they remained concentrated in border areas. Ethnic Mexicans made up 92 percent of the population of South Texas as late as 1900, before Northern farmers began arriving in numbers. Turning to Mexicans for labor was well established there: two years after Richard King purchased the Santa Gertrudis land grant in 1854, he brought the residents of an entire Mexican village—Tamaulipas—to live and work on the King Ranch. In areas to the north, however, Mexicans were seen less frequently, mainly in scattered pockets, neither widely dispersed nor numerous. As Victor Clark wrote in his 1908 Labor Department report, "As recently as 1900 immigrant Mexicans were seldom found more than a hundred miles from the border," and a study of northeastern Texas found that significant numbers of Mexicans did not live and work there for even a few months a year until after 1910. Indeed, Austin did not have a Catholic church for Mexicans until 1907, when Our Lady of Guadalupe was founded; similar examples dot the Texas landscape. In Oklahoma it was not until 1915 that three Carmelite nuns—forced out of Mexico by Pancho Villa—established a mission for Mexicans at Hartshorne and soon expanded their work to other towns; Oklahoma City did not get a Catholic church for Mexicans until 1921.[24]

They knew the lower Rio Grande Valley, however. The Texas side along Starr, Hidalgo, Willacy, and Cameron counties was developing only slowly from Reconstruction onward, but farmers were already hiring Mexicans to work in their fields of cotton, sugar cane, and vegetables. (Citrus would become a major crop only after 1920.) As David Erland Vassberg, a local resident, pointed out in his history of the valley's Mexican labor force,

> The immediate availability of a supply of cheap and willing Mexican workers was a prime factor in the development of Valley agriculture. Since labor was no problem, crops requiring a great amount of manpower could be grown. Conversely, because the Valley came to grow crops demanding large numbers of workers, the immigrant labor supply tended to increase.

True, an international border ran through the middle of the Rio Grande (called Rio Bravo by Mexicans), but it was ineffective. Illegal ferries consisting of crude rafts, often made of canvas or skins and run by *pateros* (river rats), transported customers across with ease. There were some sixty of these operating near Brownsville in the early autumn of 1907. American border guards were trying to catch bandits, not workers, and the arrival of the U.S. Immigration Service in 1921 brought only nine officers to patrol three hundred miles of riverfront.

Changes began to appear as Anglo farmers' sons reached adulthood and realized what the valley's abundant cheap labor could mean. Soon ties developed with La Laguna, a major cotton area in Mexico, so that workers would finish picking in La Laguna and travel north to get in on the cotton harvest in South Texas. The growing railroad net—with refrigerator cars now available—also enabled other crops to be raised with larger acreages, which brought further calls for Mexican help.[25]

Farther up the Rio Grande similar conditions existed, and one historian has written that by 1900 "hardly an Anglo rancher or farmer in the borderlands was without his 'meskins.'" Recruiters from areas outside Texas were beginning to show up along the border, especially in El Paso, Eagle Pass, and Laredo. "Migrant labor colonies" appeared near the river towns Del Rio and McAllen, and eventually away from the border in such cities as San Antonio and Corpus Christi. In addition to picking cotton and working in vegetable farms, Mexicans were hired to grub brush from incipient farmland, as well as to construct the spreading rail network. Historian Arthur Corwin contrasted this system with the southern slave system, for conditions developing along the border made "casual labor available at the snap of a finger but freeing the *patrón*, the crew leader or contractor from any *noblesse oblige* responsibilities."[26]

Railroads were expanding not only across Texas and the rest of the American West; bands of steel were also being laid throughout Mexico. By 1905 Mexico had 10,557 miles of track, including five railways that ran to the U.S. border. The rail network rapidly brought changes in the lives of rural Mexicans, and the initial break was probably the most significant: the new Mexican National Railroad lured workers from peasant villages for wage labor nearby, then repeatedly transported them farther from home as construction progressed. By leaving their small farms, they were drawn into a cash economy and often left railroad jobs to work in northern Mexican mines. Soon they were hearing stories about the wages farther north, beyond the border. One year the National Railroad of Mexico transported some fifteen hundred laborers north to build rail lines, but "within a year . . . practically all of them had ultimately crossed over into Texas."

In the American Southwest these Mexicans soon came to dominate railroad construction. One trackmaster in southern Kansas even called Mexicans better than Greeks or Italians for such work, surpassed only by "the American 'hobo' . . . We send a man every spring to the Rio Grande to get our men for summer." A Texas railroad official added that Mexicans were replacing Italians and Negroes—"They suit us better than any other immigrant labor we can get."[27]

To Mexicans, higher pay was the main attraction. Recruiters eagerly spread tales of northern wealth, ensuring little difficulty in signing up Mexicans. A U.S. customs collector reported in 1907 from Del Rio that an "unusual number of Mexicans" were crossing the border there, headed to interior cotton districts. The major flow into Oklahoma was under way by that year of statehood, en route to railroad construction gangs and coal mines as well as farm and ranch work. A Texas state employee examined how the recruiters operated:

> The common method used by these smugglers is to send their agents across the river to intercept any immigrants, and to prevent them from crossing illegally . . . These agents play upon the ignorance of the immigrant . . . a proposition is made to put them across the river and evade the authorities for so much per head, the amount ranging from two to ten dollars a person, according to how much the agent thinks he can get out of them . . .[28]

Whether rounded up and shipped out of state or sold to local cotton farmers, a Mexican laborer brought as much as ten dollars to the recruiter who found him and hired him.

This is how the Mexicans became *pizcadores de algodón*—pickers of cotton. They headed in large numbers for newer fields, but there was still work to do in many older areas—setting up irrigation, clearing out brush, planting new crops. In Dimmit County's "Winter Garden" district they were soon harvesting onions, spinach, and strawberries, and their wives and children fitted into the labor regimens easily. Mexican families were soon preferred.

In many parts of Texas, Mexicans began replacing whites and African-Americans in the fields. Already by the early 1900s blacks were abandoning the Texas countryside for the cities, although some who moved nearby came back annually for cotton picking. Increasingly, however, they were lost to farm labor. Cotton was the past for them; city jobs represented the future.[29]

This transformation occurred over several decades in an area of Caldwell County in central Texas called Koeglar Hill. Small farms and tenant farms had developed there during the 1860–90 years, worked by whites and some blacks into the 1880s, when the first Mexicans appeared—initially to pick cotton, as done by those who were part of a large influx in 1887. All farm tenants were Mexicans in 1900, and by 1910 no whites remained of the some three hundred who had been residents of Koeglar Hill in 1880.[30]

The changeover can be seen also at the Taft Ranch near Corpus Christi. The extensive spread on the Gulf plain began as a cattle operation but switched largely to cotton and other row crops, first replacing its Anglo cowboys with Mexicans, then shifting to the developing tenant system already widespread across the South. Now white tenants employed Mexicans as choppers and pickers. In some years Taft men went to the border areas to find Mexican workers; at other times they relied on Laredo recruiters—who sometimes brought the new laborers back by rail in locked cattle cars. White renters were provided with four-room houses; blacks working in the gins and oil plants stayed in small company houses; and seasonal Mexican workers lived in tents or two-room cottages. A hospital was built to serve both Mexicans and African-Americans. The company began holding a June 13 celebration for its Mexican workers and sharecroppers, marking St. John the Baptist Day. It also held a "June 'teenth" celebration for black employees, to commemorate the freeing of Texas slaves on June 19, 1865. These fetes were in addition to those of Christmas, New Year's, and the Fourth of July. By the time of the disruptions of the World War I era, Mexicans were an integral part of the Taft labor force.[31]

The switch to the tenant-sharecropper system began to appear in many other districts. Descended from the Old South's crop-lien system, its adaptation to new conditions again spoke to Texas's dual nature, drawing from its southern roots while moving into the new western economy of intensive agriculture. It freed the landowner from having to hire seasonal labor at harvest time, for now the tenant was responsible for bringing in the crop. In northeastern Texas the availability of cheap labor made it possible for tenants to farm bigger spreads. Mexicans could be hired for short periods as needed, often coming by train from the cities to work on the harvest, then returning—a pattern that became firmly established by the 1920s. The system would continue to evolve, and Mexican laborers were soon being drawn into the ranks of the tenantry also.

Half of Texas's farms were operated by tenants by 1910, and the system soon acquired basic subdivisions. According to an *Austin County Times* reporter in Nelsonville in 1883, "Good land can always be rented, either for money rent, from $4 to $5 per acre, or for a share of the crop—one-third of the corn and one-fourth of the cotton where the renter finds his own teams and tools, and one-half of the crop where the owner supplies everything . . ." Both types were increasing—"thirds and fourths renters" (*quarteros*, in Spanish), supplying their own equipment; "half-tenants" (*madieros*), who relied upon the owner for equipment but could sell the cotton themselves. The number of sharecroppers was also on the rise—"halver-hands," who had the crop sold for them by the landowner. Paul S. Taylor, the California scholar whose detailed examinations of southwestern migrant labor remain the major authority, wrote that while Mexican day laborers were abundant and worked for cash, more and more were placed as sharecroppers on the lands divided from former ranches, which was part of a specific plan by the landowner: "The primary purpose of maintaining Mexican share-croppers on halves is to immobilize them so that ample labor will be on hand through the year and a large nucleus to start the picking season. This was variously expressed by farmers." In this way, the tenant farmer became the "country brother of the casual worker."[32]

The growers' creativity in finding new systems to ensure completion of harvests reflected their desperation—a desperation often on display, as when an 1869 meeting of railroad leaders and planters in Memphis had called for importation of Chinese. A year later some 250 Chinese arrived to build the Houston & Texas Central Railroad, but their numbers declined rapidly, and they never played a major role in Texas agriculture. Their appearance instead revealed the anxiety of employers in Texas and elsewhere over labor uncertainties.[33]

This was true of another attempt that also ultimately failed: using convict labor. When the Democrats came back into control in Texas in the 1870s, they developed a convict lease system that eventually sent several thousand prisoners to work outside prison walls. By 1896 there were 2,463 working on farms and 317 on railroads in what had become a profitable system: half of a convict's earnings went to the farmer, half to the state.[34]

Counties were also putting their prisoners to work on farms, bringing in money in addition to freeing up jail space. But this method of getting cotton picked was not always trouble-free. In 1897 in Fort Bend County one John D. Flewellen contracted "to hire all the male county convicts of said county that were not confirmed cripples . . . and to pay therefore at the rate of $5.50 per month . . ." He also agreed not to work them "for a longer time in any one day than other laborers doing the same kind of work . . ." But of the 61 convicts in the original agreement, 7 paid their fines and were released before beginning work, and 10 others escaped. The 44 who remained could turn out only 98 bales of cotton the first year, and although they produced 400 the second year, Flewellen lost $4,000 and had to sell the plantation. Convicts had not been the answer.[35]

During the Progressive Era the leasing of prisoners to enrich the state's coffers began to be questioned. One Texas prisoner, who had been moved fifty-four times since his conviction, testified that on one occasion he had received twenty-seven licks of a whip for not picking enough cotton. A 1912 report noted that limiting the convicts' working hours, as well as "suspen[ding] the long-used method of punishment in the penitentiary—the strap," had cut convict labor's "productive efficiency" to a very large degree. Nevertheless, the report asserted, the state "owes to the persons convicted of crime and sentenced to the penitentiary the humane treatment of wholesome food, comfortable clothing and shelter, healthful surroundings and moral instruction." The report called for putting convicts to work only on state-owned farms—it owned 8,975 acres in Fort Bend County and 15,974 in Brazoria County—and ending the leasing system. The proposal was adopted, and 1912 was the last year for convict leasing in Texas.

Railroad companies branched out further, sending agents to other states and even to Germany seeking workmen. German immigrants had been present in the Texas hill country northwest of San Antonio since 1844, but for the most part they became farmers rather than farm laborers. European immigrants would not play a significant role in Texas harvest labor.[36]

Another group arriving after the turn of the century would have an impact on the labor question. These were midwesterners, primarily farmers, encouraged by railroad colonization agencies that were working with irrigation entrepreneurs and township promoters. The *New York Evening Post* noted the influx in 1906, commenting on the newcomers' unhappiness with the cold winters of the northern states but adding, "The possibilities of the land coupled with the moderate cost at which they can obtain a whole section of land, 640 acres, apparently attract them." Dry-land farming was all the rage, especially after several wet years made it seem less daunting. By 1910 the number of natives of Iowa, Illinois, Indiana, and Ohio who were now residents of Texas had climbed two-thirds from 1900's totals, to reach 79,825. But they were not coming as harvest laborers.

Many of these "snowdiggers," as they were called, were attracted to lands near new irrigation projects in the Panhandle and West Texas, although large numbers also headed to older farming regions. Soon two groups seemed to be rushing into Texas: midwesterners and Mexicans. Both movements were encouraged by chambers of commerce—such as the business group in one southwestern city that boasted to northerners of the district's "unorganizable labor in inexhaustible quantities." And a land company pointed out, "Our lands being located just across the river from Mexico, where there is plenty of cheap Mexican labor to be had, there is no trouble in getting labor." To the snowdiggers, the promoters spoke of warm weather and an abundance of cheap workers; to Mexicans, recruiters spoke of good wages.[37]

These arrivals—coming from opposite directions—fed a Texas agricultural boom but were not universally welcomed; nor, when they received them, were the welcomes identical. Many longtime residents were critical of newcomers from the North, for older *Texicans* had generally mixed amicably with *Tejanos*—native Texans of Mexican descent—even to the extent of intermarriage and were known for watching over their Mexican laborers like stern but kindly grandfathers. Studies by David Montejano, Benjamin Heber Johnson, and by Charles Harris and Louis Sadler document the worsening Anglo-Mexican relations that followed the influx of new settlers. As Montejano described it, the downturn in race relations stemmed from the appearance of "ready-made farm communities, transplanted societies from the Midwest and the North . . ." The old paternalism was replaced by a sharp division between old settlers and new settlers, and a racial divide made wider by the midwesterners' distaste for Mexicans.

A Mexican looked back on the changes years later and recalled that "since the coming of the 'white trash' from the North and Middle West we felt the change. They made us feel for the first time that we were Mexicans and that they considered themselves our superiors." Indeed, the first "Mexican School" was opened in Seguin in 1902, and school segregation of Mexican pupils spread, matching the earlier segregation of African-Americans. School attendance rules were often not enforced regarding Mexican children, who were expected to pick cotton or do other work for Anglos, not to go to school.

A letter sent back to a friend in the Midwest from a woman in Riviera, Texas, a town settled by families from Illinois, is suggestive:

> Not very long after Mr. Womack and Mr. Horstman had gone, I observed several Mexicans, mounted on prancing ponies, approaching. I closed the doors and windows and then hid myself. They rode around the building calling and knocking. I could understand only the word "carta."* I supposed they wanted a cart—maybe wanted to put me in the cart. Anyway I finally came out and talked to them and found they wanted their mail out of the post office. One of the boys could speak a few words in English.

Mrs. Womack added that "all I knew of Mexicans was from reading History and war stories. I had the impression that all Mexicans were cruel and treacherous like those I had read of."[38]

Mrs. Womack's letter touched on another post-1900 development that became part of rising anti-Mexican feelings: "war stories" increasingly were peopled with Mexicans. In the nineteenth century, Mexico had frequently been torn by revolutionary attempts, and revolts contin-

---

* *Carta* means "postal letter" in Spanish. The word for "cart" in Spanish is *carreta*.

ued into the new century, many launched by groups organized in South
Texas. In 1906 and again in 1908 bands of revolutionaries set off from
El Paso to attack Mexican government installations, rebuffed each
time. When a larger effort led by Francisco Madero failed, Madero fled
to San Antonio in 1910 and from there launched a new, successful effort fortified with recruitment drives along the border.

This warfare and the abject poverty of rural Mexico provided a volatile mix that drove waves of frightened Mexicans to flee northward. The
regime of General Porfirio Díaz (1876–1911) was exceptionally harsh
in seizing land, and efforts to overthrow him grew. The revolution that
eventually ousted Díaz began in February 1911, and some of the major
fighting took place near the Rio Grande. A full division of the U.S.
Army was eventually posted near the Rio Grande, and the federal government began subsidizing the Texas Rangers to protect the boundary
area.[39]

The Rangers already had a bad reputation among Mexicans. As the
authors of a recent study concluded, for Hispanics "the image the Rangers have historically projected is that of the most notorious instrument
of repression employed by a racist, Anglo-dominated society." Their role
as border guards increased with the outbreak of the Mexican Revolution, which was marked by further splits among Mexicans on both sides
of the border, for many *Tejanos* were linked to one or another of the
competing armies. U.S. Senator Morris Sheppard of Texas charged that
"most of the people living along the river are Mexican Americans who
are American in name but Mexican in sympathy."

Sheppard's comment reflected the widespread feeling among Anglos that Mexicans in Texas were disloyal. As the European war expanded after 1914, patriotic spasms flowed sporadically across the
United States, stimulating Anglo suspicions. As powerful as these feelings were already, publication of the Plan de San Diego on January 24,
1915, strengthened them even further. This manifesto, signed in San
Diego, a small town near Corpus Christi, called for a Mexican uprising
against the United States to bring independence to Texas, New Mexico,
Arizona, Colorado, and California—"of which States the REPUBLIC OF
MEXICO was robbed in a most perfidious manner by North American
imperialism." Filled with language guaranteed to provoke white Texans,
the plan asserted that "every North American over sixteen years of age

shall be put to death," Apache Indians would have their lands returned, and blacks would be assisted in taking over six states in the United States to form an independent republic.

In addition to growing discrimination aimed at them by theaters, restaurants, and public schools, Mexican-Americans also felt a rising anger over their loss of farms, often a result of Anglos challenging their land titles and then forcing lawsuits that poor farmers could not afford. Sometimes violence achieved results satisfying to the new Anglo farmers: land was taken from *Tejanos*, and the number of available unemployed laborers increased. Large numbers of *Tejanos* who had farmed and ranched now found themselves demoted to employment in "stoop labor." Their anger was further fueled by publicity given to successful land distribution across the border: after Carranza army successes, a large hacienda in Mexico's Tamaulipas state was broken up and some of its lands given to peasant farmers.

Raids marked by sudden ferocity began in Texas in midsummer 1915, and some of the Anglo victims were those known for showing blatant prejudice against Mexicans. Alfred Austin and his son Charles, who had a farm near Sebastian, northwest of Brownsville, had been in the area only six years; both men were active in the local Law and Order League, Alfred as president and Charles as secretary. Alfred was known to treat his Mexican workers brutally. When the raiders came, they dragged the two men away and shot both of them repeatedly. A deputy sheriff later pointed out that six of the bandits had formerly worked for Austin. Some of the attackers in different 1915 raids were local *Tejanos*, joining Mexicans from across the border. Historian Benjamin Heber Johnson concludes that while these incidents may have seemed "a random frenzy of robbery, theft, destruction, and murder," the Austins' murder by former employees "suggested that there was a method to this madness."[40]

Anglo ranchers worried by the Plan de San Diego made stronger preparations once the raids began. Numerous rifle clubs were formed, and the manager of the King Ranch requested that a Texas Ranger company be stationed nearby. He later acquired two cannons to defend the property and mounted a searchlight on a roof. The ranch's Anglo employees "go armed all of the time," according to one report. The Taft Ranch made plans to purchase a rapid-fire gun. After the violence quieted in 1916, its superintendent explained that "there is practically no danger of any disturbance now, but if we should get a cotton crop and have a thousand or two Mexican pickers here, then there might be some danger of some one trying to get them to make an uprising of some sort . . ."

In this superheated environment, as suspicions of Mexican disloyalty were spreading, the Zimmerman Telegram hit Texas like a bomb. Released in March 1917 by the British, who had broken the German code, the telegram from the German foreign secretary to a German official in Mexico promised aid to Mexico in case of a war with the United States; the eventual German-Mexican victory would return the Southwest to Mexican control. In Texas anti-Mexican hysteria exploded, with calls to restrict the entry of Mexicans. On the Taft Ranch only Mexicans accompanied by wives and children would be hired; single Mexicans were avoided.[41]

Sporadic Mexican raids into Texas increased, some related to the revolution, others carried out by bandits seeking horses or money. The climax came with Pancho Villa's attacks in 1916, murdering sixteen Americans on a train and slaying another seventeen while burning Columbus, New Mexico. These incidents led President Woodrow Wilson to dispatch a 6,000-man expeditionary force under General John Pershing to capture Villa, an effort that failed. As the Southwest border situation continued to deteriorate during America's involvement in the world war, anti-Mexican bitterness in Texas hardened.

None of the factors that swept America into war, other than the Zimmerman Telegram, centered on Mexican issues. But America's wartime superpatriotism soon had an impact on Texas farmers in ways they might not have expected. In 1917 Congress passed an immigration restriction measure, principally aimed at Europeans but also at the importation of Mexican workers—importation already technically forbidden under the seldom-enforced 1885 Contract Labor Law. Now Mexicans—as well as Europeans—arriving on U.S. soil were required to pass a literacy test (in any language) and pay an $8 head tax. Another blow at cotton farmers and others relying on an unending supply of Mexicans came with the Draft Law, passed in May 1917; initially it required registration of all American males beginning at age 21 but soon expanded to cover all men ages 18 to 45.[42]

These actions, born of war in Europe and revolution in Mexico, suddenly put the problems of harvest labor in Texas, Oklahoma, and throughout the Southwest into the national spotlight. Where could growers find enough workers, now that they depended heavily on Mexicans? Worried men talked, in East Texas communities centered on the Black Waxy, around their irrigated cotton fields in West Texas and Arizona, as they walked through the new sugar beet fields of Colorado, Kansas, and Nebraska, and in California's groves and orchards. They saw disaster ahead.

8

THE "COTTON WEST"
REACHES ARIZONA

Water gushed through the new Roosevelt Dam's conduits in 1912, producing exuberant optimism among Arizonans: just accepted as the nation's forty-eighth state, Arizona could now anticipate a brilliant agricultural future based on cotton—cotton that could thrive in a desert suddenly made productive by irrigation. But the cheers were not echoed everywhere, for as planting began the following spring, the U.S. Department of Agriculture sent a warning: if too many acres were put into cotton, "it will be impossible to secure an adequate supply of properly trained labor to pick the crop next autumn." One grower would later recall that moment vividly: "the first thing they urged was 'Be careful: do not plant too much cotton, because you can not pick it.'" Behind the advice was an implied threat, the perennial danger of the New West, as a Texas editor pointed out in discussing the news from Arizona: "If pickers cannot be secured the crop will go to waste in the fields, or if the price for labor is forced up by competition for pickers the profits of cotton culture will diminish, perhaps to the vanishing point."[1]

Not enough pickers! Not enough men, women, and children to bring in the crop! Wages pushed too high! After the South's debates over its labor supply following the end of slavery, and the search for workers in the expanding cotton acreages of Texas, now the same cry for pickers was being heard in Arizona. Anxious discussions swirled around the inadequacy of hoboes, the frenzied border recruitment drives, problems with sharecroppers. Again as elsewhere, the threat of too few harvest workers was real. It had arrived in tandem with intensive agriculture.

Irrigation was teamed with the railroad as catalyst for cotton's expansion across the Southwest. Just as railways preceded settlement as they rolled toward the Pacific, so now irrigation canals were being scraped and dug through areas that had never known more than Indian villages or scattered homesteads. Soon after their arrival in the Salt Lake Valley in 1847, the Mormons began digging ditches to carry water to their newly plowed fields. Short months after that, when placer miners in California were busily running water to their sluices and rockers, the logical next step was to divert some to farm plots, so that farmers could begin raising food for the miners. When the Southern Pacific reached Tucson in 1880, it entered an area with some irrigation canals already running. Across the Southwest the truth of an Arizona cotton grower's words to Congress became evident: "water out there is the magic word; . . . we can not raise a crop without water; we have to buy it."

Arizona was only the latest testing ground for projects to quench the West's thirst for irrigation water; efforts moved forward at varying speeds and with varying rates of success. The Salt River Project, drawing water from the Roosevelt Dam, was the first by the U.S. Reclamation Service,[*] and even bigger projects came soon after that, such as Colorado's Fort Lyon Canal, which ran 105 miles, eventually watering 120,000 acres in the Rocky Ford area. That state had been host to the first Irrigation Congress, in 1873, when participant President Ulysses S. Grant was so enthused that he proposed an irrigation canal to run all the way from the Missouri River to the Rockies.[2]

But many areas remained without irrigation. Dry farming methods were forced upon settlers moving into West Texas, the Texas Panhandle, western Oklahoma, and most districts of New Mexico and Arizona. Those conditions were seen as temporary, however, for visions of what extra moisture could accomplish soon attracted promoters with other approaches. Deep wells came first, their windmills pulling up water for cattle and garden patches, and companies experimented with sending their water to irrigation canals. The High Plains was a difficult environment, and as late as 1920 Deaf Smith, Floyd, Hale, and Bailey counties in the Texas Panhandle had only 187 irrigation wells in operation. True,

[*] Later renamed the U.S. Bureau of Reclamation.

their dry climate held back the dreaded boll weevil—which was devastating fields across the Old South—but progress still came slowly to those new cotton lands.

Irrigation was even more crucial farther west, in desert areas. There had been early small-scale attempts—centuries earlier the Hohokam Indians had built canals, which Arizonans tried to use in the 1870s to carry Gila River water to fields around Florence. By 1890 some 50,000 acres were irrigated under many small projects in the Salt River Valley, where rivers converged and where Phoenix was born. Still, Arizona's limited irrigated acreage sentenced it to last place in the West's irrigation rankings, severely restricting its agricultural development, and when the territorial governor issued his annual report to Congress ten years later, he could boast of mining and irrigation developments but still did not mention cotton. "The labor supply in Arizona is almost always equal to the demand," he noted.[3]

And then science came to the rescue. For years the United States had been importing Egyptian long-staple cotton, whose fine and silky fibers were used in hosiery and knit goods and increasingly for tires needed by the new automobile industry. Upland or short-stem cotton from the Old South was not suitable for these purposes, forcing upward imports of highly desired long-staple cotton.

In 1901 the Arizona Experiment Station began testing new seeds supplied by the U.S. Department of Agriculture, and the resulting crop yielded 400 pounds of long-staple per acre. Other types were developed, including "Pima cotton," which came from the Cotton Research Center on the Pima Indian Reservation. Commercial planting of long-staple cotton began in 1912, just as the first waters were starting to flow from the Roosevelt Dam. On September 1 the *Arizona Daily Star* of Tucson announced that a new resident from New Jersey was set to clear $15,000 from his 200 acres of Egyptian cotton near Phoenix—"the first time in the history of the valley that any party has experimented" with such large acreage, and the first large-scale test of the Egyptian variety. The newspaper predicted that expanded planting throughout the Salt River Valley would follow; this proved correct, for soon manufacturers of automobile tires began operations in the Phoenix area, near both a supply of water and the new supply of Pima cotton. When the Arizona Egyptian Cotton Company built facilities the following year, success seemed at hand.[4]

But more than water was needed to produce new cotton strains, the Agricultural Experiment Station cautioned: labor was also crucial. Labor conditions in Arizona were, it said, an "uncertainty."

Some workers were on hand. Indians, long familiar with all aspects of desert farming, including growing cotton and running irrigation canals, were veterans of working for white settlers. Although largely ignored by later historians, Indian wage labor fitted in easily with this new cotton frontier of the Southwest, as it had with Pacific Northwest hops picking. In the Southwest the Native Americans worked seasonally when they needed cash, then turned back to traditional activities and traveling. This pattern was often repeated when western Indians dealt with the incoming whites.

Wage work by Indians was "most important" to the newly arriving whites "in those regions that still lacked any densely settled, potentially competitive laboring population," according to Martha C. Knack and Alice Littlefield in their study of tribes in different areas of North America—and this situation persisted in vast areas of the West well into the twentieth century. By the 1890s, scarcely fifty years after the first settlers had arrived, southern Paiutes in the Great Basin were relying on wage earnings "for over half their provisioning." Well before century's end, the San Carlos Apaches of southern Arizona were within the dollar economy, initially laboring for farmers and mining companies, soon in railroad employment. Largely of their own accord—that is, without government pressures—these Indians turned to wage earning because it filled a crucial need. With many sources of their traditional subsistence gone or reduced, they could still control their own labor.[5]

Jeffrey Shepherd's study of the Hualapais emphasizes their efforts to fit a variety of jobs into their yearly cycles, adapting to disagreeable tasks by trading them between family or band members. He found that "the monotony of the work and a tradition of rotating hunting excursions also compelled Hualapais to change jobs frequently so that several band members shared a single position in an industry." They used wage labor to buy cloth, food, and other items needed.

Navajos also began wage labor early, and when their sheep and cattle herds declined in the 1890s, they worked on construction of the Tsa-a lee irrigation ditch north of Fort Defiance, New Mexico. Their agent reported in 1900, "They are beginning to realize that they must work [at wage labor] in order to live." Railroad construction drew many, mainly for the Santa Fe but later for the Denver & Rio Grande. The Southern Navajo superintendent determined in 1904 that "wherever labor is wanted the Navajo is employed . . . ," preferred over Mexicans and Indians of other tribes. They were picking cotton in the Salt River Valley after the First World War but in the late 1920s were replaced by Mexicans. Like many other tribes, the Navajos saw wage labor as "not an end in itself," according to Garrick Bailey and Roberta Glenn Bailey; rather, it enabled them to rebuild their herds "and carry on their former means of livelihood."

This approach meant that as the cotton boom developed after 1912, Arizona growers found Indians available for employment. Pima and Tohono O'odham Indians were hired early on, and the new Salt River Valley Water Users' Association also "found among the Yaqui Indians a particularly convenient work force . . . skilled, patient, in need of employment"—and willing to accept low wages. Driven out of the Mexican State of Sonora by Porfirio Díaz, the Yaquis quickly obtained employment in Arizona. And unlike most of the incoming whites, the Yaquis were already experienced with irrigation, so in addition to picking cotton, they kept the new canals open and running. As cotton vaulted to the top of Arizona agriculture, Yaquis found even more opportunities for employment, especially in the war years.[6]

In many other areas of the Southwest, as irrigation stimulated agricultural expansion, growers turned to Indians. In the Carson Sink Valley in Nevada, Paiute and Shoshone tribesmen became regular workers in the developing alfalfa fields. They soon were so important that area farmers—like their counterparts in Great Plains wheat districts—began visiting jails looking for Indian workmen. A Nevada Indian school director wrote to his commissioner in 1908, "It has been the custom at Fallon to arrest an Indian for being drunk and then the next morning some farmer who needed a man would pay the fine and the offender would be turned out . . ."

As the national movement for Indian education spread, some western entrepreneurs saw the pupils as potential harvest workers. Assimilation was a broad goal of these schools, and the "outing" system was one of the means employed. "Outing" combined vocational instruction in the Indian schools with work in local communities, under what one agent called "the privilege in going out in the summer" to work on ranches. In Phoenix, leaders of the Arizona Improvement Company lobbied politicians in 1890 for an Indian school to be constructed in Maricopa County, conveniently located beside lands of the Maricopa Canal Land Company. The *Arizona Republic* lectured a visiting commissioner that with the school and its two hundred pupils, "in a few years our lands, now being so extensively planted with fruit trees and vines, would give employment to many of the pupils." Squatters were pushed off the desired location, the school was established, and the outing system was soon inaugurated. Indian schoolchildren could now take jobs in the local economy to help—it was argued—with their assimilation, the girls in domestic work, the boys as field laborers.[7]

But with the rapid growth of cotton acreage after 1912, the number of Indian workers available was insufficient. A representative of the Arizona Cotton Growers Association later explained to a congressional committee that the tribes had not responded in adequate numbers:

> We have worked among the Indians continuously for seven years. We have succeeded in getting a few from some of the reservations. From the Apache Reservation at San Carlos, after seven years' work, we have gotten one; out of the Hopis we have gotten some 19; from the Navajos about 6; from the Papago Indians in the south we have had some six or seven hundred. This year it dropped to 350. The Pima Indians and some of the other tribes are growing cotton themselves to such an extent that they are competing with our labor instead of being a source of labor.[8]

Railroads delivered another possible harvest labor force: the Chinese. The Southern Pacific in its push into Arizona, New Mexico, and Texas employed Chinese tracklayers. When the rails were in place and the Chinese were let go, many found work in the copper mines, and by 1883 there were 100 Chinese (out of 400 total employees) at Arizona's famous Clifton mine.

But discrimination and rioting drove them out, and rather than moving into agriculture, most left the territory or found jobs in the new towns and cities. This did not mean that Arizonans no longer encountered Chinese, however. After passage of the 1882 ban on Chinese immigration, Nogales, in Sonora, became the popular crossing point for smugglers bringing in Chinese laborers landed at Mexican ports. Several northern Mexican villages developed Chinese communities that provided rest stops for those headed for the border. Relatives and friends assisted in these efforts, but most were apparently handled through the Six Companies in San Francisco. Ringleader of these efforts was Yung Ham, of Sonora, who is said to have helped some 6,000 Chinese cross the poorly defended boundary. Once on American soil they were whisked off to Phoenix or sent to California. But by the time Congress was urged in 1917 to admit one million Chinese laborers into the United States to handle "farm and domestic work, for which they are admirably fitted," the Chinese had lost their connections to southwestern cotton.[9]

Japanese were also considered as a possible cotton labor force, for they were present on western railroad construction crews and in the mines. Like the Chinese, they had arrived in Arizona with the Southern Pacific, in the late 1880s; while some then found copper mine employment, growing numbers saw farming opportunities along the territory's rivers, and by 1897 some one hundred Japanese were harvesting wild canaigre roots, used in producing tannic acid. From there other agricultural efforts followed—sugar beets briefly, and chicken farms, but mainly vegetables grown for townspeople. At the time of the first Egyptian cotton boom, "a number of Japanese" reportedly raised cantaloupes for a Cincinnati company that ran farms in the Salt Lake Valley. The Japanese, however, never became the cheap labor source for Arizona's new cotton fields that some growers had hoped.[10]

African-Americans did not become an important part of the Southwest's cotton labor force either. Although back in central Texas a "hybrid culture" had developed based on whites, blacks, and Mexicans, only whites and Mexicans continued to trek westward in numbers as irrigation opened new areas. Sheer prejudice was one cause for blacks' reluctance to follow cotton's migration, but northern industry also beckoned to those tired of the cotton patch.[11]

White hoboes showed up from time to time, but distances from the Midwest and the Plains were great, and the "tramp" reputation had preceded them. Hoboes found little welcome. The presence of Indian workmen, in fact, was cheered by some who did not want "floaters" moving in, even for brief stays. Transient white families sometimes appeared in the cotton fields, but never in large numbers even though western districts actually offered more opportunities for family earnings, for small children could earn up to $2 a day because there "cotton is pulled rather than picked." A family of average size made from $20 to $30 a day picking cotton.

Their lives were generally bleak. At the end of the 1920s, when Ruth Allen trudged through Texas cotton fields, she found children who "had never known a really settled existence," whose fathers had either failed at farming or been laid off from a town job. Tents were often their homes, or they might rent a room or a small house near the cotton fields. Single women—that is, widows traveling with relatives or unmarried daughters who remained with their parents—were found to never collect their own wages or "have any control over the spending of them."

And yet at the end of her interviews she concluded that the women "were not especially unhappy." One family wanted to go to Arizona, so they were paying their way by picking cotton. Several simply did not want to be tied down. Another complained of a city job she had once held, adding that such places held no fascination for her, for "the cigar smoke always makes me sick if I stay in town a few hours." Only a few women voiced strong objections to migratory life. But when Allen compared their lot to the day-to-day existence of tenants and sharecroppers, "with its deadly monotony, its grinding poverty, and ceaseless toil, who shall say that they do not choose wisely?"[12]

The hunt for workers began another tack, following trends developed in the South that had spread into Texas. Growers with large operations were increasingly dividing their land and renting out plots on a cash basis or, more typically, for a share of the crop. Under one system, the "cropper" supplied nothing but his labor and received half the proceeds when the crop was sold. As in Texas, the tenant supplied the animals and equipment himself and then paid the land owner one-fourth of the cotton and one-fourth of the corn. But there were numerous variations, including borrowing from banks, which could bring the lien system crash-

ing down on the tenant. Some tenants even subrented the land to others and wound up doing no work themselves.

Sharecropping and tenantry may be seen as a substitute, perhaps a
variation, for labors done elsewhere by hoboes, for like the men who
rode the rails to harvest wheat and fruit, large numbers of southwestern
families of tenants and sharecroppers kept on the move. A tenant often
was not fixed in place, though southwestern sharecroppers' transfers
generally occurred over a longer period; they usually did not migrate
during the picking season. In effect, they were migratory workers an-
chored only briefly to specific plots of land. A 1916 southwestern study
encountered one tenant who had moved ten times in thirteen years,
"but yet he remains at the lowest level of tenancy, a half-cropper. He is
a migratory tenant of the unsuccessful type," with "an anemic wife and
a multitude of ill-nourished children." There were tenants who did better, and some climbed the "agricultural ladder" into land ownership in
five or six years. But their numbers were minuscule amid the growing
legion of struggling tenants and sharecroppers.[13]

As cotton fields began appearing in West Texas and, bit by bit, in the
Panhandle and in western Oklahoma, tenantry increased sharply—up
from 37.6 percent of all Texas farmers in 1880 to 53.3 percent by 1920.
This expansion helped solidify Texas's production leadership among
cotton states, and by 1923 its acreage of cotton totaled four times that
of second-place Georgia, as did its total of 4,290,000 cotton bales. Tenantry continued to rise, and by 1930, 60.9 percent of all Texas farms
were tenant farms, and nearly 70 percent of Oklahoma's.

This pattern followed cotton as it spread westward, making brief
stops in New Mexico before establishing a large presence in Arizona
on newly irrigated lands. The latter state's Agricultural Experiment Station studied the Salt River Valley in 1917 and determined that 41 percent of the farmers were tenants, most in cotton farming. Tenants kept
the gins operating, but the available supply of workers still was often inadequate to keep up with the expansion of cotton acreage. As numerous
as they were, and as large as individual families tended to be, tenant
farmers still could not provide enough calloused hands for the cotton
picking.[14]

As had been the case in Texas, Mexicans became the Arizona solution. Simply stated, they had been part of the Southwest long before the Americans seized it in the 1847 Mexican War and then purchased a narrow strip along the border in 1848 for a southern railroad route, the Gadsden Purchase. The effectiveness of the border as a barrier between Arizona and Sonora was as much a fiction as was the shallow Rio Grande between Texas and Coahuila and Chihuahua. Lightly guarded, the fifteen-hundred-mile Mexican border provided little more risk to migrants than crossing a street. Even after some inspection units were installed along the border in 1903, entering Arizona was seldom a problem: if migrants were blocked at the legal entry point at Nogales, unpatrolled areas were not far away. But while Mexicans had always been present in Arizona, their numbers were small, mixed as they often were with Indian tribes of the region (and often confused with Indians by the incoming whites).

Railroads were early employers of large numbers of Mexicans who eventually showed up in Arizona, as had been true in Texas. Mexico's Sonora Railway reached the border at Nogales in 1882, where it linked with the Southern Pacific, and regional connections kept multiplying after the Mexican Central and Mexican National arrived at points along the Texas border. At the 1910 anniversary of Mexican Independence, President Porfirio Díaz announced that his country had 15,260 miles of rails in operation.[15]

By then the lure of railroad employment, and the regular paychecks that came with it, had drawn thousands of Mexican peasants off the land to railroad construction jobs on both sides of the border. Different investigators of southwestern labor during the 1920s seemed almost overwhelmed by the variety of personal work experiences they encountered. Paul Taylor came upon many such persons in his studies—one Mexican cotton picker told him he arrived from Mexico in 1890, worked with cattle, then on the railroad, wound up in Oklahoma coal mines in 1895, and later labored in the Indian Territory as well as in Texas before moving on to St. Louis and Pennsylvania. Another Mexican told Taylor that he started with the railroad in California; went to the coal mines at Gallup, New Mexico; worked in sugar beets near Greeley, Colorado; then went back to the railroad in Pennsylvania; and later was employed as a New York stevedore. Others traveled as far as the Alaskan salmon canneries and the steel mills of Pittsburgh. They fitted into the extremes of mobility already common in the American West.

Many of the Mexican immigrants interviewed by Manuel Gamio in 1926–27 described first leaving their farms and finding employment in Mexican railroad construction, then shifting to U.S. railways, going back and forth across the border between countries and jobs. Often the pathway for Mexicans led to copper and silver mines. Clifton's copper mines relied heavily upon Mexicans as well as European immigrants, especially after the whites and Mexicans drove out the Chinese in the early 1880s. Mexicans came to dominate the crews at Clifton-Morenci, but few worked in the Globe-Miami mining district, where they were on the losing side in the union-management struggles of 1907–8.[16]

Some Mexicans working for northern Mexico mines later took higher-paying jobs in U.S. coal mines, mainly in Colorado. Most Hispanics there were American-born, however, largely drawn from nearby areas of New Mexico, although increasing numbers were hired directly from mines in northern Mexico. As historian Sarah Deutsch has pointed out, despite battling workplace discrimination—which extended to giving Hispanics poorer "rooms" to work in the coal mines—"Hispanic miners could earn up to twice the monthly income of Hispanic track laborers." And from the coal mines it was a short journey to jobs in Colorado's forests, in the sugar beet fields, or in the cotton fields of Arizona.

Such cases demonstrated that mobility among Mexicans had become customary—as though leaving farms in Mexico had loosened invisible chains, giving them a freedom to roam they had never before known. Mine and smelter employment meshed well with such a mobile workforce, for machine breakdowns, fluctuations in the price of coal or ore, and conditions underground could force layoffs. Surviving company records from some Arizona mines in that era contain mainly Mexican names. In 1904 the Twin Buttes, Arizona, Mining and Smelting Company payroll revealed a pattern of great variety for its ninety-eight employees: only fourteen men had worked all 31 days in December; thirteen worked 29 days, and ten worked 28 days—a declining total that continued down to the four who worked 11 days, and one who worked 10 days, closing with the four men who had worked only a single day.

The Tip Top Mine in Pima County, Arizona, had fourteen employees in December 1906, but 104 by the following March; paydays ($2 per day) during one month went to men with 13, 24, 15, 18, 26, 18, 23, 17, 13, 21, and 21 days of labor. Frank Siqueros started in October 1913, when the mine went under lease, and worked for sixteen straight months; he left for three months, then came back and mined for five months, only to reappear four months later, in March 1916, after which he dropped out until October. Then Siqueros worked eight straight months, until March 1917, when he left again until July, then signed on again and worked until October 1917. His work schedule was scarcely unique or even unusual.[17]

Like the Pacific Northwest logger who was "starved into berries," Mexican miners in the Southwest could be starved into cotton. During mine shutdowns and economic downturns they often turned to cotton picking to tide themselves over. Although wages were lower than in mining, fieldwork at least was something they could easily grab in desperate straits, not unlike the Mexican families in Texas in the 1920s who "were traveling aimlessly through the country, living in tents and picking up whatever work they could find." Economic downturns, however, could suddenly flood a district with job seekers. Paul Taylor interviewed a Mexican, a veteran harvest worker, who complained:

> They say we live in a bad way. It is because we can't live better. The contractors come in here with other Mexicans from other places. The Americans pay them, and the Mexicans work, but no American would accept the situation [at the low wages]. It is all right for them to bring in other hands if there is danger of losing the crop, but the trouble is that it means less work for us.

By the 1920s, according to one estimate, "tens of thousands" of Mexican-Americans in Texas were displaced by incoming Mexicans and were forced to seek work elsewhere.[18]

Mexicans frequently described their hard life in *corridos*—songs they created and sang at their gatherings. Some were composed while they worked in the fields, their cotton bags dragging behind, the sun beating down. Dan Dickey translated the "Song of the Cotton Harvest"

(*Canción de las pizcas*), by an unknown Mexican, in which the singer sang:

> And I worked all over the county,
> I cried in the furrows like a baby,
> The pain in my waist,
> The pain in my waist,
> I just couldn't stand it.

But he was so desperate for money that "even by moonlight I would go out to pick . . ."[19]

With irrigation advancing and cotton fields expanding, cattlemen were being pushed out in some areas, making the work of the cowboy "increasingly irrelevant," as one historian has written. In this setting the search for Mexican cotton pickers—and competition for them—became heated. Growers were forced into a variety of recruiting strategies.

Texas farmers had long depended upon the railroads to begin the process of uprooting Mexicans and starting them north, counting on some of the workers to quit and turn to cotton when they tired of laboring on the *traque*. By the early 1900s there were already large numbers of recruiters along the Rio Grande, an activity that blossomed into a separate industry. One agency there supplied 6,474 Mexicans to four railways in the first nine months of 1907. Others went straight to the fields, as a *corrido* singer described it:

> When I came from Mexico
> In a closed train car,
> They brought me under contract
> To the cotton picking.[20]

Similar tales and songs played out in Arizona. Mexicans began moving into cotton picking as soon as the Egyptian variety proved economically worthwhile in 1912, and a reporter who visited the Salt River Valley's largest spread that year claimed that talk of a shortage of pickers was rebuffed by reality: "While there is a scarcity of colored labor, there are plenty of Mexicans." One grower said that Mexicans were showing up early to secure picking contracts, and "if he had 1000 acres instead of 200, he would not have difficulty in getting it picked." As the cotton boom developed along the Salt River, a "Mexican Employment Office" in Phoenix advertised "Mexican girls, Mexican women, Mexican men, for all kinds of work; also American help furnished."

But the continued expansion of Arizona cotton acreage eventually meant that even these local agencies could not always meet the need. Soon the Salt River Valley Egyptian Cotton Growers Association began advertising for pickers in twenty newspapers in Texas, New Mexico, Oklahoma, Arkansas, Louisiana, and Missouri. Whites as well as Mexicans were attracted, and the *Arizona Democrat* reported at the start of picking season in 1913, "Cotton pickers are arriving daily from Texas and Oklahoma." The association also sent its own agents to Texas to recruit, some traveling south of the border, although this was illegal under U.S. law.[21]

El Paso became the main recruitment center. One historian has called it "the primary labor market for organizing agricultural labor in the U.S. Southwest and the Midwest during the early twentieth century." Competition among recruiters there was heated, violent at times. Twelve Mexicans who crossed over the Rio Grande bridge from Ciudad Juárez in 1907 learned this firsthand: the *El Paso Times* reported that eleven recruiters jumped on them, yelling, grabbing, pulling them by their hair. This was the new reality of border recruiting, for it had become a desperate, raucous, unregulated, frenzied search for harvest hands that saw big winners at times, but also big losers. Gunter Peck's study found that only two Mexican-owned employment offices in the city lasted more than three years in the crucial 1905–20 period; the other seven operated an average of only 1.4 years each. There were twenty-six Anglo-American employment agencies operating at some time during those years in El Paso, but only two stayed open more than ten years, and nearly 60 percent of the others closed within a year of opening.

The cost to a cotton farmer was generally a dollar apiece for each worker delivered, a figure that meant large profits for recruiters: they sometimes marched as many as one hundred of their new cotton pickers through the streets at transfer points, from one railroad station to another. And many others found profits smuggling Mexicans across the Rio Grande; these were called *coyotes*.

Salt River cotton growers came to rely heavily upon Mexicans hired along the border, although when droughts threatened crops farther north in Texas and Oklahoma, the association saw a recruitment opening and targeted those areas with mass mailings. One year some 40,000 circular letters were sent out, advertising jobs for fall and winter, but "practically nothing" resulted—the association manager admitted that "a few white American families" came to Arizona, "but they almost invariably refused to pick cotton after they arrived . . ." Neither could the hiring gap be filled by Indians, now largely remaining on their reservations, he added. Failures such as these drove the association to rely even more heavily upon border recruiters. Largely as a result, the 1920 census revealed that more than half of Arizona's farm laborers were "foreign-born whites," that is, Mexicans.[22]

After several years during which *solos*, single men, were almost the only Mexican workers in U.S. harvest fields, families began to show up. Ruth Allen found many families among her Mexican interviewees but was surprised that at least a third of the women did not work in the fields, remaining behind in their tents or crude housing. And she encountered quite a few Mexican "casuals" as members of teams that were not necessarily immediate families: "They usually travel in large groups under the leadership of a captain who makes all business arrangements. The different parts of the group are usually but not always connected by family ties. Living conditions are unbelievably bad." Victor Clark in 1908 learned that sometimes entire villages migrated to the United States to work.

Children frequently followed their parents into the fields. Surveying Mexican immigration several years prior to the Arizona cotton boom, Clark noted that Oklahoma and Texas farmers were cultivating fields of up to eighty acres, more than their own families could handle, leading to the farmer hiring "two or three families of Mexicans that migrate from the southward at this season, camp in an outhouse or in their canvas-topped carts, and pick the fields clean, then move on northward to where the crop is just maturing . . . Children often pick as much as adults . . ."[23]

Called "a common sight throughout the Wheat Belt," hoboes such as these, riding a freight through New Rockford, North Dakota, in 1923, provided much of the West's harvest labor. (Photograph from USDA Bulletin No. 1211, May 23, 1924)

The Atchison, Topeka & Santa Fe, here seen with locomotive No. 5—the "Thomas Sherlock"—was one of the West's pioneer railroads. (Kansas State Historical Society, DaRT ID:170)

Intensive agriculture: On March 1, 1902, this California land was bare; in December, the owner stood proudly amid irrigated rows of walnut trees, dewberries, and strawberries. (California Historical Society, FN-28947/CHS2009.042.tif)

Oklahoma in midsummer: three threshing outfits in one field, straw shooting into enormous piles from machines separating wheat from chaff. (Courtesy of the Oklahoma Historical Society, No. 14333)

Shocking wheat on a large "bonanza farm" circa 1900 in the Red River Valley of the North. (Courtesy of the Minnesota Historical Society, Neg. 497-B)

Hoboes waiting to be hired for threshing—as in this 1923 scene, probably in Wichita, Kansas—were a frequent sight in Grain Belt towns. (USDA Bulletin No. 1211, May 23, 1924)

This ten-year-old Colorado boy was a "beeter," pulling up sugar beets and top-ping them with a machete. (Photograph by Lewis Hine; National Child Labor Committee Collection, Library of Congress)

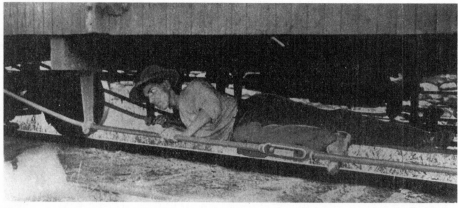

Hoboes frequently "rode the rods"—as in this 1909 photograph—as they "beat their way" around the West. (Used by permission of the State Historical Society of Missouri, Columbia)

This classic drawing of the blanket or "bindle" stiff appeared in the Industrial Workers of the World's *Industrial Worker* on April 23, 1910.

His belongings tied up in a bindle, the bindlestiff moved from job to job around the West. (Courtesy of the Bancroft Library, University of California, Berkeley)

Was this man, photographed in the early 1900s in California, a hobo, tramp, or bum? Going to a job—or avoiding work? (Courtesy of the Ticor/CHS Collection, University of Southern California, CHS-1428)

The stirrings of war in 1915 raised wheat prices, and newspapers in the Grain Belt sent out a plea for workers. From *The Survey*, July 17, 1915.

Indians from as far away as Alaska left their canoes in Tacoma's harbor, as in this photograph from 1889–90, and then worked in nearby hopyards. (Rutter photograph from the Washington State Historical Society, IndTrans 6.01.001)

Often hops picking was left to Indian women and children—as shown in this classic Asahel Curtis photograph from 1904 near Puyallup—while tribesmen hunted or worked elsewhere. (Washington State Historical Society, Neg. 441)

Sidehill harvesters with their teams of horses got a workout in the rolling Palouse hills of eastern Washington and Oregon. (Washington State Historical Society photograph, Anim-10)

Hops pickers at the Morrier Hop Ranch in Yakima in 1913. (Courtesy of the Yakima Valley Museum)

Workers in 1915 guided blocks of ice into chutes on top of the refrigerated cars—"reefers"—that would carry fruit for the Yakima Valley Fruit Growers Association. (Washington State Historical Society photograph, 1943.42.33144)

In large-scale orchards such as this one in the Yakima Valley, many ladders as well as numerous "apple knockers" were required for repeated pickings during the season. (Courtesy of the Yakima Valley Museum)

Raspberry pickers worked for the C. H. Lilly Co. in Washington State in 1920. (Washington State Historical Society, Asahel Curtis photograph 40658)

Japanese turned the Hood River Valley into one of Oregon's major fruit areas, known especially for its apples. (Washington State Historical Society, 2004.61.3)

When the Northern Rockies blew up in flames in August 1910, the new U.S. Forest Service hired firefighters from harvest fields, railroad and logging crews, and even from hobo "jungles." (Courtesy of the Museum of North Idaho)

Wagons loaded with cotton waited at the gin in Muskogee, Oklahoma, in 1906. (Robertson Studio, Muskogee, courtesy of the Oklahoma Historical Society, #19282.27)

Texas cotton pickers dragged their full bags to be weighed, then returned to their rows to continue picking. (Texas State Library and Archives, 1975/70-1049)

This elderly woman at Sacaton in 1908 was part of the Indian labor force that picked Arizona's cotton in its early years. (Will C. Barnes photograph, courtesy of the Arizona Historical Society/Tucson, #81, 022)

Indian children picking cotton at Sacaton, Arizona, in 1908 were in the federal government's "outing" system, aimed at introducing them to the American economic world. (Courtesy of the Arizona Historical Society/Tucson, #81, 021)

A Chinese crew harvesting almonds in California. (Courtesy of the California History Room, California State Library, Sacramento, California)

Children were frequently hired for gathering prune plums, as shown here in the Santa Clara Valley. (California Historical Society, FN-22169/CHS2009.044.tif)

Women packing grapes for a vineyard near Sacramento, circa 1910. (Courtesy of the California History Section, California State Library, Sacramento, California)

Prunes were sun-dried on trays at the F. H. Holmes Ranch near Sacramento in 1915. (Courtesy of the Sacramento Archives and Museum Collection Center)

Grape harvesters worked at Burbank's garden vineyards in California. (Courtesy of the California History Section, California State Library, Sacramento, California)

Richard "Blackie" Ford, sentenced to life imprisonment for inciting the 1913 Wheatland riot. (Courtesy of the California State Archives)

Sympathy for the I.W.W. largely vanished as World War I began. (From the Omaha *Bee*, May 2, 1918; reprinted in David G. Wagaman, "The Industrial Workers of the World in Nebraska, 1914–1920," *Nebraska History* 56, n. 3 [Fall 1975], 309)

Kansas Governor Lorenzo D. Lewelling issued the "Tramp Circular" in 1893, forbidding police from arresting men for having no means of support. (Kansas State Historical Society photograph, 11769)

Japanese women employed in a Folsom, California, packing house. (Courtesy of the Folsom Historical Society and Sacramento Archives and Museum Collection Center)

Mexicans, such as these men picking Santa Clara Valley oranges, were the dominant harvest labor force in California by 1920. (California Historical Society, FN-22165/CHS2009.043.tif)

The automobile's transformation of migrant labor is apparent in this Yakima hops camp in the 1920s; teepees indicate Indians were still participants. (Courtesy of the Yakima Valley Museum)

The new state of Arizona wrote into its first constitution in 1912 a rule in line with Progressive reforms then sweeping the nation: "No child under age of fourteen shall be employed in any gainful occupation during any part of the school year." Evidence gathered by Edwin Pendleton, however, indicates that for Mexican children in Arizona, this rule was largely ignored in cotton and truck garden work. "Before 1930, much of the child labor was Mexican, since school laws had rarely been enforced when Mexicans were involved," and truant officers yielded to the pressure of local cotton growers who needed their crops harvested. A 1927 report stated that as cotton picking began, Mexican children were coming down from Arizona mining camps to start working in the fields.[24]

These harvesting activities also touched family members who never left Mexico. Extended family connections—from cotton fields and railroad or mining camps in the United States back to farms and villages in Mexican states—can be glimpsed through records of money carried or mailed back home. Manuel Gamio's careful study determined that some $5 million was sent back yearly to Mexico in the 1919–27 period, with California and Texas providing the most remittances. To congressmen complaining of this loss of money for the United States, Gamio told of a response he had heard: "that the amount sent by immigrants to their relatives in Mexico is very small considering the benefit rendered by Mexican labor to American industry and agriculture . . ."

Higher wages lured Mexicans, but worsening conditions in their strife-torn nation also drove many others *al norte*. Revolutionary violence reached many Mexican areas—including some along the border—and forced enlistment into different rebel armies vied with executions and armed conflict to severely disrupt communal life. Suffering was widespread. Corn and bean production declined rapidly, inflation was rampant, and the Red Cross sent chilling news in early 1915: at Tampico all food was about exhausted, several thousands in Monterey were kept alive only through daily relief supplies, and in Jalapa some 2,500 stood in line for hours awaiting food distribution—but when supplies finally arrived they were insufficient. At one time an estimated 100,000 in Mexico City were reported to be suffering from hunger, and crowds invaded the Chamber of Deputies pleading for food. Conditions were worse in outlying areas.[25]

In this setting Arizona, far removed from the Mexican revolutionary struggles, became a refuge even more than was the case with Texas. Arizona had peace, it had adequate supplies of food, and it had employment—
but some locals complained that so many Mexicans were coming that
they were taking jobs from Americans. Investigations determined, however, that whites were not losing jobs to the incoming Mexicans. A 1920
Department of Labor study questioned employment offices in ten states
and found that unskilled jobs were going begging for workers; in twenty-
five cities "it was found that the number of Mexicans displacing white
men was negligible." Even labor unions were recruiting Mexicans in
some areas, and wages in cotton and sugar beet fields as well as railroad
work—as reported prior to the late-summer collapse of 1920—had
climbed 100 to 300 percent above prewar levels. Even in San Antonio,
where many unemployed Mexicans were destitute, there was no major
impact upon the labor market. Arguments against importing Mexicans
were unsubstantiated by facts, investigators stated; the Mexican influx
had no negative economic impact, and "Mexicans are not displacing
white laborers in any appreciable degree." The Labor Department study
also found that "white men are averse to accepting, and refuse to accept
(as they have the right to do), employment as unskilled or common laborers" except within town or city limits.[26]

These developments were appearing even before the crucial summer of
1914. In Europe during those months, as local conflicts erupted into
full-scale war, immigration from the Continent that had been topping one million annually for several years suddenly plummeted—from
southern Europe alone only 71,000 made it to America's shores in 1915,
down from 340,000 the year before. In 1914 there had been 1,058,391
immigrants from all of Europe; one year later in 1915 there were only
197,919, and by 1919 the total had fallen to 24,627.

Anguished shouts of desperation went up from American industry,
for war preparations demanded thousands more employees. Blacks
quickly learned of the high wages being offered in the North and packed
the trains heading to the industrial centers: one industrial leader estimated in mid-1917 that some 350,000 had fled the South. Canada—
drawn early into the war as a British Dominion—had much success

recruiting U.S. workmen into its fast-expanding industrial sector and also for its farms, ultimately luring some 40,000 Americans over the northern border for farm employment alone.[27]

But initially there was no need for more harvesters. As the 1914 American cotton crop neared picking stage, world markets were suddenly seized with fear. With the war expanding, the market collapsed. In September 1914 the governors of cotton states converged on Washington for a meeting with their congressmen aimed at "considering ways and means of protecting the cotton market during the period of demoralization" caused by the war. Sales fell off so sharply that "Buy a Bale" movements were launched in a futile effort to salvage some income; after the Montgomery Ward corporation offered to participate, the Commercial Club of Walters, Cotton County, Oklahoma, voted to "earnestly request Montgomery Ward to purchase a part of said 10,000 bales at Walters, Okla." The town's *Cotton County Democrat* vowed that "the wise farmer will plant very, very little cotton next year." And "night riders" rampaging near Ardmore in southern Oklahoma warned farmers to hold their cotton off the market until ten cents a pound was paid; it brought memories of a similar campaign in 1908 when gins were burned in several areas.[28]

But the tentacles of war kept reaching farther, pulling the United States toward participation, and markets began to rebound. Now southwestern cotton growers, watching their workers leave for military enlistments and high-paying industrial jobs, also had to worry about the impact of rumors on their recruitment efforts. Mexicans in the Southwest heard stories—false stories—that they would be forced to enter the American military, and passage of the U.S. Draft Law on May 18, 1917, ignited a frantic rush back to Mexico. Exact numbers in the exodus are impossible to ascertain, for many avoided crossing at official border guard points. In the first five days of June 1917 official statistics showed 5,451 Mexicans exiting southward and another 4,000 crossing in the next six days. Totals kept rising with each passing week. The Mexican consul at San Antonio then set off a new panic by telling Mexican workers that they all would be drafted into the U.S. Army—with the result that "they flew across the river like a flock of blackbirds," a Texas congressman complained. Farmers in Northwest Texas were so angry at their losses of hired hands that they formed a Farmers' and Laborers' Protective Association to fight the draft.[29]

Then nationwide criticisms of "slackers"—men who dodged military duty—added to the Mexicans' fears. New frenzies merged with
patriotism: in Alfalfa County, Oklahoma, the feeling against "slackers"
was so heated that a pacifist farmer who refused to market his grain to
aid the war effort saw a band of local patriots descend on his farm and
haul away his crop, to be sold to the government. The high school band
welcomed them into town, and placards on their wagons proclaimed
that "Hoarding Helps the Hellish Huns" and "We Are Doing This for
Uncle Sam."[30]

Anything that weakened the "war effort" was called a danger to the
nation, and efforts to stem the labor exodus could fit into that category.
The Mexican vice consul at Globe, Arizona, reported that mining companies there refused to give back passports to several hundred unemployed Mexicans, possibly blocking not only their exit but also their
chance for other employment. As cotton prices climbed higher and
higher, growers felt the taste of enormous profits—if they could only
produce the bales. Back in 1914 the argument had been whether they
should hold out for eight cents a pound, but on October 11, 1917, the
Temple (Oklahoma) *Tribune* ran a top-of-the-page headline that announced: "Cotton is Selling Today as High as 27c." Less than a month
later the same newspaper pleaded that "commercial organizations, county
councils of defense, schools—every organization and every citizen who
can possibly do so—must aid in the movement to relieve the labor
shortage." High prices for cotton collided with a shortage of pickers.
The situation was desperate.[31]

Wartime produced a crucial moment in the history of American harvest
labor, with ramifications that would affect the nation for years. The
U.S. Congress in its determination to rid the country of subversives
pushed through a border-protection bill in February 1917 that President Woodrow Wilson promptly vetoed; not to be denied in this test of
patriotism, Congress passed it over his veto. Illiterate aliens over sixteen years of age, aliens unable to pay an $8 head tax, and workers
outside the country who had already signed contracts with American
employers were barred from entry. Western railroads as well as growers
saw disaster in these rules, for few Mexicans could meet the entry re-

quirements. Industrial and agricultural spokesmen rushed to Washington and succeeded in inserting a provision permitting the commissioner general of immigration to set up new rules that would allow "otherwise inadmissible aliens" into the country—temporarily. By June 1917 the new waiver regulations were in force. At their expiration in 1921 some 80,000 Mexican laborers had been admitted into the United States, seven-eighths headed for agricultural jobs.

The new system required several actions by employers, however. Each had to first report how many men were needed, for what work, and at what wage; they also had to agree to follow existing housing and sanitation regulations and to report any employee who left early. If any workers "skipped" and were later caught, the employer had to pay their transport back to the port of entry. Initially the term of labor was to last only six months, but after growers complained it was extended to war's end. Violators would be deported—if they left agricultural labor, did not work for two weeks unless they were ill, or worked for an employer who had not been approved. Despite the complications, desperate growers eagerly signed up to participate.[32]

Paralleling these governmental actions, a campaign was launched to reassure Mexicans they would not be drafted. Texas governor James E. Ferguson signed a manifesto that Mexican citizens faced no military draft, and he urged newspapers and Mexican-American leaders to join the campaign. Notices were read in Catholic churches, and priests accompanied visiting Mexican officials to farms as well as to mines and railroad camps to explain the law: the workers had nothing to worry about. Signs in Spanish were posted. Three months of this advertising barrage calmed the situation.

Within Mexico, however, the exodus of workers northward to American war industries, railroads, and agriculture provoked a sharp reaction. The Carranza government criticized these losses at a time when suffering across Mexico was still extensive and the need was great for workers to further the recovery from revolutionary turmoil. In the northern state of Sonora, the governor tried to require each recruiter to post a $1,000 bond for every man hired for a job in Arizona; farther south, the Jalisco state government attempted to deny passports to anyone leaving for an American job. President Venustiano Carranza sought to enforce a "model contract" that would require Mexicans employed in the United States to receive medical care, a $2-per-day minimum wage, and other protections. As Lawrence Cardoso concluded, all these efforts to discourage recruitment came to naught—"the massive, growing outflow of laborers during the period is evidence of overall failure." Large numbers headed north without bothering to participate in Mexican or American legalities, while many Mexican officials cooperated with the labor recruiters and professional smugglers.[33]

Almost hidden from view then and now is the fact that many Mexicans as well as Mexican-Americans served with U.S. troops during the First World War. Spanish-language newspapers in border states presented information on how to join the military. That the war became a time of assimilation into American life would become apparent in succeeding years. Sarah Deutsch has charted how this played out in New Mexico, where some 10,000 Hispanics ultimately served with U.S. forces, making up 65 percent of the state's total. Most New Mexico villages provided men, a pattern followed in southern Colorado's Hispanic communities as well. Many could not speak English—in Taos and Mora counties in New Mexico, more than three-fourths of the men in the first draft call did not know enough English to be able to participate in drill. But community after community were drawn into a closer connection with the United States through the war. They no longer lived in a foreign country.[34]

Rather than continuing to suffer anxiety over the initial wartime challenges, farmers began to see some benefits. "Wheat will win the war!"—and it seemed that cotton would too. Commodity prices shot up; growers planted more cotton—Salt River Valley farmers went from 7,000 acres in 1916 to 180,000 acres by 1920; payments for long-staple went from 43 cents per pound in 1916 to 80 cents in 1919, which meant that the 1919 crop brought some $25,000,000 to Arizona growers. By then the Cotton Growers Association had legally imported some 7,000 workers specifically to pick cotton; many others arrived from outside the waiver system.

By assessing members $1.50 a bale for recruiting Mexicans, the association avoided competing for labor, and the supply of workers helped keep wages low. But producing an abundant crop with an adequate number of cotton pickers, while still pleading for 25,000 Mexicans for the coming 1918 cotton harvest, seemed contradictory to some observers. The *Arizona Labor Journal* blasted the employers' request, scolding that such a massive importation would "upset labor conditions in the State to such an extent that thousands of unskilled laborers would either be thrown out of work or would have to work at that rate of pay that would be paid these importees from Mexico."[35]

While cheered everywhere, the war's end on November 11, 1918, created problems on the southwestern cotton front. Not only was demand for the farmers' product reduced with the end of war production and the reopening of shipping lanes for Egyptian cotton, but tire companies discovered they did not need to rely so heavily upon the long-stem variety. In 1920 Arizona produced its largest cotton crop to date, but prices plummeted, dropping to 28 cents a pound in December 1920. Not surprisingly, the next year fewer acres were planted along the Salt River.[36]

Across the nation the sudden economic slump combined with a postwar psychological letdown to produce a resurgence of isolationism. Overnight, foreigners became undesirable, even toxic. Congress had been experimenting with limits on immigration from 1917 on, and interest was growing for country-by-country quotas. In 1924 these concepts were incorporated into the National Origins Act, and although the Western Hemisphere was not included in the restrictions, Mexicans were aliens and found themselves threatened by the national anti-immigrant mood.

In the Southwest, rising nativism combined with the declining demand for cotton to produce a crisis. Growers reduced their plantings and trimmed costs, but as always, there was a lag in the time it took for this news to reach residents of Mexican villages. Short months earlier they had heard the opposite—that jobs awaited north of the border. And so despite the changed economic situation, the migration continued unabated, only the migrants were heading northward into unemployment. Soon some 7,000 to 8,000 Mexicans were stranded in Maricopa County, where their desperation led Phoenix labor unions to feed them one meal a day for some two months. With anger at growers rising, the city manager finally led several hundred Mexican families to the Cotton Growers Association headquarters; the association transported a few hundred of them back to the border in trucks. This pattern was repeated in later months, as Mexican workers kept arriving only to find there were no jobs. The *Arizona Labor Journal* noted that when hired they had been promised return travel to Mexico, but now many were instead being charged with vagrancy and jailed. "We pause to inquire," the newspaper asked, "WHO IS GUILTY?"

Other southwestern cities were also caught in this collision: a continued surge of Mexican workers, and an agricultural depression in which few cotton pickers and other workers were needed. In Fort Worth, welfare officials put unemployment at 90 percent of its 12,000 resident Mexicans, while in Denver several thousand were stranded and starving through the 1920–21 winter. Finally the Mexican government provided $1 million to help transport Mexicans home, $17,000 of which was sent to Phoenix for the 10,000 reported out of work there.[37]

Arizona labor unions launched new efforts to block growers and other employers from importing workers. In 1914 they had led a successful campaign to enact a law that forbade mining companies to hire anyone who could not "speak the English language" and also barred any firm from having more than 20 percent of its crew as aliens. The U.S. Supreme Court, however, declared that law unconstitutional. During the relief crisis of 1920–21, the unions kept investigating and returned to their charge that cotton growers kept wages low by bringing in large numbers of Mexicans. Responding to a request for information from the American Federation of Labor, the Arizona federation's president sent a telegram with his group's analysis: "There would be no shortage of labor in the cotton industry of the Salt River Valley if cotton companies would pay living American wages. Imported Mexicans are in a virtual stage of peonage on big cotton ranches."

The California magazine *Sunset* looked at what happened in the economic collapse of July 1921 and called cotton "the roulette-and-faro crop of the Southwest," which had encouraged the Salt River Valley to economic heights "and then kicked it over the edge, on the steep side." The price rise since 1916 had created the "great cotton jab of the Southwest," writer Walter V. Woehlke charged, citing cases where local people had invested all their funds but suddenly became "dead, flat, completely and comprehensively broke."

A banker told Woehlke that the cotton gamblers created farms of up to 2,000 acres in the valley with the required labor: "Cotton brought Hindus, negroes and Mexicans by the thousand; it brought the illiterate Southern 'poor whites' with their large families of children kept out of school and worked from dawn to dark picking cotton." The banker longed instead for a Maricopa County in the future with "forty-acre farms tilled by the owners."[38]

Mexicans in this period who crossed the border *al norte* often experienced contradictory treatments—they were encouraged to come north to help harvest the crops, and they were welcomed heartily by employers, but when they ventured into town, they often met different forms of racism, some muted, some blatant. It was a perennial story for western harvest workers of whatever race or ethnicity, and as with hoboes and many other "floaters," the Mexicans often confronted this treatment with song. Justiniano Soto and Andrés O. García composed their *Corrido de pizcar algodón* ("Ballad of Cotton Picking") while at work, describing what happened when they traveled north to pick cotton:

We arrived at Abilene,
"Friends, here we eat supper,"
But they refused to serve us
Because we were Mexicans.

The *pizcadores* fought back in more forceful ways as well. Actions by Mexican workers during the postwar Arizona crisis contradicted prevailing views that they were docile, easily bossed. During the 1920 Maricopa County disruptions some 4,000 Mexicans charged that the contracts requiring decent treatment were being broken. Most of all they demanded a living wage. Their leaders were immediately arrested and jailed, and six of the ringleaders were taken by company agents and put on a train for Nogales. Growers used this protest as an excuse to avoid transporting the rest back to the border, as required under the government's waiver. Their actions did not stifle the spirit of protest, however, for a year later fourteen labor unions were formed among Maricopa County cotton pickers, who then won a wage increase to 4 cents a pound, up from the previous 2.5 cents. It represented a major victory for these unions, which had grown to 300 to 400 members each. They were aided by an announcement by Mexican officials that all the Mexican workers would be pulled away from Arizona fields and brought back home unless there was some improvement.[39]

Mexican workers laboring in other districts north of the border had, in fact, often demonstrated their willingness to fight back against unjust treatment. Many of their efforts were unreported, however, or dismissed as simply illegal behavior. Sarah Deutsch has chronicled the 1890 rides of the *Gorras Blancas*—"white caps"—in San Miguel County, New Mexico, who retaliated against the railroads' control over the political system, courts, and land, by destroying railroad ties and other equipment under their announced goal: "Our purpose is to protect the rights of the people in general and especially those of the helpless classes." There were other reports that Mexican field workers quit in a body if one member was mistreated, and individuals often protested simply by walking off the job, away from a foreman who was too harsh. Sharecroppers in disputes with landowners sometimes left even when they were under contract.

The 1920 Arizona tumult and the subsequent 1921 strike were the largest, but not the only, protest by Mexican farm laborers before the changed environment of the 1930s, when migrant worker strike activity would shift mainly to California. Harvest workers' protests dot the records of southwestern agriculture, and Mexican miners sometimes joined other ethnic groups on strike. By then numerous *mutualista* groups had been formed by Mexicans for self-help as well as protection, such as Tucson's Alianza Hispano-Americana that eventually linked 275 chapters across the region. Other groups were formed after the war, many bringing together large numbers of Mexicans and Mexican-Americans who had served in the U.S. Army. And as historian David Gutiérrez emphasizes, the veterans often excluded noncitizens, emphasizing assimilation into American life and championing their rights as U.S. citizens.

Like many of the European immigrants—at least one third of whom permanently returned home in the 1880–1930 era—many Mexicans traveled home again, carrying both money and new ideas. They caused changes in their homeland, and their stories stimulated further chain migration, the tradition whereby a pioneer traveler's stories of wealth in the United States drew others from his village to emigrate. As with European immigrants, chain migration and return migration became basic parts of the Mexican story.

And like many of the Europeans, Mexicans were directed to employment in some of the worst, most dangerous jobs in their new home. Southern Europeans dominated the drudgery and dangerous labor in steel mills, petroleum refineries, and coal mines in the eastern states. Paralleling these experiences, Mexicans found employers beckoning them to field jobs under a blazing southwestern sun as well as labor in railroad construction and mining. Frequently, they too often quit distasteful work and simply moved on.[40]

Congressmen fretting over the presence of so many aliens, so many non-English speakers on American soil, were soon alerted to the fact that multitudes of Mexicans were crossing the Rio Grande. The Republican takeover of Congress in the 1918 election placed one of its leading nativists as chairman of the House Committee on Immigration and Naturalization. This was Representative Albert Johnson, a Republican from Washington State who had first been elected in 1912. His victory at the polls came from leading a fight against the striking Industrial Workers of the World in his logging community, and for his efforts favoring U.S. citizens in local hiring. When his congressional committee opened its session on January 26, 1920—months before the economic downturn—Johnson was still working on his immigration quota bill, which he would submit the following summer.

The focus of the January hearing was "Temporary Admission of Illiterate Mexican Laborers." Most of the debate was over Joint Resolution 271, introduced by Representative Claude B. Hudspeth of Texas: "A resolution suspending the operation of certain provisions of the immigration act relating to alien contract laborers and illiterate aliens, which is said to be necessary on account of the shortage of labor in Texas." Rather than ending the wartime rule—urged by Representative Johnson—this bill would do the opposite: it would continue the waiver system allowing Mexicans into the Southwest to work. It sought, in effect, an open door.[41]

The hearing brought out issues festering since the European war began—in reality, issues bedeviling growers ever since King Cotton entered the New West, since irrigation ushered intensive farming into the "Great American Desert." Over and over witnesses stressed that without Mexican labor, Arizona, Texas, and the rest of the Southwest faced disaster. It would be "ruin and bankruptcy of these large investments and these cotton plantations," a Salt River Valley Cotton Company spokesman warned, and this feeling was echoed by a representative of Texas's Rural Land Owners Association: "We are prepared to say to you that this year's cotton crop will not be produced unless we can secure from 20,000 to 25,000 laborers from Mexico."

Representative Carlos Bee of Texas related his trips through southwestern Texas, where half of the "great cotton crop" would be "rotting in the field unless we can get Mexican labor to pick it." W. H. Knox of the Arizona Cotton Growers Association vividly depicted to eastern and midwestern congressmen the predicament of growers in a desert climate: "We depend absolutely upon the Mexican as our cotton picker. We do not have work the year around for him. We are in an isolated condition. Ours is a little green spot surrounded by hundreds of miles of desert in every direction."

Some congressmen wanted to know why whites and African-Americans were not picking the cotton. The Rural Land Owners spokesman replied that, regarding whites, "in the first place, there are not enough of them. They are otherwise employed. In the second place, it is mighty hot down there in July and August, and it is not suited to white men to work in the sun." Whites have not done such work, a South Texas Cotton Growers Association representative added, and "they will not do it . . ."

African-Americans, the committee was told, were simply unavailable. Representative Hudspeth agreed: "It is a fact that the Negro has quit the farms and gone to the cities." The wage question came under scrutiny, for several speakers referred to whites refusing employment under the existing pay scale. Attempts to lure workers from other regions had failed, the director of the U.S. Employment Service admitted: "They did not pay wages sufficient to induce people to go there, other than Mexicans, from other localities, nor was the work desirable enough for the other class of people to perform." A project to import some 1,000 whites from Texas had resulted in an enormous failure for Arizona cotton growers, the committee was told; after having their way paid to Phoenix, many refused to work, and some beat their way on to California.

Recruitment stories drew criticism from some congressmen. The 1885 Foran Act had made it unlawful "to assist or encourage the importation or migration of aliens . . . under contract or agreement . . . to perform labor or service of any kind in the United States," except for skilled workers in certain new industries, performers, and domestic servants. The act apparently had never been widely enforced in the Southwest.[42]

M. W. Clarkson of Corpus Christi described his experiences. He told the committee that in 1919 not enough workers showed up, and for the first time he had to travel to find them. He went to Laredo with an order for 100 workers that he took to a government agent. He got only 13. Then he turned to a private agent:

> Mr. Clarkson: He was a Mexican, and I could not say it [his name] if I heard you say it. He brought me 139 Mexicans and delivered to Robstown for $4 apiece and the railroad fare.
> The Chairman: What was the railroad fare?
> Mr. Clarkson: I think it is—
> Mr. Miller (interposing): About 150 miles at 2 cents a mile.
> Mr. Clarkson: It was something like $5 or $6 altogether per man.
> The Chairman: Now, this Mexican agent, whose name you can not remember and could not pronounce, where did you find him?
> Mr. Clarkson: In Laredo.
> The Chairman: Did he have an office there?
> Mr. Clarkson: I found him on the plaza . . . I told this man that I wanted 200 and I got 135.
> The Chairman: Did you pay him any money?
> Mr. Clarkson: Not until I got the Mexicans.
> The Chairman: How much?
> Mr. Clarkson: Four dollars a head.

The Chairman: Did you realize that that was against the law?

Mr. Clarkson: No.

The Chairman: Did you realize that it was against the law to get your labor in surreptitiously?

Mr. Clarkson: I never knew there was such a law in effect.[43]

Why continue with Mexicans? several congressmen asked. Why not try Chinamen? Texas Representative Joseph Mansfield and Chairman Johnson had a go-around on whether allowing Texans to import Mexicans would mean that other states could then import Chinese. This led John H. Davis of Laredo to charge that it was a "dangerous, Bolshevik idea" to bring in "the oriental peonage, and a largely diseased European population . . ."

An argument that was becoming increasingly popular was put forward to the committee: there was no long-term worry, because Mexicans went back to Mexico when the job was completed. Eighty percent would return, asserted Representative John Nance Garner (later vice president) of Texas. J. B. Vandenberger of Victoria, Texas, from the Texas Rural Land Association, explained how the Mexicans would "drift across the river" to begin cotton picking around June 1 near the Rio Grande and work their way north. "They would come across the border in ox carts, or walk across, thousands of them—and all of them, practically speaking, without any thing except what they had gathered nearer the Rio Grande. They would stay with us during the cotton-picking time, and then go back." This was echoed by Representative Bee, who recalled seeing Mexicans with their "carts and dogs, driving jacks, with their wives and children," helping with the harvest, "and then, when the fall of the year comes and the work is completed, returning again by the hundreds and going back into Mexico." When it was proposed to require Mexicans to return home within one year of American entry, Representative Mansfield also contended that it was unnecessary— "My observation is that when a Mexican gets a little money he wants to go back to Mexico to spend it."

A final argument, put forward by southwestern congressmen and growers' organizations, was that Mexicans were especially adapted for field work. Some emphasized that Mexicans' bodies were different, that they were better suited for labor among the cotton rows—work that whites somehow did not do and that blacks had abandoned. According to Representative Bee, "the Mexican is specially fitted for the burdensome task of bending his back to picking the cotton and the burdensome task of grubbing the fields." And Representative Hudspeth of Texas—sponsor of the resolution to bring in "alien contract laborers and illiterate aliens" to save the 1920 cotton crop—stated that he believed "they are an inferior race, Mr. Vaile; these Mexicans are an inferior race of people."

9

"BEETERS"

Asa's worked since he could lift a beet," a mother in Colorado told an investigator.

Young Asa was not alone. The U.S. Labor Department study in 1920 found hundreds of children, many very young, working with their parents in the sugar beet fields—on their knees thinning the plants in early summer, weeding through the hot and dry months, pulling the beets from the ground in fall, and topping them as winter neared. Sometimes performed by children as young as six, topping could be dangerous. A hook in the knife was used to pick the beet up. Once unhooked, the beet was either held away from the worker's body or laid "across his right knee as a 'chopping block.' In either case, with the knife in his right hand, he cuts off the top with one or more strokes."

Children worked on farms everywhere, but as Asa and the children topping beets were learning, the world of sugar beets was different. They were caught up in a new venture, agricultural pioneers as families took to the fields and "sugar factories" sprouted across the western Great Plains and Great Basin. At first glance it was not totally different from activities elsewhere across the West—wagonloads of families arriving for summer's early field tasks; trains disgorging Mexican workers tugging at their wide-brimmed sombreros; autumn roads clogged with wagons full of harvest bounty. These recollected other times with other western crops, in other western towns.

There was more, such as the excitement over a new sugar factory. The hoopla could match anything done to celebrate the opening of a new cotton gin or a railroad's inaugural trip. Grand Island, Nebraska, erupted with a grand jubilee on its "Sugar Night" to rejoice over the signing of papers for its first sugar factory. Bonfires brightened the city square while speechmakers competed with fireworks. Nebraska's governor sought to draw inspiration from on high: "It seems the Creator has said in nature's words: In Nebraska thou shalt raise sugar beets and manufacture sugar therefrom."

However, sugar beets were different. No other western crop drew so heavily or demanded so much of child laborers. Among the armies of cotton "choppers" and pickers were many children, as was true in the Northwest's berry patches and hopyards. But reliance upon children in sugar beets exceeded those other western examples. Left out of the publicists' glowing accounts were scenes of schoolrooms almost empty because so many of the pupils were "beeters." They also overlooked the impact of beet labor on young bodies: a six-year-old said her back was getting crooked from work "in the beets," and a father admitted that his children would "scream and cry" from fatigue after days in the beet fields. The boosters also ignored the scenes of families working into chilly autumn nights; fathers, mothers, and youngsters pushing along the rows by lantern light as they dislodged beets and tossed them into piles. Whether the beet workers were of European immigrant stock, Japanese, or Mexican *betabeleros*, the scenes were the same.[1]

At base, what made beets different as a crop was the fact that it had barely emerged from scattered beginnings across the West before it fell quickly under corporate control. While still within its pioneer period, the sugar beet came under top-to-bottom domination by the Sugar Trust, a control that has been called unique, unmatched by anything else in the region's varied agriculture. And this uniqueness was combined with newness, for unlike wheat, apples, cotton, or hops, when sugar beets were introduced, they sprang upon a population unprepared. The farm families, the townfolk, the store clerks knew nothing of sugar beets, their planting, or their harvesting. For with beets there had been no years of gestation in which folk customs could emerge from the crop's yearly cycle, no accumulation of knowledge and experience that could be passed on, father to son—no threshing dinners, no husking bees.

As with cotton, the twin pillars supporting sugar beet expansion in the West were railroads and irrigation. Beets were not native to the region or the hemisphere; in centuries long past wild sugar beets, growing

along the Mediterranean's shores, were sporadically adapted to agricultural production in Europe. Their development came too slowly for the
New World: it was cane sugar that sweetened the colonists' foods, as
early as 1791, originating mainly in Louisiana and the Caribbean islands.
But eventually European successes and American test plots of beets in
the latter half of the nineteenth century yielded strains that could
be grown in northern and western states. A small beet sugar factory
began production in 1869 in Alvarado, California, to launch the nation
into the beet world, and in 1888 Watsonville, California, started a larger
operation.

That same year the U.S. Department of Agriculture began offering
free seed, in a four-year test project to stimulate the states to grow sugar
beets. But even then a further catalyst was needed; it was provided
when the 1890 McKinley Tariff paid a cash bounty to beet growers, a
bounty quickly enlarged with payments from several states. In 1898 the
Dingley Tariff stimulated domestic production anew by levying a duty
of 78.67 percent on the market value of imported sugar. With this encouragement, beets forged ahead of cane and became the main source
of sugar in Americans' diets by 1906.[2]

In the West the arrival of railroads was crucial for the rise of beets,
perhaps as crucial as government action, for bulky objects had to be
hauled to the sugar mills: not only huge piles of heavy beets but also
enormous loads of lime rock, coke, and coal. Wagons could not carry
them for many miles, but spur rail lines could. After a sugar factory was
built in Grand Junction, Colorado, the local newspaper pointed to the
Denver & Rio Grande Railway's role: "Grand Junction will hardly be
able to repay the Rio Grande for its part in her present prosperity . . . Its
influence on the trade and prosperity of the place has been greater than
that of any other cause thus far."

Recognizing the dangers of being isolated from a rail line, the southeastern Colorado community of Rocky Ford—eventually a center for
both sugar beets and cantaloupes—actually packed up and moved itself three miles to be located squarely on the line of the Atchison, Topeka & Santa Fe, which had unfortunately missed the town. Indeed, as
sugar beets began to sprout in Great Plains soil, the new sugar factories
became rail hubs: the trend was especially visible in northern Colorado,
where the Great Western Sugar Company built its own spur lines,

linked to the Union Pacific, the Colorado & Southern, the North Western, the Burlington, and eventually the Milwaukee Road. The *Greeley Tribune* commented in 1902 that "as a direct result of the railroad" some 5,000 more acres of sugar beet contracts had been added in its district. And when a sugar factory opened at Lehi, Utah Territory, in 1891, it was eventually served by two lines, each running conveniently among the factory's buildings: the Rio Grande Western on one side and the Oregon Short Line Railroad on the other. In Utah as elsewhere across the West, railroads were crucial.[3]

Irrigation canals proved as necessary as rail lines in this semiarid region. Lehi produced the West's first sugar grown in irrigated fields, but it was not alone for long. A canal-building boom in other states provided the moisture so beet farmers could "laugh at the cloudless skies," as the Idaho state engineer predicted in 1900. Indeed, after a 200,000-acre irrigation project of Idaho's Twin Falls Land and Water Company threw open its gates in 1905, sugar beets rose to importance in the state's agricultural expansion.

By then, Nebraska had already gone from having 214 farmers on 11,744 irrigated acres in 1889, to 1,932 farmers with 148,538 irrigated acres in 1899. In 1925 a Nebraska geographer examining sugar beets could report that "the development of irrigation has made more than 400,000 acres of land available for cultivation," mainly in western Nebraska. Kansas's sugar beet birthing was linked to the arrival of a German immigrant possessing both European beet seeds and beet-raising experience, and the initial 4.7 acres planted at Medicine Lodge in 1890 produced more than 10,000 pounds of sugar. The state soon raised its bounty to one dollar per ton of beets grown in Kansas for sugar manufacture, payable to the grower instead of the manufacturer, as done previously.

State competition for irrigation leadership was fierce at times. Colorado's irrigation spurt raised it to first place in the West by 1899, when it had 1,611,271 acres irrigated, up 81 percent in a decade. Its success angered neighbor Kansas, which protested in a 1906 case before the U.S. Supreme Court that Colorado had drained off so much of the Arkansas River that only a trickle was left to flow into Kansas. The loss to Kansas's citizens had been "incalculable," the state pleaded; "the irrigation ditches are left dry and the lands uncultivated . . ." The Court disagreed. Finding only minor hurt to western Kansas, it noted that the Arkansas's waters had brought "reclamation of large areas in Colorado, transforming thousands of acres into fertile fields and rendering possible their occupation and cultivation when otherwise they would have continued barren and unoccupied . . ."[4]

With railroads, irrigation, and a protective tariff in place, reports of the sweet vapors billowing from the West's flourishing sugar factories soon reached eastern financial centers. Ignoring westerners' opposition to big business—such as the *Grand Island Daily Independent*'s vow that the city "will help knock the sugar trust out"—Henry Havemeyer soon ordered his American Sugar Refining Company westward, buying half interest of the Utah Sugar Company in 1902 and gaining dominance in northern Colorado by 1905 through his Great Western Sugar Company. The trust's control of beet sugar reached 70 percent of U.S. production by 1907—100 percent in Utah-Idaho and northern Colorado, 42 percent in southern Colorado, and 81 percent in California.[5]

Beets meant stoop labor. Growing sugar beets was also more intensive than what most farmers were used to. One veteran of the wheat fields testified before Congress in 1911 that "the farmers were accustomed to scratch the ground up a little bit and put in wheat and go back to town in the back of the saloon and play cards . . . they simply could not raise sugar beets in this fashion." As the beet plants began to emerge each spring, three separate hand operations lay ahead: blocking and thinning, usually done in May and June; hoeing and weeding, in July; and pulling and topping the plants, from late September into November and occasionally December.

Seeds were planted in early spring by a drill in a continuous row, emerging in often ragtag clusters. Each plant eventually developed four leaves. In the early period before the Sugar Trust brought a sharp expansion of acreage, local farm boys were often adequate to meet the labor needs; older ones blocked the beets into compact bunches while "the younger boys crawled behind on their hands and knees, thinning each block to a single good plant with a short-handled hoe." Later passes were made with a cultivator as well as by workers wielding long-handled hoes to chop out the ever-recurring weeds. And as the beet industry came to dominate in different districts, outside groups arrived, and other labor arrangements appeared.

The harvest got under way in fall, when testing in a field showed that at least 12 percent sugar content in the plants was reached. In the 1920s a "beet plow" or "lifter" passed down the rows to loosen the roots (earlier this lifting had been done with a hand fork); then the workers came and pulled out beets and tossed them onto a pile. Later each plant was topped with a machete-like knife. In addition to being a dangerous operation, it was also exacting, as a visitor from the Lehi sugar factory warned Nebraska sugar beet growers in 1896: "You cannot afford to let your beets go to the factory poorly topped under any consideration." And the spokesman from Utah admitted to the Nebraskans that nothing brought "more real distress" to the factory operators than to be forced "to refuse the entire crop of some poor hard working beet grower" because he delivered poorly topped, diseased, or frozen beets, or beets weighing over his factory's limit of 3½ pounds each.[6]

The government warned sugar beet farmers at the outset of the boom that having an adequate labor supply was absolutely crucial. "The raising of sugar beets requires considerably more labor than any other farm product," the Department of Agriculture stated in 1898, "and it is labor of such a kind and extent that no farmer doing considerable business could hope to perform more than a small portion of it." Three years later the USDA cautioned again that the labor question "is a serious one." A scarcity of workers would not only cause delays but could also cut yields by forcing growers to skip some of the operations.

How much labor was required—to block, thin, pull, and top? The Department of Agriculture asserted that the ratio in the beet fields was one laborer to ten acres; it noted that in one specific district with 70,000 acres cultivated, some 7,000 workers were needed—but only 2,000 were on hand. The number of workers available put limits on acreage, the USDA emphasized, for "about six times more man labor is required to raise an acre of sugar beets than an acre of corn and twelve times more than is required to raise an acre of hay." Mechanical advancements were being developed by the 1920s, and eventually mechanical planters, cultivators, and even harvesters and loaders would appear— but they were not available in the early years of sugar beets in the West.[7]

Labor requirements were only one of several burdens pressing on the farmer's shoulders, however. Beet marketing was not like that of other crops. Very soon farmers began making contracts ahead of the season with the factory, for a guaranteed price. As historian William John May explains regarding the Great Western's operations:

> There was no market for this crop other than to the sugar com-
> panies; its bulk made a long haul unprofitable; therefore, the
> production and processing of the beet was a local monopoly in a
> very real sense . . . By accident or design, the processing of sugar
> in the North and South Platte River valleys developed under the
> control of a single corporation. This interfered with the opera-
> tion of the forces of free competition that existed in other areas
> of Colorado.

What all this signified, according to Mark Fiege, was a modification of the West's family farm dream. Irrigated farming "almost invariably in-volved railroads, factories, and heavy construction"; it was "a conver-gence of the family farm ideal and industrialization." Nowhere was this more evident than with raising sugar beets.[8]

But in most areas family farms were already established, and it was to local farm families and neighbors that the early promoters of sugar beets appealed. In Utah most farmers were members of the Church of Jesus Christ of Latter-Day Saints—the Mormons—whose leaders en-couraged sugar beet development and provided early financial backing for the Lehi sugar factory. But Utah was not Kansas, Nebraska, or Colo-rado; as Leonard Arrington explains, "Utah deviated somewhat" from the labor conditions in other sugar beet areas, because "Utah's high birth rate insured an ample supply of boys whose labor in a beet field was approximately equal to that of an adult."

As in the Cotton West, various forms of tenantry and sharecropping developed early. Landowners who contracted some of the hand work on their fields came to dominate raising beets in Utah and Idaho, while tenant systems were used more widely in Colorado and California; other areas were mixed. Under contracting, a worker took on a number of acres and performed all operations, from putting in seed to pulling out and topping the beets. The cash rental system usually meant that the landlord paid real estate taxes and did building and fence maintenance, while the rent-paying tenant provided equipment and paid operating expenses but kept all proceeds from sale of the beets. With share systems, one-fourth of the proceeds usually went to the owner; the tenant provided work stock and equipment, paid operating expenses, and kept three-fourths from the sale of the crop.[9]

During early seasons, when farmers grew beets on their own small plots, landowners and their sons with occasional hired hands could generally handle the crop, not just in Utah (where the Lehi factory kept urging farmers to plant larger fields) but also in Nebraska, where irrigated farms averaged only 77 acres each by 1900. Some farmers had grown sorghum cane for sugar, but sugar beets were different—in the Grand Island operation less than half the acreage was harvested that first year "largely because a majority of the growers knew nothing whatever of the business of raising beets," the Nebraska State Board of Agriculture was informed. A Utah farmer delivered his beets to the Lehi factory and waited outside for the rest of the day, until the manager asked him why he was standing around. "For my sugar," he replied—and was informed that a sugar factory was not like a flour mill, where the farmer could receive the output of his own wheat. Finally a bag of sugar was found for him, and he was sent on his way, satisfied at last.[10]

But as the new century began, those days of small fields handled by farm boys were coming to an end. Indeed, the Great Western's opening year at Loveland, Colorado, in 1901 turned out to be a near disaster— local workers did not want to do stoop labor. It was nothing they were familiar with. Five years later, in 1906, the USDA was already warning that in many areas outside help was now required. "Just how this labor is to be secured," kept available throughout the season, and made a permanent factor, are problems "upon the correct solution of which the future of the beet-sugar industry depends to a very great extent."

Major sugar beet districts were often adjacent to Great Plains wheat fields, and not surprisingly it was to hoboes and other unattached workers that farmers first turned when looking for outside help. They called for "nomadic whites." For a decade after 1900 the Great Western recruited much "gang labor," known as "American labor," meaning American-born transients and Americanized Europeans. In 1909 the Immigration Commission found that "miscellaneous white" workers in the three main Colorado beet areas totaled 3,082 out of 15,192 workers. Growers soon learned not to depend on this source, however. Wheat-field hoboes generally wanted short-term jobs and were less interested in staying in one place for the entire cycle, from thinning through topping, while living in a shack. Later one farmer bluntly told Paul Taylor, "The whites who are available aren't any good." The Immigration Commission put it more delicately, admitting that "'American' laborers will not generally submit" to the standard of living accepted in the West by immigrant migratory workers.

Growers searched for other labor sources. As Dena Markoff Sabin found in her study of the National Sugar Manufacturing Company in Colorado: "Local children were joined by squads of boys from Pueblo's Humane Society. Tom Tynan, warden of the state penitentiary at Canon City, had a 400-acre convict farm west of town. The 200 inmates there frequently raised beets. On occasion, even the Boy Scouts helped with the crop."[11]

Indian reservations were also picked for early recruitment, and the situation in the Indian schools proved especially conducive for hiring. Soon hundreds of boys were being sent to work in sugar beets, just as they were working in Arizona cotton. (This practice contradicted the Indian Bureau's emphasis on placing male students in industrial jobs, such as in railroad shops, to connect "with the real work of the world.") Once growers learned of their availability, they hired large numbers in Colorado, Kansas, Utah, and other areas where sugar beets were grown. It was another application of the "outing" system, developed to assimilate Native Americans into the culture of the predominant society, that "evolved into a method of supplying cheap labor to white employers." The use of students as field labor made the system controversial almost from the start.[12]

An early attempt in 1891 to hire some 200 pupils from the Ute Indian School, to help with Grand Junction's first sugar beet crop, proved disastrous when the boys refused to labor in the fields; white workers from Utah had to be brought in. Reservation agents as well as Indian School leaders applied pressure, however, and later attempts had some success.

Navajos were also recruited. In 1900 some 200 went to eastern Colorado to work on American Beet Sugar Company farms; in 1902 some 2,000 Navajos and Zuñis from the reservations in New Mexico were hired for Rocky Ford's field work. Navajos continued on in Colorado sugar beets, and after 1910 more Navajo boys were recruited directly from schools—from 400 to 500 in 1910 (at 15 cents an hour), with others going into Kansas and New Mexico beet fields by 1913.

Other recruiting methods were tried on reservations, at New Mexico pueblos, and at Indian schools such as the Albuquerque Indian School. Twenty-year leases arranged by sugar companies to grow crops on the Fort Belknap, Uintah, and Wind River reservations included employer pledges to hire Indian labor. At one time the Garden City, Kansas, beet operation employed 220 Indian boys recruited by the government.[13]

Their record was generally good. When Victor Clark investigated Mexican labor for the U.S. Labor Department in 1908, he found that Indians working in the beet fields were "considered cheaper and more reliable, if not otherwise better labor." Clark quoted one employer who contended that "Indian boys from 14 to 20 years old, such as we have had here, will do as much as any laborers, Mexican, Russian, or Japanese."

Controversies built, however, when tribal spokesmen as well as outside observers objected to the use of Indian schools as hiring centers for farmworkers. In 1928 the private Institute for Government Research issued *The Problem of Indian Administration*—known as the Meriam Report after Lewis Meriam, its principal author—which lambasted the "outing" system. It admitted that in the East the system had had some successes, but in the West there were clear problems, and it cited specific examples to back up its charges:

> Reports for the summer of 1926 from three schools among the Navajos indicate that twenty-nine boys from one school returned after sixty-three days in the beet fields with average net earnings of $5.62, or less than nine cents a day, while their average gross earnings were less than fifty dollars each or less than eighty cents a day. Only one boy in this group had net earnings at the end of the period of more than twenty-five dollars and only two more had more than ten dollars, while the gross earnings of only five were more than fifty dollars.

Investigations at another school showed earnings of less than twelve
cents a day after deductions.

Not only did the work not pay, but it damaged the boys' health. It
was tedious work, for thinning beets was done "in a stooping position or
on hands and knees," and living conditions were poor. Food was provided in one case at less than 35 cents a day. The Meriam Report also
challenged arguments of earlier reformers who touted the "outing" system as having "great educational value to the boys." As a result of the
report and other reform drives, the use of boys from the Indian schools
was removed as an option for the growers of sugar beets.[14]

Japanese began moving away from coastal areas to follow railroad construction jobs inland, and they soon were showing up in agricultural
work as well. The Great Western hired some 300 Japanese for its Nebraska operations in 1904, and soon many more were taking jobs in the
rapidly expanding beet acres in Colorado. There were 3,000 laboring in
northeastern Colorado by 1909; Japanese by then formed one-sixth of
the state's beet labor force. During the same period, investors in sugar
beets in lightly settled southeastern Idaho realized they had everything
they needed but workers, and so beginning in 1903 the Utah and Idaho
Sugar Company brought in Japanese, starting with 300 the first year,
adding more as new factories opened. These workers were soon joined
by wives and children, and by 1920 Idaho had more than 1,500 Japanese residents.[15]

Years later one of the early Japanese sugar beet workers remembered
the difficulties—physical and mental—of laboring in Idaho's beet fields:

> Nothing [we had] heard in Japan prepared [us] for the Spartan
> life that awaited [us]. Sugar-beet thinning was the kind of work
> to break not only backs, but spirits, too. The rows were a full
> mile long, and the beets were thinned by stooping with a short
> handled hoe. By laboring at piece work for twelve hours a man
> earned $1.50 to $2 a day . . . At night [we] slept exhausted in a
> farmer's bunkhouse . . . [We] became badly malnourished on a
> diet of . . . flour doughball boiled in water . . . [and later] rice,
> shoyu, and a few other staples shipped in from . . . Seattle.

Nevertheless, as Utah beet acreages began expanding beyond what farm boys could handle, growers increasingly turned to Japanese. A thousand Japanese were imported to Utah in 1903 for sugar beet work, and the numbers kept expanding. Soon there were Japanese-run employment agencies across the region.

The large numbers of Japanese working in eastern Colorado established a pattern that appeared elsewhere. After some 400 Japanese were hired in 1906 to work in the fields around the sugar factory at Brush, they began leasing fields—400 acres of beets already in 1907, then growing to more than 1,700 acres the following year when approximately half paid cash rent, half gave up a share of the crop. This expanded to 2,000 acres leased around Brush in 1909, while to the north in the Greeley district the total was 4,500 acres. Across Colorado that year the Japanese had more than 20,000 acres leased for sugar beets. Many others were moving into outright ownership of land. As historian William John May found, "First they appeared as laborers, doing the hand work under contract, then became cash tenants, then finally owning the land they tilled."[16]

All of which gradually removed Japanese from the pool of stoop labor so eagerly being sought by corporations, farmers, and recruiters. They were sometimes missing from farm crews because of another factor as well: race prejudice, which soon melded with earlier western anti-Chinese sentiments. The Gentlemen's Agreement of 1907 laid down prohibitions on the immigration of Japanese workers similar to those imposed on the Chinese in 1882. Local resentments against their leases merged with other antagonisms, real and imagined. As one farmer exclaimed, "The Japanese push up wages." Another complained to interviewer Victor Clark that Japanese were demanding at least $2 a day— "about the same as a white man . . ." Similarly, another complained of the unity shown by teams of Japanese sugar beet workers, both in seeking more pay and in objecting to rough treatment. Reports circulated of Japanese suddenly abandoning contracts in an effort to force higher wages: "Every Japanese gang is a trade union; they come and quit together." By 1920 a U.S. Department of Labor committee reflected how far the growing prejudice had reached: "It is exceedingly pertinent to state that the Japanese are invading the sugar-beet industry not only as laborers but as proprietors." The committee saw a future where "large numbers of this oriental race" might possess "a considerable proportion of sugar beet and cotton areas of the country."[17]

Anti-Japanese oratory was becoming louder in the beet states as well as on the West Coast, and rumblings of banning landownership by Japanese echoed in state legislative halls. Couched in broader anti-alien terms, these complaints reflected the growing dismay that the Japanese were no longer just field labor but were becoming growers of beets who in turn competed for field workers. California's ban on aliens owning land was eventually duplicated in the 1920s by eight other states across the region—Oregon, Washington, Texas, Arizona, Utah, Idaho, Montana, and Wyoming—and upheld by the U.S. Supreme Court. Colorado abstained. In 1924 the rising anti-Japanese spirit was strong enough that Congress included an outright ban on Asian immigration in its far-reaching immigration quota act. There were some cracks in these barriers, but increasingly Japanese activity in sugar beets was finally overwhelmed by white opposition.

Another group of workers showed up in the beet fields in those early years, but like the Japanese their time as stoop laborers was brief, for from the start their goal was to eventually own land. These were Germans from Russia, the "German-Russians" who arrived by the thousands on the Great Plains as the nineteenth century closed.

Their ancestors had migrated into Russia from German districts of Europe during the eighteenth century after Russian empress Catherine II, who was German, enlisted them to launch pioneer settlements along the Volga River. Over the following decades other invitations brought Germans to the eastern Black Sea region, then to parts of the Ukraine, the Crimea, Bessarabia, and Transcaucasia. One result was that Russia soon paralleled the United States in attracting Germans—some 300 "mother colonies" were functioning by 1859. Similar to their kinfolk emigrating across the Atlantic, the Germans moving into Russia's largely vacant districts were lured by promises of abundant land, religious freedom, local self-government—and also exemption from military service. One report showed that Germans inside Russia had grown to 1.7 million by the early twentieth century.

But by that time success stories of Germans in North America were making their way back to Europe, while problems within Russia were giving its German-Russians pause. An order by the czar in 1859 removing some of their protections triggered an early emigration. In 1871 another decree ended more privileges, and soon young German men for the first time faced military service in the Russian Army. Then in 1890 Russian teachers were sent into German schools, and seven years later even their vigorously maintained German-language teaching was banned and ordered replaced by Russian.

Faced with such restrictions, the German-Russians needed little encouragement to leave. And the trip was growing easier every year: immigration agents were active throughout Europe as "America fever" swept the Continent, and new, faster steamships competed to carry emigrants swiftly across the Atlantic. German-Russians joined the exodus. Some went to South America, but North America especially beckoned: thousands of unclaimed acres in western Canada awaited the plow, and officials on the Great Plains beat a noisy drum to welcome settlers—to Nebraska (where so many settled at Sutton that it became known as "Russian Town"), to Kansas, to North Dakota, and to South Dakota especially. A 1940 estimate put the number of Russian-born Germans and their descendants in the United States at some 350,000.[18]

They may have been "a culture frozen in place in 1763 and transplanted whole to the Great Plains," as a recent writer concluded, but they adapted readily to the new world of sugar beets. A group of some 200 Volga families that settled around Lincoln, Nebraska, in the early 1890s was soon tapped to work in the beet fields supplying the new Grand Island sugar factory, and while initial employment was mainly of lone males unencumbered by families, that began to change. Soon they were joined by their wives and children, most generally returning to the Lincoln area after each harvest because there was little land for sale in western Nebraska.

Colorado sugar men took notice. Some had already tried—and failed—to sign up German immigrants on the East Coast. Occasionally Belgians, Bohemians, Poles, and Hungarians were hired, in small numbers, and a 1906 Department of Agriculture report said that Polish women who walked from their city homes out to the beet fields won praise from some employers as "the best class of labor that they are able to obtain on their farms." But news in the world of sugar beets traveled fast, and Nebraska's success with German-Russians was too enticing to ignore. On April 13, 1900, a Missouri Pacific train puffed into Sugar

City in southeastern Colorado and deposited several hundred German-Russians, most having boarded at Hastings, Nebraska; the following year the Great Western recruited fifty-four families to leave Nebraska for Colorado. Then the year after that, in 1902, four trainloads were brought to Grand Junction. Over the next several years the growing arrivals of German-Russians in the Colorado beet areas were greeted with much anticipation. They would be the long-awaited beet workers![19]

By then the sugar entrepreneurs began to see advantages in bringing families—more stability, less drunkenness among the men, and most crucially, more hands for thinning, hoeing, and pulling. In some areas single males would continue to dominate until the World War I era, but the German-Russians leaned toward working in family units. There were bumps along the road as this concept began to spread—not enough houses available, construction proceeding too slowly, off-season jobs limited. But gradually many German-Russian families settled around the beet factories.

The Immigration Commission's statistics for 1909 showed that German-Russians totaled more than half of northern Colorado's 10,724 sugar beet hand workers. In southern Colorado they numbered only 340 out of the 3,918 hand workers, but the commission admitted that the "miscellaneous white" total there of 1,215 "probably includes some German-Russians." For the entire state, German-Russians constituted two-fifths of the hand workers in sugar beets.[20]

The expansion of German-Russian settlements—with many large families—encouraged the development of sugar contracts, which began to cover more and more land. A 1915 investigation found that a couple with five or six children would cultivate 50 to 60 acres; one family with seven children worked 83 acres that year. Incomes ranging from $200 to $700 were reported among German-Russian contracting families.

Before long the German-Russians were forming stable sugar beet communities. The Immigration Commission found that while members of the group were often slow, the fact that they usually settled in family groups could provide "both a dependable labor supply and, as time goes on, a reliable class of tenant farmers." Dena Markoff Sabin has noted how sugar companies began to favor them over other ethnic groups, offering generous loans and in other ways giving them special treatment as they realized that the German-Russians' goals fit in well with company production goals: "The economic advantage of German-Russians was based on a view of the family as a working unit, an ambition to acquire property, a willingness to sacrifice and plan to achieve the goal, and policies facilitating land purchases by this group."

Indeed, at Sugar City most German-Russians rose to landowning status within five years of arrival. A 1924–25 study in northeastern Colorado's South Platte Valley found that 72 percent of the landowners were German-Russians, as were 74 percent of the tenants. These were not "floaters," not migrating hoboes.[21]

But while these European immigrant field workers initially seemed to provide the foundation for the rise of sugar beets in the West, employers saw disturbing problems, akin to some of those seen with the Japanese. Realizing that their labors were crucial to the operation of sugar factories, the German-Russians began to question company payments, sometimes aggressively, especially regarding contract work. Employers bridled at being challenged, and some played groups off against each other, as in 1903 when Japanese were hired in northern Colorado to provide competition for German-Russians. On some occasions employers used German-Russians to check other white groups, part of a broader attempt to use the heterogeneity of field workers to company advantage.

The German-Russians may have been whites, but as a foreign group whose communities were called "Little Moscow" or "Little Russia" at a time when news reports told of Bolshevik violence in Russia, they sometimes suffered the darts of local criticism. One German-Russian child who had arrived with his family in South Dakota when he was six later recalled the taunts: "We were the dumb Russians . . . We spoke German, but they never referred to us as Germans. Up until I was 10, I had many a fight, because I was called a dumb Russian."[22]

Sometimes resentment was based on envy over the fact that German-Russians scratched so hard for success. And it wasn't just the men who toiled. An investigator traveling through sugar beet country in 1921–22 found that very few German-Russian mothers did *not* work, even when pregnant—one told her that "Annie was almost born in the beet field." Another admitted she had "topped until 6 a.m., and Lucy was born at 7 a.m." One conceded that during topping season she was unable to "sleep nights because her hands and arms hurt so." Most had to prepare meals as well as work in the fields, which meant rising very early and getting to bed very late. A German-Russian woman said that on Saturday nights when the week's washing had to be done, Saturday night "became Sunday morning before they went to bed."

In many ways the German-Russians were no different from other laborers. A Department of Labor study found that "for farm owners, at least, there is a certain social stigma attached to 'working in the beets,' and they are likely to hire contract labor for the work as soon as they are able to do so." Various observers noted that different groups shied away from stoop labor after some years; German-Russians were especially determined to become landowners, a drive that then cut into their availability for weeding and pulling. The issue developed at different stages in different sugar beet districts but grew more serious in the 1910s as the United States moved toward war and labor shortages appeared. Even in German-Russian areas, growers were confronted with major challenges over finding field workers, again.[23]

While European powers lurched into war in 1914, American sugar beet growers awakened to what at first appeared to be a wonderful situation: competition from European beet sugar was diminishing, and prices for American sugar were rising. But complications soon appeared. Across much of the United States, European immigrants had long been heavily counted on to stoke the blast furnaces, mine the coal, lay down the rails, and harvest the crops. Now this seemingly unending source of cheap labor was suddenly cut off—just when production in factories and fields began to increase as the warring nations called for more and more American goods. The U.S. government tried to overcome the difficulties through regulation, finally creating a Sugar Equalization Board to set production goals and pricing for sugar. Even with controls, the price for beets rose quickly to $11.96 per ton—its highest level ever. Wheat was guaranteed at $2 per bushel for 1917, 1918, and 1919, creating a topsy-turvy world for many Plains farmers, who switched from planting wheat to planting beets, back and forth, as prices changed. And for farm labor, wartime suddenly presented new opportunities—and another crisis for growers—as rural workers left for better-paying jobs or the military. It was a strange new environment, for the sugar men enjoyed new profits but had to endure government controls amid an uncertain labor market.[24]

Growers and their recruiters reached out in many directions. Desperate, the Utah-Idaho Sugar Company saw that farm boys could no longer fill its labor needs, so it turned first to technology—a route seldom taken when cheap labor was abundant. But after spending $100,000 on new machines for field work, officers found that the devices did not top the beets correctly. The plan was a failure. At the U-I annual meeting in April 1918, officers were forced to report that for the first time "we have been compelled to import about 2,000 people, mostly Mexicans, to secure their labor for beet field work." The complexion of their field crews soon showed further changes, as hundreds of Mexicans plus many Japanese and South Asian Indians—"Hindoos"—were put to work. The same pressures were hitting Sugar City in southeastern Colorado, where the National Sugar Manufacturing Company was switching to Hispanics. Within a few years, "Mexican-Americans comprised the field work force."

Competition for these new Mexican workers—the *betabeleros*—now became intense, among different sugar firms and among different industries. The Great Western in 1916 underwent a reversal: no longer simply hiring Hispanics who showed up looking for a job, the firm began actively to seek them out. It sent agents first into southern Colorado and New Mexico, then finally on to Texas, signing up men at the border in El Paso as well as in Fort Worth and San Antonio. Often the beet companies went on their own, ignoring the agencies and sending their own "runners" to seek out Mexicans. Sugar companies and railways alike began to pay their new employees' railroad fares and build houses for them. Two Mexican recruiters had offices in Salt Lake City by World War I, sometimes traveling as far as California looking for workers.[25]

Large-scale Mexican employment in western sugar beets was under way. It was no sudden influx: for several years Hispanics had been drifting north from their homes in southern Colorado and northern New Mexico to work in Great Western's operations in Colorado and in other beet operations in Nebraska and Kansas. Increasingly workers also came from within Mexico, first recruited for railroad work before later turning to farm jobs. A 1908 report noted that workers from New Mexico had been employed laying track and harvesting crops since 1900,

"but Old Mexicans have come in more recently." The report added that
New Mexicans sometimes looked down on those hired from Mexico
because the latter, often without families, could work for lower wages.
Perhaps this contributed to the two groups' tendency to concentrate in
different areas of Colorado: the New Mexicans worked nearer home in
southeastern Colorado in the fields along the Arkansas River, while "Old
Mexicans" headed to northeast Colorado along the South Platte.[26]

Various reports indicated that employers began to favor Mexicans
over Japanese. In some cases this was because Mexicans generally
showed up as individuals and returned south to their homes when the
harvest was over; in other cases, because they were less aggressive in
dealing with foremen. Frequently they accepted lower wages. "Old Mexicans are better laborers than Japanese for a large employer because
they do not go in gangs, under a head man or agent like the Japanese,"
one grower explained. Another said that "Mexicans are cheaper, and in
many cases just as good man for man." The 1908 Department of Labor
study concluded that Mexicans "do not occupy a position analogous to
that of the Negro in the South." The study emphasized that the Mexicans "are not permanent, do not acquire land or establish themselves in
little cabin homesteads, but remain nomadic and outside of American
civilization."

The Great Western did a study of the productivity of different ethnic groups and found that a German-Russian family could cover twelve
acres of beets, while individual Japanese and Mexican men could handle only seven acres. But the Japanese and German-Russians were either moving on or obtaining their own land. Still, it had become clear to
the Great Western that a family of any ethnicity could do more than any
"solo." In 1922 the Great Western stopped hiring gangs of "solos" and
placed its total emphasis upon families in the beet fields, aiding many
to bring in furniture. Before long, 90 percent of Great Western employees consisted of families, and by the late 1920s some 10,000 Mexican
families lived in *colonias* across the region, one-third of the total families employed in beets.[27]

But bringing in a large number of Mexican families depended on
effective large-scale recruiting. In 1915 the Great Western shipped 500
Mexicans by rail, and these numbers kept increasing until 13,000 were
brought to the sugar beet areas by train in 1920, bound for operations

in Wyoming, Nebraska, and Montana as well as Colorado. The 1920 total included 5,000 from southern Mexico, 3,000 of whom had no previous experience with sugar beets. The Great Western spent $360,000 that year on recruitment.

Rumors abounded that recruited Mexicans were being guarded and forced to stay inside the rail cars. When challenged on this, a Great Western officer assured Congress that the firm lost few of the workers it brought north and had no need to place agents on the train with them: "We have never had any trouble with them at all." Hiring pressures, in fact, made agents' work easier, because now they could promise that the Mexicans would earn more—payments went from $20 per acre in 1917 as America entered the war, to $25 the following year, then up to $35 in 1920. But with the postwar economic downturn, the payments then dropped to $22 in 1921 and $18 per acre in 1922.[28]

But those decisions also pushed up the price of sugar for consumers, causing congressmen to call a hearing over their concerns. In a raucous session, the growers' argument that labor shortages were serious and were largely responsible for the rising prices finally won out. As it had with the Southwest's cotton men, American involvement in the war brought permission for the sugar beet men to import Mexicans—as long as they went back home afterward.

Behind their need for higher pay, behind their assurances that the Mexicans would all head back home, the fear continued gnawing at western growers in the early postwar era that they might soon face severe labor shortages. They had known difficulties during the war but had survived with their operations and profits largely intact. Now as peacetime settled in, the economy was souring, which seemed at first to forecast a letup in the labor crisis. But as boom times returned in the early 1920s, labor needs again rose, and the search for Mexican workers resumed on a large scale. Worries voiced earlier were heard again but now had to compete with a rising national anti-immigrant mood that did not distinguish among Mexicans, Italians, Greeks, and Poles. Growing nativist sentiment blunted the growers' arguments, complicated their recruiting across the West, and forced them to deal with local citizens and a distant Congress.

Racial discrimination meshed with the antiforeign mood. In the sugar districts it greeted many of the incoming Mexicans, similar to what they had encountered in the cotton fields of Texas and Oklahoma and in the mines. In a 1900 riot at the American Beet Sugar Company operation in Rocky Ford, groups of Mexican-Americans—called "Mexicans" despite their U.S. citizenship—had been driven from town. Three years later Rocky Ford saw enough need for field workers to acquiesce as the National Sugar Company began hiring Hispanics from New Mexico. But differences in treatment began to appear: while the company frequently helped Americans and German-Russians purchase or rent land, it more often kept Mexicans on day labor. Contracting actually restricted their chances to negotiate, because the grower had already made his agreement with the sugar factory: in effect, that earlier contract discouraged offering any more to the Mexican signing an acreage contract.[29]

Reports began to filter in to company headquarters of prejudice against its new employees. Great Western field men reported that in talking to Mexican workers "one continually heard complaints of losses of wages or delay in payment of wages . . ." Workers also were unhappy when companies that initially paid them by the day soon switched to paying them by the acre, in an attempt to get more work; finally they were paid by the ton of beets brought in. In town, stores would not serve Mexicans—some even posting "No Mexicans Are Allowed" signs— and movie theaters either excluded them or made them sit in the balcony. A farmer told Paul Taylor, "When a Mexican doesn't take his hat off to you it's time to let him go." Contradictions were numerous: even after company recruiters had desperately courted them, Mexicans found that discrimination did not disappear as they moved north from Texas.[30]

The *corridos* of the *betabeleros* provide testimony of labor amid prejudice, where an individual's muscles were valued but his humanity was not. In "Los Betabeleros," the singer pointed to promises that had been made:

> *Pero son puras mentiras / Los que vienen y les dicen.*
> *Cuando ya estamos allá / Empiezan a regañanos*
> *Y luego les respondemos: / "Nosotros nos regresamos*
> *Porque allá en San Antonio / Nosotros sólo gozamos . . ."*

But these are nothing but lies / And those who come and say
   those things are liars,
When we get there / They begin to scold us,
And then we say to them: / "We are going back
Because there in San Antonio / We just enjoyed ourselves . . ."[31]

Beset by federal laws that seemed bent on blocking the arrival of foreign harvest hands, and townspeople's bias that angered and frightened the migrants, many western growers were apprehensive. The president of the Great Western pleaded in a 1920 letter to Congress, "A great many farmers and sugar companies will undoubtedly suffer unless Mexican labor can be secured."[32]

To ease their difficulties, companies gave more thought to the conditions Mexican families would find upon arrival. When the Great Western decided to employ families and provide them with housing, it also launched a concerted effort to convince Mexican workers—and the farmers who oversaw their labors—that its policies favored them, that it was a friend to its employees. Sometimes the efforts worked, as Paul Taylor found. "I have the best Mexican house in the vicinity, and I have a good farmer to work for," one Mexican beet worker told him. Another said, "John is a good farmer to work for. You can always get your money even though he doesn't pay too well. My brother's family has been here three years." Another praised the company for paying to transport a sick worker back to Mexico.

Finding workers was an enormous challenge for the sugar companies. To keep the factories producing tons and tons of sugar each year, the sugar companies had to recruit all kinds of workers, a chore that was endless, year in and year out, whether with German-Russians or Japanese or Mexicans or others. Nonetheless the employers had enough success that one farmer could confide to a Department of Labor visitor, "There's good money in beets." The former field workers who ended up leasing or owning beet farms would have agreed.

How was such an outcome possible, at the low going rates for field work, when the corporation had a stranglehold on payments? The major reason was that much of the labor on sugar beets was so simple, requiring so few skills, that it could be done by women and children as well as men, by newcomers just off the train as well as old hands. Further, many families labored with the expectation of building up savings that they could use to lease beet fields and eventually purchase them. In this way the much-discussed "agricultural ladder" of the Midwest reemerged in beet country.

Family labor increased the number of hands working: wives, sons, daughters, and often quite small children spent their days among the beet rows, starting in early summer and laboring until the last beet was pulled and topped in late autumn. Since large families were common among the early European immigrant workers, parents and children moved like armies through the fields. Further, while other family members worked, the fathers could seek outside jobs. After examining sugar beet operations, one historian concluded, "In no other occupation has the employment of women and children been so widespread . . ." And all the while the dream of owning land drew them on. These were some of the reasons there was "good money in beets."[33]

Children had always worked on the family farm. In fact, that farm usually could succeed only when everyone worked, each with his or her own chores—gathering eggs, picking berries in the garden, milking, cooking, and of course doing field work. Even dogs and cats had specific tasks on the farm. The general secretary of the National Child Labor Committee was merely repeating a universally held view when he stated, "It has generally been assumed that if children work on the farm there can be no objection to their employment."

This belief was common across the West, where population scarcity only increased its importance. One scholar of western childhood holds that "pioneer children not only worked more; they also took on a far wider range of tasks." But studies of farm children in the West have largely ignored Indians, Hispanics, and for the most part European immigrants in such operations as leased beet fields. From the ranks of such children came many whose waking hours centered not on gathering eggs or picking berries but on income-producing tasks among the sugar beets.[34]

For the farming that the beet families experienced was of a different sort. It was intensive agriculture, whose repetition, lack of variety, and scarce opportunities for rest made it more akin to factory work. Like cotton farming, sugar beet farming rested solidly upon the collective backs of families, where children as extra hands could make the difference between a continued miserly existence or economic improvement. Families with beet contracts usually took on bigger fields than families of the same size who worked their own farms, reflecting the leasers' hard push to earn enough to become owners. Mexicans generally had smaller acreages under contract than German-Russians; also, as Sara Brown concluded, "in Spanish speaking families women and children do not work in the field to the same extent" as do the German-Russians, necessitating fewer rows to cover. This factor could slow the drive to purchase land.

But many Mexican children did work, as did many German-Russian children, Hungarian children, Polish children, and American children, in families holding contracts or sharecropping. In 1920 a judge of the Weld County Court stated that 2,500 children were working in that Colorado county's beet fields, and he estimated that statewide the total might reach 6,800. Each earned the family an average of $200, one study determined. When Sara Brown conducted her 1924 investigations in three northeastern Colorado counties, she found that of all persons working the 16,707 acres of beets, "49 per cent were children under 16 years and 10 per cent were under 10 years." The northeastern counties were proclaimed "Colorado's banner sugar beet district," but that banner was mainly held up by children.[35]

Bunching and thinning were the tasks that practically all working children performed, for these operations were well fitted for small hands. They were also operations that had to be pushed ahead forcefully, for delays would harm beet growth. Unsurprisingly, these weeks had long days, in which everyone worked to the limit. Brown found some six-year-olds thinning, and in her 1924 survey 20 percent of the children engaged in this process were under ten years old. Some crawled down the rows; others walked along bent over. Many were considered highly skilled at thinning.

Although hoeing, the next step in the yearly schedule, required more strength, Brown found that 957 of the 1,081 children worked at it, 161 of them under ten years old. The hardest work was autumn's harvest, and her study showed that 912 either pulled beets or topped them or did both. The work could not be called light—pulling the beets from the ground, knocking them together to remove clinging dirt, then throwing them into a pile so they all pointed in the same direction and were ready to be topped.

Topping was done by children as young as eight, seven, even six. In his 1915 visit to these fields, Edward Clopper noted, "The beet is fibrous and a sharp blow is required, and as the knee is not protected, children not infrequently hook themselves in the leg . . ." Since topping was the final step in field work it came late in the season, when daylight was brief and temperatures were low. Families often worked by lantern light, stumbling or crawling along ice-filled furrows. Many did not hide their unhappiness with these conditions: comments ranged from "We all get backaches" and "Hardest work there is" to a six-year-old girl's statement that her back was getting crooked from work "in the beets." Arms became so sore that at times they were almost useless; frost on the beet tops soaked the workers, and their clothing froze stiff. One worker called fall "the meanest time." Investigators from the U.S. Children's Bureau found a large percentage of orthopedic defects among the "beeters," with marked deformities in many.[36]

As criticism mounted, local politicians and business leaders sprang to the defense of the system that put such young children into the beet fields. Representative William Vaile of Colorado told a congressional committee in 1920 that when children went to work on sugar beets after being in the city all winter, "they seem to thrive under it . . ." A representative of the growers agreed, noting that his own seventeen-year-old son was once called on to help thin beets, "and you know after three or four days their back aches and they get absolutely sore, and then have to rest for a while, but we have had our own high school boys go out and try to help under those conditions." Did it hurt them to do so? he was asked. "Absolutely not."

But taking a rest after three or four days, as Vaile's son had done, was a luxury that many "beeters" did not have. Parents admitted the work was hard on children, but they needed their labor. "It wouldn't be no use, I wouldn't raise beets if the kids and the woman didn't do the hand work," one beet grower told Brown. Another confided: "Too bad for the kids, beets too much hard work, too much missa school, gotta do it to make a life on the farm."[37]

But the result was inescapable: work on the beets helped parents reach their goal of landownership. Even an investigator from the National Child Labor Committee conceded that from the efforts of parents and children, "many families earn and save enough money in a very few years to enable them to buy small farms." He added, however, that "this worthy ambition ceases to be a virtue when pursued at the sacrifice of their children's proper education and normal childhood."

Children's education was a nagging concern in the sugar beet region. Often ignored, the issue would not go away. States had compulsory school attendance laws, but enforcement varied widely. Loopholes were large in Colorado's law: while it specified that all children aged eight to sixteen years had to be in school, it made exceptions for those fourteen and fifteen years old if they had completed eighth grade, or if parents required children's help for their support, or if it was simply in their best interests to be excused. Even with these broad escape clauses, "the law . . . is not enforced in the beet sections," a 1915 study concluded.[38]

As in other parts of the West, schools made accommodations when a district's major crop was ready. The usual arrangement was a "beet vacation" for two weeks in late September and early October; in Utah, farm boys put down their books then and went to work pulling and topping. In Morgan County, Colorado, the Snyder District School opened on August 18 but then was closed from October 13 until November 10 so that students could harvest beets; some 55 percent of the district's families grew sugar beets. Other reports from across the region told of different versions of "beet vacations," ranging from a late opening for the fall term to an interruption after several weeks. Another option was for schools to run special summer classes for "beeters" to make up absences. This was customary in northeastern Colorado by 1922.

Even with such alternatives, the burdens imposed upon children by missed school days could be enormous. In northeastern Colorado's three major sugar beet counties, truancy by "beeters" was five times that of pupils not working in the fields, with totals especially great during the fall term. As a result, there was little connection between a working child's age and his or her grade in school; in one Weld County school with many "beeters," three-fifths of the children were held back. A Nebraska school reported that among the 91 children aged nine to fifteen who worked in sugar beets, 66 percent were being held back; in another Nebraska school and in a Denver school where many beet workers were enrolled, the number held back approached 80 percent.[39]

The law said children were supposed to be in school, and they were barred from employment during school time—but they kept working in their families' beet fields. This constituted a legal conundrum for some: if a father had a beet contract, and his child working with him brought in some $200 during the year, was the father an employer? Or were they simply a farm family working on the family farm? In Nebraska the Department of Inspections was perplexed, pointing out that the situation "borders closely upon a fracture of the law . . ." Whether the child was doing family work or was laboring for an employer was "impossible to determine . . ."[40]

A law had little effect when its violations were not protested. For the two major ethnic groups—German-Russians and Mexicans—the educational results were especially grim. Children in each group posted lengthy absence records, but often for somewhat different reasons.

Among German-Russian children, the problem stemmed from both family needs and local control of schooling. One man whose family arrived from Russia in 1912 recalled that his father had argued, "You were educated by the priest in Russia. You learned what he knew." Similarly, a study in the Arkansas Valley of southeastern Colorado found that many adult German-Russians simply looked down on the concept of schooling. A parent told a school principal that his boy was worth $1,000 working in the beet fields—but if he went to school he was only an expense. Another father showed no concern over having a fifteen-year-old daughter who was in third grade.[41]

Further, the system of local control over schools often meant that school boards were dominated by local beet growers. To enforce the attendance law might mean arresting one's friends, neighbors, or share-croppers. One truancy officer kept school absence notices in his pocket until harvest was over; in another district no such officer was even appointed. In communities where five-day warnings were issued, some families kept a child out until the fifth day, then placed him in school for one day, then pulled him out again for four days, repeating the process over and over.[42]

Hispanic children, generally lumped together as "Mexicans" even if they were U.S. citizens, faced a slightly different problem. Parents

needed their labor, but Mexicans were often considered outsiders, ignored in a public school system supported by local taxpayers. And like
the German-Russians, they had migrated from a culture that did not
place a high value on education. As a result, neither the surrounding
Mexican community nor the grower overseeing a contract was very concerned about forcing Mexican children to go to school. Their work was
needed, and since the Mexicans were often migratory, they might be
moving on when they were finished.

Regardless, educating Mexicans was at best a secondary concern.
Mexicans were becoming the dominant labor force in sugar beet fields,
and the western plea was now adapted to beets: "If the supply of Mexican laborers coming from old Mexico should be cut off," a director of
the American Beet Sugar Company at Rocky Ford warned in a letter to
Congress in 1920, "I am certain that the agricultural industries and
farming interests in the Arkansas Valley would be upset to such an extent that great loss would result."

Mexican laborers were now necessities. *Colonias* were becoming
communities, and the *betabeleros* found unity and protection within
them. Soon they formed *mutualista* organizations to help members
through hard times. And as nativist frenzies weakened, some of the
old prejudices seemed to weaken too. By the late 1920s along the
South Platte, most of the laboring Mexicans encountered by Paul Taylor had few problems being accepted. "Since American labor has never
been prevalent in beet culture," Taylor concluded, "and since both
German-Russians and Japanese are of diminishing importance, there
is no competing beet labor class to voice economic objections to the
Mexicans."[43]

What was clear, after two decades of development, was that sugar beets
belonged to a different agricultural world. Beets were highly perishable,
which meant that the sugar factory had to be nearby. Moreover the factory managers had to have a close relationship with the farmers, in what
has been called "a curious union of family farms and million-dollar corporations." How many acres to plant? Were the plants properly thinned?
Were the beets of the right sugar content when pulled? Expertly topped?
Delivered promptly? The written contract between beet worker and
beet company has been called unique in American agricultural labor,

with obligations and compensations carefully spelled out, from spring planting to summer weeding to fall harvest. Beyond emerging as just a "convergence of the family farm ideal and industrialization," the industry that sprouted under the umbrella of government protection developed its own umbrella against defaulting growers and, ultimately, their workers.[44]

Despite having to deal with changing groups, growers generally had located enough workers—"beeters"—to get by. Year after year, as the winter snows melted and irrigation ditches ran full through the dry land, sugar beets were planted, then thinned and blocked, and—as fall yielded to winter—they were dug and topped and hauled to the sugar factory. The system was in place: low earnings for the workers, enormous earnings for the Sugar Trust. And finally this story too would become part of the tales told—and sung—by harvest labor in the beet fields of the West.

10

THE CALIFORNIA GARDEN

To say that a white laborer cannot work in a California raisin vineyard in the raisin season is nonsense," the *Riverside Press and Horticulturist* proclaimed in 1889. All that whites needed, the editor added, was a decent wage: "Does he not work in the harvest field, day in and day out, under the same sun, and is raisin-making any harder work than harvesting?"[1]

In California, at the far end of America's westering experience, the issues of who would work the harvest, and who *should not* work the harvest, were presented in bold relief. Could "Americans" bring in the crops of this cornucopia now bursting from field and orchard, hopyard and grove? Were Chinese, Japanese, Mexicans, or any other nonwhites better workers—perhaps constructed by Nature's god to be anatomically more suited for stoop labor? Or was the wage issue—who costs less?—all-important?

Few were silent in the growing debate that veered back and forth between physiology, economics, horticulture, racial issues, and in the end, interpretations of the American dream. When a *San Francisco Chronicle* reporter toured the Napa Valley vineyards in 1883, he saw Chinese pickers squatting on their haunches to pick the low-lying grapes. For white pickers, the reporter wrote, the vines would have to be raised, but Chinese "make good pickers on account of their stolid industry and genius for plodding, and they are largely employed in the valley." The *Western Broker* agreed: "The best hand in the grape field by all odds is the little Chinamen [*sic*]. He grows close to the ground, so does not have to bend his back like a large white man. Besides, he is very supple-fingered."[2]

Or was it a matter of cheap labor—the growers' desire to pay the least amount to workers? The situation in the Ukiah Valley in Mendocino County in 1891 was typical: Chinese hops pickers were paid 90 cents per hundred pounds, Indians $1.00, and whites $1.10. The U.S. Industrial Commission reported in 1901 that in California the Chinese were paid lower wages and, unlike white crews, did not have to be fed; the Chinese "invariably feed themselves, and usually rice is the chief article of diet." In addition, the Chinese "are there Monday morning, and a good many white men are not so punctual," a California State Board of Trade official admitted.[3]

Controversies were always swirling around California harvests—from gold rush days, when wheat and cattle dominated ranch life and Indians formed a major part of the labor force, through the major epochs of California agriculture as it rose to the top of American fruit production. "I think the state is to be largely a fruit garden," predicted pioneer horticulturist John Bidwell in 1891, and his forecast became reality. By 1900 half of America's grapes, citrus fruits, plums, prunes, and peaches came from the state, along with 95 percent of its almonds, walnuts, apricots, and olives.[4]

Even before statehood in 1850 and the arrival of thousands of Americans and others in the "diggings," foundations were laid that would affect California's agriculture for decades. A cattle industry had developed in the colonial era and grew rapidly after Mexico won independence from Spain in 1822. Large landholdings became common, and Mexico authorized more than 800 private land grants before California became part of the United States in 1848. Nearly nine million acres of these grants were confirmed to their owners by the U.S. Land Commission.

Another legacy of the colonial era was the labor system of the Spanish missions, which had drawn Indians to work in their gardens through a variety of methods. These were expanded by operators of Mexican ranches. According to historian Richard Steven Street, the campesinos of the colonial era became part of "a pattern, later replicated, modified, and expanded, whereby various private, semiprivate, and official government programs would repeatedly overcome labor shortages by importing large numbers of cheap, industrious, 'trained,' Mexican workers."

When Americans began showing up in small groups in the years before the gold rush, laborers for hire were in short supply. Not surprisingly, the newcomers often turned to existing Mexican labor practices—employing Indians, holding some in debt peonage, even controlling some as slaves. John Augustus Sutter, the Swiss immigrant who hired James Marshall (who picked up the first nuggets at Sutter's Mill in 1848), employed a mixed corps of Indian and other workers on his extensive land grant in the Sacramento area. After statehood, the incoming Americans scarcely needed to be very creative, because the new legislature complied with farmers' demands and in 1850 passed an Act for the Government and Protection of Indians. If an Indian was convicted of a crime "punishable by fine," then a private employer simply paid the Indian's fine and obtained his labor; in case of a vagrancy arrest, an auction was held, and the successful bidders obtained the worker for up to four months. Indentured servitude was also common, and Indian children were kidnapped for labor under vague laws allowing them to be held as custodial wards, as "apprentices," or "adopted."[5]

As California's grain industry boomed early in the American era, wheat ranches became the new workplaces for many of these native workers. Planting, scything or mechanically cutting, tossing sheaves into wagons, threshing, tying up bags—these operations required large numbers of workers. When a plan to import black slaves from the South collapsed, employers relied on the Indian Act until, eventually, other workers could be found. Wheat became California's earliest agricultural bounty: when criticized for not planting fruit trees, a San Joaquin Valley wheat man replied, "We don't do a cent on anything but wheat in this county; we all want to get rich in two years."

And many did. By 1880, the wheat crop had twice the value of California gold, and three years later San Joaquin County claimed the world's largest wheat output: 3.4 million bushels. By then wheat raising was already dominating the flat lands of the state's interior, reaching south of San Joaquin and Contra Costa counties and stretching north to Tehama County. New labor sources were required. One estimate puts native-born Americans (i.e., "white") at 40 percent of the labor force in California's wheat fields down to the end of the century, European immigrants at 40 percent, and the remainder a diverse racial and immigrant group. Many of these came to farm work after giving up on mining along the Mother Lode. But in the 1870s, as the combine was introduced into California wheat fields, large crews were still needed at harvest time, many with special skills, and soon a permanent migrant class was forming in the Golden State. "The only laborer who can subsist for the year on seasonal agricultural work is one who 'follows the seasons;' that is, migrates from one district to another as the harvest ends in one and begins in another," noted the U.S. Immigration Commission.

Wheat, it turned out, had been too much of a good thing, as lands were cropped and recropped without fertilization. By century's end fields that had once yielded 40 to 60 bushels of wheat to the acre now turned out as few as 12 bushels. California wheat was facing strong competition, aided by the spreading rail network and the expansion of Great Plains production—California ranked second in the nation in wheat in 1889 but slipped to sixth by 1900.[6] What the railroad took with one hand, however, it empowered with the other. Simply put, the iron horse was crucial to California's changeover from wheat to fruit. "Since the birth of this State, a great economic force has come into operation," William H. Mills reminded the California Agricultural Society in 1890. "I refer to cheap and rapid communication."

Mills spoke not as a neutral observer but as chief land agent for the Southern Pacific, the state's major rail line. And by 1890 his words were the stuff not of dreams but of reality: the railroad had again steamed into a newly settled area of the West and was creating agricultural wonders. Instead of opening up Far Eastern trade, as its planners had envisioned, the western railways' most important link turned out to be between producers in the American West and consumers in the American Midwest and East.

And after the 1869 arrival of the Central Pacific–Union Pacific transcontinental, the new Southern Pacific (which swallowed the CP in the 1880s) set about not only to link the California rancher with the New York buyer but to encourage, aid, and direct California's agriculture in ways that would help both producer and consumer (and thereby the SP). Soon the railway did much more than carry produce: it advertised California to potential immigrants, it helped fight plant diseases, it sponsored workshops to educate farmers, and it especially worked to bring water to arid districts.[7]

There had been early attempts at irrigating the dry valleys, often following ditches that Indians had dug centuries before, but in the American era recognition as California's irrigation pioneers is generally given to the Mormon colony at San Bernardino in 1852. Other attempts followed; Fresno's first major project came in 1871, just ahead of the arrival of full railroad service a year later. Eventually Fresno and Tulare counties were served by 500 miles of canals with more than 5,000 miles of distributing ditches, bringing moisture from the San Joaquin and Kings rivers to 200,000 acres of cropland and orchards. Pushed by the SP and other investors and dreamers, Fresno's success was paralleled in many districts.

By 1889 California's irrigated acreage exceeded one million acres, topping all other states. A U.S. Department of Agriculture investigator in 1901 called irrigation "absolutely indispensable" to California's developing fruit industry. It led unwaveringly to intensified agriculture, for only a large output could justify the high costs of bringing in water. And these changes hurried the decline of wheat, with its sprawling fields.[8]

With both railroads and irrigation in place, soon orchards and vegetable plots were being developed, everywhere. In pre-railroad 1860 backyard trees scattered about the state had produced so much fruit that great amounts were wasted. Gingerly and carefully, farmers responded to the opportunities opened by the new transportation: the first year of railroad service saw three carloads of fruit shipped east. As long as most areas of the state still lacked rail service, it was useless to turn out large loads of fruit. Lake County boosters were well aware of this: in 1890 no rail tracks yet touched major parts of the county, and land prices remained as little as one-tenth of those in areas served by rail. "Finer fruit cannot be raised in any portion of the state," the *Middletown Independent* held, "but still people do not care to invest simply because we have no railroad."

But in those early years shipping by rail was not without its problems. The more perishable fruits with short picking seasons, such as peaches and plums, could not be moved far and still arrive in good condition. The refrigerator car was being developed, albeit slowly and with missteps. Systems with packed ice were failures until the latter 1880s, but when the first shipment of refrigerated California fruit—ripe cherries and apricots, from the Suisun Valley—went eastward in 1888, it found a ready market. Despite the occasional "ice famine" that hit some loading points, this new refrigerated car proved a major improvement. As the *Sacramento Bee* explained in 1890, "The new way costs more than the old, but shippers prefer it, as it is claimed that the fruit reaches its destination in better order and without risk, although the time required is longer, being seven or eight to Chicago, ten or eleven to New York, and about thirteen days to Boston."

Now came the bonanza years: in 1900 California shipped 50,000 carloads of citrus and deciduous fruits; this rose to 80,000 by 1920. As irrigation expert Elwood Mead proclaimed, here was proof that "the arid West is the nation's farm."[9]

Prices in Chicago, New York, and even Europe were now watched closely by California growers, their efforts made easier by new technology. Like wheat ranchers, fruit growers were now part of a world market. A former U.S. consul in Europe reminded the Southern California Pomological Society in 1899 that England was importing California oranges, apples, pears, plums, peaches, and apricots, as well as dried fruits and beeswax, hops, wheat, barley, beans, and mustard. Germany's imports ranked second, with the rest of Europe close behind.[10]

As the new agriculture developed, orchardists and vegetable growers alike quickly learned that while their farm plots were indeed much smaller than the wheat ranchers' thousand-acre spreads, the detailed requirements and extra care required in planting, cultivating, irrigating, weeding, harvesting, and transporting were much greater. Crowding plants and trees together often lured insect pests and diseases that could spread rapidly—which happened to a Sutter County farmer's vineyard one night, when eight acres of his Thompson seedless grape vines "were deprived of practically every green shoot in the course of a few hours" by cutworms. Orange groves faced continued challenges from red scale, and the number of parasites attacking pear and quince trees numbered at least fifteen, while grapevines were hosts to San Jose scale, grape scale, black rot, flea beetle, berry moth, and leafhoppers, as well as an import, the phylloxera that had devastated Italy's vineyards.

The University of California—founded in 1868 and quickly enlisted in the fight—sent experts into the field, who eventually beat back or at least held at bay most of the pests and diseases. The peach blight was one enemy that the scientists vanquished: it was ruining orchards in

1905 and 1906, whereupon plant pathologists came up with a spray that solved the problem by 1907. In time, the growers' dependence upon science for protection helped make California the nation's largest user of insecticides.[11]

High transportation costs could reduce earnings sharply, and farm groups spent much time complaining of freight rates. (One Chinese farmer recalled shipping fruit to New York and receiving—after freight and packing charges were deducted—a profit of one cent per box!) And storms and cold temperatures were another problem, severely damaging output.

Costs were enormous in this environment. Soon cooperatives were formed for each agricultural product, the better to confront high freight rates, packing problems, and insect invasions. And especially labor problems.[12]

Because harvesting machines never quite made it into the fruit orchards, and arrived only later in the hopyards and sugar beet fields, the labor question was brought to the fore rapidly and perennially. The combine reduced some of the need for threshing crews in the wheat fields, but in the orchards the work was becoming even more exacting and dependent upon human muscle and skill. Foremen in the apple orchards needed to "impress upon each worker the idea that the fruit should be handled as carefully as eggs," a university agricultural circular warned, using a phrase widely employed in the West's orchards and citrus groves. Special picking buckets and bags were required with bottoms that could be opened and thereby "emptied without bruising."

Plucking fruit from a tree, vine, or bush was only part of the process. All harvest jobs required skills, some easy to learn, others gained only through long years of experience. For example, the problems with fingernails: as citrus grower James Mills explained to the Industrial Commission, "we find from investigation that the men in picking would cut the lemons or the oranges with their finger nails. We had to get them to prune their finger nails and wear gloves, because when the fruit was punctured, the spore in countless millions being around, immediately lodged in the moist portion of the rind and began to develop." Twenty-five percent of the fruit was ruined before it got to market, he estimated.[13]

Work in the citrus groves under a broiling California sun was difficult. Pickers climbed shaky ladders, were poked in the eye by branches,
suffered cuts from lemon trees' green thorns, or were bitten by ants,
then frequently closed out the day covered with the brown smut left by
black-scale insects. The clippers used to cut the stems had to be kept
sharp and handled with care. Picking rings required the worker to pick
oranges or lemons of a certain size. A writer in the *Industrial Pioneer*
warned that orange picking "is an occupation requiring considerable
strength and agility, which bars the employment of women and children." Following a day of such labor, he added, "the 'orange glommer' is
usually 'all in,' and has not much stomach for romantic reflections."

The "romantic reflections" of the orange harvest, presented in gaudy
advertisements in national magazines, ignored not only the difficulties
and dangers facing workers, but the many tasks required to keep citrus
groves producing. At the start came clearing land—an especially strenuous job that involved digging up and removing brush, trees, and weeds,
readying irrigation ditches, and preparing intervening strips for planting
other crops, often vegetables. After the soil was prepared and water
brought in, the next step was planting trees, which then had to be
watched and pruned yearly; it took from six to eight years for an orange
tree to reach maturity. Because of the early 1870s introduction of both
the Washington navel orange (which ripened in winter), and the Valen-
cia (which ripened in summer), many groves in Southern California
could offer workers almost year-round employment.[14]

Sometimes winter brought another duty: protecting the trees from
frost. Workers tried to block the sweep of frigid air through the early
California groves by throwing blankets over trees and burning wet straw.
Increasingly they employed smudge pots, which had to be kept full and
burning around the clock. The hard freeze of December 1912 to February 1913 was long remembered, when workers were roused from their
beds and enlisted for several days and nights of steady, exhausting work.
As Limoneira Company owner Charles C. Teague recalled, "Everyone
connected with the operation was ready to drop with fatigue and loss of
sleep and only the loyalty of our men saved our crop."

Workers were tested whenever temperatures dropped. On cold days,
while waiting to be allowed to start, they often stood shivering outside

an orchard. They were not paid for this "wet time." And when picking Washington navels resumed, the oranges seemed like "ice balls," leaving their hands frostbitten.

Finding workers with the necessary skills, strength, agility, and stamina was often a challenge for growers. The major problem in California, as elsewhere, was the seasonal nature of harvesting, and the fact that the weather could suddenly shift the harvest's start and finish by days, even weeks, while workers tarried or departed. Orange and lemon groves employed large numbers of workers year round, but like the rest of California's agriculture they required even more massive crews at harvest time. If workers were not on hand, peaches and pears would rot, hops and cotton would decline in quality, and grapes would be attacked by sparrows. "One man in Fowler estimates that fifty tons of fruit have gone to waste because he can't secure fruit pickers," a Fresno packer reported, voicing the unending, nagging fear on the minds of California's orchardists.

When the Southern Pacific's William Mills addressed the State Agricultural Society in 1890, he worried about how the fruit men would deal with this "irregularity of employments." He cited as an example the giant vineyards of Senator Leland Stanford—thirty-nine of them, each covering one hundred acres, where only 135 workers were needed during the six months between harvests. But then came the harvest: "This requires the steady employment of five hundred men every part of two months, but for three weeks of that period the demand will be for seven hundred men. For steady annual employment, but seventy men are required . . . The maximum is ten times the minimum in this case." Extrapolating to the state's 200,000 acres of vineyards, Mills said the 3,500 workers employed on an annual basis were one-tenth of what was needed at harvest time. This irregularity put California "under serious disadvantage with respect of labor."[15]

Schedules for harvest labor required by California crops competed and often clashed. The Immigration Commission examined the requirements around Fresno, with its vineyards and orchards, the tasks involved with harvesting and curing crops, and finally the between-season pruning and resetting. Cultivation and hoeing began in March, as did some minimal irrigation work. Then in June picking began for some fruit, such as apricots and early peaches, followed by table grapes in early August. Then came the crush of "raisin grapes," the district's

major industry, requiring 7,000 pickers and others to carefully lay out
the grapes, which were dried on trays in the sun. That total then declined to 4,000 workers needed for curing and picking wine and table
grapes. Harvesting the grapes' second crop, running until the end of
October, required fewer pickers; even smaller numbers were needed
for pruning over the next several months.

In Fresno, life was stop and go; the area teemed with large numbers
of workers for short periods, followed by empty streets when harvest
was finished. Author Carey McWilliams would later note that harvest
workers in the state had to be able to migrate quickly, then needed the
"ability to hibernate, i.e. the seasonal worker is expected to disappear
when the crops are harvested." Their nimbleness among the grapevines
had to be matched by nimbleness in moving on, always keeping a watch
out for another job.

With these basic conditions, California enlisted significant numbers of
the various types of migrant workers seen around the West. Transients had
appeared early in the era of the wheat ranches, where those with skills
often commanded good wages. Many precedents were established—
the men were fed in the fields and often slept in the fields; and "they
come and go many times without coming in contact with any member
of the family in whose fields they labor." Conditions were little different when their job quest took them to citrus groves, vineyards, and
hopyards.[16]

This migrating army was drawn from a wide variety of sources, including the unemployed. As the nation's economy collapsed in 1893,
the *Hanford Journal* reported that the big Lucerne vineyard would need
500 grape-pickers but "already more have applied than there is work
for, many coming from as far away as San Luis Obispo county."

As the economic troubles of the 1890s deepened, a hobo-author
observed that "the Santa Clara Valley was swarming with 'tramps,' who,
laden with blankets and what else they might own on earth, traveled up
and down the dusty roads following the dim dream of work." An employment agent told him, "Carloads of them come out from San Francisco every day . . . but there's more people than work." Even in better
seasons, the sporadic nature of hobo employment left many destitute.
During the winter months just before the First World War, up to 60,000
seasonal farmworkers were "hibernating" in California's major cities,

some 10,000 of them without savings enough to carry them to the next crop season.[17]

Bindlestiffs were drifters, either by choice or from lack of alternatives. Many took jobs in the city after harvesting was finished or continued drifting. Fresno growers met in 1892 to discuss their difficulties with American workers; one speaker condemned them because "half of the white men quit [on the first day], some saying the work did not suit, others that they had a better job"; then on the next day "half the others came for their money." The head of the state's bureau of labor statistics agreed with these comments, that "good white labor" seemed to have problems staying on the job.[18]

When actual working conditions were examined, the bindlestiffs' transient nature becomes more understandable. A farmhand from Minnesota went to the coast to work but returned home complaining that he had "not been treated much better than a dog by his employers in California," his former boss reported. There was ample evidence that many in the migrant worker army felt the same way.

Pay was a continuing problem. During economic downturns prices were low, but the railroads still charged growers "all the traffic will bear." Growers had no choice but "to do to others as others do to them, and pay their labor no more than the traffic will bear." One Davisville grower told the twenty-five men working on his prune crop that because of the poor market conditions and his problems obtaining funds, "he was not able to pay more than $20 per month." The men accepted the terms, a considerable cut from the $1 to $2 per day plus board that they were used to. The grower admitted to a reporter that "he could have secured the services of a hundred men at the same wage." During the depressed conditions of 1893, men hired by a Bakersfield vineyard agreed to wait for their pay until the grapes were sold.

The wage issue was perennial. The California Bureau of Labor Statistics lectured employers in 1884 that "if they want to secure their [white] laborers," wages must be at a level "as Caucasians may expect." The following year the bureau asked San Francisco employment agencies their opinions on pay and other matters. One agency worker said, "I do not think that white men will work for $1.25 [a day], even with board." Another contended that "parties desiring to have full and faithful duty should bear in mind that the laboring class look upon good treatment from those employing them, and expect to be *well fed* and have comfortable quarters to sleep in when their day's work is done; very often a kind word will accomplish more than curses."[19]

But reports from California's orchards, groves, vineyards, and hop-yards indicated that workers usually received other than "good treatment." Food—its tastiness, its quality, the way it was served—was a frequent topic. "The milk was skimmed, flavored mainly by the drowned flies contained therein," one man told a state commission, adding that "if [the Chinese cook's] steaks were placed on the railroad track they would wreck the fastest train known." Another pointed to a lack of screens in the dining hall—"we had to beat the flies or we lost out on the food."

At times growers seemed oblivious to the realities of work on their own properties. Fresno boosters bragged of their climate (where temperatures could reach 110°F), and a cheerleader for "The Home of the Raisin" casually explained that "one should remember that 'heat' like 'sweet' is merely a relative term," adding that "sunstroke is entirely unknown." The Immigration Commission told a different story in its section on Fresno County, when investigators found several cases "where so-called Americans had become ill while engaged in picking raisins because of the heat and of the irregular camp life." The finding of a coroner's inquest in Sacramento in the middle of the hops picking season of 1913 was scarcely unique: J. Nelson, who "worked for Mr. L.D. Jacks at the Consumnes hop picking," went out by the river after dinner one evening and died—"heart failure due to heat prostration."[20]

The Immigration Commission also looked into board and lodging for California's migrant workers and found that men's housing on the larger ranches and labor camps usually consisted of "rough, unbattened, frame structures raised 5 or 6 feet above the ground," where the men bunked in rough conditions. Whites "are averse to working there even at high wages," the investigators noted.

After the State of California announced that it would investigate labor camps, over the next several years it received letters from workers describing camps they had known.[21] A typical report came from Ridgewood Ranch, Willets, on May 2, 1923: "I wish you would run up this way and inspect our quarters we have to live in. The cesspool is 12 feet from the bunk house and it is all open and the perfume from that hole is a fright and the horse barn and the stable manure is 20 feet from the sleeping and they will not clean up the place . . ." Not all labor camps had such conditions. Inspectors sometimes found enlightened employers, like the El Centro farmer who raised cantaloupes and grapes and had learned that "good housing and food as well as showers bring me a better class of labor . . ." But many inspection visits provided evidence that made the short stays, the high turnover, seem logical, predictable.

Indians, important from the outset to California agriculture, remained important in its later development. As they did elsewhere across the West, Indians in California adapted work schedules to fit their own needs, making enough to live so they could continue their traditional activities. Customary patterns of life did not disappear. From Luiseños in the south to the Pomos and other tribes grouped into the Round Lake Reservation in the north, the Indian labor pool often provided good recruiting grounds for employers, especially hops growers. Far from disappearing from the state's labor force, Native Americans remained active participants in the new California agricultural economy.

Indians were reported to be the first labor group picking hops in the Mendocino area. And they were needed, especially in places where an alternative group was present. They quickly gained a reputation for being able to handle different crops and for working in family groups. In one case, in Chico, Chinese almond harvesters had demanded more than the three cents a pound they had agreed to the previous day. Chico farmer John Bidwell fired them and brought in Mechoopda Indians: "The men can knock them [the almonds] and the boys and girls pick them up and the squaws hull them." Similarly, when Chinese struck Tulare County vineyards in 1890, the managers "went to the foothills and secured Indians" for the grape harvest. Three years later major hop-yards in Yuba County had some 3,000 hops pickers—"all are whites and Indians." Having a variety of ethnicities available could strengthen the hands of growers.

The federal Indian bureau proudly reported in 1911 that between 300 and 400 Indians had made about $1.50 a day in the bean fields around Upper Lake, one family earning $450; after that most moved on to hops and prunes. During the labor shortages that appeared as the United States entered the First World War, many Indians were recruited for California harvests, including children whose reservation schools were closed to enable them to join the crews.[22]

At such times Indians were shown to be extremely adaptable—not crushed by a new world they could not understand, not withdrawing to the reservation to await the end depicted in "Lo, the Poor Indian" tableaus. They worked in a wide variety of occupations: in the San Diego area the Luiseños, Cahuillas, Cupeños, and Kumeyaays picked fruit, cut apricots for dried fruit firms, dug canals, delivered goods, worked as sheepherders, and shipped out with whaling crews. Various accounts state that they were paid the same as whites. Through the Spanish Colonial, Mexican, and American eras, Southern California's Indians were "a dynamic force that sought and exploited opportunities and made the best of an ever-changing, volatile economy . . ."

Historian Albert Hurtado argues that these widely spread cases of harvest and other employment show that "Indian workers helped to transform a remote frontier into a quickly modernizing part of the western world." It was an accomplishment, however, they "did not ultimately benefit from."

They did not benefit because they gradually lost their land, under a pattern seen repeatedly in Manifest Destiny's westward march. It stemmed not only from being overwhelmed militarily, but also through the defeats imposed by a strange legal system. There were other factors, and disease is blamed for much of the California Indians' population decline, from 100,000 in 1848 to 30,000 in 1870, but the land issue was unrelenting. Courts blocked efforts by many tribes to keep their traditional territories—and ignorance of the law was no excuse. This was the experience of the Doaksum family, members of the Big Meadows tribe, or Nahkomas. Even though their people had occupied the lands in question "prior to October 1, A.D. 1492," and since then had continuously owned and used them "for a village site and burial-place, and for supplies of water, fuel, etc.," and even though they had never signed a treaty giving up their land—the California Supreme Court in 1886 ruled that the property had been granted to the United States by Mexico as part of the Treaty of Guadalupe Hidalgo of 1848. "If defendants had any right to the land," the Court said, "it should have been asserted in the land department . . . or by direct proceeding on the part of the government to set aside the patent." A white man who had filed a homestead claim on their land was awarded the property.

The Nahkomas had not taken the necessary legal steps. Unaware of legal requirements of the new nation, they lost the land that they and their ancestors had lived on, land they presumed was theirs. There was nothing unusual in this case in the sweep of American history. And as Indians were pushed off their homelands onto reservations, they had only their labor to fall back on.[23]

Another group was already present as intensive farming took hold: the Chinese, whose experiences would soon become entwined with the tales and folklore of California agriculture. The story of the Chinese usually leaves out the "push factors" that preceded their arrival, however. Guangdong Province, on China's heavily populated southern coast, had become a center of tragedy, as floods, droughts, famine, and other natural disasters combined with ongoing wars that finally erupted in peasant uprisings—such as the Punti and Hakka Cantonese feuds, and the long Tai P'ing rebellion from 1850 to 1864. Half a world away, similar conditions in Europe brought an exodus, crowding the ships and ship lanes to America; events in China closely paralleled the European experience. Also left out of standard accounts is the earlier presence of Chinese in the New World—their first recorded appearance was the arrival of Chinese merchants in Mexico City in 1585, the year that the first English colony in America was being launched (unsuccessfully) at Roanoke Island off modern North Carolina. Mexico City had a Chinatown by 1650, and the Spanish colonies in Mexico and Peru received Chinese in the seventeenth and eighteenth centuries.

These journeys occurred in spite of Chinese rulers' long-standing bans on "removal to foreign lands." In the nineteenth century Britain began to use Chinese labor in its Far Eastern plantations, but managers were often blocked from obtaining enough workers. It was the British who finally persuaded China in 1860 to allow Chinese laborers to travel to their colonies as laborers. This encouraged the United States, then seeking men to construct its railroads; it won similar concessions from China in the Burlingame Treaty of 1868.[24]

By then, however, interest in emigrating to the United States was already stirring in South China. News of the events of 1848 at Sutter's Mill stimulated an exodus to Gum Sahn—Gold Mountain—that China's rulers could not hold back. Lum Mu Fong later reminisced on the life-changing decision that had brought him to California: after working on his family's farm as the man of the household following his father's death, when he was twenty-two "the most exciting news in my young life was an event that my kinfolks had talked about for years—they were able to save enough money to sponsor me for the long journey across the sea to Gum Sahn!"

Many other Chinese also heard this "exciting news" and began plotting their departure. A type of indentured servitude was created, enabling many to travel under contract, to work off their shipping debt in California—but enough escaped to the gold fields after landing in San Francisco that a political scandal erupted. White miners often violently opposed the Chinese, and when the search for gold and silver went underground, the Asians were restricted to panning gold along western rivers. They often made a living from sites abandoned by others, but soon even these diggings played out.

At this juncture another employment opportunity appeared: in 1866 the Central Pacific Railroad began looking for workers to blast eastward through the Sierras to construct a roadway for the new transcontinental railway's western leg. Some 10,000 to 12,000 Chinese worked on the line before it reached Promontory Summit in Utah, where the gold spike was driven in 1869, uniting it with the Union Pacific coming from the Midwest.[25]

Thereafter many were drawn into California's developing agricultural economy. In 1852 a veteran 'forty-niner wrote an account for the *San Joaquin Republican* on future possibilities for making that valley "one vast vineyard and orchard." He saw a role for the new arrivals from Asia:

We have amongst us several thousand of the inhabitants of China; a great many of them are intelligent men, from whom much reliable information can be obtained in regard to the introduction of the tea plant into California, and the value of our tule land for the cultivation of rice . . . These emigrants are, as a class, the best people we have amongst us—they are sober, quiet, industrious, and inoffensive . . .

As the Chinese moved out of the mountains to the fields below, did they *teach* the recently arrived California agriculturists—many of whom had never farmed before—how to grow the new crops that soon dotted the landscape? Carey McWilliams admitted that the truth is difficult to discover because of the "mist of prejudice," but he argued that "by and large, it is correct to state that, in many particulars, the Chinese actually taught their overlords how to plant, cultivate, and harvest orchard and garden crops." When the Stockton Chamber of Commerce sought to become an asparagus center, for example, it called on Chinese workers' expertise in vegetable growing as well as their field skills.

Without question the Chinese fanned out rapidly over the Sacramento Valley and the San Francisco Bay area. As Sucheng Chan's studies have shown, in 1870 45 percent of the farm laborers and workers in the farm households of San Joaquin County were Chinese, as were substantial percentages in several other counties. By late 1872 San Luis Obispo had a Chinatown, where recruiters from Lompoc in Santa Barbara County traveled in 1879 to recruit all the Chinese available to pick beans. By 1880 the census recorded that Chinese made up one-third of the farm laborers in the major farming counties, while in some townships their numbers topped 80 and even 90 percent. In the heavy fruit and hops centers of Sacramento and Yuba counties, the Chinese "might indeed have constituted three-quarters to seven-eighths of the farm labor force . . . ," Chan concluded.[26]

It was a lonely time for many. As with the nineteenth-century European emigration to America, young men predominated—young men planning to make money and return home. And large numbers did return: when the steamer *City of Peking* sailed away from San Francisco one day in late 1880, it carried some 916 Chinese en route back to Hong Kong, and the *Kern County Gazette* of Bakersfield said the reasons for this "extraordinary exodus" lay in California unemployment, "persistent abuse," laws banning gambling and opium smoking, reports of China's increasing prosperity, and the approach of the Chinese New Year. But many could not afford the trip back and lived on with the unreachable dream of someday rejoining family members.[27]

Employers often heaped much praise on these Asian immigrants. Strangely, enthusiastic words came even from some who claimed they wanted the immigration stopped. While most Chinese worked in agriculture, many others found employment as cooks, clerks, peddlers, and merchants. The varieties of Chinese employment meant that many Californians simply kept quiet during the growing attacks on Chinese laborers. At an 1886 meeting of Sacramento's Boycott Safety Committee (fighting "freedom's battle"), an orator proclaimed bitterly that many supposedly pro-white employers were lying; while "crying out against the evils of Chinese labor," he said, "they were employing Chinese domestics; Chinese did their laundrying [sic]; Chinese made their cigars; Chinese did their cooking; the waiting maids of their wives and daughters were Chinese." It was a situation made for conflict, dishonesty, and some hypocrisy.[28]

As in other regions where immigrants were being hired to replace whites, some observers couched their praises by noting that those doing stoop labor had advantageous physical differences. Chinese dominance of sugar beet field work at Alvarado in 1870 and in the Sacramento Valley drew the comment that the labor involved in beet thinning "was of such a nature that only Chinamen could be obtained to do it." They could squat low, while whites were bigger, many noted. Others pointed to wage differentials and growers' inability to pay more; several reported cases where whites refused to work for going wages. In 1901 the Industrial Commission noted that the average Chinaman's daily wage was $1.25—of which he would save about $1.00, it was estimated—while whites made $1.50 to $1.75. The charge of "cheap labor" continued to echo through the anti-Chinese campaigns.[29]

Opposition to the Chinese erupted initially in the gold diggings and the workingmen's quarters of San Francisco and quickly permeated all levels of California society. In May 1870 the San Francisco Bulletin reported that "a well-dressed boy, on his way to Sunday school, was arrested and thrown into the city prison for stoning Chinamen," whereupon local reporter Mark Twain asked, "How should he suppose it was wrong to stone a Chinaman?" Twain pointed out the conditions that would seem to justify the boy's act: the state put an unlawful mining tax upon the Chinaman but "allows Patrick the foreigner to dig gold for nothing"; each arriving Chinaman had to pay $10 to be vaccinated at the San Francisco wharf, but doctors in the city would do it for 50 cents; and "everybody, individuals, communities, the majesty of the state itself, joined in hating, abusing, and persecuting these humble strangers." The rising humorist wrote that the San Francisco boy heading off to Sunday school must have said to himself: "Ah, there goes a Chinaman! God will not love me if I do not stone him."

Stonings, occasional beatings, and mounting verbal abuse led to worse violence and street campaigns. In 1871 twenty-two Chinese were killed in a daylong riot in Los Angeles, and in 1876 Sacramento's Order of Caucasians drew 4,000 to a rally. The 1877 nationwide rail strike eventually spread to California, and a July 23 San Francisco rally supporting the strikers turned into an anti-Chinese riot that went on for days. The city's Committee of Safety eventually suppressed the uprising, blaming hoodlums, thieves, and Communists as instigators, but it also proposed that "in the interest of American civilization on the Pacific Coast," the federal government needed to block further Chinese immigration.

Rioting against the Chinese spread to several other California communities, including Courtland, Rocklin, Santa Clara, Sacramento, and Chico. Throughout the waves of protests, many growers were warned that to avoid trouble, they should stop employing Chinese and instead hire whites and Indians. In Chico, major grower John Bidwell received a warning in March 1877: "discharge your Mongolian help within ten days from date, or suffer the consequences. Let this be enough." An Anaheim hops grower was told that he could employ Chinese only if no whites were available; after hiring some pickers from both races, he was warned again and replaced the Chinese with Indians.[30]

Laws began to target the Chinese, who only short years before, in 1868, had been invited to immigrate to the United States under the Burlingame Treaty. The Workingman's Party controlled a third of the delegates to California's constitutional convention in 1878–79, so new restrictions were predictable. The resulting constitution banned Chinese from voting and forbade governmental units as well as corporations with government contracts from hiring Chinese. The U.S. Congress was soon drawn into the debate, which eventually led to revision of the Burlingame Treaty: now the government could not "absolutely prohibit" Chinese laborers' entry but could regulate, limit, or suspend Chinese immigration. In 1882 such a flat prohibition was included in a new Chinese Exclusion Act, firmly cutting off Chinese laborers' immigration for ten years and forbidding their naturalization. Historians have cited this as the first step in the "racialization" of U.S. immigration policy, the transformation of the nation from an immigrant-welcoming society into a "gatekeeper" nation that sporadically barred certain racial and ethnic groups from entering.

After the 1882 federal law, many California communities passed similar statutes. The little San Joaquin River community of New York Landing, for one, banned all Chinese residency. Soon afterward a Chinese man got off a steamer and waited on the pier as the boat pulled away—and a mob dumped his bags into the river and chased him off. Many such local and state laws were declared unconstitutional, including an 1891 California statute that banned all Chinese immigration; the same fate befell a congressional enactment in 1892 requiring Chinese caught within the confines of the nation unlawfully to be imprisoned at hard labor for a year and then deported. In 1902 the temporary Chinese exclusion law was re-enacted and amended, and two years later it was made permanent.[31]

In some ways, the Chinese had the last laugh. Politicians and community elites generally kept their Chinese cooks, municipalities evaded the law to employ Chinese for road work, and growers decided they could not survive without their Asian harvesters. At the height of the rioting in 1877, a group of white farmers in the Sacramento delta responded to demands that they fire their Chinese workers by vowing that "the Chinamen were of necessity employed and found to be sturdy, sober and industrious, the whites being the very reverse." Within a year of passage of the Exclusion Act, the *Pacific Rural Press* complained that the fruit crop "taxed the labor capacity of the State to the utmost" and asked what lay ahead without the Chinese. The Horticultural Society proposed the use of high school boys, but some experienced growers criticized this idea, and others called it simply unrealistic: "Last year Chinese, school children, tramps, and all were unable to prevent hundreds of thousands of dollars worth of fruit from wasting," a letter writer to the *Pacific Rural Press* pointed out.[32]

But as the debates went on, the ticking clock of harvest was never silent. Short days before a Sacramento Boycott Safety Committee rally in 1886, the *Daily Record-Union* reported that "Chinatown has been filling up with Celestials" because of "the close proximity of the hop-picking season . . ." Then harvest began, and some Chinese crews demanded higher pay and won. "The Chinamen seem to have the best of the growers, as the hops must be picked immediately, and the pickers have evidently been studying the 'Melican man' system of labor protection, with certain improvements of their own."[33] One of the underlying realities of intensive agriculture was that without harvesters, the result was failure. Occasionally growers had to yield to that reality.

And they came to appreciate another fact: they usually did not have to hire Chinese individually but dealt with a contractor who delivered the required number of men. "The number of workers were brought to you . . . No fuss, no trouble," one raisin farmer recalled. Growers had no messy bookkeeping when dealing with Chinese contractors; they simply paid the contractors, who passed on part of the payment to the workers. This "gang" system made several Chinese contractors rich. They were usually connected to the famous Six Companies in San Francisco, often with links that extended back to workers' recruitment in China. The Chinese were part of an intricate grapevine, which helped growers obtain large gangs of workers quickly.[34]

The *Pacific Rural Press*, a major spokesman for California's growers, spelled out the dilemma over the Chinese in an editorial in 1893, by which time many of the Chinese who had arrived in the gold rush and Central Pacific Railroad era were aging, retiring from farmwork, moving to the cities, or returning to China:

> We do not argue that the Chinaman is a permanent necessity to the California fruit industry; but he is a necessity until somebody else is qualified to take his place . . . Hoodlums, tramps and ruffians can never be relied upon for any useful work . . . Under the laws which prohibit Chinese immigration our Chinese population will gradually decline and white labor will as gradually fill its place in orchard work . . .

The issue's complications were on display at the end of 1902, when the California Fruit Growers Association met in Sacramento. A proposal to import midwestern white farm boys was put forward as a cure-all for labor shortages, and a proposal was heard to induce local young white men and women to work. But a Watsonville grower argued in response, "We have degraded a certain class of labor, and there is not a man who lives in any agricultural locality who wants to get in and do this work." He called instead for sending a memorial to Congress to lift the ban on Chinese immigration. Only the Chinese could solve the labor problem. The association approved resolutions on the two plans— supporting the opening of Chinese immigration, and importing mid-western farm boys—with wide support. Around the state, growers begged Congress to allow some Chinese in.[35]

But by then there was no turning back. The anti-Chinese campaigners, most of whom were not growers, had won. The final exclusion act of 1904 put the seal on the years of rioting, debating, and shouting: the Chinese were to be kept out as unassimilable. But lengthy dependence upon laborers from China was too strong to be suddenly cut off by a scrap of paper, and reports poured in from border areas north and south that Chinese immigration was continuing—they simply traveled first to Canada or Mexico and then crossed over the border. One historian estimates that 17,300 Chinese illegally entered from Mexico and Canada in the years 1882–1920.

Such efforts were inadequate in keeping up with demand, however, and Chinese numbers were soon declining in California's orchards and hopyards. In 1880 the census counted 75,183 Chinese laborers in California; by 1900 the number had fallen to 45,753. In 1907 a Fresno labor contractor told a reporter that "Chinese labor cuts very little figure in harvest operations. Chinese are few and they are old." By 1920, according to Sucheng Chan's demographic study, "of all the places where Chinese had farmed in California, a Chinese farming community survived only in the Sacramento-San Joaquin Delta."[36]

But as the number of Chinese declined, growers were happily becoming aware that a new harvest labor force was arriving in California.

Japanese laborers missed the gold rush but began showing up on California railroad crews and farms by the 1880s. In this *Dekasegi* period of Japanese emigration, the Meiji government allowed short-term trips for labor abroad but sought both its regulation and protection. From hesitant, small-scale early ventures into California territory, the number of Japanese kept growing until 1909, when an Immigration Commission investigation concluded that the Japanese "came to dominate the labor situation in most localities devoted to intensive farming."

These Japanese, or *issei*, were arriving in a time of uncertainty, even worry, for California growers. Chinese help was sharply declining in numbers because of the Exclusion Act and the unrelenting pruning of time; growers searched anew for dependable replacements at satisfactory wages. Various plans circulated, including importing blacks from the South, whom the Southern Pacific readily agreed to transport.

Then in midsummer 1888 the Japanese consul in San Francisco announced that some of his country's unemployed would be permitted to travel to California to work. The Japanese government enacted a series of emigration protections, and while many were ineffective, others provided some help to the travelers. From such small beginnings a possible solution to California's labor shortage seemed at hand, and soon the trickle of Japanese workmen became a torrent. They came from many areas of the homeland, especially Hiroshima, Wakayama, and Kumamoto, three southwestern *ken* (prefectures) where landscape and inhabitants alike had been hurt by the long-term effects of tiny peasant landholdings. Many men from those areas had previously gone to Hawaii to labor on sugar cane plantations, and U.S. recruiters soon spotted opportunities there. From 1902 to 1907 some 37,000 Japanese left Hawaii for jobs on the West Coast, most to California.[37]

This influx of Japanese added complications to California's labor dilemma. By 1909 the *Pacific Rural Press* conceded that Japanese were needed because not enough Chinese were available: "Nearly everyone would like to see the Japanese go—but not too quickly; we would not have them branded until it appears a little more clear what labor we can have in their place . . ."[38]

The Japanese fitted quickly into the perennial needs of a diverse agriculture for short-term workers. At first these newcomers worked as migratory harvest hands like the Americans and Chinese they observed. Soon the Japanese term *Buranke-katsugi* was adapted in America as *buranketto* boys; one translation calls them the "blanke [*sic*] group." Now, as California bindlestiffs, their working, shifting, transient lives were indistinguishable in many ways from those of other migrant workers. Two brothers who arrived in San Jose in 1913 linked up with their father and worked the Santa Clara Valley: "Yoshio Ando recalled how

Japanese migrants picked strawberries in Alviso during April, moved to
the middle and far ends of the valley to the apricot and prune orchards
in July and August, and later traveled on to Fresno to pick grapes." A
similar account published in Japan recounted the struggles of one newly
arrived *buranketto* boy, who watched itinerant workers "as they carried
blankets on their backs and pressed on from job to job among California ranches, like migrating birds."[39]

Shoji Nagumo arrived in 1917. Although he had been a student in
Japan, he was forced to become a picker of muscat grapes in the "hot,
dry oven" of the Fresno area. Many foreign workers were illiterate, making Nagumo's recollections valuable. "The job itself was not hard," he
wrote, "but because of this or that obstacle my hips and back ached as
I worked in the baking hot fields in the same position, and my back and
shoulders were getting sunburned." From the grueling work to the unsanitary living conditions, he simply concluded, "What a cruel society I
have leaped into."[40]

The Japanese soon "adopted the Chinese 'boss' system," the Immigration Commission reported. The laborers now went about in "gangs."
Japanese contractors controlled them much as the Chinese "bosses"
controlled their workers, but with more flexibility, as they had no equivalent of the Six Companies. For the growers, the system was the same,
for they did not hire individuals but counted on contractors to supply
Japanese workers. As the commission explained, "In this way the employment of Asiatics has reduced the risk involved in securing laborers"
and also reduced problems over their supervision and pay. Contractors
were therefore well placed to demand better wages for their men. As
growers became aware of this possibility, they learned to spell out the
requirements in a contract; contract violations would bring a damage
charge of $1,000.

These written rules were needed because more than the Chinese or
any other group, the Japanese became known for breaking contracts to
force wage increases. "Every Japanese gang is a trade union; they come
and quit together," a sugar beet farmer complained to a U.S. Department of Labor investigator. United under leaders in this way, Japanese
workers gained a foothold in many districts by first underbidding Chinese and white workers. Once they became dominant in an area, their
wages soon rose, until even the disparity with white pay scales began to
disappear. The Immigration Commission found in 1909 that the Japa-

nese even outnumbered white men in citrus: in 23 citrus ranches investigated, the Japanese "had displaced white men on 18 ranches, white
men and Chinese on one, white men and Mexicans on another, Mexicans on two, and Chinese on the other one." For California as a whole,
"the Japanese have now come to occupy the position occupied by the
Chinese in the early nineties."[41]

Growers were at first nonplussed by Japanese threats, then embit-
tered, and finally forced into a variety of actions to thwart the contract-
breaking. At the turn of the century George Washington Pierce, Jr., a
major almond raiser near Davisville in Yolo County, confronted such a
situation. Yields from his trees were increasing steadily but white workers
were becoming scarce, so in August 1901 he contracted with Shi Kubo
for eleven Japanese, at $1.25 each per day. It seemed quite a coup;
Pierce had been paying whites $1.50 a day. On their second day gather-
ing almonds, Kubo demanded a doubling of the wage. Pierce refused to
budge, ordered Kubo's men away, put a notice in the *Davisville Enterprise* warning other orchardists, and wound up hiring ten Chinese and
five whites. In ensuing years Pierce switched to selling the entire crop
in advance to Japanese contractors, shifting responsibility to them for
getting the almonds harvested. In several years when prices were low,
Pierce won and the contractors lost in the arrangement. As historian
David Vaught concludes, Pierce's moves amid sharply changing labor
conditions "revealed just how unforgiving a horticulturist could be if
his authority in his orchards was challenged." In the process, however,
labor supply became Pierce's "Achilles heel," as it was for many other
California growers.[42]

Such negative reports were not heard yet in the Southern California
community of Oxnard, sixty-seven miles up the shoreline from Los Angeles. Oxnard had become a major sugar beet center, expanding rapidly
after the 1897 Dingley Tariff offered protection for American sugar
beets and new state bounties encouraged expanding production. Some
white workers were hired initially at the Oxnard factory and in surrounding fields, but most soon dropped out, and Mexicans, then Chinese,
and finally large numbers of Japanese showed up to fill labor needs.[43]

Their contractors accompanied them, and by 1902 nine Japanese
contractors controlled hiring of 90 percent of the men who thinned,

weeded, pulled, and topped sugar beets on farms supplying the Oxnard factory. But that year the dominant American Beet Sugar Company decided to break up this near-monopoly and joined with local bankers and business leaders to form the Western Agricultural Contracting Company (WACC). It took over hiring all beet farmworkers, replacing the Japanese contractors and in the process reducing costs—and the threat of labor disruptions—for local farmers. Japanese labor contractors were forced to subcontract through the WACC, and new hires had to pay fees both to the subcontractor and to the WACC.

An early group of Japanese, brought by the WACC from San Francisco in spring 1903, soon held a protest meeting, charging that instead of receiving the promised $1.50 per day, they were relegated to a piece-work schedule that brought them less. Thinning of beets was now pegged at $3.75 an acre; earlier rates had been $5 to $6. Further, they were paid in scrip that was accepted only at WACC company stores, where they were overcharged. The WACC's leaders refused to budge; they would finally break the contractors' power.

From these disputes came formation of the Japanese-Mexican Labor Association (JMLA), led by Japanese and Mexican contractors, with some 500 Japanese and 200 Mexican workers as initial members. Two union organizers from Los Angeles arrived to assist their efforts. It held the potential for marking a crucial turn, Tomás Almaguer writes: "The decision to form this union and challenge the WACC marked the first time the two minority groups successfully joined forces to organize an agricultural workers' union in the state."

The revolt succeeded, held together by the workers' anger at WACC pay cuts as well as by unity forged in parades and demonstrations. A violent confrontation on March 23 failed to blunt the joint Mexican-Japanese drive, and soon incoming strikebreakers were being informed of the dispute; as historian Richard Steven Street writes, those who slipped through the JMLA net were forced to leave. Arrests, threats, and cajoling failed, and final victory came to the union, now with some 1,300 members. Success was also pushed by the fact that the sugar beets did not stop growing; unless field work began soon, the company's losses would be heavy. The wage for thinning was soon reset at $5, up to a high of $6, or almost double the WACC rate, and the JMLA won the right to represent workers on 5,000 acres of Ventura County beet fields, missing only the 1,800-acre Patterson ranch. The workers had higher pay, Japanese contractors were back in control of most hiring, and both groups were in a strong position to make future demands.

It was not quite a minority-workers-vs.-white-employers confrontation: this was a multiracial event, on both sides. But the Oxnard workers' success in 1903 forced the AFL and California labor organizations at least temporarily to reevaluate their traditional fears of organizing farmworkers and signing up Asians and Mexicans as members. These fears would resurface often, however, following the United States' triumph in the 1898 Spanish-American War and the ensuing clash with the Philippines independence movement. Psychological barriers to labor unity remained.

Even the Chinese sometimes looked askance at growing Japanese successes, both within California and abroad. Japan's victories in the 1894–95 Sino-Japanese War and the 1904–5 Russo-Japanese War set off massive celebrations among Japanese in Sacramento, while in San Francisco a Japanese militia group was formed to combat hostile critics. Until then the two Asian groups had often worked together and shopped in each other's stores but had seldom fought beyond occasional brawls in gambling dens. Members of both groups were often hired through the same agencies, which sometimes increased their sense of competition.

These developments came as both groups were increasing their efforts to gain control of farmland through contracting and leasing. White orchardists often approved of this approach: it placed responsibility for bringing in the harvest on others, amid growing concerns over the future availability of workers to hire. Well before the 1894 depression, some northern California fruit men had started carving up their properties and leasing to Chinese, leaving to them the task of finding harvesters. John Bidwell finally took this route, and soon his Chinese lessees were hiring Japanese help. "The Chinese now have possession of the large majority of the orchards about Chico," the *Chico Chronicle-Record* announced in May 1894. Such reports stirred local anti-Chinese agitators anew.[44]

Before long, however, the system became more closely identified with Japanese. The *Pacific Rural Press* complained in 1909 that Japanese were leasing the best orchards around Yuba City and were taking over other Sutter County districts. While no one could blame a Japanese worker for wanting to "be his own boss," the journal admitted, Americans would have only themselves to blame if their land became "a farther Nippon," for the editor looked "with great apprehension upon the disposition to lease our fruit properties to the Japanese . . . There is no more reason why the Japanese should own our orchards than that we should become web-footed in order to own their rice fields."

The impact of these anti-Japanese statements was quite different from that of earlier anti-Chinese campaigns, however, because of the difference in the two countries of origin. China's warlord-riven society was much weaker than the unified—and proud—Japan, which was then seeking higher standing among the nations. The growing stridency of verbal attacks on Japanese workers in California rankled the Japanese government and formed part of the backdrop for the 1906–7 San Francisco school crisis. The city school board's segregation rule theoretically affected both Asian groups equally, but in 1885, when San Francisco ordered Chinese pupils to attend separate schools, the Chinese community had gone along with the order—an acquiescence that the Japanese now criticized. The Japanese refused to meekly accept such treatment.[45]

Eventually President Theodore Roosevelt entered the fray, forcing the San Francisco School Board to back down. (There were only 93 Japanese students in all 23 public schools, and 25 of these students had been born in the United States.) Roosevelt also got the California legislature to agree, for the moment, to discontinue pushing anti-Japanese proposals. Then Congress gave him the power he requested to block foreign laborers from entering the country without proper passports. This led to negotiation of the Gentlemen's Agreement with Japan in 1907–8, under which Japan agreed to issue passports "only to such of its subjects as are non-laborers"—diplomats, merchants, students and tourists—or were joining family members, or were already "settled agriculturists" in America.

The impact of this rising anti-Japanese agitation on sensibilities within Japan was great, William Howard Taft recalled several years later. Speaking to the New York Peace Society in early 1914, the former president described a meeting with a Japanese diplomat when he was secretary of war during Roosevelt's administration. The diplomat, Count Hyashi, observed that as Japan had risen in national power and prestige, its people's sensitivity as a nation had also risen, "and it makes them deeply resent an injustice or an invidious discrimination against them in a foreign country or by a foreign people." The only possible danger of the United States and Japan developing "any breach," Hyashi added, "would be one growing out of the mistreatment of our people living under the promised protection of the United States through the lawless violence of a mob directed against them as Japanese."[46]

Conditions in California agriculture were changing rapidly as the twentieth century's opening decade came to a close. Chinese and Japanese, who had provided labor for the developing boom, were now banned from further immigration; and Japanese were leaving fruit and hops picking and becoming growers, generally in orchards they leased and soon were purchasing. More laborers were discovering their power to seek better wages and living conditions as fast-ripening crops awaited harvest. A new spirit of organization was starting to appear among migrant workers of all groups.

11

MEXICANS, WOBBLIES, WAR

It was the rolled-up blanket, the "bindle," that readily identified hoboes as they traipsed along western roadways. And it was an incident involving the bindle that showed how different the decade of the 1910s was for harvest labor. It involved Pacific Northwest loggers, the bindlestiffs of the woods whose wanderings also took them to harvest jobs, fire crews, and railroad construction, among other labors. When loggers in the big woods were pressured to give up the right to strike for the duration of the Great War, they replied with a list of demands that included a guarantee of clean beds and bedding. One of them described what happened next:

> On the first of May, 1918, there was a curious ceremony performed in hundreds of camps throughout the Northwest. A holiday was taken and groups of celebrators gathered, torch in hand, to set fire to—what do you suppose?—their own blanket rolls. Thousands of old blankets and sougans* that had weighed down the backs of the loggers since the industry was established went up in smoke; the companies furnished bedding and sheets wherever this was done.[1]

It was a symbolic act, freighted with great meaning for these men, whose irregular work lives sometimes meant they were "starved into berries." For it was during that decade that many bindlestiffs had come

---

* A sougan was a type of sleeping bag made from blankets, like a bindle.

to realize, as one observer wrote, that their personal struggles left them "the finished product" of a system "cruelly efficient in turning out human beings modeled after all the standards which society abhors."[2]

The burning of the bindles in 1918 was but one upheaval of the 1910–20 period, years marked by four major developments affecting western harvest workers. First, harvest labor protests against employers were becoming more frequent, a development reflected in the rising strength of the Industrial Workers of the World. Second, urged on by Progressive activists, state and federal governments were turning their attention to seasonal workers, launching investigations aimed at reforming the migratory system. Third, Mexicans were in sharply increasing numbers becoming the dominant harvest labor group in California and across much of the West by 1920. And fourth, the outbreak of war in Europe in 1914, eventually drawing in the United States in 1917, hurried some of these trends, blocked others, and in the end served as a crucible from which emerged sharply different harvest labor conditions in the 1920s.

Some of these changes could be seen in the area formerly known as the Salton Sea (now called the Imperial Valley) in far Southern California. When the *Pacific Rural Press* looked over the region in 1909, it found that "great work" was being done there. That once-arid wasteland had been "in an absolutely desert condition in 1900," the *PRP* pointed out, but Imperial County now could boast 181,545 acres under irrigation.

The Southern Pacific was behind the drive to make this desert fruitful. As Richard Orsi has chronicled, the SP's tracks running toward Yuma, Arizona, provided the company with opportunities to acquire much land in far Southern California, which it sought to bring into production with extensive irrigation. New rail connections brought in land speculators, followed by settlers who started raising cantaloupes in the 1890s. By 1907 irrigation and a variety of new crops were beginning to match promoters' hopes—alfalfa, vegetables, eventually grapefruit and apricot trees, and finally cotton, making the Imperial Valley the latest stop in the westward march of the Cotton West. Until 1909 the agricultural census had found only seventy-nine farms in the Mountain and Pacific states (outside Texas, Oklahoma, and Arizona) growing cotton, but the following year the Imperial Valley ushered California into the census tables for the first time, with 6,000 bales grown on 9,000 acres.[3]

Heat proved a challenge. A professor at Occidental College who lost money on a Brawley area ranch admitted, "I do not believe the Imperial Valley is a white man's country and I am willing to hand it over to the Hindus and the Japanese." Agronomists experimenting with cotton worried about obtaining enough pickers in the valley's heat, but a new arrival from Texas advised that they need not worry. "We mean to get Mexicans for the work and can get all we need," he stated. "Mexicans are the best pickers we know of." Adding to such hopeful comments, the *California Fruit Grower* assured readers that Mexicans "are plentiful, generally peaceable, and are satisfied with very low social conditions."[4]

Mexicans had long been present in the valley. Many were descendants of original settlers who became Americans in the treaties after 1848, and they traveled back and forth over the unguarded border. In the Imperial Valley, hard against the Mexican frontier, Mexicans had replaced Indians as canal diggers by 1907. As more began to arrive from Sonora, Baja, and other Mexican states, they began working with vegetable crops and, increasingly, cotton. Mexicans and Japanese soon became the dominant labor groups in the Imperial Valley. Years later a Japanese veteran of that scene tellingly remembered his early schooling amid a heavily Mexican population: "So then what I first learned was *uno, dos, quatro, cinco*, so maybe I learned Spanish first. I thought it was English."[5]

The flow of Mexicans over the border, aided by extensions of the Mexican railway system, was still limited. A peasant's life remained rooted in tradition, and tradition did not yet tell him to pull up those roots to start picking cotton across the border. "A crisis had to come and tear him away from his moorings," as one sociologist later explained. That crisis was the Mexican Revolution.

As elsewhere in the Southwest, Mexicans began arriving in the valley in large numbers after 1910, fleeing violence and anarchy as fighting worsened; starvation was an added goad. The warfare between competing Mexican armies brought death to many—as high as a million and a half, by some estimates. By the mid-1920s Mexicans in the Imperial Valley numbered more than 18,000—including women and children—and the 9,000 harvest workers among them had to be joined by importation of some 15,000 others to bring in the crops. Replacements were needed frequently as workers kept deserting the scorching southern valleys for cooler districts to the north.[6]

Just as the American frontier had been hailed as a safety valve for those fleeing European wars and poverty, and then for Americans jammed into eastern cities, now this last frontier was offering an escape for Mexicans. But the slogan they shouted for their safety valve was not *Westward Ho!* but *Al norte!*

There had been pockets of Mexican workers early on—as in the Oxnard sugar beet fields—but their mass movement into California only began after revolutionary upheavals became severe. As late as 1908 a Labor Department investigator had noted that Mexicans in California were "not relatively so important a source of rural labor supply as they are in Texas," and the Immigration Commission team found in 1909 that only "a few Mexicans" were working in the Tulare citrus belt and picking grapes around Fresno. Soon the floodgates opened, however, as advertisements for labor were run in border towns and Mexicans began to arrive by the trainload. By 1914 a federal investigator could write that Mexicans were showing up even in orange groves in the Lindsay area, joining the majority "white or American type" and Japanese.

Mexicans continued moving into different areas of California, for cotton was expanding northward from the Imperial, Palo Verde, and Coachella valleys into the San Joaquin. In fact, the San Joaquin Valley would eventually join West Texas atop U.S. cotton production statistics, and an old story was repeated: by 1918 investigators were concerned over whether they could find enough workers to bring in the difficult-to-pick Egyptian cotton.

They need not have worried. Mexicans made their way toward the San Joaquin, often first taking railroad construction jobs around the Southwest. Soon drawn into California's intensive farming districts, many followed migratory routes that included thinning sugar beets in the spring, then moving on to harvest cotton and deciduous fruits, then late-summer hops, then citrus. Now the center of the nation's Spanish-speakers was no longer New Mexico; it had expanded to take in California as well as Texas and Arizona.[7]

Mexicans' movement northward was fortunate for California growers. By 1910 the number of Chinese laborers was declining sharply, and Japanese were beginning to move out of stoop labor. The 1900 census had counted only thirty-seven Japanese farms in California, with 4,674 acres, but in succeeding years more and more Japanese had left casual labor to seek out land to work for themselves—1,816 were farming almost 100,000 acres by the 1910 census. This pattern was followed closely in many of the most productive districts. In the Santa Clara Valley around San Jose, Japanese began leasing farmland soon after they arrived in large numbers in the early 1900s. What was true in the Santa Clara Valley was true in other areas, such as Florin, southwest of Sacramento, where by 1908 Japanese owned 697 of the area's 1,678 productive acres; in 1912 they had 1,065 acres.[8]

Perennially worried about finding harvest hands, many white farmers accepted any system that transferred the task of labor recruitment to someone else. As the Immigration Commission noted in its 1909 inquiry, many times "leasing has been resorted to as a method of securing a nucleus of a desired labor supply and of transferring to the tenants the solution of the problem of obtaining the other laborers needed." In eastern Colorado, Utah, and Idaho this meant leasing to German-Russians; in California it meant leasing to Chinese and increasingly by 1910 to Japanese.

Steps taken by Japanese toward eventual landownership—because that was their goal—came amid growing anti-Japanese frenzy across the state. The Gentlemen's Agreement of 1907–8 was not concluded because of fears over Japanese landholding, but as news spread of Japanese sharecropping, it was added to the arguments used against the Asians.[9] The legislature was geared to act, but worries over ruining San Francisco's chances for hosting the 1915 Panama-Pacific International Exposition— celebrating completion of the Panama Canal—initially dampened the enthusiasm for driving out the Japanese. Then pro-exclusion forces rallied again, finally wringing a statement in 1912 from presidential candidate Woodrow Wilson that he stood for exclusion. Wilson explained, "We cannot make a homogeneous population out of a people who do not blend with the Caucasian race. Their lower standard of living as laborers will crowd out the white agriculturist . . ."

After Wilson became president, however, the Japanese government complained about the tempest brewing in California and Washington State against Japanese landownership; he urged California legislators to practice caution. But it was too late: the state's Webb-Heney Act of

1913 barred land purchases by any person ineligible for citizenship, and leases of agricultural land to Japanese were limited to three-year contracts. Despite these acts, the Panama Pacific International Exposition opened to great acclaim in San Francisco on February 20, 1915, and ran until December.

California law may have banned Japanese ownership of land and may have restricted leases to three years, but white farmers continued to rent to Japanese. One-year leases, signed anew each year, were no problem. Further, Japanese who desired to quit picking fruit for others and to farm for themselves soon found ways around the bans and limits. With the 1918 Armistice, California groups angered at Japanese successes sought to clamp down further, winning wide political backing. The result was a state initiative in 1920 to amend the Webb-Heney Act, not only to block Japanese from any leasing of agricultural land but also to stop them from evading the law by placing title in corporations or in the names of their American-born children.

Voters approved the initiative by an overwhelming three-to-one margin. Another new law in 1923 made it illegal for aliens ineligible for citizenship to "acquire, possess, enjoy, use, cultivate, occupy, and transfer real property." California's toughened stance paralleled Oregon's 1923 bill banning alien landownership; it passed the house with only one vote opposed and made it through the state senate unanimously. The following year Congress approved the Johnson-Reed Act, setting an annual limit on total immigration and placing quotas on entries from specific countries—except for Japan and China. They had no quota. Their immigration was prohibited.[10]

Now the scramble for harvest help entered a new phase. Earlier, new groups from Europe and South Asia had gradually been making their way to California: Italians, Portuguese, Armenians, Dalmatians, Greeks, and Spaniards. While their numbers did not approach those of the Chinese, Japanese, and Mexicans, they often spent some years hired out for harvests before taking over farms or vineyards or drifting into the cities.

Newly arrived Armenians, Italians, and Portuguese moved in large numbers into leasing and eventual landownership, and each group was soon identified with a specific crop. With Armenians it was raisins, and by 1902 some 15 percent of the California raisin crop came from their acres. Italians initially were identified with western mining and coastal fishing, but by 1905 half of California's Italians worked in agriculture, especially in wine making and growing fruit. Newly arriving Portuguese soon veered from field labors into dairy farming and growing vegetables such as the sweet potato.[11]

East Indian Hindus and Sikhs also showed up. They had been re-cruited by the British for decades for work in the empire's far-flung plantations—in such locations as Mauritius, Guyana, Trinidad, Fiji, and the Transvaal. Eventually they were hired on construction projects in Australia and were soon building railroad lines and working in saw-mills in British Columbia. Many journeyed southward into the United States, their numbers reaching an estimated 5,000 in the West by 1912, where they labored on railroads as well as on harvest crews. They finally reached the Imperial Valley, where in 1909 a group was hired to pick melons and cotton and to dig ditches. Their work in the blazing sun won praise from their employers, as did their custom of remaining sepa-rate, not mixing with others.[12]

These groups provided workers, but the only adequate solution for Cal-ifornia's worsening harvest labor situation appeared to be Mexicans. However, employers also realized that they could not simply wait for single men fleeing the revolution. In Southern California they found the answer: they would encourage, lure, and even import Mexican fam-ilies, with wives and children.

The transformation in some ways resulted from fortuitous events. At the Limoneira Ranch, northwest of Los Angeles, single Japanese men had been housed since 1907 in a bunkhouse, but so few remained by 1910 that attention turned to Mexicans. Some were already scattered around the district—they were then building a railroad spur to the com-pany packinghouse, and when that project was finished they were hired to pick lemons. But these were single men, and somehow they were not working out, the company soon realized. As was said of American ho-boes, their Sunday often stretched into Monday.

Among the Mexican lemon pickers were a few who returned nightly to their families living nearby, and they were generally good workers. This suggested a new system. But if Limoneira's executives were going to invite large numbers of Mexican families onto their properties, different facilities would have to be provided—rundown shacks and tents would not do. They decided to construct adequate dwellings, and over the next several years the firm built 160 cottages for them. Recruitment of families began. It was a sharp break with California and western traditions, although paralleling what sugar beet employers were attempting on the Great Plains.

The businessmen found in addition to housing, Mexicans needed something approaching year-round employment. Soon Limoneira expanded its plantings along different agricultural lines, so that women and small children could stay at home while husbands and youths worked. Historian José Manuel Alamillo explains that Limoneira's acts were not simply a matter of Progressivism or company goodwill; the firm had an "economic motivation to recruit and maintain a more permanent labor force, as well to ensure a new generation of workers." For whatever motive, the idea of providing housing for Mexican families spread through California's orchards and sugar beet fields. Mexican families were on the way to becoming firmly established in California agriculture—but not as landowners, only as harvest workers.[13]

Some critics charged that placing Mexican families in the communities being created by citrus companies erected a barrier against the dream of re-creating in California the world of the midwestern farmer— a world in which white American or European immigrant families lived on small farms, supplying their own labor needs and only occasionally calling for outside help. In that world of the "agricultural ladder," hired hands could eventually become farm owners. This was the dream of Elwood Mead, who had worked long and hard to bring water to the West's arid regions. Seeking to improve the lot of the small farmer in California, Mead led a study of the challenges to land settlement. His investigators encountered both enthusiasm and frustration, contentment and defeat, in two communities newly created by the legislature. Successes were limited; several farmers had been defrauded while seeking their dream. One wrote, "I am one of the many Eastern suckers who was lied [to] by the State Official Agents in Madison Square New York, and sacrificed a good place for the chimeric visions of 'Golden' (meaning imitation) West. I cannot give the place away."

•

Later studies have ranked the availability of cheap farm labor along with farm mechanization as important to the enormous production gains recorded by American agriculture. And much of this success came from the development of "factories in the field," a reality in some California districts long before author Carey McWilliams introduced the phrase to the reading public. But despite the negative reports found by Mead's investigators, Mead's dream seems to have had some success. Historian David Vaught has pointed out that, according to one estimate, the average fruit farm had only 96 acres in 1900, a fact obscured by the large number of extensive wheat and cattle ranches across California then; for example, half of Yolo County's farms were less than 100 acres. In the years before the First World War these small farms were hardly "factories in the field" and might more appropriately be described as "workshops," where orchardists concentrated on using the latest scientific advances to wring out the highest production. With intensive agriculture small orchards could provide an owner with a decent living, and one California expert even argued that 3 to 15 acres could create a profitable cotton farm—the small scale was important, he wrote, because of maintaining soil fertility "and the problems of labor."

But holdings of enormous size were developing, especially by the time of the First World War, and they rather than small family farms would come to dominate California agriculture. They appeared at different rates in different districts and for different crops. Orange and lemon properties enlarged in Southern California ahead of other areas, while large cotton farms did not become the rule until the 1920s. In the emergence of large fields and groves, the abundance of cheap labor was a major contributing factor, even a catalyst. As Paul S. Taylor pointed out in his study of sugar beets in the West, "The availability of immigrant laborers helped to support and preserve a pattern of large-scale, industrialized farming contrasting with a long-cherished view that the tiller and owner of the soil should be one and the same."[14]

The Mexican influx adapted to small orchards as well as large operations. Both needed workers, and Mexicans were becoming the major labor force available. By 1920 Limoneira had expanded to 2,502 acres, 900 of which were in lemons. Diverse crops such as lima beans and walnuts filled up the remaining acreage and made possible many more months of work for Mexican husbands, sons, brothers. Mexican women had employment for two to three months each year packing lemons, alongside white and Japanese women; then they joined the men for a brief time harvesting walnuts. Housing areas kept expanding, and by the 1930s the firm had nine Mexican camps, each with from fifteen to forty houses. In its Ventura County operations, Limoneira also built an adobe church for Mexicans in 1921 and added a Mexican kindergarten in 1924. All remained highly segregated—Mexicans, whites, Japanese. Constructing adobe houses "throughout the valley," the manager of the American Beet Sugar Company stressed, "will very materially contribute to the solution of the great labor problem . . ." Other citrus operations soon were building their own Mexican villages.

Across the citrus belt there were some 2,300 Mexican orange pickers by 1915, and this total grew to some 7,000 by 1920, when they constituted 30 percent of the citrus labor force. Growers were providing more stable employment: winter-ripening Washington navel oranges were grown inland, summer-ripening Valencias on the coast, while lemons were picked year-round. By 1926 some 10,000 Mexican men were picking oranges and lemons, most living in communities that differed sharply from those populated by transient workers, according to historian Gilbert González: in the new arrangements, year-round labor by the entire family was not the basic production unit (Mexican women tended to stay home with children); the village had characteristics of being permanent, and jobs were usually local and ran through most of the year. The Mexican citrus community was not a hobo jungle, not a stop for bindlestiffs, not a town that stood empty once the harvest was finished. Populated by persons drawn from all parts of Mexico, the citrus village quickly developed its own personality; it became for most "the final stop of a long family journey from Mexico."[15]

Far from the West Coast, a group of America's leading radicals met in Chicago on the twenty-seventh day of June in 1905 to create a new labor movement. They were committed to overturning the American capitalist system. The call to order was delivered by William D. "Big Bill" Haywood of the western hard-rock miners:

> We are going down in the gutter to get at the mass of the workers and bring them up to a decent plane of living. I do not care a snap of my finger whether or not the skilled workers join this

industrial movement at the present time. When we get the unorganized and the unskilled laborer into this organization the skilled worker will of necessity come here for his own protection.[16]

Haywood was a pillar of the Western Federation of Miners (WFM), which had spread rapidly across the West since its founding in 1893, bringing together local hard-rock miners' unions. Many WFM locals had achieved success both in electing local officials and in pressuring state legislatures, but the entry of eastern corporations into western mining was challenging this power. Corporation leaders especially objected to the high wages and eight-hour day that the WFM had won. Bloody battles soon erupted across the mining West. As their frustration grew, WFM spokesmen urged their organization to break with the American Federation of Labor's approach of negotiating with employers and instead to place all power in the hands of workers. At the WFM's 1904 convention, frustration over trying to deal with the business tycoons then solidifying their control over Colorado, Idaho, and Arizona convinced delegates to vote their support "for the amalgamation of the entire working class into one general organization."

The WFM's bold move led to the 1905 convention in Chicago that gave birth to the Industrial Workers of the World (IWW), soon nicknamed the "Wobblies." The IWW's attacks on employers especially appealed to the western migratory workers, ignored by AFL trade unions. In fact, hoboes and other seasonal workers received little support from anyone—not from employers who expected them to move on when a job was finished; not from communities little interested in them except at harvest time; and certainly not from most city, state, and federal governmental units. Since migratory workers almost by definition could not vote, they were unable to bring pressures for governmental protection at any level. Their only "safety net" consisted of charities that sometimes provided a meal along with prayers, or kindly jailkeepers who would let a hobo sleep in a jail on a cold night. These were the men to whom Haywood appealed on that June morning in Chicago in 1905.

Some observers understood why this new movement immediately won a wide following among western workers. Carleton Parker, a California professor investigating labor conditions, said the IWW was recruiting "from the most degraded and unnaturally living of America's labor groups," itinerants who were "hunted and scorned by society." Economist Rexford Tugwell said "the blanket-stiff," a man without a home or family, had only one dream pulling him on: "the wobbly vision." After the Industrial Commission's Peter Speek spent time visiting western "jungles" where migrant workers congregated, he concluded, "The appeal of I.W.W. principles is the most alluring of the voices that offer a way out."[17]

Wobblies began to find supporters in California, putting to the test their "one big union" approach by recruiting among Asians and Mexicans. This caused rifts in the early organization, for California urban workers were being signed up as well, and they were the most vociferous opponents of Chinese and Japanese. Although the Japanese-American newspaper *The Revolution* opened its columns to the IWW, the state's leading IWW organizer argued in 1907 that recruiting Japanese "would retard our development." He was finally outvoted, however, by those seeking to make real the promise of "one big union."

There were several examples of Japanese support during the IWW's early years. When some 5,000 Japanese converged on Fresno to pick grapes in 1908, organizers were ready and signed up 2,000 into a newly born Labor League. The league promptly launched a boycott of growers paying less than the going rate of $1.65 per ton. Within a year this Labor League held a joint rally with the Fresno branch of the IWW and heard speeches by Italians and Mexicans as well as whites. When Frederick Mills came into Stockton in 1914 posing as a migrant worker to report on job conditions, he ran into an IWW organizer just down from "Sac" (Sacramento) who was handing out IWW stickers in English, Japanese, and Chinese. Four years later, in the citrus belt of Southern California, the *Los Angeles Times* reported that the entire region had been flooded with the IWW's "flaming red announcement cards" in English, Spanish, and Japanese.

This all fitted with the basic argument of J. H. Walsh, the IWW's chief organizer in Spokane, Washington, who asserted vigorously that the organization must include the Japanese, whose considerable organizational strengths were already evident. A writer in the *Industrial Worker* agreed, noting that the Japanese "are past masters in the art of bringing John Farmer to his knees. My advice is to learn the tactics used by the Japanese. Go thou and do likewise."

But while there were occasional breakthroughs, Japanese and Chinese proved less open to joining the new organization than Mexicans. Historian Cletus Daniel notes that the considerable economic strength of Japanese harvest workers was based on their separateness, on their ability to stand together unshakably as Japanese—not to merge with other races or some broader organization. The IWW had more success recruiting Mexicans.[18]

To reach migrant workers who congregated in towns after harvest time, the IWW tried street speaking, soapbox oratory. In the process they wrote a new, romantic chapter in American labor history and blazed a trail in First Amendment rights. This IWW phase began in Spokane in the winter of 1908–9, when J. H. Walsh worked to revive a struggling IWW local. Their speeches on Spokane's major streets drew enthusiastic crowds as they attacked private employment agencies: "Don't buy jobs!" The problem with agencies came out in the open when the city's mayor met with three migrant workers, Sam Moci, Pete Smith, and Fred Moskow,

> who told the mayor that they saw a sign in front of the [Carr & Hill employment] office that swampers were wanted at $2.50 a day, and that they paid fees of $2.50 each to get the jobs. When they got their tickets they say they discovered the pay was only $2, and that they were to be sent to Blackwell camp No. 1 instead of camp No. 2. They demanded their money returned, when, they say, the man in charge started to put them out forcibly.

Wobblies fought back with songs as well as the spoken (or shouted) word. Their singing became famous, adapting IWW words to old hymns, a natural decision given the frequent accompaniment nearby of the drums and trumpets of the Salvation Army (the "starvation army"), which was also seeking to win converts on the streets.

City officials responded by banning outdoor speaking. The IWW then sent out a call for workers to pack the jails of Spokane, and soon multitudes arrived, each man mounting the soapbox to be promptly arrested and placed in the local lockup. The arrests of March 8, 1909, were typical, as a local newspaper reported: "Without comment Justice

Mann pronounced sentence upon them and they were led back to their cells, where the greater part of them will serve out their sentence on a diet of bread and water, which is prescribed by city ordinance for prisoners who refused to work in the chain gang." The battle adjourned for the summer harvest season, but in the fall of 1909 it resumed, and eventually 400 Wobblies were jailed—some for reading the Declaration of Independence to a crowd. In February 1910 the financially strapped city and the IWW finally reached a compromise: public speaking in the streets would be permitted if it did not interfere with traffic, and the worst employment agencies lost their licenses to operate. Tighter controls over employment "sharks" soon appeared in other cities. Wobbly endurance, intransigence, nonviolence, and creativity had won a major victory.[19]

During the next several years the IWW staged free speech fights in other cities, from the Great Plains to the Pacific—Fresno, San Diego, Missoula, Aberdeen, Minot, Sioux City, Kansas City, and many smaller towns. And yet, observed Philip Taft (an IWW organizer in the Grain Belt who later became a labor historian), the agitation that ran sporadically from 1909 to 1915 "did not have any significant organizational results."

What occurred in San Diego supports Taft's conclusion. Scarcely an IWW stronghold, neither was it a major winter hibernation stop for migrant workers. But when the city banned street speaking in the downtown "congested district" in December 1911, the small IWW contingent saw another free speech fight aborning and called for reinforcements. In February 1912 some 150 Wobblies were jailed in an increasingly violent struggle. Vigilante action exceeded anything seen in Spokane and Fresno, both sites of Wobbly free speech victories. In San Diego armed mobs by the hundreds met incoming trains and seized hoboes, in some cases running them through vicious gauntlets. The city connived in these actions, petitioned unsuccessfully for a federal investigation of the IWW, and ultimately claimed victory. If the Fresno and Spokane free speech fights demonstrated the successful use of nonviolence, historian Melvyn Dubofsky has written, "San Diego starkly revealed the weakness of passive resistance as a tactic," when common decency was not respected, "and when no higher authority would intervene on behalf of the oppressed."

The San Diego fight brought scarcely a bump in IWW membership, but the massive publicity it generated apparently reached into the migrant labor battalions. A dedicated, transient army of workers fiercely sympathetic to the IWW was being formed. It would next have an opportunity for struggle in the hopyards near Sacramento, at a town called Wheatland.[20]

To a professor at the University of California College of Agriculture, the 1913 riot by Wheatland hops pickers was "as much a spontaneous reaction against intolerable conditions as a result of organization . . ."

Many saw it as more than that, coming as it did in an era of epic labor struggles—from the 1877 "Great Strike" of railroad workers, to Haymarket Square in 1886, to the Homestead Strike of 1892, the Pullman Strike of 1894, and the coal miners' battles of the early 1900s. California added a new element: a vigorous IWW emboldened by the notoriety gained in recent free speech battles, determined to fight back after the crushing defeat at San Diego.

Yuba County contained several large hops operations, and at each harvest time the labor force assembled on the Durst brothers' farm at Wheatland was reputed to be one of the largest in California. Nearby, however, another hopyard owned by E. Clemens Horst followed a different course, choosing technology over cheap labor to increase production. Horst developed a mechanical hops picker that he said avoided "the old method of hand picking where everything is of necessity dependent in a large measure on the uncertainty and whims of labor, possibility of strikes, etc. . . ."

But most hopyards continued to rely on hand picking, and workers—including many IWW sympathizers—began arriving for work in the yards around Yuba County at midsummer in 1913. Earlier that summer, in May, an IWW orator began speaking on a street in Marysville, not far from Wheatland; he was arrested for disturbing the peace. The Wobbly warned that he was sending for outside help, but the case faded from view as the harvest season began. It can be assumed, however, that the incident made hops growers apprehensive about the IWW's presence.[21]

Ralph Durst did not have his neighbor Horst's picking machine. Each season Durst required some 1,500 hops pickers, so he sent out advertisements throughout California as well as to neighboring Oregon and Nevada, stating that "all white pickers who make application before August 1st will be given work."[22]

And the workers piled in, more than 2,700 eventually showing up in late July 1913, according to a later investigation, including as many as one thousand women and children. About half were aliens, including Mexicans, Japanese, Syrians, Lithuanians, Italians, Greeks, Poles, Hindus, Cubans, Puerto Ricans, Swedes, and some identified as "Spanish" coming from Hawaiian sugar plantations. One foreman said he had twenty-seven nationalities in his hops gang; a witness reported that seven languages were used at a protest meeting. Carleton Parker, who wrote a report on the riot for Governor Hiram Johnson, put the Americans at around half of the number and said most were recruited from country towns (for some this was their annual "country vacation"), ranches, and mining camps, while "a small, but essentially important, fraction were American hoboes." Half of those camped at the Durst farm "were absolutely destitute," Parker wrote.

Trouble began early. Durst's advertisements had included a promise of a bonus to be paid at the end of the season to all pickers doing "satisfactory work." The going rate for California hops picking in 1913 was $1.00 per 100 pounds—and the advertisements promised "going rate paid for clean picking." But when pickers prepared to begin on Wednesday, July 30, Durst put the rate at 90 cents, with a "bonus" of 10 cents to be paid at the end. The "bonus" was eliminated if the picker left before the hops were all gone, but all knew full well that an early exit was a common situation in hops picking, sometimes for illness, fatigue, or family needs.

Unhappiness also developed quickly over labor conditions and the eating and sleeping situation. With daytime temperatures running to 106 to 110 degrees in the shade, water supplies were crucial. The five wells and two hydrants proved inadequate—two of the wells went dry early each morning. A Durst relative sold lemonade. One woman recounted that she had to walk a mile or more to get water, and that many children "cried for water and it was very pitiful to see them suffer for want of it."

Some workers had brought tents; Durst rented others at 75 cents a week. Many chose instead to sleep on straw piles. The number of camp toilets was variously reported at between five and eleven, located near the wells, and the combination of hundreds of hops pickers and the excessive heat meant that sanitary conditions deteriorated rapidly. In the field there was only one toilet. Some women had to wait up to three-quarters of an hour to use the dilapidated facilities. Several cases of malaria and typhoid were reported.

The charge was later made that Durst delayed taking care of these problems because if workers gave up and left, he would pocket the ten-cent "bonus" they had been accruing for each 100 pounds of hops.

Further angering pickers was the lack of "high-pole men," needed in hops fields like Durst's with high-wire trellises. Without these men to lift the vines off the wires, women were forced to do it themselves or to call their husbands or other men; they also had to carry their filled sacks to wagons a long distance away. Durst "refused to supply" high-pole men, "though all other hop ranches in California uniformly did so," the *Sacramento Bee* later reported.

One other major irritation goaded the hops workers: the excessively clean requirements for picking. One man testified that when he worked for Durst in 1912, the picking requirements were not as strict, and he had averaged $3 a day; in 1913 he could barely make 85 cents a day. Another said, "The hop inspectors would make me and other pickers pick the hops over again, even if they were clean. The inspectors would dump the hops out and have us pick them into another sack."

Picking began on Wednesday, July 30, and by Saturday afternoon, August 2, 1913, protests had started. At this point the presence of the IWW came into the open, its growing support among the massive work force clearly on view.

Parker later estimated that there were at least 400 workers knowl-edgeable about the IWW, familiar enough that they could sing IWW songs. Around 100 men held IWW membership cards, and "some had been through the San Diego affair, some had been soapboxers in Fresno, a dozen had been in the free speech fight in Spokane." The Durst hop-yard was seen as an opportunity "to start something," in the words of Richard "Blackie" Ford, who emerged as the Wobbly leader. Police later found that Ford and Herman Suhr had sent nine telegrams starting at 5:45 a.m. on Sunday, calling for IWW members to come to Wheatland and also alerting the *San Francisco Bulletin*: "Twenty-five hundred hop-pickers out on strike at Durst Bros ranch. Thirteen hundred to come on

Horst Co. ranch to-morrow. Strike conducted by I.W.W. Send reporter to take news."

The Saturday evening meeting on August 2 drew as many as 2,000 persons—"nearly the entire camp," one witness claimed. As a judge later wrote in his court opinion, "These meetings were in the main orderly but plainly disclosed Ford's mastery and power to lead and control the more or less excited and turbulent body of persons comprising a considerable part of the assembled masses of striking and disappointed people, looking to their leader for guidance and relief." One of the court witnesses testified that Ford told the Saturday meeting that "the conditions here are hell . . . If you people want to live in hell you can, but for my part I don't want to live in hell."[23]

Meetings resumed Sunday morning when a list of demands was read in different languages, calling for a minimum of $1.25 for each 100 pounds of hops, and improvements in living conditions. When these were taken to Durst, he agreed to all but the pay increase. One witness testified that Ford then announced that if anyone came to arrest him, "I hope you tear them into dog meat," and the crowd cheered. A constable soon showed up to arrest Ford, but when he could not produce a warrant, the crowd turned on him. Durst and the constable then drove away as rocks rained on their car amid shouts of "You big hop head."

Durst telephoned the Yuba County sheriff in Marysville, and at five p.m. Sunday automobiles arrived with the sheriff, two deputies, and the district attorney. Ford told the crowd, "Well, boys, the sheriffs are coming and I suppose they will get me . . . I don't care a tinker's damn whether they do or not but if you are loyal to this cause and want to see that this thing is carried through you will stand by me." One witness said there were shouts of "We will knock their damn blocks off if they come in here."

The ensuing melee became the key point in the resulting trial that sent Ford and Suhr to prison for life.[24] Parker reported that as the struggle developed, Ford took a baby from its mother's arms, held it up for the crowd to see, and cried out: "It's for the life of the kids we're doing this." The sheriff approached and fired into the air. The crowd attacked him, and in further shooting the district attorney and a deputy were killed, as were a Puerto Rican and a young English boy. The posse fled,

and the next morning six companies of National Guardsmen occupied
the Durst hopyards. The *San Francisco Call* headlined:

400 PICKERS
KILL DISTRICT
ATTORNEY AND
WOUND SHERIFF

Another headline proclaimed: "I.W.W. Agitators Reported to Be Ringleaders of Rioters."

Private detectives and police around the state assisted in a far-
reaching roundup of IWW members, IWW sympathizers, and others,
many of whom had been nowhere near the Durst ranch. Beatings and
torture were used. Only Ford and Suhr were ultimately convicted. The
appeals court judge admitted that neither could be shown to have killed
anyone, but, he said, their actions had instigated the revolt, and those
who did the shooting "were actuated in so doing by the encouragement
given them by Ford and his influence over them."

The trial became a cause célèbre for California labor, and AFL leaders later joined in calling for pardons for Ford and Suhr. There seemed
ample reason for at least a retrial: the judge on the original case was a
longtime friend of the slain district attorney, and the replacement district attorney had known the judge "intimately for twenty years" and
had discussed the case with him. But there had been no change of venue.
In the roundup of suspects several Wobblies were held for long periods
without access to legal aid before being released. Carleton Parker encountered a nineteen-year-old who had been caught up in the Wheatland dragnet and was still in jail after eight months, with no charges
filed and his name absent from the jail record. Parker's wife later wrote,
"How long the boy would have remained in his contaminous [*sic*] surroundings had Carl Parker not run across him no one knows."

Five years later in Chicago, when 113 IWW members went on trial
under wartime conspiracy charges (93 were found guilty, including Big
Bill Haywood), one of those ultimately convicted broke down in tears
on the stand as he recounted the Wheatland story:

Some day, when Labor's age-long fight for life and freedom is
ended, then will there be a monument raised over the graves of

the Wheatland martyrs—and it will show the little water-carrier
boy and his tin pail lying there on the ground mingling his blood
with the water that he carried, and over him, in a posture of defense, the brave Porto-Rican with the gun he had torn from the
cowardly hands of the murderers who had fired upon a crowd of
women and children . . .

The Wheatland riot was the stuff of history and legend.[25]

Wheatland had an impact also on the Commission of Immigration and
Housing (CCIH), which California's Progressive leaders had created
two months earlier. While the commission was formed specifically to
address the plight of immigrants, Wheatland steered it in a new direction that quickly elevated its executive secretary, Carleton Parker, to
prominence in that era's search for solutions to worsening labor troubles. He would later write that the Wheatland riot "began such a widespread and agitated discussion" of the casual laborers' condition that
1913 and 1914 would be known in western labor history as the "period
of the migratory worker."

The CCIH was the brainchild of Simon J. Lubin, a leading Progressive and a Sacramento businessman. In 1912 he approached Governor
Hiram Johnson with concerns that the opening of the Panama Canal
the following year would flood California with more immigrants—but
immigrants were already becoming entangled in problems of slum
housing, employment fraud, and other exploitation. Launched in June
1913, the CCIH had the troubles at Wheatland dropped on its lap during its formative months.[26]

Parker, formerly with the University of California economics department, and Lubin were philosophical twins in their belief that basic labor conditions were at the heart of both the immigration question and
the Wheatland riot. Lubin once observed that when a California hops
grower wanted 2,000 pickers for three or four weeks of work, he had no
thought about what would happen to them afterward; nor did he worry
about their housing while they were working for him. As a result, "his
jobs are sought in great part by tramps and bums. The self-respecting
man avoids such employment."

Parker early put his focus on day-by-day conditions behind the prob-

lems besetting agricultural labor. Hoboes were not hoboes because of
personal failings; nor did they suffer from some innate disability that
made them prefer living in "jungles" and flitting from job to job. From
complaints that were already coming in, the CCIH was blunt in its
conclusion that "the Durst camp was no exception" to labor camp conditions in California. Parker wrote that the IWW revolt "could be called
without injustice a hunger riot." It was not a union-inspired riot: although IWW recruiters targeted migratory workers, they were actually
poor labor union material—always on the move, lacking reserve money
or energy, "incapable of sustained interest . . ." They would either sink
into hopelessness or revolt, as they had at Wheatland.

Parker's report to the governor was specific in locating the remedy
for labor riots:

> It is the opinion of your investigator that the improvement of liv-
> ing conditions in the labor camps will have the immediate effect
> of making the recurrence of impassioned, violent strikes and ri-
> ots not only improbable, but impossible, and furthermore, such
> improvement will go far towards eradicating the hatred and bit-
> terness in the minds of the employers and in the minds of the
> roving, migratory laborers.[27]

And so the CCIH under Lubin and Parker threw itself into labor
camp improvements. It set up a model labor camp at Shingle Springs,
sent investigators around the state—at least one of them incognito—
and got back reports that of 876 camps visited, 297 were classed as
"good," 316 as "fair," and 263 as "bad." And soon praise began to arrive
from growers who discovered that their workers appreciated the improvements. "We have recently had marked evidences of this in the fact
that some of our men who early in the Spring thought there were better
wages elsewhere have returned to us more satisfied than they were before," wrote one grower. "This includes all the classes of help which we
employ, the Japanese in their quarters, the Mexicans in their camp, and
the Americans in the dormitory."

In the hot, dry Imperial Valley, a rancher who had installed better
housing for his workers agreed that during the previous summer's labor
shortage "we scarcely felt the shortage at all . . . We attribute this largely

to our housing accommodations . . ." This rancher pointed out, however, that many valley growers had pioneered there, "without a cent, developed their own land, lived on the desert in ramada houses or tents and without any of the facilities and comforts" now common. He added, "It is no wonder that these pioneers have found it hard to see why ordinary cotton pickers should be furnished with accommodations" better than the ones they had once lived with.

The seven inspectors sent out during the first summer of 1914 found that upon reinspection, 72.3 percent of the camps were up to minimum standards. The commission was especially gladdened by news from the Durst hopyards at Wheatland, for the CCIH inspector reported that "Ralph Durst is very pleased with the new latrines and likes the design. He has given me full authority to hire as many men as I need, and also purchase all the material I need." Five years later the CCIH claimed it had "revolutionized" labor conditions and noted that "no serious labor disturbances" in California had taken place since Wheatland.[28]

Historian David Vaught points out, however, that the inspectors could not reach many camps, and large numbers of California's harvest workers did not live in camps. Not only were they beyond the reach of CCIH inspectors, but they seemed outside the thought processes of Lubin and Parker, who generalized for the entire state from Durst's operations at Wheatland—both before the riot and after the improvements there—and at a few of the better camps.

While the situation seemed to be improving in many labor camps, complaints were increasing about private employment agencies, the main targets of the Wobblies' earlier free speech campaigns. Many of these "labor sharks" were believed to be in league with employers, with whom they would split a worker's fee, then see to it that he was quickly fired from his new job. And then the two—agent and employer—would await their next victim.

Parker sent a former student dressed as a hobo into this world of migrant workers to report on such issues. During Frederick Mills's travels that summer of 1914, as described by historian Gregory R. Woirol, he rode the rails about California, "rustled" oranges in a packing plant, lived in a "jungle," and slept alternately on the grass and in a boxcar. And he tried to "buy a job." He encountered an agent in Reedley who sent men to work "with the certainty that they will not hold the job." Crooked or not, Mills concluded, "it is a most absurdly inefficient way of obtaining labor."[29]

The CCIH eventually established free public employment agencies in several California cities and barred misrepresentation by private agencies, but problems remained: employers had too many ways to evade the law when dealing with desperate job seekers. The private agencies were under attack throughout the West, and Washington State banned employment agents from receiving payments from those wanting work; however, the law was overturned by the U.S. Supreme Court.

Parker was fired after a year as CCIH's executive secretary; thereafter the earlier enthusiasm for the CCIH weakened among California legislators.[30] But Parker's star began to rise again when he was hired at the University of Washington and used as a mediator in lumber camp disputes during the early weeks of America's involvement in the war. His determination to bring employers and employees together led to the wartime creation of the Loyal Legion of Loggers and Lumbermen (the "4-L's"), a government-organized type of company union joining employers and employees. Logging companies—whose turnover rates sometimes approached 1000 percent a year—reluctantly limited workdays to eight hours and provided loggers with decent housing, sanitary facilities, and better food. As noted at the beginning of this chapter, loggers responded by burning their bindles on May 1, 1918. They had been expected to launch strikes when all work stoppages were banned during wartime, but once the 4-L organization was launched, with few exceptions work in Pacific Northwest forests continued at full force for the duration of the war.[31]

American entry into the Great War brought an end to many things—to the CCIH's vigorous drive to improve labor camps, to tolerance for the IWW's soapbox oratory, to the unfettered passage of Mexicans coming across the border. Suddenly western farmers, orchardists, and ranchers found they had a host of new anxieties, as many young men left for the army and others took high-paying jobs in war industries.

In another development that would affect the harvest scene, the nation was gripped by a growing wave of xenophobia and suspicion of foreigners. A million immigrants a year had generally found welcome on America's shores in the years leading up to 1914, but now the public mood was shifting.

Congress responded in 1917 by levying an $8 head tax on each person entering the country, a project aimed not at raising money but at discouraging poverty-stricken immigrants. Beyond this, Congress banned entry of any alien over age sixteen who could not read English or some other language. When western growers protested that most of the immigrants they needed could neither meet the literacy requirement nor pay the $8 charge, the commissioner general of immigration established a waiver: to hire Mexicans who met neither requirement, a grower had to pay prevailing wages, provide adequate housing, and limit any imported workers to six months of labor. This rule became the growers' salvation.

They found, however, that importing workers was expensive: incoming Mexicans had already heard of higher-paying jobs around the region, and so guards rode the trains to block desertions en route to the harvest fields. Fresno's raisin grape growers developed an elaborate organization to advertise and recruit, bringing in more Japanese than had ever before worked in the area, plus large numbers of Mexicans and even Hindus. One surprise at Fresno was the successful wartime recruitment of whites. Now offering piecework rates that could bring up to $14 per day in earnings, the growers luxuriated in a corps of white workers who "bent their backs and in so doing have given the utmost satisfaction." Recruiting was aided by a new Federal Employment Service that eventually opened fifty-three offices in California.[32]

While screaming newspaper headlines told of battles in Europe, in the American West concern also focused on labor shortages. Businessmen in Yakima, Washington, closed their doors on specified days and sent employees out to harvest peaches. More women and children were recruited, and the federal government created the Women's Land Army of America (WLAA), with "If you can't fight, farm!" as its banner slogan. They marched to work wearing uniforms; labored under strict rules governing housing, hours of work and overtime pay; and generally made growers happy. In California, twenty-eight camps for the WLAA were set up at different times in such harvesting centers as Lodi, Vacaville, Florin, Hamilton City, and Acampo. It worked. Harvests were brought in and packed, newspapers poured praise on both workers and growers, and a farmer's comment encapsulated the spirit of a nation at war: "Why, I feel like saluting every time one of 'em goes past."[33]

There was also ample precedent for employing children. Reform schools in California had been contracting out their youthful charges for fruit picking for years, and the superintendent of the Preston School of Industry at Ione reported that some of his reform school boys made $59 during a season doing such work. The concerns of child labor reformers were now drowned out by patriotism's shouts. Indian reservation schools in some areas were closed, and "many hundreds of Indian children were secured" for harvest work. The federal government also created the Boys' Working Reserve as the youthful male counterpart of the WLAA; in California it eventually had fifty units in operation, recruited and supervised by Boy Scouts and the Young Men's Christian Association.

But child labor had drawbacks. In such jobs as thinning sugar beets, constant supervision was needed. After most of a group of twenty-four high school boys had quit one camp, a CCIH staff member said the lesson was that "they cannot depend upon high school boys for such back-breaking work in the heat and alkali dust as is this asparagus cutting." An old man at the site commented that "this work requires a man with a strong back and a weak mind."[34]

If the war years brought job opportunities and higher pay to many— men, women, high school students, and children; Mexicans, Japanese, Hindus, and whites—in many ways it proved a disaster for the main labor organization for harvest workers, the Industrial Workers of the World. The label "un-American" had long been thrown at the IWW by employers trying to fend off work disruptions, and wartime brought abundant opportunities to hurl that epithet again. With the national slogan "Food Will Win The War," growers and their allies around the West resurrected the old disloyalty attacks whenever IWW rumors appeared. Now any questioning of the war effort—especially refusal to fight, but also reluctance to push forward with production—was condemned as unpatriotic. The *Yakima Morning Herald* warned that since the nation needed Yakima's crops, "Hampering the harvest is treasonable . . ." Elsewhere around the nation Americans feared secret German agents; in the West, they also worried about harvest disruption. And the blame for any such disruptions—or hints of such actions—was put on the Wobblies.

Back on the Great Plains, the IWW had been increasing its activities among wheat harvesters since 1914, forming an Agricultural Workers Organization (AWO Local 400) in April 1915 to carry out its own recruiting. Thorstein Veblen, sent to investigate by the wartime President's Mediation Commission, estimated that "probably a large majority" of transient farm labor was in the AWO. This IWW offshoot initially demanded a minimum wage of $3 a day in the wheatfields, with 50 cents an hour overtime beyond ten hours; adequate board and good sleeping accommodations; and no discrimination against IWW members. Significantly, realizing that California free speech fights had not brought in many new members, the AWO on the Plains voted to ban "soap-boxing" by members.

While the AWO met aggressive hostility in many districts, in North Dakota it forged a working alliance with the Non-Partisan League, a farmers' organization that frequently criticized big business. Others in the Grain Belt held back criticizing the organization in early years, but the mood began to change as American involvement in the European fighting increased. This was clear in the about-face taken by Victor Rosewater, editor of the *Omaha Evening Bee*, who had written on July 31, 1916, that migratory workers had a "habit of life forced on them by circumstances" and became wanderers because their work was seasonable in nature. His question was: "What to do, *not with, but for them* . . ." Vague on solutions, editor Rosewater sympathetically sought a "better balance" in industry: "Then the I.W.W. will vanish, or at least retreat to the condition of mere annoyance."

When the U.S. entered the war, Rosewater did not shift views suddenly. But as U.S. soldiers began to die in battle, as national stress mounted, and as debates heated up in Great Plains communities between wheat men and the AWO (renamed the Agricultural Workers' Industrial Union No. 110), he saw things in a new light. He wrote on November 15, 1917, "The prompt action of the federal authorities in arresting the I.W.W. gang assembled in Omaha will have the approval of right minded folks." Rosewater called the unionists "malcontents and apostles of disloyalty" and added that in peacetime the nation "suffers enough" from "Bolshevikism"—but in wartime its advocates were "intolerable."[35]

His reference to the victors in the Russian Revolution was evidence that a new charge of subversion was being added to the Wobblies' burden: now supposed Bolshevik machinations were merged with those of the German Huns, whose spies some charged were already running rampant across the nation, and both were linked to the Wobblies. Bolsheviks, Germans, the IWW—the trio was trying to overthrow America. In California, even the CCIH was drawn into the antisubversive campaign, and papers of Director Simon Lubin contain reports from staff members telling of hidden radios, shoreline hideouts, criticism of the government, and opposition to the war.

In Charter Oak, near the San Dimas orange district in Los Angeles County, an attempt by a small group of IWW members in late 1918 to seek $4 for an eight-hour day drew attacks that they were "Russian Bolshevik agitators." Other evidence, however, indicated that un-Bolshevik thoughts might have been driving some of the demands, for the county health inspector criticized the poor housing provided Mexican citrus workers. Recruitment of some of these Mexicans into the IWW drew attacks on the organization as a violent group—although the *Pomona Bulletin* contradicted claims that the strikers had fired into orchards to frighten other pickers, noting that the constable "does not believe the men have any arms."

But the Russian connection remained the main line of attack. "Russian agitators" had been fired, the newspaper reported, and the *Los Angeles Times* announced, "BOLSHEVIK CONSPIRACY BARED," describing the "Russian House" where the group of male and female strikers lived "in the most approved Bolshevik manner, sans clothing." When the strike was broken in February 1919, the *Los Angeles Record* declared that "every I.W.W. . . . should be kicked out of the country," and the *Times* cheered the police for blocking the IWW, "which is the American arm of the Bolsheviki . . ." The citrus belt was saved.

The Survey, a Progressive journal that reported on labor issues, had concluded in 1915 that "baiting the I.W.W. has become a pastime in nearly every place in the United States where that organization has made its appearance." As the Charter Oak events showed, the baiting only worsened as the United States entered the war, and soon "bolshevism" and "violence" were the twin denunciations hurled at the organization. When someone tried to dynamite the California governor's mansion in Sacramento, federal authorities automatically rounded up forty-five IWW members—despite "strenuous objection on the part of local and state agents" as well as a Department of Justice representative.[36]

While the IWW never took a stand for or against the war, its scorn for the government left the impression that it hoped for a U.S. defeat. A song that first appeared in its *Little Red Songbook* in 1917 sent an antiwar message:

> Onward, Christian soldiers! Duty's way is plain;
> Slay your Christian neighbors, or by them be slain.
> Pulpiteers are spouting effervescent swill,
> God above is calling you to rob and rape and kill,
> All your acts are sanctified by the Lamb on high;
> If you love the Holy Ghost, go murder, pray and die.

Other verses in the song by John F. Kendrick told Christian soldiers to "Rob with bloody fingers, Christ O.K.'s the bill; Steal the farmers' savings, take their grain and meat; Even though the children starve, the Savior's bums must eat."[37]

The growing swirl of allegations of violence, bolshevism, and antiwar rhetoric proved more than local authorities could ignore, and jail records across the region provide ample evidence of this justification for corraling Wobblies. Police arrest citations were often marked simply "I.W.W.," although often charges were listed: "Remarks against President Wilson and American soldiers," "Agitating I.W.W.sms," or "Defaming flag and country."[38]

Paralleling the arrests of IWW members and their sympathizers along western rail lines, IWW meeting places and offices were spied upon throughout the era. The climax came the morning of September 5, 1917, in coordinated Justice Department raids. Major IWW offices in Chicago, Fresno, Seattle, and Spokane were ransacked, and even rubber bands and paper clips were taken; less important IWW meeting spots and members' homes were also invaded. With evidence seized on these and other raids, the federal government convinced a

Chicago grand jury to indict 166 IWW members. After a trial lasting almost five months, with charges of some ten thousand crimes, the Chicago jury took less than an hour to return a verdict of guilty for each man charged on each count; as Wobblies were brought to trial in other cities, juries returned similar verdicts. "Criminal syndicalism" laws were passed as states joined the parade to remove the IWW threat. Melvyn Dubofsky concluded that with the 1917 raids, "probably no group of labor agitators before or since has as suddenly or as disastrously experienced the full wrath of state and national authorities."[39]

The large-scale attack on the Industrial Workers of the World was one of the major events closing out the decade, but there were other aspects of the 1910–20 record that were important for western harvesters. In California, Progressives had created a new state agency to improve the conditions in which migrant workers lived and worked. Further, a new ethnic group had risen to dominance in many agricultural districts; as a San Antonio onion farmer told a congressional committee, "I never wanted outside Mexicans until two or three years ago, and the war changed conditions." Responding to western growers' demands for more workers, the Mexican influx grew steadily, and increasing numbers arrived with their families.[40]

Many changes were under way. But the war had thrown all of them into a conglomeration that was still being sorted out as the 1920s began.

12

ARRIVAL OF THE "GASOLINE TRAMPS"

Now the bindlestiffs had competition as they slogged along the road-ways searching out harvest jobs. As early as 1917 they had seen it in the Fresno vineyards: families arriving in "machines," packing tents so they could camp out. Both the parents and the children who emerged from these automobiles and slept in tents went to the vineyards and picked grapes.[1]

A new day was dawning in the West. The automobile's intrusion into the world of the hobo and fruit tramp did not come suddenly, but by the mid-1920s it was turning the traditional labor market upside down. A 1928 report from Aberdeen, South Dakota, told of streets at harvest time filled with cars from Delaware and California and states in between, including many who had "made 'er up from Texas." Almost all carried several men, who had gone in together to purchase the jalopy they adorned with such slogans as "Danger, 10,000 Jolts," and "Three More Payments and She's Ours to Love and Cherish."

It was a new labor system. An inquiring reporter found that migrant workers' lives on the Great Plains were now counted in "eight days in Oklahoma, two weeks in Kansas and then a hop across Nebraska into South Dakota for another two weeks before making for the Red River of North Dakota," then perhaps into Canada's prairie provinces. In 1926 a Department of Labor agent in Kansas estimated that at least 65 per-cent of the harvest workers came by automobile—just short years after the freight trains had been loaded each summer with farmworkers beat-ing their way to the wheatfields. Changes were coming rapidly, and it was even becoming rare to see large numbers of men languishing around a country town after a job was finished. Now the men could drive straight to a farm, get to work, and when finished head up the road to another harvest job.[2]

New types were showing up in western fields and orchards: "gasoline tramps," "automobile floaters," or "flivver harvesters," their arrivals indicating that the second frontier was ending. Fifty years earlier the appearance of the steam locomotive had marked the close of the pioneer epoch and launched the second period of western history; now the internal combustion engine, with its automobile and tractor offspring, signaled that another new era was aborning.

Changes were seen in the fields too. After the war headers came into widespread use on the Great Plains, but gradually the combine-harvester gained in popularity, joining two processes in the traditional threshing run. In its first year of widespread use, 1926, it displaced 33,227 workers, one study found, and by 1930 that total had climbed to 100,900.

Many migrant workers found the new vehicle to be liberating. For years use of the automobile had been spreading from community elites into the general population, even into rural areas. In 1914 Frederick Mills was given a lift by "a young mechanic in a machine" as he trudged along a country road near Tulare, California. Mills wrote that it was "impossible to hobo in peace thru this country. Willy-nilly one is picked up and carried along by kind-souled auto-owners. The country just swarms with machines." Fruit pickers were making the change as well, and in 1921 "auto campers" were numerous enough to start playing major roles in harvests along the California foothills. What was happening in Tulare was happening across the West. Soon, from Fresno's vineyards to Yakima's berry patches to Aberdeen's wheatfields, newly mobile urban families were discovering that they could use their new "machine" to take a harvest break from the city in summertime.[3]

The automobile also played a role in establishing Mexicans as the dominant group in western migrant labor. The presence of Mexicans had been growing for two decades, but not until the turmoil of the Mexican Revolution did the movement *al norte* become massive, drawing Mexicans from deep within their homeland as well as from border areas.

They had become mobile, and from 1910 to 1930, according to some estimates, three-quarters of a million Mexicans entered the American labor market. They were warmly welcomed in the Colorado-Nebraska-Kansas sugar beet areas, where their predecessors from other ethnic groups were becoming landowners. In the expanding cotton districts of Texas, New Mexico, Arizona, and Southern California, Mexicans began replacing Indians and Asians, until farm journals were referring to 1920 as the year of the "Mexican harvest." Eventually they would start to appear in the Pacific Northwest.

By the 1920s the pattern was set: across broad areas of the American West, Mexicans no longer were strangers. Certainly not in California, where by 1924 the state's bureau of labor statistics reported that "the largest proportion" of families coming to pick fruit were Mexican, "bundled and huddled together in cheap and troublesome used autos . . ." Once Texas farmers had seen Mexicans by the hundreds moving along roadways "with their carts and dogs, driving jacks," but the new era brought changes: a nurse looked out of her California home one day in 1928 as Mexican fruit pickers passed by in "three trucks, several flivvers, and a mule-drawn covered wagon, all filled to overflowing with perspiring Mexicans and sundry household goods . . ."[4]

At first many argued that the influx of Mexicans was nothing to worry about—it was only temporary. They were "homers" who came only to earn some money to carry back to their families in Mexico. This was the thrust of growers' arguments, when wartime labor needs clashed with new federal limits on immigration. The temporary reprieve they received then was scheduled to be dropped once peacetime conditions returned. But when the war ended, growers still felt panic. "A great many farmers and sugar companies will undoubtedly suffer unless Mexican labor can be secured," the president of the Great Western Sugar Company wrote in 1920 to a congressional committee. He added that congressmen need not worry about changes in the U.S. population—the lawmakers could rest assured that the migrants' presence would only be temporary because "after the work is done these laborers are returned to Mexico."[5]

But later studies in Colorado beet areas found that Mexicans—as opposed to Spanish-Americans from New Mexico—largely came from landless families, and when the harvest was done, they seldom went back to Mexico. Many became charity cases in nearby cities, there to await the call for *betabeleros* to come back to the beet fields. "This migratory pattern permitted members of each culture to deny their membership in and responsibility for the other," Sarah Deutsch has pointed out, enabling American farmers to "keep the doors to Mexican reserve labor open."[6]

A major change had taken place, and the two governments seemed unaware of it: the Rio Grande was no longer the border between the United States and Mexico—the real border was becoming racial rather than geographical. Voters in neither country had approved the change. Rather, Mexican laborers had voted with their feet, and U.S. farmers and companies such as the Great Western had voted with their hiring practices. Mexicans were showing up farther north, soon heading to midwestern industrial centers. In 1930 the U.S. Census Bureau classified Mexicans as a separate racial group; then, during the Depression, high U.S. unemployment sparked campaigns to deport many back to Mexico. But eventually the *bracero* program brought them back again. Arguments on the need for Mexicans would take several different forms, and their presence would become a national issue for the rest of the century, and beyond.[7]

These issues were debated in 1926 when Congress, still reflecting the nation's xenophobic mood, again confronted the Mexican question. At a hearing on whether to apply immigration quotas to Latin America, I. D. O'Donnell spoke for Montana and Wyoming farm organizations, insisting that if the government would permit them to bring in the Mexican harvest worker, "he is going to drift back; I do not think they are going to stay here permanently." And a Colorado sugar beet spokesman rebutted a congressman's warning that Mexicans would lower American standards—"That presupposes something that does not exist, because they simply would not stay." This point was stressed repeatedly by a Fresno spokesman: "the Mexican does not remain," S. Parker Frisselle asserted; "he always goes back."[8]

Another recurring argument was that these workers were physically better adapted to such work than whites; as presented to Congress, this plea even carried a sense of destiny—Mexicans were made to harvest crops. Representative Addison T. Smith of Idaho assured his fellow congressmen on this point when he was asked if paying higher wages would draw white men to work in the beet fields:

Mr. Smith: I do not think so . . . for the reason that it is very tiresome work for anyone except persons who are small in stature,
because they have to get down on their knees a great deal of
the time and crawl along the rows and weed out the extra
plants, and a large man such as you or myself, figuratively speaking, would have a good deal of difficulty in engaging in that
sort of work with any degree of comfort 12 or probably more
hours per day. We might stand it two hours.

Mr. Sabath: Are the Mexicans very much smaller in stature than
the Americans?

Mr. Smith: Very much, and they are also wiry.

Mr. Sabath: Isn't it a fact that they can bend better? It is tiresome
work and they are used to it?

Mr. Smith: Not only can they do it better than anybody else, but
there is scarcely any other work they can do as successfully.[9]

(The persistence of this argument was demonstrated more than four
decades later, in a U.S. Senate debate over the 1960s bracero program
to bring in Mexican harvest workers. Senator George Murphy of California stated that Mexicans were physically suited to farm labor—they
were "built lower to the ground," so it was "easier for them to stoop.")[10]

When those pushing for easy entry for Mexicans were challenged
over whether their real goal was to create an abundance of "cheap labor," they became almost testy. Frisselle, describing the employment of
Mexicans on the 5,000 acres he farmed near Fresno, called them "anything but cheap labor," and Representative Edward Taylor of Colorado
agreed: "They are not cheap labor. They know the value of their labor
and they demand and get well paid for it," before, of course, returning
to Mexico.[11]

Regardless of whether Mexicans were physically better suited to
stoop labor—and whether they were cheap labor and would go back
home—by the 1920s they were considered essential for western harvests. No other racial or ethnic group could challenge them. Fred Cummings, representing some 3,000 Colorado beet growers, recalled
potato-digging season in years past when "you could pick up a number
of fellows" to work. No more—"they are not there. The floating element
of labor in our country is gone." Committee chairman Representative
Albert Johnson of Washington, from a Washington State logging district

and a leader of the anti-immigrant forces, seemed incredulous: "It is gone entirely?" Cummings's answer was blunt: "Yes, sir."

There was no way out, it seemed. Crops had to be harvested; only the Mexican was available. The aging Chinese had moved to town. The Japanese had their own truck farms. Many of the Indians had returned to the reservation or taken other jobs. "Hindoos," Italians, Armenians, Portuguese—they were pursuing other economic enterprises. In the sugar beet areas of the Great Plains, German-Russians had provided the labor as recently as a decade earlier, but now "the Russians have all become owners or renters and there is very little Russian help left," Representative O'Donnell informed the committee. Growers were left with no alternative except to hire Mexicans, said J. T. Whitehead of Nebraska's North Platte Valley, where 52,000 acres of sugar beets re-quired 4,500 laborers. "Now, we must have help or the American farmer must quit."

Over and over farmers argued that there was no one else. Whites would not do the work—back from the war, or acclimated to the wages of factory work, they had turned their backs on the groves and fields forever. The Fresno district's Frisselle seemed exasperated by congres-sional doubts as to whether only Mexicans could harvest western crops—"We have gone east, west, and north, and south and [the Mexi-can] is the only man power available to us. We take him because there is nothing else available."

The growers won. Immigration quotas remained in force for Europe but not for the Western Hemisphere. Chinese and Japanese were banned, and rigid limits were set for Italians and Greeks. But Mexicans would be allowed to enter.

Facing the increased Mexican presence in the West, continued attacks by superpatriots and police, and now the shift by migrant workers to automobiles, the Industrial Workers of the World staged one final burst of activity in the 1920s. It was impressive, given their numerous defeats in courtrooms and jails. But the fact that the organization still could rally pointed again to the grim realities of the harvest worker's life, con-ditions that now only the Wobblies seemed intent on changing. This combination of factors, this series of hard blows, gave the final struggles of the IWW a sense of tragedy.

The IWW resurgence began on the Great Plains. Stumbling away from end-of-war battles with the government, the IWW's Agricultural Workers' Industrial Union (AWIU) got Kansas wheat harvesters' daily pay raised to $5 from the farmers' initial offer of $4.50 in 1921.[12] Historian Greg Hall notes that staying clear of the large cities and concentrating instead on rural areas was at least partly responsible for this success, and it stoked the membership total beyond ten thousand. As they finished up the southern Plains grain fields and began to move north, "it became clear to harvest Wobblies that this would be a resurgent year for their industrial union," Hall writes, and the organization eventually broke through the South Dakota $3 daily maximum by at least a dollar. By the time they reached North Dakota, however, tumbling wheat prices led to a series of confrontations and harassments, although Wobblies' control of freight train ridership often kept the competing forces fairly even. When they took up their cause anew in Washington's Palouse, Wenatchee, and Yakima areas, they again faced police attacks, but at least the organization won one criminal court case, virtually nullifying the state's syndicalism law.

Successes were sporadic and uneven, and violence in some spots checked Wobbly progress. This was especially true in Yakima, Washington, and Enid, Oklahoma. In Oklahoma they faced an opponent rare in anti-IWW confrontations: the Ku Klux Klan, operating with such enthusiastic local support that it smashed AWIU drives with methods reminiscent of San Diego in 1912. But the Wobblies stumbled on into 1923, only to be weakened again by poor crops on the Plains.

In Pacific Northwest forests, wartime successes symbolized by the burning of the bindles proved to be short-lived, for the organization withered before a determined employer and local government onslaught, improved logging camp conditions including housing for families, and a disastrous market for lumber.[13] It was left to the harvest Wobblies on the Plains to carry the IWW banner.

In 1924 a new push across the Grain Belt raised AWIU spirits again, bringing another membership surge and enlarging the IWW's treasury; the AWIU now enlisted a third of the IWW's members but provided half the organization's income. The Great Plains was seen as the base for a new burst of Wobbly energy and growth.

Within the national leadership, however, an ideological split was in the making. In the end, 1924's internal clashes weakened the IWW

more than government spies and small-town vigilantes had done. Melvyn Dubofsky concludes, "It is nearly impossible to fathom the issues
dividing the two main I.W.W. factions in 1924." Fights centered on
whether to have national control under "One Big Union" or to develop
a more decentralized structure; and whether the migrant worker or the
"homeguard" worker in a factory or other urban job should be the focus
of recruitment. Added to those divisive issues was the vigorous support
by some Wobblies for the new Soviet Union. While in the end the
IWW did not endorse Communist ties, the fight left a residue of bitterness that would linger for years. The 1924 national IWW convention in
Chicago split into separate meetings, each rival group claiming to be
the authentic organization. Whatever the causes, Dubofsky writes, there
is no argument over the result: the "total collapse" of the Industrial
Workers of the World.

    Various reasons have been cited for this debacle. Perhaps changes
in the migrant labor force provided an underlying prod to the debates.
Some members complained about the rise of "automobile tramps," as in
Wenatchee, where apple-picking families now arrived in automobiles,
stayed in employers' automobile camps, and avoided the hobo "jungles"
of old. But those jungles had long served as recruiting centers—now
"all attempts to organize the men prove futile," lamented a report in an
IWW newspaper.[14]

    While a migrant family's automobile and tent might have improved
some aspects of their lives, other evidence points to a general 1920s
backsliding rather than an advance in harvest labor conditions. The
1920s legacy to the 1930s on that score would not be pretty, for much
of the "normalcy" of the 1920s meant abandoning Progressive-Era protections for workers. The California Commission of Immigration and
Housing was typical: it was left with neither much strength nor interest
in the issues for which it had once worked so vigorously. A CCIH commissioner who toured labor camps in the mid-1920s and found facilities
"very bad" for Mexican workers learned that persons concerned about
migrant labor conditions felt that the CCIH had "ceased to function."
There was no longer a Carleton Parker to serve as the workers' advocate.

Old habits die hard, and in many farming districts traditional treatment
of migrant labor simply continued. The situation was basically un-

changed from the time two decades earlier when a delegate to the California Fruit Growers Convention conceded, "We have degraded a certain class of labor, and there is not a man who lives in any agricultural locality who wants to get in and do this work." By 1926 the head of that state's employment bureau admitted there was still a tendency "to hold the men down to the lowest standards through a mistaken idea on the part of farmers that all temporary workers must necessarily be of the lowest order of labor." A year later, when Paul Taylor studied Mexicans in the sugar beet fields of Colorado's South Platte Valley, he found that employers continued to play on workers' ignorance of the going wage rate, because "when the Mexicans are in dire need they will work for almost anything." Nothing had changed in local communities, either: some South Platte towns dependent upon seasonal labor "are eager for the laborers to move in when they are needed, and almost equally eager for them to move out when they are no longer needed." It was an old, old story.[15]

Perhaps the public was incapable of abandoning traditional beliefs that men who were only temporarily out of work were useless vagabonds or dangerous criminals. This tradition was carried West by settlers, occasionally reinforced by such enactments as Massachusetts's 1880 law that defined tramps as "all persons who rove from place to place begging or living without labor or visible means of support . . ." Women, children, the blind, and "persons seeking charity" were excluded, but for the others the penalty was six months to two years in a workhouse or house of correction. As the railroad network spread through the East, more such men seemed to rove the land, and even stronger penalties were soon under discussion, including confining those with no visible support in "labor colonies."[16]

Around the turn of the century, some observers began arguing that hoboes should not be included in such classifications: the hobo was en route to a job, unlike the tramp who "dreams and wanders" and the bum who "drinks and wanders." But the new definition did not find acceptance in the law enforcement community; on the contrary, the vagrancy statute in California's penal code snared anyone "except a California Indian" who lacked "visible means of living" and did not work over a ten-day period or "when employment is offered him . . ."[17]

Jack London was not a hobo traveling around to harvest jobs, but he was a well-known author who rode the rails and understood migrant labor's problems better than any other writer in the era. In his travels he frequently encountered the vagrancy law, notably on a visit to Niagara Falls in 1894. There London was "pinched" when he could not tell a policeman which hotel he was staying in. The next morning, as he awaited his turn in police court, he watched hoboes each being sentenced to thirty days of hard labor for vagrancy. One was a Lockport teamster out of work since the 1893 Depression, who had traveled to the "lakes" to find work. As the judge left the courtroom, he asked the Lockport man why he had quit his job. When the teamster replied, "Your Honor, isn't that a funny question to ask?" the judge added another thirty days to his sentence. "The machine of justice was grinding smoothly," London wrote.[18]

While the hoboes' predicament was similar in many parts of the nation, the West provided the first major opposition by government officials to their usual treatment. Texas governor James Stephen Hogg, from the reform wing of the Democratic Party, challenged the railroads' harsh anti-tramp measures: he asserted that "food, not fines, will be the treatment of the law-loving, law-abiding element in this state when men commit no greater crime than traveling as tramps for lack of work." Hogg's sympathy for hoboes drew a retort from *Railway World* that he was showing "more courtesy to the chronic tramp than to the men employed by railroads, the tourists who ride on railroads, or the investors who have sunk money in railroads." And in a measure of the editor's great distance from the real world of harvest labor, the journal added: "Are the tramps benefited by their custom of boarding trains or sauntering along the tracks of railways?"[19]

Populists, gaining ground in the 1890s among western farmers angered by railroad policies, began to question whether men without work—such as those searching for wheat-threshing jobs each summer—were criminals. The most famous case of a politician challenging traditional condemnations of the jobless involved Populist Governor Lorenzo D. Lewelling of Kansas. Son of an Iowa Quaker minister, orphaned at an early age, he attended business college in New York State, then worked his way back West in various jobs until he arrived in Kansas in 1887. Lewelling was nominated by the Populists in the Kansas governor's race in 1892 and won with Democratic Party endorsement, but lost his re-election bid two years later when the latter party deserted him over his support for women's suffrage.

Lewelling's 1893 letter to Kansas police commissioners was given the name "The Tramp Circular," and while it has been widely reprinted in recent document collections, its contemporary reception was decidedly negative. A journalist examined the responses of one hundred newspapers and found that ninety-three disapproved, some treating it as a joke, others accusing the governor of courting the anarchist/lawless element for political gain. It nevertheless remains a pointed reminder of how, in Lewelling's argument, vagrancy laws were misapplied in American industrial society:

> In this country, the monopoly of labor-saving machinery and its devotion to selfish instead of social use have rendered more and more human beings superfluous, until we have a standing army of the unemployed numbering, even in the most prosperous times, not less than one million able-bodied men; yet, until recently, it was the prevailing notion, as it is yet the notion of all but the work-people themselves, and those of other classes given to thinking, that whosoever being able-bodied and willing to work, can always find work to do, and section 571 of the General Statutes of 1889 is a disgraceful reminder how savage, even in Kansas, has been our treatment of the most unhappy of our human brothers.

Under Kansas state law and similar city laws, Lewelling explained, "thousands of men, guilty of no crime but poverty, intent upon no crime but seeking employment, have languished in the city prisons of Kansas or performed unrequited toil on 'rock piles' as municipal slaves, because ignorance of economic conditions had made us cruel." While freedom of movement—whether seeking work or following "a mere whim"—was a constitutional guarantee to all Americans, judges regularly violated this when they ordered men to leave town.

Only the rich could afford lawyers, he argued, but "the first duty of the government is to the weak." Lewelling's "Tramp Circular" spoke for the thousands of bindlestiffs, hoboes, fruit tramps, and others making their way along western roads and rail lines:

> If voluntary idleness is not forbidden; if a Diogenes preferred poverty; if a Columbus choose hunger and the discovery of a

new race, rather than seek personal comfort by engaging in "some legitimate business," I am aware of no power in the legislature or in city councils to deny him the right to seek happiness in his own way, so long as he harms no other, rich or poor; but let simple poverty cease to be a crime.[20]

In the years since the railroad provided a means to move more easily around the vastness of the West, migrant workers had attempted in many different ways to deal with the exploitation, the indignities, the taunts, and the coercion of their lives. A railroad engineer praising the hobo's skills in railroad construction asserted, "The hobo seldom strikes. If he does not get what he considers his rights, he leaves; usually without comment." Most hoboes were "Americans," white native-born, or were Irish, Scandinavian, German, or other immigrants from northern Europe. Their ethnicity may sometimes have won them milder treatment from police, and yet in some ways they lacked the protections available to the rising numbers of nonwhites.[21]

Chinese and Japanese were most often hired through contractors of their own group; these bosses kept them from straying and were frequently able to pressure employers and win them more pay. In the end many Asian workers clung together simply because it was their best protection, in a land that may have been short of harvest labor but was still prejudiced against them. Fear of the outside world provided the glue of unity. Blacks moving West with the spread of cotton could find themselves facing a similar situation, although since they lacked a boss or *padrone* to enforce unity, such protections were often incomplete.

Critics' complaints of clannishness among the Asians only pointed to its effectiveness. Their ability to stay together was demonstrated in various ways, including uniformity of payments: when Japanese tunneling the Milwaukee Road through the Northern Rockies in 1910 were hurriedly enlisted at Avery, Idaho, to battle a massive forest fire, each one worked the same number of hours each day—twelve hours for Hamauchi as well as Sato, twelve for Yamaseta as well as Takahashi and the rest. When discharged, each had the same 118 hours recorded for his labors. But the same Forest Service record book shows much more variegated totals for those with "American" names like Conway, Lindstrom, Dunn, Maloney, and Eberle. They all shared the same experiences on the fire line, but the Americans did not demonstrate the uniformity of the Japanese.

Mexicans and Indians also achieved a degree of unity, perhaps not as tightly bound as the Asians. Increasingly heading north in families and small groups, Mexican migrants usually stayed with their own people because of their common language and Catholicism, preferring to congregate in barrios. These strangers arriving from different areas of Mexico "founded a dynamic and creative community with a distinctive lifestyle, organization, traditions, and customs," drawing on their mutual heritage, telling their stories in *corridos*. A study of the Los Angeles barrio called it "a positive accomplishment. The barrio gave a geographic identity, a feeling of being at home, to the dispossessed and the poor. It was a place, a traditional place, that offered some security . . ."[22]

Protection through sticking together was theoretically open to American migrant workers as well. Very often, however, the cords binding the Americans together were weak or wasted and lacked reinforcement. Alien workers often had long-standing shared dreams and goals that were forged and strengthened in the journey to America. But if the Americans' common English language provided a base for unity, their individualism was pronounced enough to draw comments from observers, and their dreams and goals could veer off in a multitude of directions. Where immigrants saw only a few narrow chances to succeed in their new home, the Americans were aware of myriad possibilities; they knew the lay of the land and were aware of pitfalls as well as opportunities. And so while men "beating their way" in the same boxcar may all have been U.S. citizens, they likely came from quite different backgrounds: a Wisconsin dairy farm, a town in the Texas hill country, a village perched beside a Missouri levee. They were Methodists and Catholics, Southern Baptists and Primitive Baptists, Lutherans and atheists, Democrats and Populists and Socialists and Republicans, even anarchists. Not surprisingly, they did not always get along.

It was the genius of the Industrial Workers of the World to point out to these disparate elements that regardless of their different backgrounds they had common interests, important ones; that these had been fused by hard knocks; and that unity should emerge simply because of the lives they led.

Early on the IWW discovered singing as a route to unity, and it be-

came the single lasting element that continues to draw later generations to the Wobblies' story. Former hobo Nels Anderson recalled it as
"a song-promoting movement" and saw the hoboes' ballads and protest
songs bringing "a unanimity of sentiment and attitudes, the strongest
form of group solidarity in the hobo world." Carleton Parker noted the
importance of singing in his report on the 1913 Wheatland riot, observing that even lacking a tightly bound membership, "where a group of
hoboes sit around a fire under a railroad bridge, many of the group can
sing I.W.W. songs without the book."[23]

Two religious leaders discovered this fact when they sought to lead
Spokane's hoboes to Jesus. After their speeches to a street-corner as-
semblage had met only silence, the pair of divines followed the crowd
down the street to the IWW hall, where a Wobbly speaker attacked the
Supreme Court, "The Star Spangled Banner," and the Constitution. At
that point, a newspaper reporter noted, "The presence of the preachers
in the hall led to the singing of an I.W.W. song, the title of which is the
'Long Haired Preacher.' It was sung through with much enthusiasm to
the tune of 'In the Sweet By and By.'"[24] The song, by Wobbly bard Joe
Hill, is still popular today in folksong gatherings and has been called
the IWW's "signature song." Its first verse announces:

Long-haired preachers come out every night,
Try to tell you what's wrong and what's right;
But when asked how 'bout something to eat
They will answer with voices so sweet:

CHORUS: You will eat, bye and bye,
In that glorious land above the sky;
Work and pray, live on hay,
You'll get pie in the sky when you die.[25]

During the war, an agent of the California Commission of Immigration and Housing spied on hundreds of Wobblies preparing a pageant
at IWW headquarters in San Francisco, and concluded that "a movement which is able to write its own songs, and sing them with religious
fervor, as well as staging their own plays is a force which sooner or later
will have to be reckoned with."[26]

The Wobblies also became known for the IWW hall, a fixture in many cities and towns across the West. It paralleled the roles that ethnic meeting places were playing across the nation—the Finn halls of northern Minnesota, Sons of Italy centers in New York, Buddhist temples in California, African Baptist churches in Mississippi. Without such a meeting place, hoboes trudging in from the hopyards and logging camps found a welcome only in the saloon and heard a friendly greeting only from bartenders and prostitutes. Most town residents, their organizations, their churches, shunned them.

As Richard White has written, "The Wobblies survived because they understood the nature and the needs" of this migratory labor force, and their union halls served as dormitories, social clubs, mess halls, and even libraries and mail drops. A Wobbly writing to the *Industrial Worker* in 1910 emphasized the importance of IWW halls to western workers, the majority of whom "do not know what a home is. The only home most of us have is the roll of blankets which we carry on our backs." In the IWW hall one could enjoy some of the aspects of home—that made the difference. When Spokane's Wobblies set up their first hall, membership began to grow, for it showed the worker "that we were looking after his material welfare, that we were practicing what we preached, and when he went back to the camp he told his companions in the bunkhouse . . ."[27]

In the era marked by the coming of the railroad until the mid-1920s, when migrant workers began traveling by automobile, the West had been transformed. Because of the iron horse it became a new West, a Second Frontier, an economy marked by intensive agriculture where the role of harvest workers was absolutely crucial. The two—railroads and bindlestiffs—acted together in what the scientific world labels symbiosis, two dissimilar organisms in an intimate association that is necessary for the survival of each. For the western population remained light and scattered, and by the 1920s large cities were still few across the vast region, but with the thrusts of intensive agriculture, it was a world in the making. As one of Willa Cather's characters exclaims when he first views the rolling plains of Nebraska, "There was nothing but land: not a country at all, but the material out of which countries are made." The railroad was the essential element in bringing together scattered materials to create this new western country, but to do this it required one of those other elements, the hobo.[28]

The American frontier had always been characterized by a heterogeneous conglomeration of shifting groups, and what occurred in the Second Frontier as the line of settlement crossed the Missouri and marched toward the Pacific was not unique. In 1802, when the Frenchman François-André Michaux traveled through midcontinent, he was struck by the fact that everyone came from somewhere else, and when his horse would pull up before a collection of people, he was "presented with a glass of whiskey, and then asked a thousand questions, such as Where do you come from? Where are you going? What is your name? Where do you live? . . ." Such fellowship among strangers was common in new settlements, and after the 1870s the incoming railroads continued that mix of peoples, stimulating and encouraging it.[29]

In part this was because the agriculture that the railroads made possible forced upon the West a perennial hunt for workers. Irish, Chinese, and other groups were hired to lay down the rails and then move on, but unlike railways the new growers required harvest help each year. "We are sparsely settled here and have not enough people," a woman in the Texas Winter Garden district told Paul Taylor as she explained the need for Mexican farm help.[30] As fields and orchards grew in size, the West's search for workers became unending: the Old South had imported slaves, but western growers lacked that possibility. And so they were forever recruiting, always alert to potential new groups to bring in their harvests, finally seeking help outside U.S. borders.

The crucial role played by harvest labor in the West begs a question: If it was so important, why were wages generally so low? Why were workers so poorly treated? Only sporadically, for brief periods, were they paid above what would be considered bottom-level wages, and this was true with all crops across the West. The war years briefly brought higher wages, but at other times orchard and field laborers usually could advance economically only when an entire family took to the field. And their living conditions were generally both uncomfortable and unsanitary.

Several reasons for their continued economic weakness appear from the Western harvest story. Seldom part of the local community, those arriving for harvest jobs were seen as outsiders, not expecting or receiving much sympathy from townspeople, town leaders, or law enforcement. Growers therefore did not lack allies when they rejected workers' complaints. Perhaps this opposition from the citizenry seems strange in a community that was not only dependent upon the surrounding agriculture but whose members had generally known recent mobility. Transients seeking work, however, were not settlers, not classed as residents.

Further, criminal elements were also traveling the roadways, and in physical appearance, the migrant worker by day was usually indistinguishable from the burglar who came by night. Railroad records of the period do more than report the deaths of hoboes who fell beneath the wheels; the pages are also filled with lists of items stolen from boxcars and depots, and brakemen killed by men beating their way. Communities could have trouble distinguishing between honest and dishonest hoboes.

Also, racism was woven into the fabric of American life, present long before covered wagons rolled over the Plains, and new communities were only extensions of what had gone before. Wage levels reflected this fact: whites were paid the most, then descending rates were set for other racial groups.

It is sometimes difficult for scholars to place bindlestiffs in the working class because of their mobility in and out of wage labor, and their enormously high turnover rates. Quitting a job could result in finding a different occupation, going from hopyard to railroad construction to factory labor, becoming a settled farmhand, or returning to a distant home and leaving wage labor behind. Was this working class? Or just a temporary experiment? Hobo Carl Sandburg became a poet, hobo Nels Anderson a pioneering sociologist, and hobo William O. Douglas made it to the U.S. Supreme Court. Also, as noted, migrant workers usually arrived as individuals and bargained as individuals; class feeling was discouraged in such a setting, as the Industrial Workers of the World discovered. For Asians and Mexicans, class feeling took second place to ethnic identity but could be merged with it.

And one must add that the hobo was often his own worst enemy. His migratory instincts blocked him from staying in one spot and working to improve his own standing through group action. Carleton Parker noted this and said that each hobo possessed the "instinct of migra- tion . . . To every man the coming of Spring suggests moving on."[31]

What resulted was a heterogeneous western population that has only recently begun to be examined in all its diversity. One recent study acknowledged that to know the West's history, "we must adopt a view that accounts for the incredible variety of its peoples."[32] And although immigration streams from many lands headed to America, nowhere was the multiplicity of origins more evident than within western harvest crews. Carleton Parker was struck by this point when he investigated Wheatland: not only were there many "American" migratory workers, along with hoboes and even some middle-class families, but he learned that a hop inspector had counted twenty-seven different nationalities in his gang of 235 hop pickers.[33]

One struggles to find a unifying factor in such diversity, in this "na- tional sandwich," as a Kansas newspaper described the United States in 1869, when ships were unloading Europeans on the East Coast and Chinese on the West Coast. Perhaps only myth can unify a people lack- ing a common ancestry. Patricia Nelson Limerick has examined the "popular origin myth" of white Americans, that the West was settled by "hardy pioneers, bringing civilization to displace savagery"—a myth that she contends goes against the truth of conquering native peoples, bear- ing "little resemblance to the events of the Western past." Then there is the old saw "Go West and grow up with the country"—a common nineteenth-century saying that played to the vision of the West as a land of opportunity and freedom. Understandably weaker among Indi- ans, these dreams and beliefs fused and traveled across plains and mountains but did not march only in a westerly direction: a look at the pathways of Chinese, Japanese, and Mexicans who filled out the har- vest crews reveals that they carried dreams of success also. Whether one was gazing across the Atlantic, the Pacific, or the Rio Grande, one might have seen picking hops, oranges, or cotton as a large first step up a ladder to a better life. That, after all, was why they came.[34]

Such complicated stories, entwined with the dreams and struggles of diverse peoples, placed the West outside the white-black division assigned to many major events of American history. True, East Texas was a land where southern whites and blacks walked cotton rows amid the lingering shadows of the Old South, but once irrigation and farming began inching westward, even that story became complicated. Europeans arrived, Indians were recruited from their new reservations, German-Russians fled the czarist regime, Chinese piled into West Coast ports, Japanese followed, and Mexicans fleeing revolution pushed across the Rio Grande, while thousands of hoboes came beating their way—and a new story was created. Within this western granary, this sugarlands, the Cotton West and Garden West, a different history was being created by migrant workers.

The story is still unfolding, for growers' search for harvest help never ends. In a region where irrigation now combines with hybrids, fertilizers, and herbicides to produce a large share of America's food, finding workers is a perennial struggle. New controversies over western harvest labor erupt with each generation. Despite the mechanical cotton picker and other technological wonders, the basic issues do not change in agriculture, unlike the case of many urban jobs being transformed by technology. Complaints of harvest workers' harsh treatment and low pay are raised again and again, as are recurring efforts to bend national laws and local statutes to ward off disaster for farmers.

California reformers were reminded of the difference between factory labor and harvest labor in 1912, when they challenged the state's eight-hour law for women's work, because it covered factory jobs but excluded their labor in orchards and fruit packing. In rejecting this complaint, the California Supreme Court noted that agricultural labor was different, because "unless the work is done at the proper time, great loss must ensue from the perishable nature of the products to be preserved."[35] Fear of a "great loss" put western growers and migrant workers forever on a collision course. Much of the western story grew out of that reality in the years of the Second Frontier; it continues to do so today.

The accomplishments, the struggles, and the experiences along the many pathways taken by the region's harvest workers suggest that perhaps someone has been left out of the usual pantheon of western heroes. Those heroes have long been justly celebrated—such personalities as Sitting Bull and Buffalo Bill, Sam Houston and Sacajawea, James

Marshall and Collis P. Huntington, Narcissa Whitman, Billy the Kid, Chief Joseph, Wild Bill Hickok. Western heroes are cowboys and Indians, explorers and entrepreneurs, first settlers and gunslingers.

Might we add the harvest worker? He, she, needs no further justification, no defense, to join this group. Whether a hobo beating his way atop a freight train, a Texas mother herding her children along cotton rows, a German-Russian wielding a machete on sugar beets, an Asian orange glommer edging up a creaky ladder, a Mexican poking through a Fresno vineyard, or an Indian paddling a long canoe en route to the hopyards—harvest workers were essential in creating a new West. This worker was "one of the heroic figures of the frontier," ex-hobo Nels Anderson concluded.[36] With a bindle on his shoulder and his eye on the road, always scouting a job at the next orchard or farm, this hobo, bindlestiff, fruit tramp—this John Chinaman, this *buranketto* boy, this *pizcador*—was also part of the American West.

NOTES

1: GREAT EXPECTATIONS

1. *Junction City* [Kan.] *Union*, July 6, 1867, 2.
2. Howard R. Lamar, ed., *The Reader's Encyclopedia of the American West* (New York: Thomas Y. Crowell, 1977), 992–98; Richard J. Orsi, *Sunset Limited: The Southern Pacific Railroad and the Development of the American West 1850–1930* (Berkeley: University of California Press, 2005), 74–79.
3. *Oroville Register* quoted in *California State Board of Horticulture Annual Report . . . for 1892* (Sacramento: State Printer, 1892), 379–80. See also *California State Agricultural Society Transactions, 1904* (Sacramento: State Printer, 1905), 77; Robert G. Athearn, *Union Pacific Country* (Chicago: Rand McNally, 1971), 223, 317; *Junction City Union*, July 6, 1867, 1; *Salina* [Kan.] *Herald*, March 1, 1879, 3; John Fahey, *The Inland Empire: Unfolding Years, 1879–1929* (Seattle: University of Washington Press, 1986), 35; Gunther Peck, *Reinventing Free Labor—Padrones and Immigrant Workers in the North American West 1880–1930* (New York: Cambridge University Press, 2000), 40–41; Orsi, *Sunset Limited*, 17.
4. Hiram M. Drache, "The Economic Aspects of the Northern Pacific Railroad in North Dakota," *North Dakota History* 34, no. 4 (Fall 1967), 326–27; Athearn, *Union Pacific Country*, 145; Amos S. Lapham, "Looking Backward," *Kansas State Historical Society Collections, 1923–25* (Topeka: State Printing Office, 1925), 16: 504–8.
5. Fahey, *Inland Empire*, p. 36; Michael A. Tomlan, *Tinged with Gold: Hop Culture in the United States* (Athens: University of Georgia Press, 1992), 34–36; *Ashland* [Ore.] *Tidings*, April 18, 1884, quoted in Wallace D. Farnham, "The Development of an Oregon County, 1852–1890: Mines, Farms, and a Railroad," *Pacific Historical Review* 25, no. 1 (February 1956), 42–43.
6. David Vaught, *Cultivating California: Growers, Specialty Crops, and Labor, 1875–1920* (Baltimore: Johns Hopkins University Press, 1999), 11; Ray Allen Billington and Martin Ridge, *Westward Expansion: A History of the American Frontier*, 5th ed. (New York: Macmillan, 1982), chap. 29 passim.
7. *Fort Worth* [Tex.] *Gazette*, September 30, 1877, 2; Fahey, *Inland Empire*, 33, 35; L. A. Burk, interview in U.S. Works Progress Administration, *Oklahoma Indian-Pioneer Project*, 17:374, Oklahoma Historical Society; Carlos A. Schwantes and

James P. Ronda, *The West the Railroads Made* (Seattle: University of Washington Press, 2008), 114.

8. *Northwest Pacific Farmer* [Portland, Ore.], October 3, 1901; "Report of John Isaac, Special Agent," *California State Board of Horticulture Annual Report . . . for 1892* (Sacramento: State Printer, 1892), 376.

9. *Junction City Union*, June 23, 1866, 2; July 21, 1866, 2; December 29, 1866, 3, quoting *Atchison* (Kansas) *Free Press*.

10. Thomas E. Sheridan, *Arizona: A History* (Tucson: University of Arizona Press, 1995), 104; Mrs. Caroline Warnike Asling, quoted in Clara M. Fengel Shields, "The Lyon Creek Settlement," *Kansas State Historical Society Collections* 14 (1915–18), 157; and Leslie A. Fitz, "The Development of the Milling Industry in Kansas," *Kansas State Historical Society Collections* 12 (1911–12), 53–55; *Northwest Pacific Farmer*, March 7, 1901.

11. Joseph A. McGowan, *The Sacramento Valley—A Student's Guide to Localized History* (New York: Teachers College Press, 1967), 30–31; William H. Mills, "Annual Address," *California State Agricultural Society Transactions, 1890* (Sacramento: State Printer, 1891), 187–88.

12. Fahey, *Inland Empire*, 16; Hiram M. Drache, *The Day of the Bonanza—A History of Bonanza Farming in the Red River Valley of the North* (Fargo: North Dakota Institute for Regional Studies, 1964), 15, 26; and Vaught, *Cultivating California*, 76–77. For further inventions assisting the raisin pack, see *Fresno* [Calif.] *Herald and Democrat*, August 14, 1907, 10.

13. *Fort Worth Gazette*, August 8, 1894, 7; Fahey, *Inland Empire*, 49.

14. *California State Agricultural Society Transactions, 1891* (Sacramento: State Printer, 1892), 128–29; Harold Barger and Hans H. Landsberg, *American Agriculture, 1899–1939: A Study of Output, Employment and Productivity* (New York: National Bureau of Economic Research, 1942), 121n; Reverend F. W. Gookin, *Pacific Baptist*, September 15, 1888, quoted in Farnham, "Development of an Oregon County," 44; *Northwest Pacific Farmer*, June 30, 1904; *Puyallup Republican*, July 17, 1908, 1.

15. Orsi, *Sunset Limited*, 328–31; Fahey, *Inland Empire*, 118–19; Lawrence J. Jelinek, *Harvest Empire: A History of California Agriculture* (San Francisco: Boyd & Fraser, 1979), 57–58; *U.S. Industrial Commission, Reports*, vol. 10, *Agriculture and Agricultural Labor* (Washington, D.C.: GPO, 1901), 956–57.

16. Francis J. Swehla, "Bohemians in Central Kansas," *Kansas State Historical Society Collections* 13 (1913–14), 477; Steven Stoll, "Insects and Institutions: University Science and the Fruit Business in California," *Agricultural History* 69, no. 2 (Spring 1995), passim, esp. 222–23; Fahey, *Inland Empire*, 55; Albro Martin, *James J. Hill and the Opening of the Northwest* (New York: Oxford University Press, 1976), 278–79; Orsi, *Sunset Limited*, 55, chap. 11 passim.

17. *Puyallup Republican*, July 17, 1908, 2; Robert C. Nesbit and Charles M. Gates, "Agriculture in Eastern Washington 1890–1910," *Pacific Northwest Quarterly* 37, no. 4 (October 1946), 286–87; Greg Hall, *Harvest Wobblies: The Industrial Workers of the World and Agricultural Laborers in the American West, 1905–1930* (Corvallis: Oregon State University Press, 2001), 42; M. Catherine Miller, "Riparian Rights and the Control of Water in California, 1879–1928: The Relationship Between an Agricultural Enterprise and Legal Change," *Agricultural History* 59, no. 1 (January 1985), 7.

18. *Report of the Governor of Arizona to the Secretary of the Interior for the Year Ended June 30, 1902* (Washington, D.C.: GPO, 1902), 24–25; *U.S. Eleventh Census* (1890), vol. 1, *Agriculture,* 22–32; *U.S. Twelfth Census* (1900), vol. 6, *Agriculture,* 2:823–26; Colorado Bureau of Labor Statistics, *Tenth Biennial Report (1909–10),* 53.

19. Vaught, *Cultivating California,* 36–38; Tomlan, *Tinged with Gold,* 85–89; Daniel Flint, "Hops," *California State Agricultural Society Report, 1905* (Sacramento: State Printer, 1906), 60; *U.S. Department of Agriculture Yearbook, 1922* (Washington, D.C.: GPO, 1922), 750; Leonard J. Arrington, *Beet Sugar in the West: A History of the Utah-Idaho Sugar Company, 1891–1966* (Seattle: University of Washington Press, 1966), 22.

20. See the discussion of this transformation in California in California State Relief Administration, *Migratory Labor in California* (San Francisco: State Relief Administration, 1936), 4–6. See also *Fresno Herald and Democrat,* August 13, 1907, 2; R. I. Bentley, general manager, California Fruit Canners Association, in *U.S. Commission on Industrial Relations Final Report* (1916), 5:4917.

21. W. J. Spillman, "Seasonal Distribution of Labor on the Farm," *U.S. Department of Agriculture Yearbook, 1911* (Washington, D.C.: GPO, 1912), 271. A migratory farm laborer is defined as "a worker whose principal income is earned from temporary farm employment and who in the course of his year's work moves one or more times, often through several States." President's Commission on Migratory Labor, *Migratory Labor in American Agriculture* (Washington, D.C.: GPO, 1951), 1; *Spokane Inland Herald,* June 11, 1910, 4; *U.S. Department of Agriculture Yearbook, 1917* (Washington, D.C.: GPO, 1917), 539; *Puyallup Republican,* July 20, 1906, 1.

22. California Bureau of Labor Statistics, *First Biennial Report 1883–84* (Sacramento: State Printer, 1884), 9–10.

23. President Frederick Cox, "Opening Address," *California State Agricultural Society Transactions, 1891* (Sacramento: State Printer, 1892), 98–99, 386–87.

24. William H. Mills, "Annual Address," 199–200.

25. Arrington, *Beet Sugar in the West,* 20–21; C. O. Townsend, "Conditions Influencing the Production of Sugar-Beet Seed in the United States," *U.S. Department of Agriculture Yearbook, 1909* (Washington, D.C.: GPO, 1910), 183.

26. *Junction City Union,* July 6, 1867, 3; Mark Wyman, *Hard-Rock Epic: Western Miners and the Industrial Revolution, 1860–1910* (Berkeley: University of California Press, 1979), 59.

27. Vaught, *Cultivating California,* 68; Don D. Lescohier, *The Labor Market* (New York: Macmillan, 1923), 63.

28. The most-quoted paean to unfettered wandering is Walt Whitman's "Song of the Open Road"; the theme also runs through his "Leaves of Grass." See Whitman, *Complete Poetry and Collected Prose* (New York: Library of America, 1982), 71, 297. See also E. Keough, Burlington Railroad Roadmaster, "Characteristics of the Hobo," and F. E. Crabbs, North Western Railroad Roadmaster, "Good Board Essential in Hobo Camps," in *Railway Age Gazette,* June 21, 1912, 1566–67; testimony of E. Clemens Horst and George E. Hyde, in *U.S. Commission on Industrial Relations Final Report* (1916), 5:4928, 4930, 4962; Carleton H. Parker, "Preliminary Report on Tentative Findings and Conclusions in the Investigation of Seasonal, Migratory and Unskilled Labor in California," *Report to the U.S. Commission*

on *Industrial Relations*, December 2, 1914, 8 (microfilm copy in State Historical Society of Wisconsin).

29. William M. Duffus, "Labor Market Conditions in the Harvest Fields of the Middle West," *Report to the U.S. Commission on Industrial Relations, December 1, 1914*, 32.

30. John A. Fitch, "Old and New Labor Problems in California," *Survey*, September 19, 1914, 609–10.

2: "WHEAT FARMS AND HOBOES GO TOGETHER"

1. *Salina* [Kan.] *Herald*, May 21, 1881; September 10, 1881, 3; Peter A. Speek, *Report on the Preliminary Investigation of the Harvest Hand Situation in the States of Kansas and Missouri, June 25–July 5, 1914* (microfilm copy in State Historical Society of Wisconsin, P71-1684/S7).

2. Allen G. Applen, "Migratory Harvest Labor in the Midwestern Wheat Belt, 1870–1940" (Ph.D. diss., Kansas State University, 1974), 22–26; E. Dale Odom, "The Economic Impact of Railroads on Denton County, Texas," *East Texas Historical Journal* 29, no. 2 (1991), 59.

3. *Junction City* [Kan.] *Union*, October 1, 1870, 2.

4. There are many sources for the farming machinery revolution of the nineteenth century and how it played out in grain harvesting. I have mainly relied upon the following: Harold Barger and Hans H. Landsberg, *American Agriculture, 1899–1939: A Study of Output, Employment and Productivity* (New York: National Bureau of Economic Research, 1942), 195–221; Fred A. Shannon, *The Farmer's Last Frontier—Agriculture, 1860–1897* (New York: Harper Torchbooks, 1945, 1968), chap. 6; William M. Duffus, "Labor Market Conditions in the Harvest Fields of the Middle West," *Report to the U.S. Commission on Industrial Relations*, December 1, 1914, in *Commission Reports* (microfilm copy in State Historical Society of Wisconsin); John Fahey, *The Inland Empire: Unfolding Years, 1879–1929* (Seattle: University of Washington Press, 1986), 61–63; Greg Hall, *Harvest Wobblies: The Industrial Workers of the World and Agricultural Laborers in the American West, 1905–1930* (Corvallis: Oregon State University Press, 2001), 14–17; Thomas D. Isern, *Bull Threshers and Bindlestiffs: Harvesting and Threshing on the North American Plains* (Lawrence: University Press of Kansas, 1990), 8–21, 26–29, 45–50, 58–63. J. Sanford Rikoon, *Threshing in the Midwest, 1820–1940: A Study of Traditional Culture and Technological Change* (Bloomington: Indiana University Press, 1988), 65–88.

5. Selje is a municipality of 58,000 acres, located 120 miles north of Bergen on Norway's west coast. Some 26 percent of its emigrants returned to reside again in Norway. Interviews with returnees are discussed in Knut Djupedal, "Tales of America," *Western Folklore* 49, no. 2 (April 1990), 177–89.

6. *Salina* [Kan.] *Herald*, October 8, 1881, 2. No more railroad shipments to Chicago were allowed for a period in 1881 because its grain storage facilities were full, the newspaper said. Applen, "Migratory Harvest Labor," 27.

7. Applen, "Migratory Harvest Labor," 58–59, 103–5. The *New York Sun* proposed shipping Bowery derelicts to the West to supply harvest labor.

8. Hiram M. Drache, *The Day of the Bonanza: A History of Bonanza Farming in the*

Red River Valley of the North (Fargo: North Dakota Institute for Regional Studies, 1964), 25ff, 70–71, 108–22, 210.

9. Don D. Lescohier, "Conditions Affecting the Demand for Harvest Labor in the Wheat Belt," *U.S. Department of Agriculture Bulletin*, no. 1230 (April 1924), 19; Applen, "Migratory Harvest Labor," 42–43, 70–71; Drache, *Day of the Bonanza*, 116–18.

10. Testimony of M. F. Greeley, secretary of the South Dakota Board of Regents of Education, *U.S. Industrial Commission Reports*, vol. 10, *Agriculture and Agricultural Labor*, (Washington, D.C.: GPO, 1901), 934; Drache, *Day of the Bonanza*, 115, chap. 8 passim.

11. William R. Draper, "Solving the Labor Problem of the Wheat Belts," *American Monthly Review of Reviews*, July 1902, 72; William Culver Wilson, diaries, June 12, 1893, ms. 0723, Nebraska State Historical Society.

12. Applen, "Migratory Harvest Labor," 127; Lescohier, "Conditions Affecting," 22–23; *Salina Herald*, June 21, 1879, 3; July 2, 1881, 3; September 3, 1881, 2.

13. Applen, "Migratory Harvest Labor," 127; Washington L. McClary, diary, September 6, 1892, ms. 3775, Nebraska State Historical Society.

14. *Salina Herald*, June 26, 1880, 3; June 25, 1881, 3; *Nebraska State Journal*, July 12, 1897, 4. *U.S. Industrial Commission Report*, vol. 10, *Agriculture and Agricultural Labor*, 275–76.

15. *Salina Herald*, July 30, 1881, 3; May 21, 1881, 3.

16. Martha C. Knack and Alice Littlefield, "Native American Labor—Retrieving History, Rethinking Theory," in Littlefield and Knack, eds., *Native Americans and Wage Labor* (Norman: University of Oklahoma Press, 1996), 31–32; Victor S. Clark, "Mexican Labor in the United States," *U.S. Bureau of Labor Bulletin* 78 (September 1908), 483; *Cherokee* [Okla.] *Republican*, May 18, 1912, 3; Isern, *Bull Threshers*, 136–44.

17. *Lincoln* [Neb.] *Star*, July 12, 1912, 14; *Alliance* [Neb.] *Police Day Book*, vol. 1 (1923), August 23 and September 4, 1923; in Nebraska State Historical Society, Record Group 353, Subgroup 3; Paul S. Taylor, *An American-Mexican Frontier—Nueces County, Texas* (1934; reprinted New York: Russell & Russell, 1971), 140–41.

18. Speek, *Report on . . . the Harvest Hand Situation in the State of Kansas*, 11–12.

19. Representative William P. Holaday, House Committee on Immigration and Naturalization, *Seasonal Agricultural Laborers from Mexico*, 69th Cong., 1st sess. (Washington, D.C.: GPO, 1926), 174.

20. Gavin Wright, "American Agriculture and the Labor Market: What Happened to Proletarianization?" *Agricultural History* 62, no. 3 (Summer 1988), 198; Peter Speek, "Report on Psychological Aspect of the Problem of Floating Laborers (An Analysis of Life Stories)," 82, in *Report to U.S. Commission on Industrial Relations, 1914* (microfilm in State Historical Society of Wisconsin, P71-I684/S7).

21. Nels Anderson, *On Hobos and Homelessness* (Chicago: University of Chicago Press, 1998), 28–29. Some of Anderson's writings in this collection appeared in his path-breaking first book, *The Hobo: The Sociology of the Homeless Man* (Chicago: University of Chicago Press, 1923).

22. *Hendryx v. The Kansas City, Fort Scott & Gulf Railroad Company*, 45 *Kansas Reports* 377–80; F. N. Finch, Livingston, Mont., report, September 2, 1907, in Northern

Pacific Railroad Company Records (11 A 5 5B), (138.H.8.7[B]), "Labor—Correspondence Concerning Injuries," in Minnesota Historical Society; President D. Miller, Chicago, to Peter A. Speek, "Report on Transportation of Laborers," in *Reports to the U.S. Commission on Industrial Relations* (microfilm copy in State Historical Society of Wisconsin, P71-T684/S7); Duffus, "Labor Market Conditions," 32. Eric H. Monkkonen argues that the term "beating his way" came from beating the railroad company out of a fare; see Eric H. Monkkonen, ed., *Walking to Work: Tramps in America, 1790–1935* (Lincoln: University of Nebraska Press, 1984), 9. It seems more likely that the term is carried over from the experience of walking through difficult terrain, heavy brush, when a person would have to use his arms to slash open a trail; that is, rough going.

23. The classic account is Jack London, *The Road,* in London, *Novels and Social Writings* (New York: Library of America, 1982), 210–11. *The Road* first appeared in 1907. Also, see descriptions in Carl Sandburg's autobiography, *Always the Young Strangers* (New York: Harcourt, Brace, 1953), 395 and passim. Almost all recent accounts of hobo life contain descriptions of riding the rails. See Roger A. Bruns, *Knights of the Road—A Hobo History* (New York: Methuen, 1980), 36ff; Clark Spence, "Knights of the Tie and Rail—Tramps and Hoboes in the West," *Western Historical Quarterly* 2, no. 1 (January 1971), 8–10; Todd DePastino, *Citizen Hobo: How a Century of Homelessness Shaped America* (Chicago: University of Chicago Press, 2003), 66–67. Thanks to Mike Matejka for assistance in understanding hobo riding spots and techniques.

24. Personal Injury Register, Union Pacific Railroad, Record Group 3761, Subgroup 125, v. 1, v. 8 (1895–1902), 20, Nebraska State Historical Society. Case of James R. Read, Albany, N.Y., May 10, 1897, in Grand Island Jail Registers, Hall County Records, Nebraska State Historical Society, Record group 260, Subgroup 10, Series 1. Chief of Special Agents, Secret Service Record Books, Registers, Northern Pacific Misc. files, v. 5 (1914–16), case 16330; v. 7 (1917–19), case 23818.

25. *Atchison, Topeka & Santa Fe Railroad Company v. John R. Johnson*, 3 *Oklahoma Reports* 41 (1895); Speek, "Report on Transportation," 16; Jim Tracy, interview, Livingston, Mont., June 2, 2002. Tracy formerly worked as a Northern Pacific special agent. Work by a hobo in exchange for a ride is covered in *George W. Woolsey, Administrator, v. Chicago, Burlington & Quincy Railroad Company*, 39 *Nebraska* 798 (1894). See also *Harry O'Banion v. the Missouri Pacific Railway Company*, 65 *Kansas Reports* 352, 69 *Pacific* 353 (1902).

26. Chief of Special Agents, Secret Service Record Books, Registers, Northern Pacific Misc. files; v. 6, case 22394; *Spokane Press*, April 14, 1912, 1–2; Personnel—Box 32:FF 1397; Discharged Employees, 1888, Denver & Rio Grande Collection, Colorado Historical Society; Josiah Flynt, "Tramping with Tramps: The American Tramp Considered Geographically," *Century,* January 1894, 106; Warren McGee, Livingston, Mont., interview with author, June 2, 2002; Applen, "Migratory Harvest Labor," 127–29.

27. UP Personal Injury Registers, 1907–15, 132; *John Conchin v. El Paso & Southwestern Railroad Co.* (1910), 13 *Arizona* 259, 108 *Pacific* 260.

28. Discussion of hoboes and tramps mainly relies on Anderson, *On Hobos*, 61; Speek, "Report on the Psychological Aspect of the Problem of Floating Laborers," 23–24. "How to Tell a Hobo from a Mission Stiff," *Survey* (March 21, 1914), 781; Alexander Cleland, "The Time to Deal with Vagrancy," *Survey* (December 9, 1916), 268–69.

29. Carleton H. Parker, "Preliminary Report on Tentative Findings and Conclusions in the Investigation of Seasonal, Migratory and Unskilled Labor in California," *Report to the U.S. Commission on Industrial Relations*, 1914 (microfilm in State Historical Society of Wisconsin, P71-1684, P2), 7–8.

30. A. L. Beier, *Masterless Men: The Vagrancy Problem in England, 1560–1640* (London: Methuen, 1985), chap. 1 passim, 69–70. On the colonial American background of treatment of vagrants, see Douglas Lamar Jones, "The Strolling Poor: Transiency in Eighteenth-Century Massachusetts," in Monkkonen, *Walking to Work*, 21–55. See also Bram Stoker, "The American 'Tramp' Question and the Old English Vagrancy Laws," *North American Review* (November 1909), pp. 65ff; Tim Cresswell, *The Tramp in America* (London: Reaktion Books, 2001), 57.

31. Speek, "Report on Transportation," 24. On the links between business cycles and tramps, see John C. Schneider, "Omaha Vagrants and the Character of Western Hobo Labor, 1887–1913," *Nebraska History* (Summer 1982), 264. See also DePastino, *Citizen Hobo*, esp. 5–13; Sidney L. Harring, "Class Conflict and the Suppression of Tramps in Buffalo, 1892–1894," *Law and Society* Review 11 (1977), 878; Alan Dawley, *Class and Community: The Industrial Revolution in Lynn* (Cambridge, Mass.: Harvard University Press, 1976), 140; Kevin Kenney, *Making Sense of the Molly Maguires* (New York: Oxford, 1998), 261; Walt Whitman, "The Tramp and Strike Questions," in *Complete Poetry and Collected Prose* (New York: Library of America, 1982), 1063–65; C. G. Tiedeman, "Police Control of Dangerous Classes, Other Than by Criminal Prosecutions," *American Law Review* (July–August 1885), 561–62.

32. Harring, "Class Conflict," 879–81; Elbert Hubbard, "The Rights of Tramps," *Arena* 53 (April 1894), 593–96; Cresswell, *Tramp in America,* 46n, 50–54.

33. *Salina Herald*, June 14, 1879, 2; May 15, 1880, 2; Orlando F. Lewis, "The Vagrant and the Railroad," *North American Review* (July 1907), 610–11.

34. Dagmar Pedersen Frye, *As I Remember It* (River Falls, Wis.: privately published, 1996), 19–20; *Nebraska State Journal* [Lincoln], July 24, 1894, 8.

35. Flynt, "Tramping with Tramps," 100; Anderson, *On Hobos and Homelessness*, 49; *Nebraska State Journal*, June 30, 1915, 6; Jeff Davies, in *Hobo News*, quoted in Cresswell, *Tramp in America*, 57.

36. Ned B. Bond, "The Hobo's Vindication," *Industrial Worker* [Seattle], February 20, 1910, 2.

3: THE WESTERN HOBO

1. Ned B. Bond, Imperial, California, "The Hobo's Vindication," *Industrial Worker* [Seattle], February 20, 1910; and T. J. O'Brien, "Organization and Tactics," *Industrial Worker* [Seattle], February 20 and 26, 1910, 2.

2. Peter A. Speek, "Report on Transportation of Laborers," 15, in *Reports to U.S. Commission on Industrial Relations, 1914* (microfilm copy in State Historical Society of Wisconsin, P71-I684/S7); William M. Duffus, "Labor Market Conditions in the Harvest Fields of the Middle West," *Reports to the U.S. Commission on Industrial Relations, December 1, 1914,* 37–38 (microfilm copy in State Historical Society of Wisconsin, P71-1684/+I45/D9).

3. Josiah Flynt, "Tramping With Tramps: The American Tramp Considered Geographically," *Century,* January 1894, 106.

4. *L. Miller & Co. v. Texas & New Orleans Railway Co.*, 83 *Texas Reports* 518, 520; *Nebraska State Journal*, July 23, 1894, 3. The best descriptions of wage labor's role in the West, although heavily focused on logging and mining, are Carlos Schwantes, "The Concept of the Wageworkers' Frontier: A Framework for Future Research," *Western Historical Quarterly* 18, no. 1 (January 1987); and Melvyn Dubofsky, "The Origins of Western Working Class Radicalism, 1890-1905," *Labor History* 7, no. 2 (Spring 1966).

5. Allen G. Applen, "Migratory Harvest Labor in the Midwestern Wheat Belt, 1870–1940" (Ph.D. diss., Kansas State University, 1974), 125–26; Hall County Jailor's Records, v. 3 (1914), Grand Island, Nebraska State Historical Society, Record Group 260, Subgroup 10, Series 1; Duffus, "Labor Market Conditions," 10, 40–41; Speek, "Report on Transportation," 19; Special Agent Depart., Reports 1909–1914, Al. G. Ray to All Special Agents, Sept. 20, 1909, Great Northern Railway records, Record Group 132.B.19.16F, File 11154, Minnesota Historical Society.

6. "Wherever diversified farming is practiced the amount of transient labor is relatively decreasing, and the duration of employment is increasing." *U.S. Industrial Commission Reports*, vol. 10, *Agriculture and Agricultural Labor* (1901), xix.

7. John C. Schneider, "Omaha Vagrants and the Character of Western Hobo Labor, 1887–1913," *Nebraska History* (Summer 1982), 261–62; Spokane [Wash.] Police Department, Crime Scrapbooks, v. 3, n.d., circa January 1913. See discussion of ethnic backgrounds in Frank Tobias Higbie, "Indispensable Outcasts: Seasonal Laborers and Community in the Upper Midwest, 1880–1930" (Ph.D. diss., University of Illinois, 2000), 146–48. Carlos Schwantes points out that the West had the nation's highest percentage of foreign-born residents in 1890; "Concept of Wageworkers' Frontier," 46–47. Hall County Jailor's Records, v. 3 (1914), Record Group 260, Subgroup 10, Series 1: Jail Registers–Grand Island.

8. Peter A. Speek, "Report on the Preliminary Investigation of the Construction Camps in the States of Dakota and Montana from July 25 to August 10, 1914," 9, in *Reports to the U.S. Commission on Industrial Relations, 1914* (microfilm copy in State Historical Society of Wisconsin, P71-1684, HF. 4I45 S7); Howard Lamar, "From Bondage to Contract: Ethnic Labor in the American West," in Steven Hahn and Jonathan Prude, eds., *The Countryside in the Age of Capitalist Transformation: Essays in the Social History of Rural America* (Chapel Hill: University of North Carolina Press, 1985), 294. Schwantes examines factors making the wage-labor force different in the West, in "Concept of Wageworkers' Frontier," passim.

9. Oscar Friedrichs Inquest, Sacramento County Coroner's Inquests, 1906, Box 25, Folder 1; 1907, Folder 2; Unknown Man, Custer County (Mont.) Coroner's Inquest Book No. 1, 1893–1940, August 30, 1915.

10. Flynt, "Tramping with Tramps," 106–7; arrest of Prairie Chicken, June 1, 1884, Custer County [Mont.] Jail Registers, v. 1, 1881–1908; Union Pacific Personal Injury Register, 1895–1902, p. 77, Nebraska State Historical Society, Record Group 3761, Subgroup 125, vol. 1; Duffus, "Labor Market Conditions," 13–14; Speek, "Report on the Preliminary Investigation," 8. See discussion of Speek's conclusions in Greg Woirol, "Peter Speek and Migratory Labor: An Estonian Revolutionary Finds the Real America," *Journal of the Gilded Age and Progressive Era* (July 2005), 304–6.

11. *Carrington Record*, August 12, 1915, 5, quoted in Kristine Stilwell, "'If You Don't Slip': The Hobo Life, 1911–1916" (Ph.D. diss., University of Missouri–Columbia, 2004), 196.

12. *Lincoln* [Neb.] *Star*, July 10, 1912, 3; Speek, "Report on the Preliminary Investigation," 6; Hiram M. Drache, *The Day of the Bonanza—A History of Bonanza Farming in the Red River Valley of the North* (Fargo: North Dakota Institute for Regional Studies, 1964), 115; Thomas D. Isern, *Bull Threshers and Bindlestiffs: Harvesting and Threshing on the North American Plains* (Lawrence: University Press of Kansas, 1990), 162–64; Duffus, "Labor Market Conditions," 6–7; *Salina Herald*, September 10, 1881, 2; California Commission of Immigration and Housing, CTN 57.4, Labor Camps—Complaints (April 9, 1923) in Bancroft Library; *Nebraska State Journal*, July 25, 1894, 3; August 13, 1894, 2; August 14, 1894, 2.

13. *U.S. Department of Agriculture Yearbook, 1918* (Washington, D.C.: GPO, 1918), 697. Averages for both 1910 and 1918 are given here. In 1920 the *USDA Yearbook* reported that the percentage of yearly hired farm labor totals made up of daily harvest labor hiring was 16.9 percent in the West and 15.9 percent in the western North Central states; the national average was 10.5 percent. Harvest time, and the workers hired for just that short period, was more important in the West. Also see the wage analysis by Isern, *Bull Threshers*, 153–57.

14. Duffus, "Labor Market Conditions," 3–4; Don D. Lescohier, *The Labor Market* (New York: Macmillan, 1923), 63–64.

15. George Dawson and Richard Glaubman, *Life Is So Good* (New York: Penguin, 2000), 96; Paul S. Taylor, "Migratory Agricultural Workers on the Pacific Coast," *American Sociological Review* 3, no. 2 (April 1938), 225.

16. Vagrancy arrests are taken from the following: *Nebraska State Journal*, June 30, 1915, 6; Grand Island [Neb.] Police Judge's Docket, v. 5, 1893–1896; Alliance [Neb.] Police Day Book, v. 1, July 26 and August 24, 1923, both in Nebraska State Historical Society, Record Group 300, Series 1; Spokane Police Department scrapbooks, v. 2, June 29, 1907 (name of paper not given); Livingston [Mont.] Police Docket Books, v. 2, February 26, 1914; October 1, 1917; Denver Police Magistrate Court Record, v. 1 and 2, DeWitt C. Webber, Police Magistrate—No. 9232, June 12, 1895; no. 10042, September 24, 1895; no. 10629, November 25, 1895, in Colorado State Archives; Custer County [Mont.] Jail Register, v. 1, November 12, 1899; Sacramento [Calif.], Police Department, Jail Registers, v. 1896–99, Sacramento Archives and Museum Collections.

17. Dawson and Glaubman, *Life Is So Good*, 157–58, 160; Jack London, *The Road*, 202, in London, *Novels and Social Writings* (1907; reprint by New York: Library of America, 1982). Since London seldom rode the rails with the aim of working, to call him a hobo may be inaccurate, but he did occasionally take jobs as he traveled. His aim seems to have been to find adventure. Herbert L. Pease, *Singing Rails* (New York: Thomas Crowell, 1948), 101.

18. *Southern Pacific R.R. Co. v. Svendsen*, 13 *Ariz.* 111, 108 *Pacific* 262 (1910); *Golden v. Northern Pacific Railway Co.*, 9 *Montana* 435, 104 *Pacific* 549 (1909); *W.P. Richardson et al. v. The Missouri Pacific Railway Co.*, 90 *Kansas* 292 (1913).

19. Coroner's Docket, Inquisition [sic] into death of Chauncy W. West, October 6–8, 1894, Silver Bow County Coroner's Register, in Butte-Silver Bow Public Archives, Butte, Montana; Speek, "Report on Transportation," 35.

20. Jon C. Schneider, "Tramping Workers, 1890–1920: A Subcultural View," in Eric H. Monkkonen, ed., *Walking to Work: Tramps in America, 1790–1935* (Lincoln: University of Nebraska Press, 1984), 212–34. There are many collections of hobo slang. Roger A. Bruns includes "A Glossary of the Road" in his *Knights of the Road: A Hobo History* (New York: Methuen, 1980), 200–4. Contemporary articles about hoboes often mentioned hobo terms, and more recent studies of the Industrial Workers of the World take up the issue as well. Hobo fence markings have frequently been described; an early newspaper account appeared in *Chicago Mail* and was reprinted in *Helena* [Mont.] *Daily Herald*, January 9, 1889, 2. On hobo songs, see Carl Sandburg, *The American Songbag* (New York, 1927; reprint by New York: Harcourt Brace Jovanovich, 1955); also the recent collection, *The Big Red Songbook*, edited by Archie Green, et al. (Chicago: Charles H. Kerr, 2007). IWW songs are discussed below, in Chapter 12.

21. Dawson and Glaubman, *Life Is So Good*, 96, 160; Speek, "Report on Transportation," 20; and "Psychological Aspect," 74; Clark Spence, "Knights of the Tie and Rail—Tramps and Hoboes in the West," *Western Historical Quarterly* 2, no. 1 (January 1971), 13–14; Duffus, "Labor Market Conditions," 42.

22. Unkown man, Custer County Coroner's Inquest Book no. 1, October 31, 1911; death of Samuel Hutton, Inquest March 6, 1891, Spokane County Medical Examiner Coroner's Inquests, 1891; Yakima County Coroner's Records 1911–1916. Similar comments appear throughout coroners' inquest reports. See also Northern Pacific injuries correspondence, May 20, 1907; *Omaha Daily Bee*, July 26, 1884, 8.

23. Death of Zachery Finn, Coroner's Inquest, in Spokane County Medical Examiner, Coroner's Inquests 1891, Eastern Washington Archives, Cheney, Accession 001-0558, Box 1.

24. Reverend Frederic R. Howard, Portland, Ore., letter to *Survey* 34 (April 10, 1915), 57.

25. Stilwell, "If You Don't Slip," 71ff, on women hoboes; Sandburg, *Always the Young Strangers* (New York: Harcourt, Brace, 1953), chap. 19 passim.

4: "LABOR SHORTAGE MENACE" IN THE NORTHWEST

1. *Puyallup* [Wash.] *Republican*, September 6, 1907, 5.

2. D. W. Meinig, *The Great Columbia Plain—A Historical Geography, 1805–1910* (Seattle: University of Washington Press), chap. 1 passim. Spokane's boosters included the mining districts of northern Idaho—the famous Coeur d'Alenes—as part of the Inland Empire.

3. John S. Cochran, "Economic Importance of Early Transcontinental Railroads: Pacific Northwest," *Oregon Historical Quarterly* 71, no. 1 (March 1970), 62; *Northwest Pacific Farmer* [Portland, Ore.], October 3, 1901, 1; Oregon Bureau of Labor Statistics, *Second Biennial Report, Oct. 1, 1904 to Sept. 30, 1906* (Salem, 1906), 89–90; *Wenatchee* [Wash.] *Republic*, September 12, 1912, 2.

4. *Pacific Northwest Farmer*, July 23, 1903, 1; *U.S. Department of Agriculture Yearbook, 1918* (Washington, D.C.: GPO, 1918), 374–75.

5. *Yakima Morning Herald*, August 21, 1915, 4; August 28, 1915, 3–4; September 18, 1915, 3; July 28, 1917, 6; and September 2, 1917, 8. *Puyallup Republican*, August 10, 1906, 4–5; Michael A. Tomlan, *Tinged with Gold: Hop Culture in the*

United States (Athens: University of Georgia Press, 1992), 33; *U.S. Department of Agriculture Yearbook, 1918,* 552–53.

6. *Reports of the U.S. Immigration Commission,* vol. 22: *Recent Immigrants in Agriculture* (Washington, D.C.: GPO, 1911), 24:149; Peter A. Speek, "Report on Psychological Aspect of the Problem of Floating Laborers," in *Reports to U.S. Commission on Industrial Relations, 1914,* 73 (microfilm copy in State Historical Society of Wisconsin, P71-1684 S7).

7. Harry Schwartz, *Seasonal Farm Labor in the United States, with special reference to hired workers in fruit and vegetable and sugar-beet production* (New York: Columbia University Press, 1945), 67; *Coeur d'Alene Evening Press,* May 25, 1910; *Spokane Inland Herald,* July 19, 1910, 16; *Spokane Spokesman-Review,* August 23, 1901, 6; August 15, 1907, 6; October 20, 1916, 12; October 20, 1918, 10; July 28, 1920, 10. *Puyallup Republican,* July 20, 1906, 4.

8. This account of railroad development relies heavily upon John Fahey, *The Inland Empire: Unfolding Years, 1879–1929* (Seattle: University of Washington Press, 1986), 13–15, 39, chap. 2 passim; William Dietrich, *Northwest Passage: The Great Columbia River* (New York: Simon & Schuster, 1995), 243, chap. 10 passim; Dorothy O. Johansen and Charles M. Gates, *Empire of the Columbia: A History of the Pacific Northwest* (1957; New York: Harper & Row, 1967), chap. 19; and Ralph W. Hidy, Muriel E. Hidy, and Roy V. Scott, *The Great Northern Railway: A History* (Boston: Harvard Business School Press, 1988), chap. 11 passim.

9. U.S. Census data compiled by University of Virginia Library, Geospatial and Statistical Data Center, www.Fisher.lib.Virginia.edu/Collections/stats/histcensus (accessed November 15, 2006); Fahey, *Inland Empire,* 38–40; Cochran, "Economic Importance," 41, 59, 63; Johansen and Gates, *Empire of the Columbia,* 374–75, 608; Washington State Department of Agriculture, *Atlas of Washington Agriculture* (Olympia, 1963), 10.

10. *Wenatchee Advance,* May 26, 1894, 1–4; October 19, 1901, 2.

11. Meinig, *Great Columbia Plain,* 251ff, chap. 14 passim; Wayne D. Rasmussen, "A Century of Farming in the Inland Empire," in David H. Stratton, ed., *Spokane and the Inland Empire: An Interior Pacific Northwest Anthology* (Pullman: Washington State University Press, 2005), 119–22; J. H. Arnold, "Farm Practices in Growing Wheat," *U.S. Department of Agriculture Yearbook, 1919,* 136–50; Oregon Bureau of Labor Statistics, *Second Biennial Report, 1904–6,* 91; *Third Biennial Report, 1906–8,* 55–56; *Wenatchee Advance,* August 9, 1907, 1.

12. Hayes Perkins, "Here and There—An Itinerant Worker in the Pacific Northwest, 1898," *Oregon Historical Quarterly* 102, no. 3 (Fall 2001), 352–68.

13. Frederick Bracher, "How It Was Then: The Pacific Northwest in the Twenties," *Oregon Historical Quarterly* 84, no. 4 (Winter 1983), 341–58.

14. *Inland Herald,* July 22, 1910, 11; *Wenatchee Advance,* July 13, 1901, 1; August 31, 1901, 8; August 3, 1907, 2, 6.

15. Judith Austin, "Desert, Sagebrush, and the Pacific Northwest," in William G. Robbins, Robert J. Frank, and Richard E. Ross, eds., *Regionalism and the Pacific Northwest* (Corvallis: Oregon State University Press, 1983), 139; Robert C. Nesbit and Charles M. Gates, "Agriculture in Eastern Washington 1890–1910," *Pacific Northwest Quarterly* 37, no. 4 (October 1946), 286–87; *Yakima Herald* quoted in *Wenatchee Advance,* January 11, 1902, 2; Fahey, *Inland Empire,* 87–92,

97–98; Dietrich, *Northwest Passage*, 243–46; Meinig, *Great Columbia Plain*, 379–81.

16. Fahey, *Inland Empire*, 89–91; Nesbit and Gates, "Agriculture in Eastern Washington," 289; John Fahey, "Irrigation, Apples, and the Spokane Country," *Pacific Northwest Quarterly* 84 (January 1993), passim.

17. Johansen and Gates, *Empire of the Columbia*, chap. 24 passim; Nesbit and Gates, "Agriculture in Eastern Washington 1890–1910," 287–90; Dietrich, *Northwest Passage*, 244–47; Fahey, *Inland Empire*, 92–95; Fahey, "Irrigation, Apples, and the Spokane Country," 18; *Wenatchee Advance*, June 22, 1901, 4; *U.S. Twelfth Census* (1900), vol. 2, *Agriculture*, 803, 820.

18. Johansen and Gates, *Empire of the Columbia*, 376; U.S. Census data, 1900 and 1910, University of Virginia Library compilation; Nesbit and Gates, "Agriculture in Eastern Washington 1890–1910," 290.

19. Tomlan, *Tinged with Gold*, pref., 5–6, 26–30, 62–64, 66–71; *Yakima Morning Herald*, May 2, 1915, 4; Carl F. Reuss, Paul H. Landis, and Richard Wakefield, *Migratory Farm Labor and the Hop Industry on the Pacific Coast with Special Application to Problems of the Yakima Valley, Washington*, Rural Sociology Series in Farm Labor, no. 3 (Pullman: State College of Washington Agricultural Experiment Station, 1938), 5–6.

20. *Yakima Morning Herald*, May 5, 1915, 4; *Herald* want ad section, August 31, 1917, 7; *Puyallup Republican*, September 6, 1907, 5; Ezra Meeker, *Hop Culture in the United States—Being a Treatise on Hop Growing in Washington Territory, From the Cutting to the Bale* (Puyallup, Washington Territory: E. Meeker & Co., 1883), 6–7, 20; Annie Marion MacLean, "With Oregon Hop Pickers," *American Journal of Sociology* 15, no. 1 (July 1909), 88–89; Oregon Bureau of Labor Statistics, *Second Biennial Report*, 104–6; *Third Biennial Report*, 51; *Seventh Biennial Report*, 13.

21. Meeker, *Hop Culture*, 18; *Washington Farmer*, July 25, 1890, reprinted in *Pacific Rural Press* [San Francisco] 40, no. 6 (August 9, 1890), 119; *Northwest Pacific Farmer*, September 12, 1901; Margaret Willis, ed., *Chechacos All: The Pioneering of Skagit* (Mount Vernon, Wash.: Skagit Valley Historical Society, 1973), 133; A. G. Rogers, letter to *People's Paper*, Santa Barbara, Calif., reprinted in *Puyallup Republican*, July 27, 1906, 1.

22. *Reports of the U.S. Immigration Commission*, vol. 24, *Immigrant Labor in the Western States* (Washington, D.C.: GPO, 1911), 25:163–64; Paige Raibmon, *Authentic Indians: Episodes of Encounter from the Late-Nineteenth-Century Northwest Coast* (Durham, N.C.: Duke University Press, 2005), 79, 104; Coll Thrush, *Native Seattle: Histories from the Crossing-Over Place* (Seattle: University of Washington Press, 2007), 47–49, 70–73, 106–9, 112; *Puyallup Republican*, September 7, 1906, 4.

23. Raibmon, *Authentic Indians*, 79, 83, 87–88, spelling as in original.

24. Rebecca T. Richards and Susan J. Alexander, *A Social History of Wild Huckleberry Harvesting in the Pacific Northwest* (U.S. Forest Service, Pacific Northwest Research Station, 2006), 5–10; Kevin R. Marsh, "Ups and Downs of Mountain Life: Historical Patterns of Adaptations in the Cascade Mountains," *Western Historical Quarterly*, 35:2 (Summer 2004), 200–1; Kent Richards, "History of the Snoqualmie Valley," unpublished environmental impact research, Central Washington University, 74–75; Raibmon, *Authentic Indians*, 105–6. Continued journeys into

the mountains were likely misunderstood by whites, however. To a *Yakima Herald* reporter, it was simply a summer respite. "Many Indians of the reservation are departing at this time for a vacation in the mountains," he wrote in August 1917; but most would return by hops-picking time, he wrote reassuringly. *Yakima Morning Herald*, August 10, 1917, 6; Kenneth Tollefson, "The Snoqualmie Indians as Hop Pickers," *Columbia* 39 (Winter 1994–95), 40–44 passim.

25. *Seattle Times*, August 31, 1891, 3.
26. *Pierce County News*, July 28, 1882; *Puyallup Republican*, September 14, 1906, 4, 8; Thrush, *Native Seattle*, 110–12.
27. Robert B. Campbell, "Newlands, Old Lands: Native American Labor, Agrarian Ideology, and the Progressive-Era State in the Making of the Newlands Reclamation Project, 1902–1926," *Pacific Historical Review* 71, no. 2 (May 2002), 204–5; Philip J. Deloria, *Indians in Unexpected Places* (Lawrence: University Press of Kansas, 2004), 6–7, 14, 225, 231; Alice Littlefield and Martha C. Knack, eds., *Native Americans and Wage Labor* (Norman: University of Oklahoma Press, 1996), chap. 1 passim, esp. 13–15; Agent J. B. Lane, Siletz Indian Agency, Oregon, in U.S. Office of Indian Affairs, *Annual Report of the Commissioner, 1887* (Washington, D.C.: GPO, 1887), 188–90. The confederated Indians of the Siletz were remnants of some twenty-eight different tribes, according to agent T. J. Buford in *Annual Report . . . 1893*, 269; Raibmon, *Authentic Indians*, 76, 108.
28. Reuss et al., *Migratory Farm Labor and the Hop Industry*, 7; Tomlan, *Tinged with Gold*, 109–11, 119. See discussion in Gunther Peck, *Reinventing Free Labor: Padrones and Immigrant Workers in the North American West, 1880–1930* (New York: Cambridge University Press, 2000), chap. 5 passim. References to Japanese and Chinese in Pacific Northwest hops-growing centers are sporadic, leading to the conclusion that they worked there mainly in fruit picking and sugar beet harvesting. See *U.S. Immigration Commission Reports*, vol. 22, *Immigrant Labor in the Western States*, 24:163–64; Tollefson, "Snoqualmie Indians as Hop Pickers," 43; *Yakima Morning Herald*, September 28, 1915, 8; *Puyallup Republican*, August 26, 1909, 10.
29. Joan M. Jensen, *Promise to the Land: Essays on Rural Women* (Albuquerque: University of New Mexico Press, 1991), chap. 6 passim; *Pacific Northwest Farmer*, September 12, 1901; Raibmon, *Authentic Indians*, 79, 119–20; *U.S. Department of Agriculture Yearbook, 1914*, 271.
30. Annie Marion McLean's story is told in "With Oregon Hop Pickers."
31. Carlos A. Schwantes, "The Concept of the Wageworkers' Frontier: A Framework for Future Research," *Western Historical Quarterly* 18, no. 1 (January 1987), 41.

5: THE NORTHWEST BECOMES AN ORCHARD

1. *Puyallup Republican*, July 31, 1908, 5. Idaho approved women's suffrage in 1905, Washington in 1909, and Oregon in 1912.
2. *Yakima Morning Herald*, August 3, 1915, 6; August 22, 1915, 7.
3. See first page of *Wenatchee Advance* for July 12, 1902, and January 5, 1911. See also John Fahey, *The Inland Empire: Unfolding Years, 1879–1929* (Seattle: University of Washington Press, 1986), 118.
4. Linda Tamura, *The Hood River Issei: An Oral History of Japanese Settlers in Oregon's Hood River Valley* (Urbana: University of Illinois Press, 1993), 80–81; Lauren Kes-

sler, *Stubborn Twig—Three Generations in the Life of a Japanese American Family* (New York: Random House, 1994), 3–4, 25; *Wenatchee Advance*, May 26, 1894, 3–4; January 3, 1903, 2.

5. Moses Folsom, GN Immigration Agent, speech reprinted in *Wenatchee Advance*, March 9, 1895, 1; *Spokane Inland Herald*, June 12, 1910, 4 (advertisement); *Leavenworth Echo*, quoted in *Seattle Post-Intelligencer*, reprinted in *Wenatchee Advance*, August 9, 1907, 4; W. T. Clark, quoted in *Wenatchee Republic*, June 26, 1913, 2; *Wenatchee Advance*, May 26, 1894, 3–4; January 3, 1903, 2; Works Progress Administration, *Index of Spokane Newspapers*, vol. 11, *Fruit Industry* (copy in Spokane Public Library), February 3, 1917, probably *Spokane Spokesman-Review*; *Wenatchee Republic*, August 29, 1912, 2; *U.S. Department of Agriculture Yearbook, 1900*, 732; *Yearbook, 1918*, 374–75; *Yearbook, 1923*, 734.

6. *Northwest Pacific Farmer*, September 11, 1902; August 4, 1904; *Puyallup Republican*, July 20, 1906, 1; August 24, 1906, 1; *Spokane Inland Herald*, June 11, 1910, 4.

7. Carl F. Reuss, "The Farm Labor Problem in Washington, 1917–18," *Pacific Northwest Quarterly* 34, no. 4 (October 1943), 340. Canadian railroads before the war were erecting signs in northern states offering cheaper rail fares to harvest hands willing to move to Canada. Evelyne Stitt Pickett, "Hoboes Across the Border—A Comparison of Itinerant Cross-Border Laborers Between Montana and Western Canada," *Montana* 49, no. 1 (Spring 1999), 26–27; Nellie L. Beck, term paper reprinted in *Yakima Morning Herald*, August 1, 1915, 9.

8. *Yakima Herald*, August 2, 1917, 8. E. B. Elton, Route # 2, The Dalles [Ore.] to Warm Springs Agency, June 4, 1940, in U.S. Bureau of Indian Affairs, Warm Springs (Ore.) Indian Agency, Old Decimal Files 1908–52, Folder 989 Berry Picking; E. L. Scobee, Hood River [Ore.] to Warm Springs Agency, May 18, 1928, in Folder 980 Employment, private, off reservation; C. A. Roos, Hood River [Ore.] to Warm Springs Agency, May 27, 1926, in Folder 989 Berry Picking, all in National Archives and Records Administration (NARA), Seattle.

9. *Wenatchee Republic*, August 10, 1911, 4; October 19, 1911, 4; "Prunes in Oregon," *Oregon Agricultural Experiment Station Bulletin* 45 (June 1897), 35–36; "The Apple from Orchard to Market," *Oregon Agricultural Experiment Station Bulletin* 94 (February 1907), 4–5, 8–9.

10. *Yakima Morning Herald*, July 30, 1915, 6; August 1, 1915, 4; August 31, 1915, 2; September 1, 1915, 3; September 8, 1915, 2; September 21, 1917, 2; September 27, 1917, 6. *Spokane Inland Herald*, July 26, 1910, 4, quoting *Yakima Democrat*. *Wenatchee Republic*, August 8, 1912, 1; September 19, 1912, 3.

11. "As Told in the Valley," outside communication to *Puyallup Republican*, July 17, 1908, 4. *Wenatchee Advance*, September 15, 1900, 7, 8; September 6, 1907, 1. Oregon Bureau of Labor Statistics, *Seventh Biennial Report, 1914–16* (Salem, 1916), 88.

12. Oregon Bureau of Labor Statistics, *Fourth Biennial Report, 1908–10*, 8–9. C. K. Hauke, second assistant commissioner, Office of Indian Affairs, Washington, to S.A.M. Young, Superintendent, Yakima Indian School, Fort Simcoe, Wash., May 2, 1911, in Superintendent's Correspondence, U.S. Bureau of Indian Affairs, Yakima Indian Agency, Record Group 75, Box 69, in NARA, Seattle. In 1938 the Washington State College Agricultural Experiment Station could still report that one-eighth of the hops pickers interviewed in the Yakima Valley were under age

fifteen—"even though the public schools of the county already had opened." It conceded that "child labor is no novelty in the hop fields." Carl F. Reuss, Paul H. Lundis, and Richard Wakefield, *Migratory Farm Labor and the Hop Industry on the Pacific Coast, With Special Application to Problems of the Yakima Valley, Washington*, Rural Sociology Series in Farm Labor, no. 3 (Pullman: State College of Washington, Agricultural Experiment Station, 1938), 26; *Yakima Morning Herald*, September 14, 1915, 1; *Spokane Spokesman-Review*, October 18, 1916, 10.

13. *Yakima Herald*, October 16, 1917, 6; October 17, 1917, 6; October 21, 1917, 6; Oregon Bureau of Labor Statistics, *Eighth Biennial Report, 1916–18*, 44; E. V. Wilcox, "Plan of the Department of Agriculture for Handling the Farm Labor Problem," *American Economic Review* 8, no. 1 (March 1918), 166–67.

14. Michael A. Tomlan, *Tinged with Gold: Hop Culture in the United States* (Athens: University of Georgia Press, 1992), 110; Dorothy O. Johansen and Charles M. Gates, *Empire of the Columbia: A History of the Pacific Northwest* (1957; New York: Harper & Row, 1967), 348–49; Kenneth Tollefson, "The Snoqualmie Indians as Hop Pickers," *Columbia* 39 (Winter 1994–95), 43; Marie Rose Wong, *Sweet Cakes, Long Journey: The Chinatowns of Portland, Oregon* (Seattle: University of Washington Press, 2004), 44–50.

15. *Reports of the U.S. Immigration Commission*, pt. 25, *Japanese and Other Immigrant Races in the Pacific Coast and Rocky Mountain States* (Washington, D.C.: GPO, 1910), 3:389; Joan S. Wang, "The Double Burdens of Immigrant Nationalism: The Relationship Between Chinese and Japanese in the American West, 1880s– 1920s," *Journal of American Ethnic History* 27, no. 2 (Winter 2008), 30; Wong, *Sweet Cakes, Long Journey*, 176–81; D. W. Meinig, *The Great Columbia Plain—A Historical Geography, 1805–1910* (Seattle: University of Washington Press, 1968), 505n; Sarah M. Griffith, "Border Crossings: Race, Class, and Smuggling in Pacific Coast Chinese Immigrant Society," *Western Historical Quarterly* 35, no. 4 (Winter 2004), 473–92 passim; Spokane County Sheriff's Docket, Criminal, 1897–1902, passim; Barbara Yasui, "The Nikkei in Oregon, 1834–1940," *Oregon Historical Quarterly* 76, no. 3 (September 1975), 229–34. Census information was taken from U.S. Census publications, 1880–1920; data were also obtained from www2 .census.gov/prod2/decennial/documents/33405927v1ch12/pdf, and from the on-line site of the University of Washington Center for the Study of the Pacific Northwest: www.washington.edu/uwired/outreach/cspn/Website/Resources/curriculum/ Asian/Section5.html; Asian/Documents/50.html and Asian/Documents/57.html.

16. Eiichiro Azuma, "A History of Oregon's *Issei*, 1880–1952," *Oregon Historical Quarterly* 94, no. 4 (Winter 1993–94), 315–19; Yasui, "Nikkei in Oregon," 230; Yuji Ichioka, *The Issei: The World of the First Generation Japanese Immigrants 1885– 1924* (New York: Free Press, 1988), 66–68.

17. Azuma, "History of Oregon's *Issei*," 321; Yasui, "Nikkei in Oregon," 234; Kessler, *Stubborn Twig*, 10.

18. This information on the Hood River Japanese is taken mainly from Tamura, *Hood River Issei*, 33–85 passim, and Kessler, *Stubborn Twig*, 12–14, 29–32, 56–59.

19. Information on the Japanese in Yakima County is drawn mainly from Louis Fiset and Gail M. Nomura, eds., *Nikkei in the Pacific Northwest: Japanese Americans and Japanese Canadians in the Twentieth Century* (Seattle: University of Washington Press, 2005), chap. 3 passim; H. A. Millis, *The Japanese Problem in the*

United States—An Investigation for the Commission on Relations with Japan Appointed by the Federal Council of the Churches of Christ in America (1915; reprinted New York: Arno Press, 1978), 88, 95–96; Oregon Bureau of Labor Statistics, Fifth Biennial Report, 1910–12, 11–13; Wenatchee Republic, September 19, 1912, 3.

20. Tamura, Hood River Issei, 89–90; Wendy Ng, "Collective Memory, Social Networks, and Generations: The Japanese American Community in Hood River, Oregon" (Ph.D. diss., University of Oregon, 1989), 24–34.

21. Puyallup Republican, September 14, 1906, 8; Wenatchee Advance, September 13, 1907, 4; October 4, 1907, 2; Oregon Bureau of Labor Statistics, Sixth Biennial Report, 1910–12, 17; Eighth Biennial Report, 1916–18, 31; Yakima Herald, July 27, 1915, 6; July 31, 1915, 1; August 31, 1915, 6.

22. Hayes Perkins, "Here and There—An Itinerant Worker in the Pacific Northwest, 1898," Oregon Historical Quarterly 102, no. 3 (Fall 2001), 368; Yakima Herald, August 5, 1917, 6; August 17, 1917, 5; August 19, 1915, 6; October 23, 1917 (want ads), 7.

23. Yakima Herald, October 9, 1917, 8; October 10, 1917, 6; October 11, 1917, 5. Typical reports of brief strikes appear in Spokane Spokesman-Review, October 20, 1916, 12; October 20, 1918, 10.

6: HOBOES BATTLING FOREST FIRES

1. Will Barnes, in Vivian Gornick, The Romance of American Communism (New York: Basic Books, 1977), 68–69.

2. Yakima Herald, September 12, 1917, 1; September 14, 1917, 6.

3. Wenatchee Advance, July 13, 1907, 2; Yakima Herald, September 9, 1917, 4.

4. Harry Schwartz, Seasonal Farm Labor in the United States with special reference to hired workers in fruit and vegetable and sugar-beet production (New York: Columbia University Press, 1945), 84.

5. Samuel Schrager, "Migratory Lumberjack: A Portrait of Michigan Bill Stowell," Forest and Conservation History 35 (January 1991), 9; Carleton H. Parker, "Preliminary Report on Tentative Findings and Conclusions in the Investigation of Seasonal, Migratory and Unskilled Labor in California," Reports to U.S. Commission on Industrial Relations, 1914, 10 (microfilm copy in State Historical Society of Wisconsin, P71-1684 P2).

6. William D. Hagenstein, interviewed by Elwood Maunder, 1960, provided by Forest History Society; Carleton H. Parker, The Casual Laborer and Other Essays (New York: Harcourt Brace and Howe, 1920), 79; Parker, "Preliminary Report," 10; Richard A. Rajala, "Bill and the Boss: Labor Protest, Technological Change, and the Transformation of the West Coast Logging Camp, 1890–1930," Journal of Forest History 33, no. 4 (October 1989), 170; Spokane Inland Herald, July 6, 1910, 1; July 31, 1910, 3.

7. William G. Robbins, Hard Times in Paradise: Coos Bay, Oregon, 1850–1986 (Seattle: University of Washington Press, 1988), 55–57; Schrager, "Migratory Lumberjack," 9; Father Andrew Mason Prouty, "Logging with Steam in the Pacific Northwest—The Men, The Camps, and The Accidents 1885–1918" (M.A. thesis, University of Washington, 1973), 22, 178.

8. President's Mediation Commission, *Report . . . to the President of the United States*, in
   U.S. Department of Labor Reports . . . 1918 (Washington, D.C.: GPO, 1919), 22;
   R. J. O'Farrell, "The Evolution of Logging—Some Personal Glimpses," *University of
   Washington Forest Club Quarterly* (Autumn 1929), quoted in Prouty, "Logging with
   Steam," 35–36; Vernon H. Jensen, *Lumber and Labor* (1945; reprint New York:
   Arno Press, 1971), 106–7; Parker, *Casual Laborer*, 74–75; Rexford G. Tugwell,
   "The Casual of the Woods," *The Survey* 44, July 3, 1920, 473.

9. See Prouty citation above with the following court cases: *Robert T. Haverland v.
   Potlatch Lumber Company*, 200 *Pacific* 129, *Idaho Reports* 237 (July 29, 1921);
   Melissa Wall et al. v. Idaho & Washington Northern Railway Co., Spokane County
   Superior Court, October 31, 1908; *Asa Delozier v. Phoenix Lumber Co.*, Spokane
   County Superior Court, n.d., circa 1900, the latter two in Washington State Ar-
   chives, Eastern Region, Cheney. See also *Spokane Press*, April 2, 1910, 1.

10. Hercules Mining Company personnel records, in Wallace District Mining Mu-
    seum, Wallace, Idaho.

11. Testimony of Charles E. Plumtree, Coroner's Inquest over death of Samuel Hut-
    ton, March 6, 1891, Spokane County Medical Examiner, Coroner's Inquests,
    1891; in Washington State Archives, Eastern Region.

12. The *Spokane Inland Herald* reported on August 6, 1910, that some 500 USFS men
    were battling fires on the Coeur d'Alene reserve, plus "an equal number of men
    employed by mining and lumber companies and the railroads." Stephen J. Pyne,
    Year of the Fires: The Story of the Great Fires of 1910 (New York: Viking, 2001), 201;
    Coeur d'Alene Evening Press, August 23, 1910, 1, 4.

13. *Spokane Press*, July 13, 1910, 2; July 14, 1910, 1. *Spokane Inland Herald*, July 9,
    1910, 2; July 19, 1910, 2; July 20, 1910, 10; July 21, 1910, 1, 3. Elers Koch, "His-
    tory of the 1910 Forest Fires in Idaho and Western Montana," 2, 10 (prepared for
    USFS; copy in K. Ross Toole Archives, University of Montana); *Spokane Spokesman-
    Review*, July 20, 1910, 10.

14. Koch quote in Pyne, *Year of the Fires*, 85. Firefighting Time Book, August 1910,
    William Rock, Ranger, Avery, Idaho; copy provided by Carl Ritchie, district archae-
    ology technician, USFS, Coeur d'Alene, Idaho.

15. Wade Bilbrey, "1910 Fire Graves," unpublished account provided by author; Pyne,
    Year of the Fires, 84, 101, 161ff, 212–15; *Spokane Press*, August 25, 1910, 2; Au-
    gust 27, 1910, 2; August 30, 1910, 1.

16. B. W. Clark, "Memorandum for the District Forester, October 9, 1919," and F. R.
    Ingalsbe, Mineral Examiner, "Memorandum for District Forester," 1919, in USFS
    District I Archives, Missoula, Montana; J. C. Urquhart, "Firefighting Experiences,"
    USFS, *Early Days in the Forest Service* (1962), 3:264–74; Rajala, "Bill and the
    Boss," 171–72; District Forester Rutledge, in "Statements of U.S. Forest Service
    Supervisors Expressing Satisfaction with IWW Labor Performance in Montana,"
    in *Papers of the President's Mediation Commission, 1917–18*, 8; L. M. Steward,
    Memoir, *Early Days in the Forest Service* (1962), 3:243–47; entries from 1917
    through 1924, Shoshone County Jail Register, 1917–1965, Wallace, Idaho.

17. John McLaren, National Forest Examiner, "Memorandum," September 11, 1919;
    Elers Koch, "Notes on Steamboat Fire," Coeur d'Alene National Forest, Septem-
    ber 16, 1919; Joe B. Halm, "Report on Camp Martin Fire," 1919; Report of Board
    of Review—Fire Season 1919, 24-25, in USFS District I Archives.

18. J. W. Girard, USFS logging engineer, Missoula; Major F. A. Fenn, assistant district forester; Mr. Rutledge, acting district forester; "Statements of U.S. Forest Service Supervisors Expressing Satisfaction with IWW," 1–9; B. W. Clark, "Memorandum for the District Forester," USFS, Missoula, Mont., October 9, 1919; T. J. Watkins, Forest Ranger, Uncompahgre National Forest, Ouray, Colorado, to District Forester, Missoula, October 14, 1919; L. R. Lessel, Forest Examiner, Flagstaff, Ariz., October 7, 1919, report on District I visit. All 1919 USFS records are from District I Archives, Missoula; Lt. Horace F. Sykes, quoted in Pyne, *Year of the Fires*, 84.

19. *Spokane Men* [YMCA newsletter] 4, no. 10 (November 19, 1908), 2; no. 14 (December 17, 1908), 2.

20. Spokane County Sheriff, Jail Registers 1909–10 and 1919, passim (stored in Spokane sheriff's garage); Spokane City Prison Register, v. 3 (July 1, 1898–December 31, 1899), and Spokane Police Register, 1899–1900, both in Washington State Archives, Eastern Region.

21. Spokane City Prison Register, v. 3 (1898–99); newspaper clipping dated December 23, 1907, in Spokane Police Department Crime Scrapbooks, v. 2 in Northwest Museum of Arts & Culture, Spokane. *Spokane Inland Herald*, July 7, 1910, 6; *Spokane Spokesman-Review*, January 23, 1911, 6, in WPA, *Newspaper Index*, Spokane Public Library.

22. *Spokane Press*, August 25, 1910, 2; August 30, 1910, 1.

23. Clipping dated December 3, 1907, in Spokane Police Crime Scrapbooks; *Spokane Press*, April 2, 1910, 1; *Spokane Spokesman-Review*, January 14, 1909; July 24 and December 30, 1911; February 1, 1913; December 30, 1914; January 10 and 15, 1915, in WPA, *Newspaper Index*; *Spokane Men* 4, no. 18 (January 14, 1909), 2.

24. *Spokane Spokesman-Review*, January 10, 11, 12, 13, 14, 16, 20, and 21, 1909, in WPA, *Newspaper Index*; *Spokane Men* 4, no. 18 (January 14, 1909), 1; clippings from unidentified Spokane newspaper, January 16, 1909, in Spokane Police Crime Scrapbooks, v. 2.

7: KING COTTON MOVES WEST

1. J. B. Coltharp, "Reminiscences of Cotton Pickin' Days," *Southwestern Historical Quarterly* 73, n. 4 (April 1970), 539–42; *Fort Worth Democrat*, October 10, 1877, 4; Homer L. Boyd, Sulphur, Okla., interviewed May 26, 1937, Works Progress Administration, *Oklahoma Indian-Pioneer Project*, 16:71, in Oklahoma Historical Society; *Fort Worth Gazette*, October 1, 1891, 5.

2. Thad Sitton and Dan K. Utley, *From Can See to Can't: Texas Cotton Farmers on the Southern Prairies* (Austin: University of Texas Press, 1997), 34–35; *Bellville Times-Standard*, July 7, 1893, 8.

3. James Smallwood, "The Southern Plains and the Expansion of the Cotton Kingdom," *West Texas Historical Association Year Book* 56 (1980), 36; Raymond E. White, "Cotton Growing in Texas to 1861," *Southwestern Historical Quarterly* 61, no. 2 (October 1957), 257; Thomas D. Clark, "Cotton Culture," in Howard R. Lamar, ed., *The Reader's Encyclopedia of the American West* (New York: Crowell, 1977), 264–65; Seymour V. Connor, *Texas: A History* (New York: Crowell, 1971), 70–79.

4. Sitton and Utley, *From Can See to Can't*, 10; Robert A. Calvert, "Nineteenth-Century Farmers, Cotton, and Prosperity," *Southwestern Historical Quarterly* 73, no. 4 (April 1970), 509, 512; George O. Coalson, *The Development of the Migratory Farm Labor System in Texas: 1900–1954* (San Francisco: R & E Research Associates, 1977), 5; Gaston Litton, *History of Oklahoma at the Golden Anniversary of Statehood* (New York: Lewis Historical Publishing Co., 1957), 1:516; Walter L. Buenger, "Texas and the South," *Southwestern Historical Quarterly* 103, no. 3 (January 2000), 313–14; and Buenger, *The Path to a Modern South: Northeast Texas between Reconstruction and the Great Depression* (Austin: University of Texas Press, 2001), xvi; "Native White Population of the United States, Distributed According to State or Territory of Birth," Table 11, *U.S. Tenth Census* (1880), 484–87; "Native Colored Population of the United States, Distributed According to State or Territory of Birth," Table 12, ibid., 488–91. Southern states are here considered to be Alabama, Florida, Georgia, Kentucky, Louisiana, Mississippi, North Carolina, South Carolina, Tennessee, and Virginia. Native Americans were not counted in this census.

5. Neil Foley, *The White Scourge: Mexicans, Blacks, and Poor Whites in Texas Cotton Culture* (Berkeley: University of California Press, 1997), 4–5; Buenger, *Path to a Modern South*, 134–35; Roger N. Conger, "Waco: Cotton and Culture on the Brazos," *Southwestern Historical Quarterly* 75, no. 1 (July 1971), 56. For a different view of this issue, see John C. Hudson, "A Longitudinal Approach to Great Plains Migration," *Great Plains Quarterly* 22, no. 4 (Fall 2002), 245–58.

6. Gregory R. Graves, "Exodus from Indian Territory: The Evolution of Cotton Culture in Eastern Oklahoma," *Chronicles of Oklahoma* 60, no. 2 (Summer 1982), 188–89; Cameron L. Saffell, "When Did King Cotton Move His Throne (And Has It Moved Back)?" *Agricultural History* 74, no. 2 (Spring 2000), 295–99; Litton, *History of Oklahoma* 1:152; Gilbert C. Fite, "Development of the Cotton Industry by the Five Civilized Tribes in Indian Territory," *Journal of Southern History* 15, no. 3 (August 1949), 342, 346, 349–53. A community "cotton picking" was at the center of an 1886 Texas court case, involving "a great many people" who picked for Thomas Ross and then enjoyed dinner. One witness described the arrangements in the field: "The cotton pickers were classified. The old folks formed one class, the youths and maidens another class, and the children the third class." *Louis Davidson v. The State*, Texas Court of Appeals, 22 Tex. Ct. App. 372, 3 S.W. 662, 1886 Tex. Crim. App. LEXIS 265 (November 20, 1886). On the social values connected with cotton picking, see Ruth Allen, *The Labor of Women in the Production of Cotton* (Austin: University of Texas *Bulletin* 3134, September 8, 1931), 207; Connor, *Texas*, 178–81, 270–71, 274; White, "Cotton Ginning in Texas," 265.

7. On railroad expansion, see Buenger, *Path to a Modern South*, chap. 2 passim; William D. Angel, Jr., "Vantage on the Bay: Galveston and the Railroads," *East Texas Historical Journal* 22, no. 1 (1984), 4–5, 8–9, 14; L. Tuffly Ellis, "The Revolutionizing of the Texas Cotton Trade, 1865–1885," *Southwestern Historical Quarterly* 73, no. 4 (April 1970), 478–485, 502–3; Odie B. Faulk, "Texas," in Lamar, *Reader's Encyclopedia*, 1172; Conger, "Waco," 56; Richard J. Orsi, *Sunset Limited: The Southern Pacific Railroad and the Development of the American West, 1850–1930* (Berkeley: University of California Press, 2005), 22; L. A. Burk, Muskogee, interview, WPA, *Oklahoma Indian-Pioneer Project*, 17:373–74; Ellis, "Revolutionizing,"

493, 506; *Austin County Times* [Bellville, Tex.], September 15, 1883, 3; Benjamin Heber Johnson, *Revolution in Texas: How a Forgotten Rebellion and Its Bloody Suppression Turned Mexicans into Americans* (New Haven, Conn.: Yale University Press, 2003), 30–31; *Corpus Christi Weekly Gazette*, August 22, 1874, 2.

8. A. Ray Stephens, *The Taft Ranch: A Texas Principality* (Austin: University of Texas Press, 1964), 15–16, 79, 93, 150, 174, 190-91, 197. For planting and tending cotton plants, see Samuel Lee Evans, "Texas Agriculture, 1865–1880" (master's thesis, University of Texas, 1955), 26–33; Rebecca Sharpless, *Fertile Ground—Narrow Choices: Women on Texas Cotton Farms, 1900–1940* (Chapel Hill: University of North Carolina Press, 1999), 169–74; *U.S. Department of Agriculture Yearbook, 1921* (Washington, D.C.: GPO, 1921), 342; U.S. Department of Labor Children's Bureau, *The Welfare of Children in Cotton-Growing Areas of Texas*, Bureau Publication no. 134 (Washington, D.C.: GPO, 1924), 12–15; and Calvert, "Nineteenth-Century Farmers," 514–15.

9. *Fort Worth Gazette*, July 13, 1891, 8; *Cotton County Democrat*, Walters [Okla.], November 12, 1914, 5.

10. Paul S. Taylor, *An American-Mexican Frontier: Nueces County, Texas* (1934; reprinted New York: Russell & Russell, 1971), 98; U.S. Department of Labor, *Welfare of Children*, 12–13; Coltharp, "Reminiscences," 539–40.

11. *Garland News* quoted in *Fort Worth Gazette*, October 1, 1891, 5; *Corpus Christi Weekly Gazette*, October 27, 1877, 2; *Bellville Times*, June 5, 1913, 5; *U.S. Eleventh Census* (1890), vol. 1, *Agriculture*, 47; Buenger, *Path to a Modern South*, 58–59.

12. *Taylor County News*, August 18, 1905, 4; Stephens, *Taft Ranch*, 197; Sharpless, *Fertile Ground*, 182–83; *Houston Post*, September 13, 1891, 1; Testimony of Joe Worsham, Dallas to House Committee on Immigration and Naturalization, *Temporary Admission of Illiterate Mexican Laborers*, 68th Cong., 2d sess., Hearings on H.J. Res. 271 (1920), 250.

13. *San Antonio Evening Light*, January 14, 1882, 4; *Bellville Times*, July 3, 1913, 4; and *Cherokee Republican*, June 15, 1917, 2. Alfalfa County was also wheat country.

14. *Houston Telegraph*, quoted in *Marshall Tri-Weekly Herald*, August 24, 1880, 2; September 30, 1880, 2.

15. Reports in *Marshall Tri-Weekly Herald*, January 3, 1880; January 6, 1880, 1; August 21, 1880, 2.

16. Coalson, *Development of Migratory*, 4, 6; *U.S. Eleventh Census* (1890), vol. 1, *Agriculture*, 100; "Farmers Union," *Handbook of Texas Online*, www.tsha.utexas.edu/handbook/online/articles/FF/aafr.html (accessed June 4, 2007).

17. William F. Holmes has done the major study on the 1891 strike; much of the material presented here follows his "The Arkansas Cotton Pickers Strike of 1891 and the Demise of the Colored Farmers's Alliance," *Arkansas Historical Quarterly* 32, no. 2 (Summer 1973), 107–19.

18. *Houston Post*, September 7, 1891, 1.

19. *Houston Post*, September 8, 1891, 4, 6; September 9, 1891, 2; September 14, 1891, 2; September 15, 1891, 2; *Bellville Times*, September 19, 1891, 3. A 500-pound bale at 8 cents a pound comes to $40, however. *Dallas Times-Herald*, September 12, 1891, 4.

20. *Houston Post*, September 11, 1891, 4; September 12, 1891, 4; September 13,

1891, 1; September 15, 1891, 2. *Brenham Banner* quoted in *Bellville Times*, September 19, 1891, 3.

21. W. E. Blevins, Paula Valley, interviewed December 16, 1937, WPA, *Oklahoma Indian-Pioneer Project*, 8:495–96. Various studies are examined by Sharpless, *Fertile Ground*, 162–69; Allen, *Labor of Women*, 141–43, 146. See U.S. Department of Labor, *Welfare of Children*, 44–48. Rusk County is in northeast Texas, south of Longview; Hill County is north of Waco.

22. Allen, *Labor of Women*, 141–43, 146; and U.S. Department of Labor, *Welfare of Children*, 44–48.

23. "Cousins' League" department, *Texas Farm and Ranch* [Dallas], November 24, 1894; October 12, 1895. U.S. Department of Labor, *Welfare of Children*, 7–9, 11–12; Sharpless, *Fertile Ground*, 177; Allen, *Labor of Women*, 176–77.

24. Connor, *Texas*, 254; David Erland Vassberg, "The Use of Mexicans and Mexican-Americans as an Agricultural Work Force in the Lower Rio Grande Valley of Texas" (master's thesis, University of Texas, 1966), 25–26; Johnson, *Revolution in Texas*, 26–27; Victor S. Clark, "Mexican Labor in the United States," *U.S. Bureau of Labor Bulletin* 78 (September 1908), 466; Buenger, *Path to a Modern South*, 142; David C. Humphrey, *Austin—An Illustrated History* (Austin, Tex.: Austin Sesquicentennial, 1988), 14; Michael M. Smith, *The Mexicans in Oklahoma* (Norman: University of Oklahoma Press, 1980), 56–58.

25. Vassberg, "Use of Mexicans," 14–17, 25, 29–31, 53–54; Clark, "Mexican Labor," 475; Emilio Zamora, *The World of the Mexican Worker in Texas* (College Station: Texas A&M University Press, 1993), 16.

26. Arthur F. Corwin, "Early Mexican Labor Migration: A Frontier Sketch, 1848–1900," in Corwin, ed., *Immigrants—and Immigrants: Perspectives on Mexican Labor Migration to the United States* (Westport, Conn.: Greenwood Press, 1989), 29–30.

27. Clark, "Mexican Labor," 469–71, 473, 477; John Chala Elac, *The Employment of Mexican Workers in U.S. Agriculture, 1900–1960: A Binational Economic Analysis* (1961; reprint Los Angeles: UCLA, 1971), 88–89; Coalson, "Development of Migratory," 14, 15.

28. Smith, *Mexicans in Oklahoma*, 9–10; Texas Bureau of Labor Statistics, *Sixth Biennial Report . . . (1919–20)*, 16, quoted in Coalson, *Development of Migratory*, 16–17.

29. Juan Gómez-Quiñones, *Mexican-American Labor, 1790–1990* (Albuquerque: University of New Mexico Press, 1994), 51, 74; Walter L. Buenger, "'This Wonder Age': The Economic Transformation of Northeast Texas, 1900–1930," *Southwestern Historical Quarterly* 989, no. 4 (April 1995), 541; Buenger, *Path to a Modern South*, 171; Stephens, *Taft Ranch*, 191.

30. Foley, *White Scourge*, 51; Zamora, *The World of the Mexican Worker in Texas*, 34–35. Recent sources anglicize the spelling to *Keglar* Hill.

31. Foley, *White Scourge*, 35, 39, 96–97, 113, 118–19, 123; Buenger, *Path to a Modern South*, 64–65; Stephens, *Taft Ranch*, 178, 183, 196–98.

32. Foley, *White Scourge*, 86, 118–19; Sitton and Utley, *From Can See*, 45–47; Buenger, *Path to a Modern South*, 141–43. See the discussion of sharecropping's role in supplying labor in Gavin Wright, "American Agriculture and the Labor Market: What Happened to Proletarianization?" *Agricultural History* 62, no. 3 (Summer 1988), 205–6. See also James R. Green, "Tenant Farmer Discontent and Socialist Protest

in Texas, 1901–1917," *Southwestern Historical Quarterly* 81, no. 2 (October 1977), 137; *Austin County Times*, September 15, 1883, 2; Taylor, *American-Mexican Frontier*, 120–21; Charles W. Holman, "The Tenant Farmer: Country Brother of the Casual Worker," *Survey* 34 (April 17, 1915) 62ff.

33. Edward J. M. Rhoads, "The Chinese in Texas," *Southwestern Historical Quarterly* 81, no. 1 (July 1977), 1–36 passim.

34. The convict labor description is drawn from Donald R. Walker, *Penology for Profit: A History of the Texas Prison System 1867–1912* (College Station: Texas A&M University Press, 1988), 14–17, 20–32, 45, 70–71, 93–94, 126–29, 189; Texas State Penitentiaries, *Reports . . . Embodying the Proceedings of the State Penitentiary Board, and Statistical and Financial Exhibits . . . for Two Years Ending October 31, 1884* (Austin: State Printer, 1885), 39–40, 51–52; *. . . Ending October 31, 1896* (Austin: State Printer, 1896), 8; *Fort Worth Gazette*, July 16, 1891, 1; Texas 33d Legislature, *A Record—Evidence and Statements Before the Penitentiary Investigating Committee Appointed by the Thirty-Third Legislature of Texas* (Austin: State Printer, 1913), 2–3, 6, 12–13, 15, 22–23.

35. *John D. Flewellen et al. v. Fort Bend County*, Court of Civil Appeals of Texas, Houston; 17 Tex. Civ. App. 155; 42 S.W. 775; 1897 Tex. App. LEXIS 335.

36. *Galveston News* quoted in *Marshall Tri-Weekly Herald*, July 21, 1880, 2; September 7, 1880, 1; Terry G. Jordan, "A Religious Geography of the Hill Country Germans of Texas," in Frederick C. Luebke, ed., *Ethnicity on the Great Plains* (Lincoln: University of Nebraska Press, 1980), 109–28.

37. *New York Evening Post* quoted in Donald E. Green, *Land of the Underground Rain: Irrigation on the Texas High Plains, 1910–1970* (Austin: University of Texas Press, 1973), 67; colonization projects are discussed on 65–69. See also *U.S. Twelfth Census* (1900), sec. 11; *U.S. Thirteenth Census* (1910), sec. 9, ch. 6; Johnson, *Revolution in Texas*, 28–29; *Benjamin Post*, March 22, 1912, 4; Lawrence Leslie Waters, "Transient Mexican Agricultural Labor," *Southwestern Social Science Quarterly* 22, no. 1 (June 1941), 66.

38. David Montejano, *Anglos and Mexicans in the Making of Texas, 1836–1986* (Austin: University of Texas Press, 1987), 75–99, 106–28 passim, and 160. Montejano's quote from the Riviera letter is taken from Stirling W. Bass, "The History of Kleberg County" (M.A. thesis, University of Texas, 1931), 187–88. See also Charles H. Harris III and Louis R. Sadler, *The Texas Rangers and the Mexican Revolution: The Bloodiest Decade, 1910–1920* (Albuquerque: University of New Mexico Press, 2004), 214–15; Johnson, *Revolution in Texas*, 181.

39. Connor, *Texas*, 307–11; Corwin, *Immigrants*, 38–39. On the Texas Rangers along the Mexican border, and the Mexican Revolution, see Harris and Sadler, *Texas Rangers*, chaps. 2 and 3 passim.

40. Harris and Sadler, *Texas Rangers*, 3. The Sheppard quote is on 136–37; the Plan de San Diego is reprinted on 210–12. Also see Johnson, *Revolution in Texas*, 33–36, 66–69, 80–81, 114ff, 128–29, and chap. 4.

41. The Taft rapid-fire gun was never purchased, apparently. See Stephens, *Taft Ranch*, 198–99; Harris and Sadler, *Texas Rangers*, chap. 12; Foley, *White Scourge*, 41, 133.

42. Montejano, *Anglos and Mexicans*, 118–25; Corwin, *Immigrants*, 52. Information on the World War I legislation and immigration orders is taken from Otis M. Scruggs, "The First Mexican Farm Labor Program," *Arizona and the West* 2, no. 4

(Winter 1966), 319–26; and George C. Kiser and Martha Woody Kiser, eds., *Mexican Workers in the United States: Historical and Political Perspectives* (Albuquerque: University of New Mexico Press, 1979), 1–5.

8: THE "COTTON WEST" REACHES ARIZONA

1. *Bellville*, [Tex.], *Times*, June 19, 1913, 3; House Committee on Immigration and Naturalization, *Temporary Admission of Illiterate Mexican Laborers*, 66th Cong., 2d sess. (1920), 182.

2. Testimony of C. S. Brown, Mesa, Arizona, in House Committee on Immigration and Naturalization, January–February 1926, *Seasonal Agricultural Laborers From Mexico*, 69th Cong., 1st sess. (Washington, D.C.: GPO, 1926), 35. See also Everett Dick, "Going Beyond the Ninety-fifth Meridian," *Agricultural History* 17, no. 2 (April 1943), 107–9.

3. Donald E. Green, *Land of the Underground Rain: Irrigation on the Texas High Plains, 1910–1970* (Austin: University of Texas Press, 1973), 68–71, 82–83, 99, 108–10; Walter L. Buenger, "'This Wonder Age': The Economic Transformation of Northeast Texas, 1900-1930," *Southwestern Historical Quarterly* 98, no. 4 (April 1995), 532; Melissa Keane, "Cotton and Figs: The Great Depression in the Casa Grande Valley," *Journal of Arizona History* 32, no. 3 (Autumn 1991), 268; Thomas E. Sheridan, *Arizona: A History* (Tucson: University of Arizona Press, 1995), 199–201; Edwin Charles Pendleton, "History of Labor in Arizona Irrigated Agriculture" (Ph.D. diss., University of California, 1950), 12; Arizona Territory, *Report of the Governor of Arizona to the Secretary of the Interior for the Year Ended June 30, 1902* (Washington, D.C.: GPO, 1902).

4. Virginia Rice, "The Arizona Agricultural Experiment Station—A History to 1917," *Arizona and the West* 20, no. 2 (Summer 1978), 139–40; Malcolm Brown and Orin Cassmore, *Migratory Cotton Pickers in Arizona* (Washington, D.C.: Works Progress Administration, 1939), 49; *Arizona Daily Star* [Tucson], September 1, 1912, 2; *Arizona Democrat* [Phoenix], August 21, 1913, 3; September 22, 1913, 4; September 27, 1913, 2.

5. Pendleton, "History of Labor in Arizona," 92–93; Donald Worster, *Rivers of Empire: Water, Aridity, and the Growth of the American West* (New York: Pantheon Books, 1985), 172; Martha C. Knack and Alice Littlefield, "Native American Labor—Retrieving History, Rethinking Theory," in Littlefield and Knack, eds., *Native Americans and Wage Labor* (Norman: University of Oklahoma Press, 1996), chap. 1 passim.

6. Jeffrey P. Shepherd, "Land, Labor, and Leadership: The Political Economy of Hualapai Community Building, 1910–1940," in Brian Hosmer and Colleen O'Neill, eds., *Native Pathways: American Indian Culture and Economic Development in the Twentieth Century* (Boulder: University Press of Colorado, 2004), 214–15; Garrick Bailey and Roberta Glenn Bailey, *A History of the Navajos: The Reservation Years* (Santa Fe: School of American Research Press, 1986), 155–60; Sheridan, *Arizona*, 214; Leah S. Glaser, "Working for Community: The Yaqui Indians at the Salt River Project," *Journal of Arizona History* 37, no. 4 (Winter 1996), 337–39; House Committee on Immigration and Naturalization, *Temporary Admission of Illiterate Mexican Laborers*, 262.

7. Walter Van Voorhis, superintendent of Fallon School, to commissioner of Indian affairs, May 5, 1913, quoted in Robert B. Campbell, "Newlands, Old Lands: Native American Labor, Agrarian Ideology, and the Progressive-Era State in the Making of the Newlands Reclamation Project, 1902–1926," *Pacific Historical Review* 71, no. 2 (May 2002), 224, 215; Robert A. Trennert, "'And the sword will give way to the spelling-book'—Establishing the Phoenix Indian School," *Journal of Arizona History* 23, no. 1 (Spring 1982), 42–46; Knack and Littlefield, *Native Americans and Wage Labor*, 254.

8. House Committee on Immigration and Naturalization, *Temporary Admission of Illiterate Mexican Laborers*, 189.

9. Sheridan, *Arizona*, 123, 169; George E. Paulsen, "The Yellow Peril at Nogales: The Ordeal of Collector William M. Hoey," *Arizona and the West* 13, no. 2 (Summer 1971), 113–15; Clifford Alan Perkins, *Border Patrol: With the U.S. Immigration Service on the Mexican Boundary 1910–1954* (El Paso: Texas Western Press, 1978), 8–9, 21; Patrick Ettinger, "'We Sometimes Wonder What They Will Spring on Us Next': Immigrants and Border Enforcement in the American West, 1882–1930," *Western Historical Quarterly* 37, no. 2 (Summer 2006), 167, 169, 171; Pendleton, "History of Labor in Arizona," 86, 115.

10. Jack August, "The Anti-Japanese Crusade in Arizona's Salt River Valley 1934–35," *Arizona and the West* 21, no. 2 (Summer 1979), 113–15; Eric Walz, "The Issei Community in Maricopa County: Development and Persistence in the Valley of the Sun, 1900–1940," *Journal of Arizona History* 38, no. 1 (Spring 1997), 2–5; *Arizona Democrat*, August 26, 1913, 3.

11. Ruth Allen, *The Labor of Women in the Production of Cotton* (Austin: University of Texas *Bulletin* No. 3134, 1931), 192–93, 206; Neil Foley, *The White Scourge: Mexicans, Blacks, and Poor Whites in Texas Cotton Culture* (Berkeley: University of California Press, 1997), 32.

12. Allen, *Labor of Women*, 102–15; Campbell, "Newlands, Old Lands," 216.

13. Foley, *White Scourge*, 9-11, chap. 3 passim; William E. Leonard, "Migratory Tenants of the Southwest," *Survey* 35 (January 29, 1916), 511–12.

14. Otis M. Scruggs, "The First Mexican Farm Labor Program," *Arizona and the West* 2, no. 4 (Winter 1966), 324; *U.S. Department of Agriculture Yearbook, 1923* (Washington, D.C.: GPO, 1923), tables 293 and 294; Texas State Historical Society, *Handbook of Texas Online*, www.tsha.utexas.edu/handbook/online/articles/TT/npt1.html (accessed September 8, 2007); Gregory R. Graves, "Exodus from Indian Territory: The Evolution of Cotton Culture in Eastern Oklahoma," *Chronicles of Oklahoma* 60, no. 2 (Summer 1982), 196–97; Pendleton, "History of Labor in Arizona," 57; Oklahoma Historical Society, "Encyclopedia of Oklahoma History & Culture," "Tenant Farming and Sharecropping," http://digital.library.okstate.edu/encyclopedia/entries/T/TE009.html (accessed March 5, 2009).

15. Ettinger, "'We Sometimes Wonder,'" 160–62; John Chala Elaz, *The Employment of Mexican Workers in U.S. Agriculture, 1900–1960: A Binational Economic Analysis* (1961; reprinted Los Angeles: UCLA, 1971), 88–89.

16. Paul S. Taylor, *An American-Mexican Frontier—Nueces County, Texas* (1934; reprinted New York: Russell & Russell, 1971), 114–15; Manuel Gamio, comp., *The Mexican Immigrant: His Life-Story* (1931; reprinted Chicago: University of Chicago Press, 1969), 123–25; chap. 1 passim; Sheridan, *Arizona*, 170–73.

17. Sarah Deutsch, *No Separate Refuge: Culture, Class, and Gender on an Anglo-Hispanic Frontier in the American Southwest, 1880–1940* (New York: Oxford University Press, 1987), 32; Gunther Peck, *Reinventing Free Labor—Padrones and Immigrant Workers in the North American West 1880–1930* (New York: Cambridge University Press, 2000), 42; Arizona Copper Company wage records, v. 89–93 (1903–21); Tip Top Mining Company ledgers, v. 5 (February 1907–July 1926); Twin Buttes Mining and Smelting Company, box 34 (Payrolls, 1904–11, 1913); all in University of Arizona Library, Special Collections.

18. Pendleton, "History of Labor in Arizona," 139; U.S. Department of Labor Children's Bureau, *The Welfare of Children in Cotton-Growing Areas of Texas* (Washington, D.C.: GPO, 1924), 62, 65; Paul S. Taylor, *Mexican Labor in the United States—Dimmit County, Winter Garden District—South Texas* (Berkeley: University of California Publications in Economics 6, 1928–30), 354; Johnny M. McCain, "Texas and the Mexican Labor Question, 1942–1947," *Southwestern Historical Quarterly* 85, no. 1 (July 1981), 47.

19. "*Canción de las pizcas,*" composer unknown, late 1920s or early 1930s, sung by Miguel Salinas, Edinburg, Texas, in Dan Dickey, "Corridos y Canciones de las Pizcas—Ballads and Songs of the 1920s Cotton Harvests," *Western Folklore* 65, nos. 1 & 2 (Winter and Spring 2006), 131–32. Translations of the *corridos* are by Dickey.

20. David Montejano, *Anglos and Mexicans in the Making of Texas, 1836–1986* (Austin: University of Texas Press, 1987), 90; "*Hay Mexicanos en Texas,*" composer unknown, late 1920s, as sung by Bernardo Martínez, Laredo, Texas, in Dickey, "Corridos y Canciones," 121–22.

21. Pendleton, "History of Labor in Arizona," 105, 108–10; George O. Coalson, *The Development of the Migratory Farm Labor System in Texas: 1900–1954* (San Francisco: R&E Research Associates, 1977), 34; *Arizona Daily Star*, September 1, 1912, 2; *Arizona Democrat*, June 7, 1913, 2; September 20, 1913, 3.

22. Samuel Bryan, "Mexican Immigrants in the United States," *Survey* 28, no. 23 (September 7, 1912), 727–28; Peck, *Reinventing Free Labor*, 41, 44–45; Foley, *White Scourge*, 45–47; Coalson, *Development of Migratory Farm Labor System*, 16; testimony of E. J. Walker, manager, Arizona Cotton Growers' Association, before Congress in 1926, discussing methods used since 1912, quoted in Pendleton, "History of Labor in Arizona," 105, 112–13.

23. Allen, *Labor of Women*, 209–29; Victor S. Clark, "Mexican Labor in the United States," *U.S. Bureau of Labor Bulletin* 78 (September 1908), 482–83, 515.

24. See discussion of this and other parts of the Arizona Constitution in H.A.E. Chandler, "With Arizona's First Legislature," *Survey* 28 (August 17, 1912), 647–48; Pendleton, "History of Labor in Arizona," 128.

25. Manuel Gamio, *Mexican Immigration to the United States* (1930; reprinted Chicago: University of Chicago Press, 1960), 4–5, 30; U.S. Department of Labor, *Report of Special Committee Appointed by the Secretary of Labor to Investigate Complaints Against the Temporary Admission of Aliens for Agricultural Purposes* (Washington, D.C.: GPO, 1920), 4–5; Allen, *Labor of Women*, 215–16; "Mexico Sick of Plague and Famine," *Survey* 34 (June 12, 1915), 241; Lawrence A. Cardoso, "Labor Emigration to the Southwest, 1916 to 1920: Mexican Attitudes and Policy," *Southwestern Historical Quarterly* 79, no. 4 (April 1976), 400–401.

26. Department of Labor, *Report of Special Committee . . . to Investigate Complaints Against the Temporary Admission of Aliens*, 6, 10–11.

27. *Historical Statistics of the United States—Colonial Times to 1957* (Washington, D.C.: 1960), table C88–114; Buenger, "'This Wonder Age,'" 354; E. V. Wilcox, "Plan of the Department of Agriculture for Handling the Farm Labor Problem," *American Economic Review* 8, no. 1 (March 1918), 158.

28. *Cotton County Democrat* [Walters, Okla.], September 10, 1914, 4; September 17, 1914, 7; September 24, 1914, 2; October 8, 1914, 1; October 22, 1914, 1, 9; *Hartshorne* [Okla.] *Sun*, October 15, 1908, 2.

29. Cardoso, "Labor Emigration to the Southwest," 413–15; House Committee on Immigration and Naturalization, *Temporary Admission of Illiterate Mexican Laborers*, 138–39; Charles H. Harris III and Louis R. Sadler, *The Texas Rangers and the Mexican Revolution: The Bloodiest Decade, 1910–1920* (Albuquerque: University of New Mexico Press, 2004), 326, 410–12.

30. *Cherokee* [Okla.] *Republican*, April 12, 1918, 1; April 19, 1918, 1.

31. Mexican vice-consul quoted in George C. and Martha Woody Kiser, eds., *Mexican Workers in the United States: Historical and Political Perspectives* (Albuquerque: University of New Mexico Press, 1979), 14–15; *Cotton County Democrat*, November 19, 1914, 6; *Temple* [Okla.] *Tribune*, October 11, 1917, 4; October 18, 1917, 1; November 1, 1917, 1.

32. Scruggs, "First Mexican Farm Labor Program," 320–21; Elac, *Employment of Mexican Workers*, 34; Carey McWilliams, *North from Mexico: The Spanish-Speaking People of the United States* (1949; reprinted Philadelphia: Lippincott, 1975), 173–74; Mark Reisler, *By the Sweat of Their Brow: Mexican Immigrant Labor in the United States, 1900–1940* (Westport, Conn.: Greenwood, 1976), chap. 2 passim.

33. Cardoso, "Labor Emigration to the Southwest," 400–16 passim; Carole E. Christian, "Joining the American Mainstream: Texas's Mexican Americans During World War I," *Southwestern Historical Quarterly* 92, no. 4 (April 1989), 572–73.

34. Christian, "Joining the American Mainstream," 573; Deutsch, *No Separate Refuge*, 112.

35. *Arizona Labor Journal*, February 1, 1918, 1, quoted in Pendleton, "History of Labor in Arizona," 116–17; Reisler, *By the Sweat of Their Brow*, 25, 39; Brown and Cassmore, *Migratory Cotton Pickers*, 49–50; Sheridan, *Arizona*, 214–15; House Committee on Immigration and Naturalization, *Temporary Admission of Illiterate Mexican Laborers*, 262.

36. Brown and Cassmore, *Migratory Cotton Pickers*, 50.

37. Sheridan, *Arizona*, 215–16; *Arizona Labor Journal*, January 20, 1921, 4, quoted in Pendleton, "History of Labor in Arizona," 132, 135–37; Carey McWilliams, *Ill Fares the Land: Migrants and Migratory Labor in the United States* (Boston: Little, Brown, 1942), 78–79; Reisler, *By the Sweat of Their Brow*, 51–55; Scruggs, "First Mexican Farm Labor Program," 324–26.

38. Sheridan, *Arizona*, 176–79; Pendleton, "History of Labor in Arizona," 107–8; *Arizona Labor Journal*, April 16, 1920, 1, quoted in ibid., 123; Walter V. Woehlke, "What Cotton Did to Arizona," *Sunset* 47, no. 1 (July 1921), 21–23.

39. "*Corrido de pizcar algodón*," composed by Justiniano Soto and Andrés O. Garcia, 1926, collected and translated by Dan Dickey and Carla Hagen, in Dickey, "Corridos y Canciones," 108–9; McWilliams, *Ill Fares the Land*, 76–77; Scruggs, "First

Mexican Farm Labor Program," 325; Foley, *White Scourge,* 49; Juan Gómez-Quiñones, *Mexican-American Labor, 1790–1990* (Albuquerque: University of New Mexico Press, 1994), 130–31, 141, 144–45.

40. Deutsch, *No Separate Refuge,* 25, and chap. 4 on Hispanics in Colorado coal fields; Sheridan, *Arizona,* 179–86; Gómez-Quiñones, *Mexican-American Labor,* 57; David G. Gutiérrez, *Walls and Mirrors: Mexican Americans, Mexican Immigrants, and the Politics of Ethnicity* (Berkeley: University of California, 1995), 74–77, 96–97; Christian, "Joining the American Mainstream," 594–95.

41. John Higham, *Strangers in the Land: Patterns of American Nativism, 1860–1925* (1955; reprinted New Brunswick, N.J.: Rutgers University Press, 1994), 177–79, 307; Elliott Barkan, *From All Points: America's Immigrant West, 1870s–1952* (Bloomington: Indiana University Press, 2007), chap. 19 passim. Citations on the following pages are from the 1920 House Committee on Immigration and Naturalization, *Temporary Admission of Illiterate Mexican Laborers,* as follows: 15, 19, 28, 35–36, 43–44, 65, 75, 79, 80, 189 (Knox statement), 194–96 (Knox-Box exchange), 210, 279–83.

42. Maldwyn Allen Jones, *American Immigration* (Chicago: University of Chicago Press, 1960), 251–52; House Committee on Immigration and Naturalization, *Temporary Admission of Illiterate Mexican Laborers,* 9–10.

43. House Committee on Immigration and Naturalization, *Temporary Admission of Illiterate Mexican Laborers,* 13, 16–17, 19, 59 (Roberts statement), 68–69, 71, 82, 134–35 (Clarkson testimony), 166–67.

9: "BEETERS"

1. Sara A. Brown, *Children Working in the Sugar Beet Fields of Certain Districts of the South Platte Valley, Colorado* (New York: National Child Labor Committee, 1925), 38; U.S. Department of Labor Children's Bureau, *Child Labor and the Work of Mothers in the Beet Fields of Colorado and Michigan,* Bureau Publication No. 115 (Washington, D.C.: GPO, 1923), 19, 25, 31–32; *Grand Island* [Neb.] *Daily Independent,* December 7, 1989, 4; August 26, 1890, 4; September 16, 1890, 4; Governor Silas A. Holcomb, *Proceedings of the Second General Convention of the Nebraska Beet Sugar Association, Feb. 5–6, 1896* (Omaha: Bechtold, 1896), 29–36.

2. *U.S. Department of Agriculture Yearbook, 1909* (Washington: GPO, 1909), 173; Harold Barger and Hans H. Landsberg, *American Agriculture, 1899–1939: A Study of Output, Employment and Productivity* (New York: National Bureau of Economic Research, 1942), 90; Leonard J. Arrington, *Beet Sugar in the West: A History of the Utah-Idaho Sugar Company, 1891–1966* (Seattle: University of Washington Press, 1966), 3–6, 19; William John May, Jr., *The Great Western Sugarlands: The History of the Great Western Sugar Company and the Economic Development of the Great Plains* (New York: Garland, 1989), 5; Daniel Thomas Moreno, "Social Equality and Industrialization: A Case Study of Colorado Beet Sugar Industry" (Ph.D. diss., University of California, Irvine, 1981), 28–29.

3. *Grand Junction News,* February 28, 1899, 2, quoted in May, *Great Western Sugarlands,* 73–74, 115–16, 118–24; Arrington, *Beet Sugar in the West,* 10, 47; Dena Markoff Sabin, *How Sweet It Was! The Beet Sugar Industry in Microcosm: The National Sugar Manufacturing Company, 1899 to 1967* (New York: Garland, 1986), 21.

4. Arrington, *Beet Sugar in the West*, 3–4; Mark Fiege, *Irrigated Eden: The Making of an Agricultural Landscape in the American* West (Seattle: University of Washington Press, 1999), 11–12, 42; Sam S. Kepfield, "El Dorado on the Platte: The Development of Agricultural Irrigation and Water Law in Nebraska, 1860–1895," *Nebraska History* 75, no. 3 (Fall 1994), 232, 241; Esther S. Anderson, "The Beet Sugar Industry of Nebraska as a Response to Geographic Environment," *Economic Geography* 1, no. 3 (October 1925), 379. Later Minnesota, on the edge of the Plains, became a sugar beet center. See also "Sugar," in *Kansas: A cyclopedia of state history, embracing events, institutions, industries, counties, cities, towns, prominent persons, etc.* (Chicago: Standard Publishing Co., 1912), v. 2, on Kansas State Historical Society website, http://skyways.lib.ks.us/genweb/archives/1912/s/sugar.html (accessed August 6, 2008); *U.S. Twelfth Census (1900)*, vol. 6, *Agriculture*, 2:820; *Kansas v. Colorado et al.*, 206 U.S. 46; 27 S. Ct. 655; 51 L. Ed. 956; 1907 U.S. LEXIS 1145; May 13, 1907.
5. *Grand Island Daily Independent*, December 6, 1889, 2; Sabin, *How Sweet It Was!*, iii–iv, 14–15; May, *Great Western Sugarlands*, chaps. 4 and 5 passim.
6. May, *Great Western Sugarlands*, 357 (1911 quotation); Lawrence Leslie Waters, "Transient Mexican Agricultural Labor," *Southwestern Social Science Quarterly* 22, no. 1 (June 1941), 57–58; Wayne D. Rasmussen, "Technological Change in Western Sugar Beet Production," *Agricultural History* 41, no. 1 (January 1967), 31–32; Arrington, *Beet Sugar in the West*, 23–25, 133; C. A. Granger, in *Second General Convention of the Nebraska Beet Sugar Association*, 62.
7. U.S. Department of Agriculture, *Special Report on the Beet-Sugar Industry in the United States* (Washington, D.C.: GPO, 1898), 170; *United States Department of Agriculture Yearbook, 1901*, 489–90; *USDA Yearbook, 1906*, 270; *USDA Yearbook, 1923*, 194–95; *Grand Island Daily Independent*, December 17, 1889, 2; U.S. Department of Labor, *Report of Special Committee Appointed by the Secretary of Labor to Investigate Complaints Against the Temporary Admission of Aliens for Agricultural Purposes* (Washington, D.C.: GPO, 1920), 4; Fiege, *Irrigated Eden*, 140–41; May, *Great Western Sugarlands*, 433–34.
8. May, *Great Western Sugarlands*, 433–34.
9. Arrington, *Beet Sugar in the West*, 5, 12, 23–25; *USDA Yearbook, 1923*, 200.
10. *Second General Convention of the Nebraska Beet Sugar Association*, 36–41, 60–66; Kepfield, "El Dorado on the Platte," 241; Arrington, *Beet Sugar in the West*, 25n.
11. *USDA Yearbook, 1906*, 270–71; May, *Great Western Sugarlands*, 384; *Reports of the U.S. Immigration Commission*, U.S. 61st Cong., 2d sess. (1909–10) (Washington, D.C.: GPO, 1911), 24:114, 151; Paul S. Taylor, "Mexican Labor in the United States: Valley of the South Platte—Colorado," *University of California Publications in Economics* 6, no. 2 (1929), 102, 153–54; Mary Lyons-Barrett, "Child Labor in the Early Sugar Beet Industry in the Great Plains, 1890–1920," *Great Plains Quarterly* 25, no. 1 (Winter 2005), 31; Paul S. Taylor, "Hand Laborers in the Western Sugar Beet Industry," *Agricultural History* 41, no. 1 (January 1967), 21; J. C. Bailey testimony, Senate Committee on Immigration, *Restriction of·Western Hemisphere Immigration*, 70th Cong., 1st sess. (Washington, D.C.: GPO, 1928), 136, quoted in Dennis Nodín Valdés, "Settlers, Sojourners, and Proletarians: Social Formation in the Great Plains Sugar Beet Industry, 1890–1940," *Great Plains Quarterly* 10, no. 2 (Spring 1990), 116; Sabin, *How Sweet It Was!*, 120.

12. *U.S. Office of Indian Affairs Annual Report, 1910* (Washington, D.C.: GPO, 1911), 8–9; Robert A. Trennert, Jr., *The Phoenix Indian School: Forced Assimilation in Arizona, 1891–1935* (Norman: University of Oklahoma Press, 1988), 72–73; Martha C. Knack and Alice Littlefield, "Native American Labor—Retrieving History, Rethinking Theory," in Littlefield and Knack, eds., *Native Americans and Wage Labor* (Norman: University of Oklahoma Press, 1996), 16.

13. May, *Great Western Sugarlands*, 382; Moreno, "Social Equality and Industrialization," 98; Garrick Bailey and Roberta Glenn Bailey, *A History of the Navajos: The Reservation Years* (Santa Fe: School of American Research Press, 1986), 156–57; Alice Littlefield, "Learning to Labor: Native American Education in the United States, 1880–1930," in John H. Moore, ed., *The Political Economy of North American Indians* (Norman: University of Oklahoma Press, 1993), 54–55.

14. Victor S. Clark, "Mexican Labor in the United States," *U.S. Bureau of Labor Bulletin* 78 (September 1908), 484, 500; Lewis Meriam, director, *The Problem of Indian Administration* (1928; reprinted Johnson Reprint Corporation, 1971), 389–90, 524–26; Knack and Littlefield, "Native American Labor," 31–32; *Office of Indian Affairs Report, 1910*, 9.

15. Eric Walz, "From Kumamoto to Idaho: The Influence of Japanese Immigrants on the Agricultural Development of the Interior West," *Agricultural History* 74, no. 2 (Spring 2000), 406–7.

16. Quoted in Mary S. Henslall, "Pioneer Portraits," *Idaho Yesterdays* 19 (Spring 1975), 21, reprinted in Walz, "From Kumamoto to Idaho," 406, 408. Yamato Ichihashi, *Japanese in the United States* (1932; reprinted New York: Arno, 1969), 170–71; May, *Great Western Sugarlands*, 394–95.

17. Clark, "Mexican Labor in the United States," 499; May, *Great Western Sugarlands*, 395; U.S. Department of Labor, *Report of Special Committee . . . Complaints Against the Temporary Admission*, 5.

18. Information on the German-Russian background is drawn principally from Peter H. Griess, "The First Settlement of Russian Germans in Nebraska," *Nebraska History* 49, no. 4 (Winter 1968), 399; and Theodore C. Wenzlaff, ed., "The Russian Germans Come to the United States," *Nebraska History* 49, no. 4 (Winter 1968), 379–82.

19. Timothy Egan, *The Worst Hard Time* (Boston: Houghton Mifflin, 2006), 62–63; Dennis Nodín Valdés, "Betabeleros: The Formation of an Agricultural Proletariat in the Midwest, 1897–1930," *Labor History* 30, no. 4 (Fall 1989), 547; Lyons-Barrett, "Child Labor in the Early Sugar Beet Industry," 31; C. O. Townsend, "Methods of Reducing the Cost of Producing Beet Sugar," *USDA Yearbook, 1906*, 271; *U.S. Immigration Commission Reports*, 24:119; Sabin, *How Sweet It Was!*, 58; Juan R. Garcia, *Mexicans in the Midwest 1900–1932* (Tucson: University of Arizona Press, 1996), 11.

20. Taylor, "Mexican Labor—South Platte," 134–35; Sabin, *How Sweet It Was!*, 62–66, 102–4; *U.S. Immigration Commission Reports*, 24:114.

21. Edward N. Clopper, "'Beeters'—What field labor means to 5,000 children in the Colorado sugar beet districts," *Survey* 35 (March 4, 1916), 657; *U.S. Immigration Commission Reports*, 24:121; Moreno, "Social Equality," 94–95; Sabin, *How Sweet It Was!*, 129, 131; Brown, *Children Working in the Sugar Beet Fields*, 86–87.

22. *U.S. Immigration Commission Reports*, 24:120. Brehm/Lapella family tree, www

.lapella.net/wordstoryscheidtjohnnotrelated.doc, remembrance by Dave Scheidt (accessed August 6, 2008.)

23. José Aguayo, "Los Betabeleros (The Beetworkers)," in Vincent C. De Baca, ed., *La Gente: Hispano History and Life in Colorado* (Denver: Colorado Historical Society, 1998), 107; *Child Labor and Work of Mothers,* 8–9, 12–13, 54–55.

24. Sarah Deutsch, *No Separate Refuge: Culture, Class, and Gender on an Anglo-Hispanic Frontier in the American Southwest, 1880–1940* (New York: Oxford University Press, 1987), 108–9; Matthew C. Godfrey, "The Utah-Idaho Sugar Company: Political and Legal Troubles in the Aftermath of the First World War," *Agricultural History* 75, no. 2 (Spring 2001), 191; Anderson, "Beet Sugar Industry," 379–80.

25. Arrington, *Beet Sugar in the West*, 88, 90; Jorge Iber, *Hispanics in the Mormon Zion 1912–1999* (College Station: Texas A&M University Press, 2000), 8; Sabin, *How Sweet It Was!* 183; Deutsch, *No Separate Refuge*, 108–9; *Child Labor and Work of Mothers,* 116–19; Michael M. Smith, "Beyond the Borderlands: Mexican Labor in the Central Plains, 1900–1930," *Great Plains Quarterly* 1, no. 4 (Fall 1981), 244; Iber, *Hispanics in the Mormon Zion*, 9–10.

26. Clark, "Mexican Labor," 483. Clark explains in a footnote, "For convenience the term 'Old Mexicans' is used in this article to designate persons of Mexican descent born in Mexico, and 'New Mexicans' to designate those of Mexican descent born in the United States, and mainly in New Mexico." Valdés, "Settlers, Sojourners, and Proletarians," 114; May, *Great Western Sugarlands*, 286–87, 381; Taylor, "Mexican Labor . . . South Platte," 104–5; García, *Mexicans in the Midwest*, 12; Smith, "Beyond the Borderlands," 241, 244–45.

27. May, *Great Western Sugarlands*, 363, 414–15; Clark, "Mexican Labor," 481, 483–85, 499; U.S. Department of Labor, *Report of Special Committee . . . Complaints Against the Temporary Admission*, 5; Aguayo, "Los Betabeleros," 107, 112; George O. Coalson, *The Development of the Migratory Farm Labor System in Texas: 1900–1954* (San Francisco: R & E Research Associates, 1977), 35; Deutsch, *No Separate Refuge*, 34, 127; Brown, *Children Working in Sugar Beet Fields*, 70; Taylor, "Mexican Labor—South Platte," 134, 137; Valdés, "Settlers, Sojourners," 116.

28. Taylor, "Mexican Labor—South Platte," 131–33, 142; U.S. Department of Labor, *Report of Special Committee . . . Complaints Against the Temporary Admission*, 221.

29. Deutsch, *No Separate Refuge*, 33; Sabin, *How Sweet It Was!* 128–29; Bertram H. Mautner and W. Lewis Abbott, *Child Labor in Agriculture and Farm Life in the Arkansas Valley of Colorado* (Colorado Springs: Colorado College General Series no. 164, Studies Series no. 2, 1929), 151; Moreno, "Social Equality," 71.

30. May, *Great Western Sugarlands*, 366–67, 388; Taylor, "Mexican Labor—South Platte," 155; Iber, *Hispanics in the Mormon Zion*, 12; Mautner and Abbott, *Child Labor in Agriculture*, 151; Valdés, "Betabeleros," 556–57.

31. *"Los Betabeleros"* ("The Beet-Field Workers," no composer listed), *corrido* collected by Manuel Gamio, prepared by Margaret Park Redfield, in Gamio, *Mexican Immigration to the United States* (1930; reprinted Chicago: University of Chicago Press, 1960), 86–88.

32. House Committee on Immigration and Naturalization, *Temporary Admission of Illiterate Mexican Laborers*, 66th Cong., 2d sess. (Washington, D.C.: GPO, 1920), 78.

33. *Child Labor and Work of Mothers*, 63; Waters, "Transient Mexican Agricultural Labor," 118.

34. Owen R. Lovejoy, *Proceedings of the Fifth Annual Meeting of the National Child Labor Committee* (Philadelphia: American Academy of Political and Social Science, 1909), 59; Elliott West, *Growing Up with the Country—Childhood on the Far Western Frontier* (Albuquerque: University of New Mexico Press, 1989), xviii–xix, 74. In a later publication, West points out that the 1900 census found that nearly one-fifth of the children aged ten to fifteen were "gainfully employed." See West, *Growing Up in Twentieth-Century America: A History and Reference Guide* (Westport, Conn.: Greenwood Press, 1996), 31. Such places as the beet fields could be considered the western equivalent of eastern factories where children labored.

35. *Child Labor and Work of Mothers*, 6–7. The criterion used in these studies put age sixteen as the cutoff: "children" were those under sixteen. Brown, *Children Working in Sugar Beet Fields*, 9, 17, 67. Brown's findings paralleled those in *Child Labor and Work of Mothers*. Colorado Bureau of Labor Statistics, *Seventeenth Biennial Report, 1919–20*, quoted in *Child Labor and Work of Mothers*, 2n, 9, 61–63. The study noted that for many families a house was provided, sometimes with a cow and garden plot.

36. *Child Labor and Work of Mothers*, 19, 26, 31, 76–77. The Scottsdale, Nebraska, school nurse gave a more favorable view of the health of the children to geographer Esther Anderson. See Anderson, "Beet Sugar Industry," 384–85.

37. U.S. Department of Labor, *Report of Special Committee . . . Complaints Against the Temporary Admission*, 231–32; Brown, *Children Working*, 41, 111; Aguayo, "Los Betabeleros," 113; *Child Labor and Work of Mothers*, 27.

38. Clopper, "'Beeters,'" 655–56, 658; *Child Labor and Work of Mothers*, 4–5.

39. Clopper, "'Beeters,'" 687; Brown, *Children Working in Sugar Beet Fields*, 158–59; Arrington, *Beet Sugar in West*, 24; Anderson, "Beet Sugar Industry," 384; May, *Great Western Sugarlands*, 372; *Child Labor and Work of Mothers*, 37–42, 52–53.

40. Nebraska Bureau of Labor and Industrial Statistics, *Fourteenth Biennial Report, 1913–14*, 28; *Bulletin no. 25 (1912)*, 46.

41. Brehm/Lapella website, Scheidt remembrance; Clopper, "'Beeters,'" 657; Mautner and Abbott, *Child Labor in Agriculture*, 153–54.

42. Clopper, "'Beeters,'" 688; *Child Labor and Work of Mothers*, 37–38.

43. Mautner and Abbott, *Child Labor in Agriculture*, 154–57; Aguayo, "Los Betabeleros," 109–10, 119; U.S. Department of Labor, *Report of Special Committee . . . Complaints Against the Temporary Admission*, 237; Taylor, "Mexican Labor—South Platte," 154.

44. Taylor, "Mexican Labor—South Platte," 152–53.

10: THE CALIFORNIA GARDEN

1. *Riverside Press and Horticulturist*, January 12, 1889, 2.

2. Lawrence J. Jelinek, *Harvest Empire: A History of California Agriculture* (San Francisco: Boyd & Fraser, 1979), 63–64.

3. Michael A. Tomlan, *Tinged with Gold: Hop Culture in the United States* (Athens: University of Georgia Press, 1992), 127; Marie Rose Wong, *Sweet Cakes, Long*

Journey: The Chinatowns of Portland, Oregon (Seattle: University of Washington Press, 2004), 58–59; *U.S. Industrial Commission, Reports*, vol. 10, *Agriculture and Agricultural Labor* (Washington, D.C.: GPO, 1901), 954–55, 978.

4. David Vaught, *Cultivating California: Growers, Specialty Crops, and Labor, 1875–1920* (Baltimore: Johns Hopkins University Press, 1999), 13–14; Jelinek, *Harvest Empire*, passim; Michael J. Gillis and Michael F. Magliari, *John Bidwell and California: The Life and Writings of a Pioneer* (Spokane: Arthur H. Clark, 2003), 162.

5. Frank Adams, "The Historical Background of California Agriculture," in Claude B. Hutchison, ed., *California Agriculture* (Berkeley: University of California Press, 1946), chap. 1 passim; John Walton Caughey, *California* (1940; reprinted Englewood Cliffs, N.J.: Prentice-Hall, 1953), chap. 10 passim; Carey McWilliams, *Factories in the Field—The Story of Migratory Farm Labor in California* (1935; reprinted Hamden, Conn.: Archon Books, 1969), 12–13; Richard Steven Street, *Beasts of the Field: A Narrative History of California Farmworkers, 1769–1913* (Stanford, Calif.: Stanford University Press, 2004), 15, 20; Albert L. Hurtado, "California Indians and the Workaday West: Labor, Assimilation, and Survival," *California History* 69, no. 1 (Spring 1990), 4–5; Gillis and Magliari, *John Bidwell*, 250–53; Michael Magliari, "Free Soil, Unfree Labor: Cave Johnson Couts and the Binding of Indian Workers in California, 1850–1867," *Pacific Historical Review* 73, no. 3 (August 2004), 351–57.

6. Farms in California were referred to as "ranches." *U.S. Immigration Commission Reports*, vol. 24, *Immigrants in Industries* (Washington, D.C.: GPO, 1910), 15; Harold Barger and Hans H. Landsberg, *American Agriculture, 1899–1939: A Study of Output, Employment and Productivity* (New York: National Bureau of Economic Research, 1942), 198–200; Hutchison, *California Agriculture*, 35–36; Richard Steven Street, "Tattered Shirts and Ragged Pants: Accommodation, Protest, and the Coarse Culture of California Wheat Harvesters and Threshers, 1866–1900," *Pacific Historical Review* 67, no. 4 (November 1998), 578; Mills speech, *California State Agricultural Society Transactions, 1890*, 188–89; California Bureau of Labor Statistics, *Fifth Biennial Report . . . 1891–1892* (Sacramento: State Printer, 1893), 15; *Fresno Republican*, June 29, 1899, quoted in *Pacific Rural Press* (*PRP*), July 8, 1899; *Santa Maria Times*, September 27, 1890, quoted in *PRP*, October 4, 1890, 298; Elwood Mead, *Irrigation Investigations: A Discussion of the Economic and Legal Questions Created by the Growth of Irrigated Agriculture in the West* (1903; reprinted New York: Macmillan, 1972), 163; Timothy J. Lukes and Gary Y. Okihiro, *Japanese Legacy: Farming and Community Life in California's Santa Clara Valley* (Cupertino: California History Center, 1985), 16; *PRP*, September 6, 1890, 202; Jelinek, *Harvest Empire*, 40–41.

7. Mills speech, *California State Agricultural Society Transactions, 1898*, 187; Richard J. Orsi, *Sunset Limited: The Southern Pacific Railroad and the Development of the American West 1850–1930* (Berkeley: University of California Press, 2005), 24ff.; Vaught, *Cultivating California, 19*.

8. Mead, *Irrigation Institutions*, 183–84, 199–200, 216–17; Steven Stoll, *The Fruits of Natural Advantage: Making the Industrial Countryside in California* (Berkeley: University of California Press, 1998), 33–34; *Fresno Morning Republican*, January 1, 1896, "Progress Edition"; Donald Worster, *Rivers of Empire: Water, Aridity, and the Growth of the American West* (New York: Pantheon Books, 1985), 98–101,

108–9. Orsi, *Sunset Limited*, 209–20, provides a detailed look at the SP's extensive irrigation activities. See also *Salinas Democrat*, August 29, 1891, 1. Statistics of irrigation's growth are taken from surveyor general's reports and U.S. Census; see Paul S. Taylor and Tom Vasey, "Historical Background of California Farm Labor," *Rural Sociology* 1, no. 3, (September 1936), 282–84; *U.S. Industrial Commission Report*, vol. 10, *Agriculture and Agricultural Labor* (Washington, D.C.: GPO, 1901), 953.

9. *Middletown Independent*, September 6, 1890, quoted in *PRP*, September 13, 1890, 234; *Sacramento Bee*, September 27, 1890, quoted in *PRP*, October 4, 1890, 298; Hutchison, *California Agriculture*, 158; *Fresno Herald and Democrat*, August 23, 1907, 5; Mead, *Irrigation Institutions*, 3.

10. *Marysville Evening Democrat*, April 4, 1912, 6; *PRP*, June 10, 1899, 365.

11. *Marysville Evening Democrat*, May 2, 1912, 4; Steven Stoll, "Insects and Institutions: University Science and the Fruit Business in California," *Agricultural History* 69, no. 2 (Spring 1995), 222–23, 239; Hutchison, *California Agriculture*, 277–78.

12. H. K. Wong, *Gum Sahn Yun—Gold Mountain Men* (n.p., Fong Brothers Printing, 1987), 141; David Vaught, "'An Orchardist's Point of View': Harvest Labor Relations on a California Almond Ranch, 1892–1921," *Agricultural History* 69, no. 4 (Fall 1995), 579; José Manuel Alamillo, "Bitter-Sweet Communities: Mexican Workers and Citrus Growers on the California Landscape" (Ph.D. diss., University of California, Irvine, 2000); Hutchison, *California Agriculture*, 37–40, 151–53; A. H. Naftizer, president and general manager, Southern California Fruit Exchange, in *U.S. Industrial Commission Report*, vol. 10, *Agriculture and Agricultural Labor* (1901), 953; *Riverside Press and Horticulturist* (January 12, 1889), 2; H. Vincent Moses, "'The Orange-Grower Is Not a Farmer'—G. Harold Powell, Riverside Orchardists, and the Coming of Industrial Agriculture, 1893–1930," *California History* 74, no. 1 (Spring 1995), 24–25; Stoll, *Fruits of Natural Advantage*, xiv.

13. Warren P. Tufts, *The Packing of Apples in California* (University of California College of Agriculture, circular no. 178, October 1917), 8–9. On picking lemons "as carefully as eggs," see Alamillo, "Bitter-Sweet Communities," 109. James Mills, Willows, Calif., testimony before U.S. Commission on Industrial Relations, *Final Report and Testimony*, Senate Doc. 415, U.S. 64th Cong., 1st sess. (1916), 5:4956.

14. Street, *Beasts of the Field*, 505–7; Street quotes an article by J. A. Stromquist in *Industrial Pioneer*, March 1921, 24–25. See Alamillo, "Bitter-Sweet Communities," 106–7. Information on orange grove labors is drawn from Hutchison, *California Agriculture*, 13; 217–19; Street, *Beasts of the Field*, 504–14; and Jelinek, *Harvest Empire*, 37, 50–51.

15. *Fresno Herald and Democrat*, August 13, 1907, 2; Mills speech, *California Agricultural Society Transactions, 1890*, 200–201.

16. Immigration Commission, *Reports*, 24:573–75; McWilliams, *Factories in the Field*, 107; California Bureau of Labor Statistics, *Fifth Biennial Report, 1891–92*, 15. See discussion on the basis for casual labor in M. R. Benedict, "The Economic and Social Structure of California Agriculture," in Hutchison, *California Agriculture*, 400–405.

17. *California Agricultural Society Transactions, 1891*, 196; *PRP*, August 26, 1893, 158; September 9, 1893, 190–91; California Bureau of Labor Statistics, *Second*

Biennial Report, 1885–86, 66; Fifth Biennial Report, 1891–92, 9, 18; Morrison I. Swift, *What a Tramp Learns in California—Social Danger Line* (San Francisco: Society of American Socialists, 1896), 1; Harry Schwartz, *Seasonal Farm Labor in the United States With Special Reference to Hired Workers in Fruit and Vegetable and Sugar-Beet Production* (New York: Columbia University Press, 1945), 57.

18. Vaught, *Cultivating California,* 75; Indian Hill Citrus Union report, 1908–9, quoted in Street, *Beasts of the Field,* 588; California Bureau of Labor Statistics, *Second Biennial Report, 1885–86* (Sacramento: State Printer, 1887), 56; *PRP,* September 16, 1905, 183.

19. California Board of Horticulture, *Biennial Report, 1901–02,* 281, quoted in La-Wanda F. Cox, "The American Agricultural Wage Earner, 1865–1900: The Emergence of a Modern Labor Problem," *Agricultural History* 22, no. 2 (April 1948), 103; *PRP,* August 26, 1893, 150; September 2, 1893, 175; September 9, 1893, 207; California Bureau of Labor Statistics, *First Biennial Report, 1883–84,* 11; *Second Biennial Report, 1885–86,* 45–47, 62–63; R. L. Adams and T. R. Kelly, *A Study of Farm Labor in California* (University of California Agricultural Experiment Station, March 1918), Circular 193, 29–30.

20. *California Agricultural Society Transactions, 1891,* 196–97; *Fresno Morning Republican,* January 1, 1896, "Progress Edition"; *U.S. Immigration Commission Reports,* 24:600n. Death of J. Nelson, August 22, 1913, in Sacramento Archives and Museum Collection Center, Coroner's Inquests Case Files, Box 30, Folder 15.

21. *Immigration Commission Reports,* 24:378. The following were taken from California Commission of Housing and Immigration Papers, Carton 57, Folders 1–5: Labor Camps 1914–37, Complaints, MSS C-A 194, Bancroft Library.

22. William J. Bauer, Jr., "'We Were All Migrant Workers Here': Round Valley Indian Labor in Northern California, 1850–1929," *Western Historical Quarterly* 37, no. 1 (Spring 2006), 43–63 passim; Tomlan, *Tinged with Gold,* 126–27; *PRP,* September 6, 1890, 204; September 2, 1893, 175; Gillis and Magliari, *John Bidwell,* 319; U.S. Office of Indian Affairs, *Annual Report . . . 1911* (Washington, D.C.: GPO, 1912), 15–16; Adams and Kelly, *Study of Farm Labor,* 59.

23. Richard L. Carrico and Florence C. Shipek, "Indian Labor in San Diego County, California, 1850–1900," in Alice Littlefield and Martha C. Knack, eds., *Native Americans and Wage Labor* (Norman: University of Oklahoma Press, 1996), 198–217 passim; Hurtado, "California Indians," 4; *Alexander Thompson v. Doaksum,* 68 Cal. 593, 10 Pacific 199, 1886 Cal. LEXIS 498, Feb. 25, 1886; Todd Benson, "The Consequences of Reservation Life: Native Californians on the Round Valley Reservation, 1871–1884," *Pacific Historical Review* 60, no. 2 (May 1991), 222.

24. Liping Zhu, *A Chinaman's Chance: The Chinese on the Rocky Mountain Mining Frontier* (Niwot: University Press of Colorado, 1997), chap. 1 passim; Wong, *Gum Sahn Yun,* 5; Levi Varden Fuller, "The Supply of Agricultural Labor as a Factor in the Evolution of Farm Organization in California," (Ph.D. diss., University of California, 1939), 71n; Sylvia Son Minnick, *Samfow: The San Joaquin Chinese Legacy* (Fresno: Panorama West Publishing, 1988), 2–9.

25. Wong, *Gum Sahn Yun,* 139; Zhu, *Chinaman's Chance,* 23; Alexander Saxton, *The Indispensable Enemy: Labor in the Anti-Chinese Movement in California* (Berkeley: University of California Press, 1971), 3–5; Minnick, *Samfow,* 60–63.

26. "Tule" refers to land overgrown with brush. *San Joaquin Republican,* March 3,

1852, quoted in Minnick, *Samfow*, 58, 183; McWilliams, *Factories in Fields*, 71–72; Sackman,"'*Nature's Workshop,'*" 31; Street, *Beasts of the Field*, 235ff; Sucheng Chan, *This Bittersweet Soil: The Chinese in California Agriculture, 1860–1910* (Berkeley: University of California Press, 1986), 304–13; Patricia Mary Ochs, "A History of Chinese Labor in San Luis Obispo County and a Comparison of Chinese Relations in This County with the Anti-Chinese Movement in California, 1869–1894" (master's thesis, California State Polytechnic College, San Luis Obispo, 1966), 6, 17–18.

27. *Kern County Gazette* [Bakersfield], November 6, 1880, 7; letters of Liang Kwang-jin, quoted in Ronald Takaki, *A Different Mirror: A History of Multicultural America* (Boston: Little, Brown, 1993), 219–20.

28. *Sacramento Daily Record-Union*, in 1886: August 13, 3; August 17, 3; August 21, 1.

29. *Riverside Press and Horticulturist*, January 12, 1889, 2; Tomlan, *Tinged with Gold*, 127; Wong, *Sweet Cakes, Long Journey*, 58–59; U.S. *Industrial Commission Reports*, 10:954–55.

30. Mark Twain, "Disgraceful Persecution of a Boy," *Galaxy* (May 1870), reprinted in Twain, *Collected Tales, Sketches, Speeches, & Essays 1852–1890* (New York: Library of America, 1996), 379–82; Alexander Saxton, *The Indispensable Enemy: Labor and the Anti-Chinese Movement in California* (Berkeley: University of California Press, 1971), chap. 6 passim; Minnick, *Samfow*, 128–29; Tomlan, *Tinged with Gold*, 128–29; Gillis and Magliari, *John Bidwell*, 335.

31. Minnick, *Samfow*, 128–29; Elliott Barkan, *From All Points: America's Immigrant West, 1870s–1952* (Bloomington: Indiana University Press, 2007), chap. 4 on anti-Chinese laws; "Labor Laws Declared Unconstitutional," U.S. *Department of Labor Bulletin*, no. 91 (November 1910), 934–35; William H. Siener, "Through the Back Door: Evading the Chinese Exclusion Act along the Niagara Frontier, 1900 to 1924," *Journal of American Ethnic History* 27, no. 4 (Summer 2008), 36.

32. Minnick, *Samfow*, chap. 5 passim; Chan, *Bittersweet*, 373; *PRP*, September 8, 1883, 192; April 21, 1888, 354; quoted in Fuller, "Supply of Agricultural Labor," 105, 112.

33. *Sacramento Daily Record-Union*, August 13, 1886, 3; August 17, 1886, 3; August 21, 1886, 1; testimony of E. Clemens Horst of Wheatland, California, U.S. *Commission on Industrial Relations Reports* (1916), 5:4951.

34. George Chu, "Chinatowns in the Delta: The Chinese in the Sacramento-San Joaquin Delta, 1870–1960," *California Historical Society Quarterly* 49, no. 1 (1970), 24, 29–30; Street, *Beasts of the Field*, 259–61; Vaught, *Cultivating California*, 54–55; Chan, *Bittersweet Soil*, 344–45; Saxton, *Indispensable Enemy*, 8; Thomas Turnbull testimony, U.S. *Industrial Commission Reports* (1901), 10:978.

35. *PRP*, September 16, 1893, 199; Cletus Daniel, *Bitter Harvest: A History of California Farmworkers, 1870–1941* (Ithaca, N.Y.: Cornell University Press, 1982), 51–54; Vaught, *Cultivating California*, 54–59; Resolution of Pajaro Valley Fruit-Growers' Association, reprinted in Fuller, "Supply of Agricultural Labor," 331–34; H. A. Millis, *The Japanese Problem in the United States—An Investigation for the Commission on Relations with Japan Appointed by the Federal Council of the Churches of Christ in America* (1915; reprinted New York: Macmillan, 1978), 129.

36. Barkan, *From All Points*, 65–67; *El Paso Times*, July 23, 1903, 5; Erika Lee, "The 'Yellow Peril' and Asian Exclusion in the Americas," *Pacific Historical Review* 76,

no. 4 (November 2007), 543; Street, *Beasts of the Field*, 396–97; Chan, *Bittersweet Soil*, 386; *Fresno Herald and Democrat*, August 14, 1907, 10.

37. Yuji Ichioka, *The Issei: The World of the First Generation Japanese Immigrants 1885–1924* (New York: Free Press, 1988), 3–4, 63–66; *U.S. Immigration Commission Reports*, 23:10, 13, 63; 24:25–26; Schwartz, *Seasonal Farm Labor*, 55; Fuller, "Supply of Agricultural Labor," 116–19. Small numbers of African-Americans arrived in California under this plan.

38. *PRP*, February 24, 1909, 122; Mitziko Sawada, "Culprits and Gentlemen: Meiji Japan's Restrictions of Emigrants to the United States, 1891–1909," *Pacific Historical Review* 60, no. 3 (August 1991), 339–59 passim.

39. Bill Helfman, "'Sun Rising in an Eastern Sky'—Japanese Americans in Washington Township, 1920–1942," *California History* 73, no. 1 (Spring 1994), 55, 62. Helfman's interviews are from his *In the Cookhouse and Fields: The Workers of Patterson Ranch* (East Bay Regional Park District, 1990). David Mas Masumoto, *Country Voices: The Oral History of a Japanese American Family Farm Community* (Del Ray: Inaka Countryside Publications, 1987), 16; Lukes and Okihiro, *Japanese Legacy*, 21; Shoji Nagumo, *A Pioneer's Autobiography*, trans. Misue Sautter (Japan: Aimei Insatsu Kabushiki Gaisha, 1978; translation, 1982), 16; Ichioka, *Issei*, 82–83.

40. Nagumo, *Pioneer's Autobiography*, 12–15.

41. *Los Angeles Olive Growers Association v. Pacific Surety Co.*, 24 Cat. App. 95; 140 Pacific 295; 1914 Cal. App. LEXIS 336 (Feb. 25, 1914). *U.S. Immigration Commission Reports*, 23:62–63; 24:358–59. A copy of a contract is on 24:586–89. Victor S. Clark, "Mexican Labor in the United States," *U.S. Bureau of Labor Bulletin*, 78 (September 1908), 499. *U.S. Immigration Commission Reports*, 23:12–13, 63; 24:26–27. Gilbert G. González, *Labor and Community: Mexican Citrus Worker Villages in a Southern California County, 1900–1950* (Urbana: University of Illinois Press, 1994), 27.

42. Vaught, "'An Orchardist's,'" 573, 577–79; Fuller, "Supply of Agricultural Labor," 168–70, 172; *Marysville Evening Democrat*, April 5, 1912, 2.

43. Information on Oxnard and the 1903 strike is drawn principally from the work of Richard Steven Street, *Beasts of the Field*, chap. 18. Also useful was Tomás Almaguer, "Racial Domination and Class Conflict in Capitalist Agriculture: The Oxnard Sugar Beet Workers' Strike of 1903," *Labor History* 25, no. 3 (Summer 1984), 325–50; Almaguer, *Racial Fault Lines: The Historical Origins of White Supremacy in California* (Berkeley: University of California Press, 1994), chap. 7 passim; Ichioka, *Issei*, 96–99.

44. Joan S. Wang, "The Double Burdens of Immigrant Nationalism: The Relationship Between Chinese and Japanese in the American West, 1880s–1920s," *Journal of American Ethnic History* 27, no. 2 (Winter 2008), 38–41; Gillis and Magliari, *John Bidwell*, 330–31.

45. *PRP*, July 3, 1909, 2. Information on the 1906–7 controversy is drawn from Wang, "Double Burdens," 35–36; Roger Daniels, *The Politics of Prejudice: The Anti-Japanese Movement in California and the Struggle for Japanese Exclusion* (1962; reprinted Berkeley: University of California Press, 1977), 33–44; Sawada, "Culprits and Gentlemen," 339–59 passim; *U.S. Immigration Commission Reports*, 23:16–19; and Ichioka, *Issei*, 69–72.

46. "Taft Would Protect Aliens Living Here," *New York Times*, January 23, 1914, 7.

11: MEXICANS, WOBBLIES, WAR

1. Ralph Winstead, "Enter a Logger: An I.W.W. Reply to the Four L.'s," *Survey* 44 (July 3, 1920), 475; *Commission on Industrial Relations, Final Report*, vol. 5, *The Seasonal Labor Problem in Agriculture*, Senate Doc. 415, 64th Cong., 1st sess. (Washington, D.C.: GPO, 1916), 4924. On the wartime strike controversy in Pacific Northwest forests, and the employers' switch to providing bedding, see Robert L. Tyler, "The United States Government as Union Organizer: The Loyal Legion of Loggers and Lumbermen," *Mississippi Valley Historical Review* 47, no. 3 (December 1960), 444 and passim.

2. Carleton H. Parker, *The Casual Laborer and Other Essays* (New York: Harcourt Brace and Howe, 1920), 123–24. The modern sleeping bag came into use later.

3. *Pacific Rural Press (PRP)*, October 9, 1909, 231; John Chala Elac, *The Employment of Mexican Workers in U.S. Agriculture, 1900–1960: A Binational Economic Analysis* (1961; reprint Los Angeles: UCLA, 1971), 60; Juan L. Gonzáles, Jr., *Mexican and Mexican American Farm Workers: The California Agricultural Industry* (New York: Praeger, 1985), 14–15; Joan M. Jensen, *Passage From India: Asian Indian Immigrants in North America* (New Haven, Conn.: Yale University Press, 1988), 36–37; Richard Steven Street, *Beasts of the Field: A Narrative History of California Farmworkers, 1769–1913* (Stanford, Calif.: Stanford University Press, 2004), 474–75; *U.S. Department of Agriculture Yearbook, 1911*, 579; *Yearbook, 1918*, 532; Richard Orsi, *Sunset Limited: The Southern Pacific Railroad and the Development of the American West 1850–1930* (Berkeley: University of California Press, 2005), 226ff.

4. Jensen, *Passage from India*, 36; R. L. Adams and T. R. Kelly, *A Study of Farm Labor in California* (University of California Agricultural Experiment Station, March 1918), circular 193, 8; *Imperial Valley Press*, October 29, 1910, quoted in Paul S. Taylor, "Mexican Labor in the United States—Imperial Valley," and in Taylor, *Mexican Labor in the United States* (Berkeley: University of California Press, 1930), 12; Mark Reisler, *By the Sweat of Their Brow: Mexican Immigrant Labor in the United States, 1900–1940* (Westport, Conn.: Greenwood Press, 1976), 6–7.

5. Taylor, "Mexican Labor—Imperial Valley," 7–8; Street, *Beasts of the Field*, 485; Tom Oshiro interview, March 27, 1993, Florin Japanese-American Citizens League Oral History Project, California State University–Sacramento Special Collections.

6. Max Sylvius Handman, "Economic Reasons for the Coming of the Mexican Immigrant," *American Journal of Sociology* 35, no. 4 (January 1930), 605; Lawrence A. Cardoso, "Labor Emigration to the Southwest, 1916 to 1920: Mexican Attitudes and Policy," *Southwestern Historical Quarterly* 79, no. 4 (April 1976), 400–401; Gilbert G. González, *Mexican Consuls and Labor Organizing: Imperial Politics in the American Southwest* (Austin: University of Texas Press, 1999), 11; California Bureau of Labor Statistics, *22nd Biennial Report, 1925–26* (Sacramento: State Printer, 1926), 126.

7. Victor S. Clark, "Mexican Labor in the United States," *U.S. Bureau of Labor Bulletin* 78, (September 1908), 485; Carleton Parker, "Seasonal, Migratory and Unskilled Labor in California," *Report to the U.S. Commission on Industrial Relations, 1914*, 8–9; *U.S. Immigration Commission Reports: Japanese and Other Immigrant Races in the Pacific Coast and Rocky Mountain States* (Washington, D.C.: GPO, 1911), 24:30; Street, *Beasts of the Field*, 490–91; John W. Gilmore, *Cotton in the*

San Joaquin Valley (University of California Agricultural Experiment Station, February 1918), Circular 192, 3, 6; Cameron L. Saffell, "When Did King Cotton Move His Throne (And Has It Moved Back)?" *Agricultural History* 74, no. 2 (Spring 2000), 296; California Bureau of Labor Statistics, *22nd Biennial Report, 1925–26,* 126; Walter Nugent, *Into the West* (New York: Knopf, 1999), 198ff.

8. Yuji Ichioka, *The Issei: The World of the First Generation Japanese Immigrants 1885–1924* (New York: Free Press, 1988), 146–53; Eiichiro Azuma, "Japanese Immigrant Farmers and California Alien Land Laws: A Study of the Walnut Grove Japanese Community," *California History* 73, no. 1 (Spring 1994), 14–15; Timothy J. Lukes and Gary Y. Okihiro, *Japanese Legacy: Farming and Community Life in California's Santa Clara Valley* (Cupertino: California History Center, 1985), 29–30; Wayne Maeda, *Changing Dreams and Treasured Memories—A Story of Japanese Americans in the Sacramento Region* (Sacramento: Sacramento Japanese American Citizens League, 2000), 103–5.

9. *U.S. Immigration Commission Reports,* 24:48, 303; California Department of Industrial Relations, Division of Immigration and Housing Records, 1912–1919, Complaints 16958, 16597, 16575, as examples (in Bancroft Library); Street, *Beasts of the Field,* 492–93; *U.S. Industrial Commission, Final Report* (1916), 5:4955.

10. Roger Daniels, *The Politics of Prejudice: The Anti-Japanese Movement in California and the Struggle for Japanese Exclusion* (1962; reprinted Berkeley: University of California Press, 1977), 87–91; Cecilia Tsu, "Grown in the 'Garden of the World': Race, Gender, and Agriculture in California's Santa Clara Valley, 1880–1940" (Ph.D. diss., Stanford University, 2006), 172–73; Daniel P. Johnson, "Anti-Japanese Legislation in Oregon, 1917–1923," *Oregon Historical Quarterly* 97, no. 2 (Summer 1996), 190–200.

11. Elliott Barkan, *From All Points: America's Immigrant West, 1870s–1952* (Bloomington: Indiana University Press, 2007), 168–70, 186–88.

12. Jensen, *Passage from India,* 9–10, 24–28, 35–40; David Vaught, "'An Orchardist's Point of View': Harvest Labor Relations on a California Almond Ranch, 1892–1921," *Agricultural History* 69, no. 4 (Fall 1995), 581–86; H. A. Millis, "East Indian Immigration to the Pacific Coast," *Survey* 28 (June 1, 1912), 384–85; *Akhay Kumar Mozumdar v. United States,* 299 F. 240, 1924 U.S. App. LEXIS 2546 (June 16, 1924), 241.

13. José Manuel Alamillo, "Bitter-Sweet Communities: Mexican Workers and Citrus Growers on the California Landscape, 1880–1941" (Ph.D. diss., University of California–Irvine, 2000), 156–58; Taylor, "Mexican Labor," 55–56; Gilbert G. Gonzalez, *Labor and Community: Mexican Citrus Worker Villages in a Southern California County, 1900–1950* (Urbana: University of Illinois Press, 1994), 36–40.

14. Ian Tyrrell, *True Gardens of the Gods—Californian-Australian Environmental Reform, 1860–1930* (Berkeley: University of California Press, 1999), 3, 9, 155–56; Vaught, "'Orchardist's Point of View,'" 567; Vaught, "Factories in the Field Revisited," *Pacific Historical Review* 66, no. 2 (May 1997), passim; Carey McWilliams, *Factories in the Field—The Story of Migratory Farm Labor in California* (1935; reprinted Hamden, Conn.: Archon Books, 1969); Elac, *Employment of Mexican Workers,* 55–56, 77; Gilmore, *Cotton in San Joaquin Valley,* 4, 6; Paul S. Taylor, "Hand Laborers in the Western Sugar Beet Industry," *Agricultural History* 41, no. 1 (January 1967), 24.

15. Margo McBane, "The Role of Gender in Citrus Employment: A Case Study of Recruitment, Labor, and Housing Patterns at the Limoneira Company, 1893 to 1940," *California History* 74, no. 1 (Spring 1995), 76–79; Frederick Noble, manager, Oxnard Factory, to CCIH, September 17, 1918, in CCIH Papers, Carton 57, Labor Camps 1914–37 Complaints (in Bancroft Library); Gonzalez, *Labor and Community*, 7–13, 28, 61–65, 75.

16. Information on the early organization of the IWW is taken from the two major studies of the organization: Paul F. Brissenden, *The I.W.W.—A Study of American Syndicalism* (1918; reprinted New York: Russell & Russell, 1957), chap. 2 passim, app. 2; and Melvyn Dubofsky, *We Shall Be All: A History of the Industrial Workers of the World* (Chicago: Quadrangle Books, 1969), chaps. 4 and 5 passim. Origins of the "Wobbly" name are lost to time. The most frequent explanation used by historians is based on a tale of a Chinese cook's unsuccessful attempt to pronounce "I.W.W."

17. Parker, *Casual Laborer*, 15; Rexford G. Tugwell, "The Casual of the Woods," *Survey* 44 (July 3, 1920), 472; Peter A. Speek, "Report on Psychological Aspect of the Problem of Floating Laborers," in *Reports to the U.S. Commission on Industrial Relations*, 1914, 83.

18. Street, *Beasts of the Field*, 599–600; Brissenden, *I.W.W.*, 208–9, 271; Dubofsky, *We Shall Be All*, 127; Ichioka, *Issei*, 110–13; Gregory R. Woirol, *In the Floating Army: F.C. Mills on Itinerant Life in California, 1914* (Urbana: University of Illinois Press, 1992), 122–23; Nelson Van Valen, "The Bolsheviki and the Orange Growers," *Pacific Historical Review* 22, no. 1 (February 1953), 40; Daniel Rosenberg, "The IWW and Organization of Asian Workers in Early 20th Century America," *Labor History* 36, no. 1 (Winter 1995), 77–79, 80–87; Cletus Daniel, *Bitter Harvest: A History of California Farmworkers, 1870–1941* (Ithaca, N.Y.: Cornell University Press, 1982), 82–83, quoting *Industrial Worker*, May 18, 1911, 3; Manuel Gamio, comp., *The Mexican Immigrant: His Life-Story* (1931; reprint Chicago: University of Chicago Press, 1969), 128–30.

19. Dubofsky, *We Shall Be All*, chap. 8 passim. Spokane cases are from unnamed local newspaper, clippings of March 9, 1909, and June 11, 1911, in Spokane Police Department Crime Scrapbooks, vol. 2 (1888–1913). Similar cases were numerous from 1909 on.

20. Philip Taft, "The I.W.W. in the Grain Belt," *Labor History* 1, no. 1 (Winter 1960), 53. The Fresno and San Diego information is drawn from Dubofsky, *We Shall Be All*, 184–97; Street, *Beasts of Field*, 604–21; and Ione Elizabeth Wilson, "The I.W.W. in California, With Special Reference to Migratory Labor (1910–1913)," (master's thesis, University of California, 1946), 10–43.

21. M. R. Benedict, "The Economic and Social Structure of California Agriculture," in Claude B. Hutchison, ed., *California Agriculture* (Berkeley: University of California Press, 1946), 413; E. Clemens Horst, *Scenes from E. Clemens Horst Company's Hop Ranches During Harvesting Time* (n.p., circa 1920), 8, 10, 14; *Sacramento Bee*, May 12, 1913, 8.

22. Unless otherwise noted, the Durst riot information is taken from the following: Parker, *Casual Laborer*, 171–99; Dubofsky, *We Shall Be All*, 294–98; Daniel, *Bitter Harvest*, 88–94; David Vaught, *Cultivating California: Growers, Specialty Crops, and Labor, 1875–1920* (Baltimore: Johns Hopkins University Press, 1999), 132–42;

Greg Hall, *Harvest Wobblies: The Industrial Workers of the World and Agricultural Laborers in the American West, 1905–1930* (Corvallis: Oregon State University Press, 2001), 48–54, and *U.S. Commission on Industrial Relations Final Report*, 5:4932–47.

23. *People v. Richard Ford*, 25 Cal. App. 388; 143 Pacific 1075; 1914 Cal. App. LEXIS 354 (September 14, 1914).

24. Street says the penalty was twenty years in prison; other sources say life imprisonment. Street, *Beasts of Field*, 625; *U.S. Commission on Industrial Relations Final Report*, 5:4980.

25. *People v. Ford*; Parker to Paul Scharrenberg, June 5, 1914, in CCIH Papers, Carton 5, File 31; Parker, *Casual Laborer*, 19–20. James P. Thompson, who spoke of the Wheatland victims, was an IWW lecturer; his speech is in Harrison George, *The I.W.W. Trial* (1918; reprinted in New York, Arno Books, 1969), 71–72. McWilliams, *Factories in Field*, 163.

26. Parker, *Casual Laborer*, 62; Simon Lubin to Henry M. Goldfogle, New York, August 24, 1912; Lubin to Philip Davis, Boston, Mass., November 22, 1913, in Simon J. Lubin Papers, Box 4, Letters 1912–14, Bancroft Library.

27. Lubin to Mr. Fels, January 17, 1914, in Lubin Papers, Box 4; Parker, *Casual Laborer*, 86–87, 103, 197–98; CCIH, *First Annual Report, 1913–14* (Sacramento: State Printer, 1915), 19.

28. The 1918 grower reports are in Carton 57, Labor Camps, 1914–1937, CCIH Papers; J. J. Rosenthal to Lubin, April 27, 1914, in Rosenthal 1914 folder, Letters to Lubin (M–Z), Box 3, Lubin Correspondence, Lubin Papers, Bancroft Library; Don Mitchell, *The Lie of the Land: Migrant Workers and the California Landscape* (Minneapolis: University of Minnesota Press, 1996), 53–55; Vaught, "Factories in Field Revisited," 173–74.

29. Vaught, "Factories in the Field Revisited," 173–74; Woirol, *Floating Army*, 65.

30. California Bureau of Labor Statistics, *Twenty-Second Biennial Report, 1925–1926* (Sacramento: State Printer, 1926), 31, 40–41; Don D. Lescohier, *The Labor Market* (New York: Macmillan, 1923), 147.

31. "Regulations Promulgated for the War Industry, of Woods and Mills of the Northwest, March 1, 1918," Exhibit D, in Papers of the President's Mediation Commission, 1917–18 (University Publications of America microfilm, Reel 3, Research Collections on Labor Studies); Dubofsky, *We Shall Be All*, 446–47; Oregon Bureau of Labor Statistics, *Eighth Biennial Report* (1916–18), 28–31; Mitchell, *Lie of the Land*, 121; Daniel, *Bitter Harvest*, 98–99; Robert S. Gill, "The Four L's in Lumber: A War Heritage of Industrial Unionism that Includes the Employer," *Survey* 44 (May 1, 1920), 165–70; Parker, *Casual Laborer*, 19; Tyler, "United States Government as Union Organizer," 444.

32. Juan Gómez-Quiñones, *Mexican-American Labor, 1790–1990* (Albuquerque: University of New Mexico Press, 1994), 84; Otis Scruggs, "The First Mexican Farm Labor Program," *Arizona and the West* 2, no. 4 (Winter 1966), 322; Adams and Kelly, *Study of Farm Labor*, 56–57, 59–60; Lescohier, *Labor Market*, 173–75; Vaught, *Cultivating California*, 181; Hall, *Harvest Wobblies*, 80–81.

33. Vaught, *Cultivating California*, 166–67; *Yakima Herald*, September 2, 1917, 1; Fuller, "Supply of Agricultural Labor," 299; Mitchell, *Lie of Land*, 83–84; A. H. Hendrickson, *Small Fruit Culture in California* (University of California Agricul-

tural Experiment Station, Circular 164, April 1917), 3; Adams and Kelly, *Study of Farm Labor*, 61.

34. Vaught, *Cultivating California*, 181; McBane, "Role of Gender," 75; McWilliams, *Factories in Fields*, 175–76; Van Valen, "Bolsheviki," 44; Adams and Kelly, *Study of Farm Labor*, 66–67, 64–65; George Bell to Mrs. F. A. Gibson, CCIH Staff, Carton 6:5, Gen Corr May–June 1917, CCIH Papers.

35. *Yakima Morning Herald*, August 19, 1917, 4; David G. Wagaman, "The Industrial Workers of the World in Nebraska, 1914–1920," *Nebraska History* 56, no. 3 (Fall 1975), 297; *Omaha Evening Bee*, July 31, 1916, 4; July 14, 1917, 4; November 15, 1917, 8, quoted in Wagaman, 307–8, 310, 316–17; Dubofsky, *We Shall Be All*, 314–17; Thorstein Veblen, "Farm Labor and the I.W.W.," Papers of the President's Mediation Commission, 1917–1918, (Research Collections on Labor Studies, University Publications of America, 1985) 4–6.

36. The strike in the San Dimas area in 1918–19 is described in Van Valen, "Bolsheviki," 39–50. See also *Survey* (March 6, 1915), 634–35; *Yakima Morning Herald*, August 18, 1917, 1; "Additional Confidential Memoranda Regarding Western I.W.W. Situation," Papers of the President's Mediation Commission, 1917–18; Wagaman, "Industrial Workers in Nebraska," 306; *Cherokee* [Okla.] *Republican*, May 25, 1917, 1.

37. John F. Kendrick, "Onward, Christian Soldiers," reprinted in Archie Green et al., eds., *The Big Red Songbook* (Chicago: Charles H. Kerr, 2007), 168–70.

38. Jail records investigated for the war years and after were from Livingston, Montana; Wallace, Idaho; Spokane, Washington; and Wenatchee, Washington.

39. Dubofsky, *We Shall Be All*, ix, 406–7, 436–44. One of the defendants in the Chicago trial published his extensive notes of the proceedings: see Harrison George, *The I.W.W. Trial*, cited above at note 25.

40. J. C. Minus, San Antonio, Texas, in House Committee on Immigration and Naturalization, *Temporary Admission of Illiterate Mexican Laborers*, 66th Cong., 2d sess. (Washington, D.C.: GPO, 1920), 118.

12: ARRIVAL OF THE "GASOLINE TRAMPS"

1. R. L. Adams and T. R. Kelly, *A Study of Farm Labor in California* (University of California Agricultural Experiment Station, Circular 193, March 1918), 59.

2. John J. Hader, "Honk Honk Hobo," *Survey* 60 (August 1, 1928), 453–55.

3. Gregory R. Woirol, *In the Floating Army: F.C. Mills on Itinerant Life in California, 1914* (Urbana: University of Illinois Press, 1992), 83; Levi Varden Fuller, "The Supply of Agricultural Labor as a Factor in the Evolution of Farm Organization in California" (Ph.D. diss., University of California, 1939), 245.

4. Gilbert G. González, *Labor and Community: Mexican Citrus Worker Villages in a Southern California County, 1900–1950* (Urbana: University of Illinois Press, 1994), 6–7; California Bureau of Labor Statistics, *Twenty-First Annual Report, 1923–24* (Sacramento: State Printer, 1924), 95; House Committee on Immigration and Naturalization, *Temporary Admission of Illiterate Mexican Laborers*, 66th Cong., 2d sess. (Washington, D.C.: GPO, 1920), 16–17; Juan Gómez-Quiñones, *Mexican-American Labor, 1790–1990* (Albuquerque: University of New Mexico Press, 1994), 84; Alice Evans Cruz, "The Romanzas Train Señora Nurse," *Survey* (August 1, 1928), 468.

5. House Committee on Immigration and Naturalization, *Temporary Admission of Illiterate Mexican Laborers*, 6, 26, 78.

6. Sarah Deutsch, *No Separate Refuge: Culture, Class, and Gender on an Anglo-Hispanic Frontier in the American Southwest, 1880–1940* (New York: Oxford University Press, 1987), 131–32, 156–59.

7. William H. Siener, "Through the Back Door: Evading the Chinese Exclusion Act Along the Niagara Frontier, 1900 to 1924," *Journal of American Ethnic History* 27, no. 4 (Summer 2008), 36.

8. House Committee on Immigration and Naturalization, *Seasonal Agricultural Laborers from Mexico*, 69th Cong., 1st sess. (Washington, D.C.: GPO, 1926), 10, 14, 75, 95.

9. Ibid., 225–26.

10. *Time* (October 16, 1964), 36.

11. Quotes in the following paragraphs from the 1926 congressional hearings are from House Committee on Immigration and Naturalization, *Seasonal Agricultural Laborers from Mexico*, 6–7, 60–61, 73–74, 90–91, 104, 266–67.

12. The IWW's rise and fall in the 1920s is based on accounts in Greg Hall, *Harvest Wobblies* (Corvallis: Oregon State University Press, 2001), 195ff; and Melvyn Dubofsky, *We Shall Be All: A History of the Industrial Workers of the World* (Chicago: Quadrangle Books, 1969), 462–68.

13. Richard A. Rajala, "A Dandy Bunch of Wobblies: Pacific Northwest Loggers and the Industrial Workers of the World, 1900–1930," *Labor History* 37, no. 2 (Spring 1996), 228–29, 233–34.

14. Hall, *Harvest Wobblies*, 224ff; *Industrial Solidarity*, n.d., quoted in Hader, "Honk Honk Hobo," 455.

15. Cletus E. Daniel, *Bitter Harvest: A History of California Farmworkers, 1870–1941* (Ithaca: Cornell University Press, 1982), 51–54; Anderson quoted in *Sacramento Bee*, October 4, 1926; CCIH commissioner Walter G. Mathewson, San Francisco, to Executive Officer R. W. Kearney, Bureau of Labor Statistics, March 11, 1926, in Carton 3:6, Bureau of Labor Statistics Correspondence, 1918–1935, California Commission of Immigration and Housing (CCIH) Papers, BANC MSS C-A 194, Bancroft Library; Paul S. Taylor, "Mexican Labor in the United States—Valley of the South Platte—Colorado," in Taylor, *Mexican Labor in the United States* (Berkeley: University of California Press, 1930), 1, no. 2, 136, 144.

16. The Massachusetts law is discussed in the *Salina* [Kan.] *Herald*, May 15, 1880, 2; Orland F. Lewis, "The Vagrant and the Railroad," *North American Review* 185 (July 1907), 610–11.

17. *Ex parte* McCarthy, Supreme Court of California, 14 Pacific 96, May 31, 1887; Grand Island [Neb.] Police Judge's Docket, August 3, 1894, 381, Nebraska State Historical Society, Record Group 300, Subgroup 1, v. 5. Spokane [Wash.] Police Scrapbook, v. 11, May 31, 1903. Spokane [Wash.] Jail Register, 1909–10: March 29 and April 6, 1909; September 15, and October 4, 1910.

18. Jack London, *The Road*, in *Jack London: Novels and Social Writings* (New York: Library of America, 1982), 230–43.

19. Robert C. Cotner, *James Stephen Hogg: A Biography* (Austin: University of Texas Press, 1959), 425–27; *Railway World* [Philadelphia], November 4, 1893, 1035.

20. Walter J. Costigan, "Lorenzo D. Lewelling," *Kansas Historical Collections* 1901–1902, 7:121–126 (the Tramp Circular is reprinted on 125–26); Elbert Hubbard, "The Rights of Tramps," *Arena*, no. 53 (April 1894), 593ff.

21. E. R. Lewis, Michigan Central Railroad, "The Ability of the Hobo," *Railway Age Gazette* (June 21, 1912), 1566–67.

22. William Rock, USFS forest ranger, time book, fire crews working out of Avery, Idaho, August 1910, provided by Carl Ritchie, USFS. González, *Labor and Community*, 75; Richard Griswold del Castillo, *The Los Angeles Barrio, 1850–1890* (Berkeley: University of California Press, 1979), 62–63, quoted in David G. Gutiérrez, *Walls and Mirrors: Mexican Americans, Mexican Immigrants, and the Politics of Ethnicity* (Berkeley: University of California, 1995), 22.

23. Nels Anderson, *On Hobos and Homelessness* (Chicago: University of Chicago Press, 1998), 209–10; and *The Hobo—The Sociology of the Homeless Man* (1923; reprinted Chicago: University of Chicago Press, 1967), 214; Carleton H. Parker, *The Casual Laborer and Other Essays* (New York: Harcourt Brace & Howe, 1920), 190.

24. Clipping from unidentified periodical, circa February 1912, in Spokane Police Department Scrapbooks, v. 3.

25. "The Preacher and the Slave" is based on the gospel song "Sweet Bye and Bye," by Joseph P. Webster and S. Fillmore Bennett. Archie Green et al., eds., *The Big Red Songbook* (Chicago: Charles H. Kerr, 2007), 99.

26. J. Vance Thompson to George Bell, February 25, 1917, in "IWW Investigations" folder, Simon J. Lubin Papers, MSS C-B 1059, Bancroft Library.

27. *Industrial Worker* [Seattle], February 26, 1910, 2; Richard White, *"It's Your Misfortune and None of My Own"—A New History of the American West* (Norman: University of Oklahoma Press, 1991), 294.

28. Jim Burden arriving at Black Hawk, Nebraska, in Willa Cather, *My Ántonia* (1918; reprint New York: Library of America, 1987), 718.

29. François-André Michaux, *Travels to the West of the Alleghany Mountains* (1805), vol. 3 of Reuben Gold Thwaites, ed., *Early Western Travels 1748–1846* (Cleveland, Ohio: Arthur H. Clark, 1904), 247–48.

30. Paul S. Taylor, *Mexican Labor in the United States—Dimmit County, Winter Garden District—South Texas* (Berkeley: University of California Publications in Economics, v. 6, no. 5, 1930), 444.

31. Parker, *Casual Laborer*, 148; Toby Higbie, "Indispensable Outcasts: Harvest Laborers in the Wheat Belt of the Middle West, 1890–1925," *Labor History* 38, no. 4 (Fall 1997), passim; and Higbie, "Rural Work, Household Subsistence, and the North American Working Class: A View from the Midwest," *International Labor and Working-Class History* 65 (Spring 2004), passim.

32. Editor Scott C. Zeman, introducing the Cultures in the American West series, in Jorge Iber and Arnoldo De León, *Hispanics in the American West* (Santa Barbara, Calif.: ABC-CLIO, 2006). New books bear such titles as *From All Points: America's Immigrant West, 1870s–1952; Into the West: The Story of Its People; From Different Shores;* and a host of books examining Asians and Mexicans in the West.

33. Parker, *Casual Laborer*, 173–74.

34. *Junction City* [Kan.] *Union*, July 17, 1869, 1; Patricia Nelson Limerick, *The Legacy of Conquest: The Unbroken Past of the American West* (New York: Norton, 1987), chap. 10 passim; White, *"'It's Your Misfortune,'"* 285.

35. F. A. Miller, Writ of Habeas Corpus; 162 Cal. 687; 124 Pacific 427; 1912 Cal. LEXIS 584 (May 27, 1912).

36. Anderson, *On Hobos*, 31.

ACKNOWLEDGMENTS

Writing about harvest labor in the West builds up many debts. Bringing the story together was made easier by the work of several historians who pushed ahead earlier, real trailblazers. Melvyn Dubofsky pointed out new directions for studying western labor, as did Carlos Schwantes, William Robbins, and David Vaught, and I am glad I can publicly thank them for their pioneering work.

Librarians and archivists play crucial roles for any researcher. At Illinois State University's Milner Library, my work was helped enormously by Chris Young, Angela Bonnell, Vanette Schwartz, Ryan Peters, and Michael Lovell. Maps were made by Jill Freund Thomas of the university's department of geography-geology, her work excellent as always.

David Rademacher's photo skills were indispensable.

Several people read early versions of parts of the manuscript, and I leaned heavily on their historical and geographical expertise: Michael Magliari, Al Lowman, Walter Buenger, Bill Lang, LeRoy Ashby, Arlan Helgeson, Ed and Judy Jelks, Lance Lippert, and Mark Plummer. Mike Matejka kept me on track regarding railroads and hoboes' travels thereon; Carl Ritchie, a Forest Service archaeologist, provided material from the 1910 Northern Rockies fire; veteran railroader Warren McGee helped me understand the hoboes' work on the Northern Pacific in Montana; Ivan Doig suggested new research directions in the Pacific Northwest; and Rick Dettwiler deserves special mention for saving aged Spokane County sheriff files from the Dumpster.

Archivists who were especially helpful were David Kessler, Bancroft Library; Kathryn Kenefick, Center for American History at the University of Texas; Rayette Wilder, Northwest Museum of Arts and Culture in Spokane; Pat Johnson and Carson Hendricks, Sacramento Archives and Museum Collection Center; Patricia Churray of the Public Records section, Nebraska State Historical Society; Jene Robbins of Texas State Archives; Ellen Crain of the Silver Bow Public Archives in Butte; Amanda Burbank of the USFS Region One Archives; Brigid Clift (in Ellensburg) and Susan Beamer (in Cheney) of the Washington State Regional Archives; Elaine Miller, Washington State Historical Society; and John Ferrell (in Seattle) and Nicholas Natanson (in Washington, D.C.) of the National Archives and Records Service.

Several people not noted above gave crucial aid at various phases of this project: Walter Nugent, R. David Edmunds, Donald Worster, Malcolm Rohrbough, John Mack Faragher, Wade Bilbrey, Robert Walls, Teresa Hamann, Karen Zoltenko, John Fryer, Jim Tracy, Bob Blenz, Pat and Esther McLatchey, Roger Myers, Charles Harris, and Ken Holder.

Staffs of the following institutions assisted me, often extensively: the libraries of Illinois State University, of the University of Illinois (Main, Law, and Agriculture libraries), and of the universities of Texas, California, Washington, Montana, Arizona, and Utah; the state historical societies of Nebraska, Kansas, Colorado, Oklahoma, Arizona, California, Oregon, Washington, Montana, Wisconsin, and Minnesota; the state archives of Texas, Arizona, and California; the Yakima Valley Museum; the Museum of North Idaho; the Wallace (Idaho) District Mining Museum; the Skagit County Historical Museum; the Sacramento Archives and Museum Collection Center; the Forest History Society; and the public libraries of Denver, Lincoln, Spokane, Fort Worth, and Sacramento.

My agent, Deirdre Mullane—an experienced editor herself—not only improved the manuscript but guided me expertly through the search for a publisher.

I thank all of them for helping create this book.

INDEX